RELIGION AND CHANGE

David L. Edwards

Revised Edition

HODDER AND STOUGHTON
LONDON SYDNEY AUCKLAND TORONTO

To Hilary

RELIGION AND CHANGE

Preface
(1974)

In this book I try to consider the challenges to religion which have resulted from changes in the twentieth century. These changes have, I think, made our time the *secular* century, in a sense which is without precedent in history. Many people draw the conclusion that the religion which survives is doomed to disappear. In my introductory chapter, I try to consider the challenge of the current feeling that man is 'coming of age', and the challenge of the growing unity of the world. Will the one world of the future be completely secular?

Since I maintain that these matters should not be treated in a bloodlessly intellectual way, I begin my more detailed chapters by studying the social character of traditional religion and the social character of traditional religion's defeat in industrial Europe, Russia, China and some other areas; but I note that the impact of this century has not led to religion's complete defeat. Then I turn to the psychological impact of secularisation, and I try to illustrate this both from the writings of Sigmund Freud and from the perplexities of some religious writers, Muslim or Jewish as well as Christian; but I note that even under this impact the religious passion has survived rather strongly. Perhaps, then, the 'death of God' is an exaggerated report? After these sociological and psychological observations, I feel free to turn to the intellectual challenge to religious doctrine. I take as the key example the challenge to Christian dogmatism, briefly recording and assessing some of the responses of Christian theologians during the twentieth century.

My own conclusion is that the old shape of Christian life and thought—as in Protestant Fundamentalism, for example, or in conservative Catholicism—is not likely to become again the powerful religion of the West. But although many of the old customs and images of religion are dead, I regard the 'post-Christian' West as a society which is still in search of an object to worship, and in two chapters I examine the possibilities that the old religions of the East, specially Hinduism and Buddhism, may come to the rescue, or that a new and more or less secular kind of 'religion' without the traditional God may be evolved within the West. The evidence seems to suggest that, great as are Christianity's current problems, the problems faced by Westerners who try to find a religious (or quasi-religious) substitute for Christianity are at present greater. Both the religious missionaries from the East and the West's own humanists have a long way to go before they can close down the churches. I believe, therefore, that Christianity still has a chance of filling the religious vacuum in the West, and of expanding its world-wide influence, if Christianity will accept the necessary changes.

In my last two chapters, Part Two of the book, I try to be constructive rather than analytic, for I attempt to discuss what these necessary changes in Christianity may be—while recognising that major changes in such a sphere must have origins beyond the reach of any commentator who is not a prophetic genius.

I try to summarise first the very extensive discussion which has already taken place about a new shape for the Christian Church. Finally, although still disclaiming the role of a religious prophet, I draw on some recent theology in order to offer an outline of a restatement of Christian belief which tries to take into account the criticism of Christianity mentioned earlier in the book.

Religion and Change is only an introduction to a vast field of study, which I want to explore and which I invite others to explore with me. The chapters were delivered in an abbreviated form as eight Hulsean Lectures in the University of Cambridge in the Michaelmas Term, 1967. I am grateful to the Vice-Chancellor and to my senior colleagues in the

Faculty of Divinity at Cambridge for the high honour which they conferred on me by electing me to stand in the succession of Lecturers since the benefaction by the Reverend John Hulse in 1777.

This book was first published in 1969, in the series of *Twentieth Century Studies* under the creative editorship of Donald Tyerman. It was reprinted in 1970 and also published in the United States and Germany. Some reviewers of the book thought it too Christian and others thought it not Christian enough, but to my delight reviewers were on the whole encouraging about it and readers seem to have found it useful, if in places frustrating or annoying. When preparing this new edition I have taken the opportunity to revise and shorten the text and to cut out many of the suggestions for further reading.

D. L. E.

Acknowledgments

The author is grateful to the following for permission to use material from their publications:

Faber and Faber Ltd., for material from *The Social Reality of Religion* by Peter Berger.

Allen & Unwin Ltd., for material from *A Preface to Morals* by Walter Lippman.

Harper & Row, Publishers, Incorporated, for material from *The Eclipse of God* by Martin Buber.

Marvell Press, Hessle, Yorks., for lines from 'Church Going' in *The Less Deceived* by Philip Larkin.

SCM Press Ltd., for material from *The Reality of God* by Schubert M. Ogden.

Mr. M. B. Yeats and Macmillan & Co. Ltd., for lines from 'The Circus-Animals' Desertion' from *Collected Poems of W. B. Yeats*.

Contents

PART ONE

CHAPTER ONE

Religion and the World's Coming of Age

Secularisation

If space were even more limited than it is in this book, and if we were asked to produce one word which would characterise the twentieth century, we should indeed despair. But if circumstances forced us either to produce one word or else to accept some horrific punishment (such as having to keep silent), we should eventually utter—but in how great an anxiety lest we should be misunderstood!—the one word *secular*. The twentieth century, we should say, is the secular century. Originally, in Latin, this word meant no more than that the thing being described belonged to its own time. However, something more than a glimpse of the obvious is being attempted when the twentieth century is described as secular.

Secularism as a word seems to have been coined by George Jacob Holyoake, who once spent six months in an English prison for public blasphemy and who died in 1906. For him it was 'the doctrine that morality should be based on regard to the well-being of mankind in the present life, to the exclusion of all considerations drawn from belief in God or a future state'. This definition is quoted by the *Oxford English Dictionary*; and it implies the doctrine which used to be called 'atheism' and which, since it has become established and respectable, is now usually known as 'humanism'. *Secularisation*, however, is a word which may be used to describe a situation when 'the exclusion of all considerations drawn from belief in God or a future state' reflects the main emphasis in a society, but not necessarily the opinions of all its members. Secularisation, it can be argued, does not necessarily make everyone embrace atheistic doctrines with all his heart and mind and strength. Thus Ronald Gregor Smith, a theologian who applauded secularisation and what he called 'secularity', wrote that 'modern secularism is not secular enough'.[1] He meant that secularisation ought not to lead to *any* doctrine—not even to secularism. Secularisation ought to emphasise the worldly and the human, but leave people free to think their own thoughts about God, in a liberal type of society which may be described as 'open' or 'pluralistic'. A suspicion at once crosses the mind. Is this distinction between the process of 'secularisation' and the doctrine of 'secularism' more than a clever theologian's play with words? It will be our task in this book to see, but at least we can agree now that secularisation means the displacement from a society's centre of belief in the eternal God, in the 'after-life' as man's great hope and in supernatural force as man's great ally. *Secularisation occurs when supernatural religion—that is, religion based on 'belief in God or a future state'—becomes private, optional and problematic.*

We cannot put it more simply than that, by saying that under the impact of secularisation all religion disappears. A great many people still do participate in religious ceremonies. They do so in African villages, in the deserts of Arabia, on the banks of the Ganges; they even do so in London and Moscow. And all this religious observance certainly indicates some religious belief, which is probably far more widespread than the statistics of the observance suggest. Christianity, Islam, Hinduism and Buddhism all continue to command great popular respect, which can flame into ardent devotion in exceptional circumstances and which normally results in some influence of religious beliefs and values on the psychology of the masses. The

[1] *Secular Christianity* (London, 1966), p. 172.

younger generation arising in the secularised West during the 1960s and 1970s is often interested in religion—mostly of an unorthodox kind—as an enlargement of human consciousness and as a liberation from a soul-destroying materialism.[1]

Nevertheless, the fact remains that in many countries of the modern world those who set the pace for society are usually not much influenced by this continuing or reviving religion; and in a million subtle ways the media of mass communication and of public instruction spread a secular emphasis. Although time may be given to religious worship and teaching, the mass-media and the schools excite worldly curiosity and desire. In addition to intellectual and cultural awakenings, people are encouraged in 'the lust of the flesh, the lust of the eyes and the pride of life', in the New Testament's ancient but accurate phrase; and the activities of organised religion are not connected with the things which matter most. The thinking of the people is influenced, however obscurely and slowly. All over the modern world the sea of traditional faith in the supernatural God or gods seems to be ebbing. Even in the great plains of India, millions hear the 'melancholy, long, withdrawing roar' which in Victorian England sounded for Matthew Arnold on Dover beach. Many modern people are, however, fascinated by a more cheerful spectacle. Before their delighted eyes, the mainstream of modern life appears to flow from its own inexhaustible sources and at its own irresistible pace, towards an ocean which may even now be glimpsed, serene and shining—the ocean of human health, freedom, dignity and dominance over the earth and over space. This mainstream of secular energy is what really excites many people today. They judge themselves and others basically by their ability to take part in the progress to secular knowledge and secular prosperity. Here is the system of beliefs and values into which the churchgoing of the

[1] See Theodore Roszak, *The Making of a Counter Culture* (New York, 1969); Andrew M. Greeley, *The Persistence of Religion* (New York, 1972); Kenneth Leech, *Youthquake* (London, 1973).

United States (for example) may have to be fitted; for it has been suggested that if the real attitudes of most American churchgoers are to be reflected, the motto which is familiar on United States dollar notes should be expanded to read: '*In God we trust*—all others pay cash.' Thus the fascination of our study lies in the question: *will the religion which survives in this mainly secular century disappear before too long?* The question is crucial and urgent, for—whatever the theologians may now say—many observers of contemporary trends are convinced that secularism will gradually prove to be the universal consequence of secularisation.[1]

Before we try to answer that central question, however, we must ask another of almost equal interest: *Is this degree of secularisation a new phenomenon?* Is this century in fact the first secular century?

There are no clean breaks in history. Just as religion has not in fact disappeared from our largely secular civilisation, so also the secular emphasis was in fact prominent in past ages which we regard as heavily religious. According to the evidence of history, there have been no ages of faith—if we have in mind a whole society's acceptance of a religious faith, and if we define religious faith as the deliberate subjection by a freely acting individual of his whole personality, thought and conduct to the dominance of 'belief in God or a future state'. In every age both the clever and the rich have often been critical of religion, and again and again—as in the poetry of Lucretius, who died half a century before the birth of Jesus, or amid the 'Enlightenment' of eighteenth-century Europe and America—the death certificate of the God of popular religion has been signed by the élite with a flourish. Among the masses the observance of religious ceremonies and the profession of religious beliefs would often seem to have been more or less unthinking. Popular religion was largely the product of convention, inspired by the wish to be like others rather than to be like God; and popular religion was limited even in its popu-

[1] See, e.g., Vernon Pratt, *Religion and Secularisation* (London, 1970).

larity. Where reliable records of popular religion can be recovered (for example, statistics of church attendance) we discover that in times or areas which appear to have been heavily religious (for example, Victorian England), in fact considerable numbers had few or no connections with organised religion. On Sunday, 30 March 1851, a census of places of worship in England, the last of its kind to be taken, indicated that only about thirty-six per cent of the population attended services. It is a mistake to suppose that there has ever existed a large society of saints, or that mass movements of intense religious belief have been anything other than freaks. Most people, for most of the time, have preferred to concentrate not on unseen powers but on the everyday powers of earth and flesh and mind. When people have turned in large numbers to religion, it has often been in order to use religion for secular aims. Religion has meant to them the solidarity of their clan or class or nation, in contrast with others; and religion has enabled them to express the loyalty and the hatred in their hearts. Human nature being what it is, crusades of righteous indignation have been specially liable to use the weapons of excommunication, mob fanaticism, oppressive legislation and violence in order to impose their visions on lesser breeds. The inevitable consequence of this intense form taken by the internal secularisation of religion has been a revulsion. Men have been revolted by the foul corruption of the religious idea, and have turned back to the enjoyment of life without raising dangerous questions of theology. The religious vision of the saints, we may conclude, has scarcely been glimpsed by the mass of mankind. Religion, like music, has been a bond of unity for human societies, and a basic religious sense, like a simple pleasure in tunes, is human; but a deeply religious sense, like a deep appreciation of music, has been for the few. Most history, including most religious history, was secular.

However, the secularisation of our time seems to be novel in two ways: (1) in its conviction that *the world is 'coming of age'*, and (2) in its conviction that *the world is becoming one.* We must consider these two features of the twentieth century in turn; for, between them, they have produced, if not a totally new situation of universal secularism, then at least a world-wide challenge to religion from a new power of secularisation.

Coming of Age

The idea of the world's 'coming of age' has a long history, for the comparison of the life of mankind with the life of an individual has been a stock theme in literature and rhetoric. To cite a fairly modern use of the idea: Pope Leo XIII, when he condemned 'Americanism' in 1899, linked that heretical tendency with the suggestion that 'the Church should adapt herself more to the civilisation of a world that has reached the age of manhood'. But the use of the 'coming of age' catchword by the German Protestant theologian Dietrich Bonhoeffer in a letter on 8 June 1944,[1] has made it echo in many places, and the discussion has shown that many interpretations can be given to it.

The best interpretation makes 'the world's coming of age' refer to modern man's sense that his powers are increasing, and that, however inadequate they may be at present, his only real hope lies in their increase, for no greater power will help him. In the last 150 years or so, the technical and social revolutions have created a new psychological situation. This climate of opinion has given an unprecedented encouragement to the intoxicating sense of freedom, power and progress. Even before the technical and social revolutions of the nineteenth century began, optimism already marked in their different ways the Renaissance in Italy, the political revolutions in America and France, the intellectual revolutions of idealism and romanticism in Germany and almost the whole life of an England whose revolutions were (after the execution of Charles I) a fairly painless evolution in prosperity. Again and again during the nineteenth century,

[1] *Letters and Papers from Prison* (1951; revd. Eng. trans., London, 1971), pp. 324–9.

from the defeat of Napoleon to the Golden Jubilee of Queen Victoria, progress in peace to greater and greater riches seemed inevitable for an England, a Europe and a North America reaping the new harvests of the industrial factories and the illimitable prairies. Optimism has continued to be the prevailing note of the West in the twentieth century. Exuberant proclamations of self-confidence marked the birth of the century. Around 1910 there was the 'great unrest' because new powers were stirring in the industrial society. After the catastrophe of World War I, optimism revived in the reconstruction of a world 'safe for democracy'; and many clung to this optimism through the 1930s. Optimism grew as never before in the 1950s, with their vision of affluence in the West.

The intoxication has now spread to Asia and Africa, where hundreds of millions have celebrated independence and a new chance to reach better living standards. And running beneath the official rhetoric of triumph there has been the assumption of increasing numbers of people, in increasing numbers of moods, that things have been getting better—and will get better still. Nor has this quieter optimism lacked solid justification. Diseases have been tamed; crops have been blessed by science and given vastly greater markets; democracy has moved its objective from the vote for all to security for all; women are being emancipated, and children educated. And for the first time in his history, man is becoming predominantly a city dweller. In vast conurbations such as Tokyo, man has had to adapt himself to a new civilisation. Despite all the squalor which he has created in the cities, and despite all the misery which he has experienced there, urban man has grown increasingly independent of the elemental forces of nature. The fruits of nature have become the raw material of manufacturing. Apart from the sky, some decorative gardens and some natural food, everything around the city-dweller has been man-made. Even his children have been planned. The dream has grown of the city as a place fully adequate to man's dignity, from its skyscrapers to its subways; that dream has been the magnet to the paupers of Calcutta or the shanty-dwellers of Rio; and that dream has begun to come true. Villagers the world over also share in this dream, looking up at aeroplanes, listening to the radio, tasting the first trickle of the amenities of modern life. Even simple people nowadays regard science as magic and salvation, creating the good life in the City of Man.

This century has, of course, witnessed many setbacks to the realisation of its dream. That prince of English secular humanists, Professor Gilbert Murray (a scholar who attributed the rise of the 'mystery' religions, including Christianity, to a 'failure of nerve' among the ancient Greeks), lived to see his daughter Rosalind a convert to Roman Catholicism and the author of *The Good Pagan's Failure*. Led by Oswald Spengler with his turgid lament for *The Decline of the West*, innumerable prophets have arisen to proclaim the end of the modern era of optimism and energy. Apparently overwhelming problems have been posed by man's inability to civilise the contacts between nations and races, to relate his breeding capacity to the availability of food, to avoid the pollution and exhaustion of the resources of this fragile planet and to secure fair shares for all. The gap between the rich and the poor nations has widened tragically; the twentieth century may be recorded as the prelude to an explosion of hungry anger from the poor two-thirds of mankind. Wars and political fanaticisms, famines and economic depressions have brought tragedies to millions in Europe and even in North America, so that a harsh disillusionment has followed the agonies of the rich society during and since 1914. In the trenches of France and Flanders, in the Wall Street crash of 1929, in the British queues for the unemployment dole, in the ruin of central Europe under the Kaiser or the Führer, in Auschwitz and Hiroshima, in Stalin's Russia, in the Vietnam war and the riots in American cities, many false optimisms have been buried. Today—as we are so often told—the mushroom cloud of nuclear annihilation casts its shadow over all civilisation, but a more likely fate appears to be that by the end of the century there will be no oil left at a price that can be afforded, so that the machines will stop running and the horse will have the last laugh against the car.[1]

Yet many of the prophecies of doom have been falsified, for progress has continued. Many millions, greatly shocked but not crushed by our time of troubles, have insisted on making *this* 'the century of hope' (the label which was attached to the nineteenth century). In the United States the early prophets of prosperity have been outdistanced by the speed of the actual growth in the country's economy. Elsewhere, hopes have often been very modest—a cure for an eye disease, regular meals instead of empty bellies, a home with a minimum of security, a better chance for the children. But many of these hopes have actually come true before men's eyes in our time.

The economic recovery of Europe with a speed which no one prophesied in 1945 has been a symbol of the whole century's resilience. Twice over, Europe has bled itself white, yet from somewhere fresh blood has come, and Europe half a century later was immensely stronger than the continent was in the fateful summer of 1914. For all Spengler's gloom, in the long run the West has *not* declined. It has staggered, it has picked itself up, and it has run on. 'Man,' Professor Bateson once told the scientists assembled in the British Association, 'is just beginning to know himself for what he is—a rather long-lived animal with great powers of enjoyment if he does not deliberately forego them. Hitherto superstition and mythical ideas of sin have predominantly controlled these powers.'[2] That address was delivered in August 1914. A half-century followed of bloody tragedies with an inter-war 'waste-land'; sin became not a 'mythical idea' but a thing of steel and fire, bayonets, mud and poison gas; yet at the end of this ordeal of the West the optimistic professor's words seemed plausible again. Even the many warnings in the 1970s of an

[1] See, e.g., Hugh Montefiore, *Can Man Survive?* (London, 1970).
[2] Quoted in S. Radhakrishnan, *An Idealist View of Life* (London, 1932), p. 43.

ecological doom to come could not get the average man, or the average thinker, really worried. Surely the West, which had survived so much and achieved so much, could survive the new and the future problems! Surely man would cope!

The East has kept much of its own pessimism, but that has been a pessimism about the basic condition of man, a despair inherited from the ages. For the East, this century began with Japan's defeat of Russia, a momentous symbol of what modernised Asians could do. Since then the East has felt, amid its often overwhelming material problems and its continuing fatalism of the spirit, that famine is not inevitable; in other words, the East has known a hope so great and so new that the masses have felt that they have entered history for the first time since the golden ages of their half-legendary past. And the proof of this is that even in the 1970s the population explosion has not produced panic in the 'developing' nations. The world's population is now doubling every thirty years—but so, it would seem, is the world's hope.

This is, therefore, a time of *humanism*. In many previous ages the arts which ease, illuminate and adorn life flourished for the few, and the twentieth century has seldom reached the standards of excellence then established. Many Muslims look to the past for the glory of Islam, and many Chinese or Indians confess that the twentieth century cannot match the high culture of their vanished empires. Modern Europe has not produced a Shakespeare or a Beethoven, an Athens or a Florence. Below that level of excellence, middle-class culture as a whole has not reached the solid strength which it knew in nineteenth-century England, France and Germany. But the achievement of our time—most dramatic in Russian and Chinese Communism's liberation of the peasants, but as powerful in the growth of Western capitalism—has been the extension of humanism to include humanity. Although many forms of privilege remain in the world, excluding the masses from the good things of life and challenging reformers to fights enough for many centuries, yet popular expectation and popular education have made immense advances already, and all the signs are that their progress will accelerate. This means that teaching, travel, television and radio, printing and other forms of preservation and reproduction can now place the sublime achievements of genius within the reach of the people. Above all, it means that men, women and children are now valued more highly *for themselves*. Increasingly the individual is courted as an elector by politicians; he is caressed by doctors, dentists, oculists and psychiatrists; he is pampered by merchants whose sole hope of fortune lies in attractively feeding, clothing, transporting and amusing the customer with money in his pocket, in his millions. Increasingly the individual is tolerated even when in character or in opinion he is not normal within his society. The quest for human dignity is what is vital—more vital even than economic motivation. Our age is accordingly the age of the revolt of the poor against the rich; of the coloured against the white; of the women against the men; of the deviants against the respectable. It means something that fully a quarter of all the human beings who have ever survived infancy are now alive—thanks to the fact that over ninety per cent of all the scientists who have ever lived are living now. But it means more that in the unprecedented social response to the unprecedented economic change, the masses grasp at an equality of respect.

What has survived from the prophecies of doom, and from the facts of many disasters, has been a sense that progress to an equal prosperity for all is not automatic. And this sense of ambiguity and danger, so clear in the political and economic worlds, is another key to what the unprecedented 'coming of age' means spiritually. Dietrich Bonhoeffer, the Christian pastor who was writing in a Nazi prison cell ten months before his execution, would have been the last person to endorse all the inane prophecies of inevitable human progress. (He had been repelled by his personal experience of American religious optimism.) But exactly in its ambiguity and danger has lain our time's resemblance with the coming of age of an individual. New powers stir; they can lead either to fantastic progress or to utter catastrophe. That is the thrill, and when things go wrong that is the poignancy. 'Coming of age' is the beginning of battle, not the consummation of victory; it is promise, not perfection. The power is there; if disaster comes, it will be because the power was not used in a sufficiently intelligent plan. The great transition into modernity comes through the loss of that sense of intellectual and physical powerlessness which in the past accompanied man's dependence on God or the gods. Now that man is powerfully—and perhaps tragically—mature, there is no going back to any Paradise which existed before man defied the divine prohibition and ate the fruit of knowledge. 'The future cannot be predicted,' writes Dennis Gabor, 'but futures can be invented . . . We cannot stop inventing because we are riding on a tiger. We must now start thinking of social inventions to anaesthetise the tiger, so that we can get off its back.'[1]

Above all, a society, like an individual, can feel that now, if things do go wrong, if the tiger-ride out of Paradise does end in catastrophe, there is no one else to blame. This is a sober thought, often forgotten as the champagne for independence flows, but when the party is over the thought remains, to give a society, like an individual, an adult pride in taking responsibility, even for mistakes. Even if ballistic missiles with nuclear warheads horrifically devastate our civilisation and pollute the earth, it will remain true that with unprecedented skills twentieth-century men made them and sent them on their journeys. If industry uses up all the fossil fuels or all the fresh water, it will remain true that human industry accomplished this—and probably could have avoided it. Human nature is the key—and may be the curse. As Dennis Gabor points out: 'About three-quarters of the population of the globe are still engaged in the age-old occupation of mankind, in the fight against a stingy and hostile Nature. The "most advanced" quarter has almost defeated Nature, which fights back only as a

[1] *Inventing the Future* (London, 1963), pp. 185–6.

rotting corpse does; by pollution. In the rich, industrialised countries the fight has turned, almost imperceptibly, into one against human nature.'[1] And here lies the transforming element in this 'coming of age' for the future of religion. As man's consciousness of his powers, or at least of his potential, has grown, so his reliance on supernatural force has shrunk, or at least has been seen to need a radical readjustment and restatement. Professor Gabor, for example, pins his hopes on education, to train or re-train people on severely pragmatic lines for life in the new society.

In history, the beating heart of religion has lain deeper than the intellect, deeper even than the conscience. The heart of religion has been a primal sense of awe before a tremendous and fascinating mystery, a sense of absolute dependence on the mercy of a power infinitely greater than man. And the essence of practical religion has been petitionary prayer. A villager knowing that he was really empty-handed but burning a little incense or leaving a few flowers before an idol, with a petition for a crop or a son, has been the typically religious man. This has been the case even in India, where the official philosophy has been based on the eternal identity of *Atman* and *Brahman*, the human and divine spirits. Even Buddhism, which in its founder's intention was a godless philosophy, has largely become in subsequent practice an emotion surrounding a request for supernatural aid in the affairs of this life—which means that it has become a practical religion. Even Confucianism and Taoism, which originally were philosophies of the good life in the family and society and in communion with nature, with references to 'Heaven' (*tien*) so vague that they have won the approval of modern Western atheists, became in Chinese history religions to some extent like the practical religion of India: systems of petitionary prayer sliding quite easily into magic. And even in Islam, where prayer is meant to be adoring submission to the will of Allah, men in practice ask for things. We stand in caves painted by primitive men and we know that their beliefs cannot be recovered by us,

[1] *The Mature Society* (London, 1972), p. 6.

despite the ingenuity of the anthropologists; yet one psychological reality we think we can often recognise in the scenes of hunting and of pregnancy preserved on the amazing walls of those caves—and that is, a confession that already, when nature had scarcely yet turned into history, *homo sapiens* was *homo religiosus*, for he needed supernatural help to survive, to hunt animals and to rear offspring. From primitive magic to the prayer of the Christian to the heavenly Father for daily bread, the central theme of practical religion could be expressed as a cry for help.[1]

In the nineteenth and twentieth centuries of the Christian era, increasing numbers of people have either experienced no such need of supernatural force, or else they have believed that it would be futile to expect their need to be satisfied as a consequence of petitionary prayer. Of course, the situation is often confused, with the old and the new mingling, the old surviving, the new failing. But that there has been a shift of emphasis in modern civilisation can scarcely be doubted. When modern people feel sick, they want medicine; when their crops are poor, they want fertilisers; when they are ignorant, they want education; when their relationships are entangled, they know that they ought to profit by a cool, scientific study of the underlying economic or emotional problems. And when they want rain, they do not beat drums. At least to the unreflective, all this seems a world away from the Church of England's Litany, which echoed in the language of the Tudor age the petitions of all the religious centuries to the God of a thousand names:

> That it may please thee to succour, help, and comfort,
> all that are in danger, necessity, and tribulation;
> *We beseech thee to hear us, good Lord.*

What is strong in the modern world seems to have come by the exploitation of man's inherent powers, not by a gift from God. The prayer of the religious centuries was for

[1] See, e.g., *Dialectic in Practical Religion*, ed. E. R. Leach (Cambridge, 1968).

illumination. Out of illusions they asked to be led into
reality, out of darkness into light, and thus out of death into
life; and to this day the Latin motto of the University of
Oxford affirms that the Lord is its light. But now the vast
conquests of science have been won without any reference to
a supernatural source of illumination. Indeed, it has been
of the essence of the scientific method that every object,
however impressive, should be analysed as just one object in
nature, and that supernatural causes should not be ascribed
to any event in the universe. To many in this age of science,
God has been the great illusion, and the worship of God has
seemed a cause of darkness and death to the mind of man.
Even religious believers have had to do their science as if
God did not exist. The activity of God, as the astronomer
Laplace remarked to Napoleon, is a hypothesis of which the
scientist has 'no need'; and 'to bring religion into it' has
seemed the chief of sins in the age of science. Thus scientific
man seems to have understood nature as merely natural.
Without supernatural illumination, he can boast that he has
created our glittering and hugely pregnant civilisation.

To secularists it does not seem to be conclusive evidence
against 'man's coming of age' to say that the achievements of
the scientific civilisation matter little in comparison with the
continuing tragedy of the human situation taken as a whole.
The common argument designed to overthrow humanist
arrogance and to commend religious humility—the argument used by many religious conservatives against Bonhoeffer—rests on the point that man's basic problem remains
his finitude, experienced through his deep loneliness, his disappointments with the good things of life, his exposure to
accidents and diseases and his inevitable ageing to death.
It is urged that man's basic problem can be overcome only
through religious faith for it is only by such faith that man
feels himself to be in touch with a power which, being
supernatural and immortal, sustains him through all the
losses inflicted by chance and decay. All other happiness, it
is suggested, is unsubstantial and transitory. The vitality of
religious life and thought in the twentieth century has shown

that many people still find truth in that religious analysis of the condition of man. Many humanist advertisements of the glories of life in the age of science seem, in comparison with that ancient vision, brash and trivial. Twentieth-century life is often still tragic, and for everyone life is in one way or another frustrated. Everyone dies. Further advances in technology or in the humane and social sciences will cure few of such complaints. But it is crucial for the future of religion that its defenders should see that the main weight of their case can no longer rest on the weakness of man. Many twentieth-century people have succeeded, to a greater or lesser extent, in pushing their mortality to the back of their minds. Life for them is ultimately death, but they think that there is nothing that they can do about this unfortunate circumstance, and meanwhile they are merry enough, with many duties to perform and many enjoyments to explore in this teeming and fascinating world. All their important things are the things before the last things. Against all the abstractions of the metaphysical philosophies and against all the hell-fire or angel-voices of the 'old-time' religion, this physical joy, this earthiness, has usually been the position on which the average sensual man has taken his stand; and in the twentieth century the earth's consolations for the absurdity of man's ultimate place in the scheme of things have multiplied. Amid the surrounding wilderness and the silence of the infinite spaces, this earth has become more of a garden of delights.

Admittedly, some sensitive artists and intellectuals have gone deeper than that. They have explored the full, sad consequences of atheism. Thomas Hardy and A. E. Housman did it in England; sex brought misery to them, and in their misery they saw the tragedy of all our days. Jean Paul Sartre and Albert Camus did it more thoroughly, when French intellectuals had to rebuild their whole view of the world under the pressure of the ethical dilemmas posed by three appalling problems: the necessity of committing evil in order to resist the Nazis, the necessity of countenancing evil in order to support social justice through Communism's appeal to the working-class and the necessity of denouncing one's own country as the French empire sank into ruin amid futile cruelties in South East Asia and North Africa.

As the depths of the human situation have been probed by Hardy or Housman, Sarte or Camus, man has been seen as thrown into the world without an explanation, compelled to make decisions but not allowed long satisfactions, subjected to passions with no hope of peace while in that bondage, experiencing guilt but not forgiveness, drawn to the grave with all his dreams. That tragic vision has produced 'nausea'; and the right response to the 'absurdity' has seemed not acceptance but rebellion. Yet many have refused to escape from the 'nausea' by the method adopted by Housman, when he buried himself in pedantic scholarship— or by Sartre, when he chose the cause of Soviet Russia. On the contrary, Camus before his accidental death in 1960 spoke for many in our generation with his profounder analysis of the proper task and scope of the human rebellion. Rebellion there must be, but Camus taught that the real rebellion against the real enemies of man is betrayed if the mind and conscience capitulate to a political creed of fanaticism and violence. Modern man must be a rebel; but just as he betrays his body if he commits suicide, so he betrays and kills his intelligence if he embraces the consolations of religion or of the Marxist substitute for religion. In an absurd world, we must learn to live with a lucid authenticity, to think and to feel among our fellow-men—to think and to feel, *but not to hope*. In the plague of life, man must be a doctor, but a doctor without heroics.[1]

Camus saw modern man as being like Prometheus, who stole fire from the Greek gods—but also like another mythological hero, Sisyphus, who in Hades was doomed to roll a stone to the top of a hill and see it always roll down again. The necessity of rebellion, with its hopelessness, were expressed for our time in Franz Kafka's novel *The Castle*; and the anxiety of guilt with its permanence had been put

[1] This is taught in the great novel or allegory by Albert Camus, *The Plague* (1947; Eng. trans., London, 1948).

a year before (1925), in Kafka's *The Trial*. Can human nature assert its own dignity under such anguishing conditions? Is it possible in such a tragic solitude *to be a man*? Kafka seems merely to have asked the question; and Sartre has given an ambiguous reply, for Sartre's individualism needed to be rescued by his Communism. Camus (like Freud) showed his undeterred humanism by his disillusioned *yes*. But, we may add, Camus (like Freud) saw how difficult it is for the vital energies of man to accept a civilisation which renounces both the passions which energise and the illusions which console; he saw how difficult it was for others to say *yes*. In 1951, on the first page of *The Rebel*, Camus recorded his sympathy (although also his disagreement) with the violence of the revolts against modern man's fate. 'One might think that a period which, within fifty years, uproots, enslaves or kills 70 million human beings, should only, and forthwith, be condemned,' he wrote, adding: 'But also its guilt must be understood.' The violence in modern man's rebellion against his destiny was understood by Camus— understood, but not endorsed, for whether or not men could say *yes* to the human situation, they must renounce illusions about it.

Existentialism such as that of Camus sounds differently from an earlier optimism, for it is fully atheistic. Hegel in 1802 observed that the religion of modern times rested on the feeling that God himself is dead, and Feuerbach's *Essence of Christianity* (1841), which George Eliot translated in 1854, publicly celebrated the fact that the feeling was true, so that at last man could come into his own. But it needed genius of the stature of Nietzsche and Dostoevsky to begin to probe the consequences in the depths of the emotional life. 'God is dead! God remains dead!' cried the madman in Nietzsche's *Joyful Wisdom* (1882) to those scoffers in the market-place who merely did not believe in God. 'And we have killed him! The holiest and the mightiest that the world has hitherto possessed has bled to death under our knife . . . Is not the magnitude of the deed too great for us? Shall we not ourselves have to become Gods, merely to seem worthy of it? There never was a greater event, and on account of it, all who are born after us belong to a higher history than any history hitherto!' So Superman could come—when 'everything is permitted', as Ivan Karamazov said in Dostoevsky's last book.

Nietzsche's madman concluded that he had shouted too early about the murder, for 'this deed is as yet further from them than the furthest stars—*and yet they have done it!*' But the twentieth century has been the time of the widespread experience of the 'death' of God. That experience has seemed to many a liberation, so that what the madman said sounds like the Gospel of life. Millions have felt some of the excitement of the liberation; they have felt godlike, because now, like a man come of age, they could do things which are not done in the nursery or at school. This has, however, not been the predominant mood in the great artists, poets, dramatists and novelists. These have often known despair. Nietzsche himself went mad. Dostoevsky, who might easily have given way to despair, instead shared the vision which Father Zosima tries to describe in *The Brothers Karamazov*, a vision of purity and peace beyond men's folly and evil. Other artists have chosen other ways to protest against the emptiness of life. In a crudely materialist and commercial society, many artists have projected their own feeling of alienation, and have made out of their personal sorrows works of art which state that when everything is possible, little is achieved; when everything is permitted, little is enjoyed. While the main note of public opinion in the twentieth century has been a note of hope, or at least of adult pride in responsibility, we should also reckon with the conviction of these artists that man's hope is (like everything else) chiefly an illusion, and that his lonely responsibility is a tragedy. As Nietzsche's *Joyful Wisdom* put it: 'The total nature of the world . . . is to all eternity chaos.'

Some twentieth-century secularists, sensitive to the anxiety of man after the 'death' of God, have expressed sympathy with religion. These thinkers have appreciated religion's age-old and continuing attempt to comfort the heart's sufferings in this plague which is life, and to raise the mind's vision to a destiny above the long littleness of our days. They have been patient with religion's difficulties as it has struggled to convey its vision through imperfect symbols, for to a considerable extent they look on religion's problems from inside—nor from the superior point of view of outside critics who can afford to sneer and to destroy without needing to replace.

Thus we find Sir Julian Huxley, the eminent zoologist who was Director-General of UNESCO, editing *The Humanist Frame* (London, 1961). This book was a collection of extracts from the works of atheists or agnostics ancient or modern, and might be regarded as some sort of secular Bible. The extracts advocated many moral attitudes which many religious believers would heartily endorse, and in his Introduction to the volume Sir Julian summed up criticisms of religion which many believers would admit to be valid. But he believed that 'what the world now needs is not merely a rationalist denial of the old but a religious affirmation of the new', for he saw clearly the strength and value of religion. 'All religions,' he wrote, 'involve the emotion of sacred mystery . . ., the sense of right and wrong; and feelings of guilt, shame, or sin. They are always concerned in one way or another with the relation between the individual and the community, and with the possibility of his escaping from the prisoning immediacies of space, time and selfhood by relating himself to some broader frame of reference, or in some self-transcending experience of union or communion with a larger reality.'

Here is an estimate of religion which is far more positive than was the attitude of the critics who reduced religion to 'nothing but' ignorance, superstition, illusion or nonsense. 'This reformulation of traditional religious concepts and beliefs and ceremonies,' Huxley writes, 'their translation into a new terminology and a new framework of ideas, is a major task for Humanism.'[1] So far, we must reluctantly add, the

[1] *The Humanist Frame*, p. 43.

'new religion' which has dominated history since 1914 has been militantly political and defiantly irrational—it has been the European militarism of 1914 or the Nazism of 1939, it has been the imperialism of the 1900s or the Afro-Asian nationalism of the 1950s; and in the 1970s a third of the world's population lives under governments which subscribe to the Communist doctrines. In our age of violence, it is a 'rough beast' who (as in that famous nightmare, *The Second Coming*, of W. B. Yeats) 'slouches towards Bethlehem to be born'. But perhaps in the more peaceful future man will reconstruct religion on a scientific basis, as Sir Julian Huxley advises. At any rate, it is vital that we should appreciate the force of this demand for a new religion, whether irrational or scientific.

Yet there is real danger in speaking about Huxley's evolutionism (or any other secular creed) as a 'religion'— and that is, the danger of tempting believers in the old religions to minimise the threat offered by the new belief to the old. At most a secular creed is, in Paul Tillich's phrase, a 'quasi-religion'. We cannot call it simply a 'religion' unless we are to agree on a definition of religion which represents a clean break with the past. When a humanist like Sir Julian Huxley witnesses to the importance, indeed to the necessity, of religion in history and in the future, he is of course resolute to avoid any endorsement of what has been the heart of religion: 'belief in God or a future state'. He writes, clearly enough: 'Religious experiences such as those of communion with some higher reality, or inspiration from outside the personality, or a sense of transcendent power or glory, or sudden conversion, or apparently supernormal beauty or ineffable sacredness, or the healing power of prayer, or repentant adoration, or, above all, the deep sense of inner peace and assurance in spite of disorder and suffering, can no longer be interpreted in the traditional terms of communication with a personal God or with a supernatural realm of being . . . They are the outcome of human minds in their strange commerce with outer reality and in the still stranger and often unconscious internal struggle between their components.'[1]

Many nowadays share this sympathetic scepticism towards the claims of supernatural religion to be true. In the heyday of rationalism, it was fashionable to reduce religion to 'nothing but' a pre-scientific attempt to cope with nature, or to 'nothing but' a social discipline, or to 'nothing but' repressed sex. Today that crudely secularist reductionism still lingers on in some quarters. It is aided to some extent by the fervour with which theologians still tend to denounce those varieties of religion to which they owe no allegiance. (Karl Barth, in particular, claimed that God's Word comes as 'the abolition of religion' as he defined 'religion', and Bonhoeffer's speculation that the day of *homo religiosus* might be over had some of its roots in this Barthian polemic.) But many who have pondered the significance of religion in history and in human nature today seem to be agreed that both the rationalists and the theologians were wrong in their contempt for the phenomenon of religion, which is in truth central to the whole story of *homo sapiens*. Religion has roots in nature, in society and in sex, but it is concerned primarily with the attempt to pierce the mystery which surrounds man and which conceals his destiny from him. It should not be reduced to one simple element and then dismissed as illusory apart from that element; it should be taken much more seriously. Indeed, it is widely agreed that religion is to a certain extent self-authenticating. Many millions of lives, producing many millions of words of recorded testimony, have borne witness that through religion men experience a power which produces not only righteousness but also love, joy and peace. F. H. Bradley, a philosopher who was superior enough to the 'appearances of the Absolute' which are honoured in popular religion, once remarked that the man who asks for a reality more solid than that given in religious experience does not know what he is seeking.[2]

[1] *The Humanist Frame*, p. 45.
[2] *Appearance and Reality* (Oxford, 1893), p. 449.

But what *is* 'the Absolute' which we experience in religion? A common attitude among the thoughtful in our time combines with a seriousness in appreciating the psychological reality of religious experience a scepticism, greater or less, about the extent to which the power or 'Absolute' experienced is really supernatural, really absolute. At least, it is agreed that if some part of the power experienced in religion extends beyond nature, the existence of that transcendent power is a matter not of direct experience but of what William James called 'over-belief'. At the very end of his widely influential *The Varieties of Religious Experience* (London, 1902), a book based on Gifford Lectures which set for our century a new standard of sympathetic seriousness in religious studies, James said: 'The ideal power with which we find ourselves in connection, the "God" of ordinary men, is . . . assumed as a matter of course to be "one and only" and to be "infinite" . . . Nevertheless in the interests of intellectual clearness, I feel bound to say that religious experience, as we have studied it, cannot be cited as unequivocally supporting the infinitist belief. The only thing that it unequivocally testifies to is that we can experience union with *something* larger than ourselves and in that unity find our greatest peace.'

If the tendency grows to separate the experience of this 'something' from the 'infinitist' belief in the eternal God, then the future of traditional religion is plainly dubious. In a brilliant essay of 1897 James described the 'will to believe', but it may be doubted whether modern men are likely to wish to believe in this 'something' which is vaguely 'larger'. The God of traditional religion—at least among Jews, Christians, Muslims and many Hindus and Buddhists—was certainly more than the 'Absolute' of the metaphysical philosophers, for he had a personal character and will; but he was also more than the 'something' of the mystical consensus, for religious believers found their peace in his infinite power. William James was primarily a psychologist, not a propagandist, but the belief in 'something' which he advocated with great modesty and courtesy may not be far

removed from Sir Julian Huxley's more brutal dismissal
of the 'dead' God in favour of a new, secular 'religion'. It
can be said about William James (as Heine said about
Kant) that he brought the sacraments to a dying God.

The lack of truth in the old, supernatural religion arouses
in some twentieth-century people *The Tragic Sense of Life*
—to use the title of Miguel de Unamuno's great book of
1912. Man's heart, Unamuno declared, craves God and
immortality, but his intellect is sceptical. Unamuno's
solution is that 'the man of flesh and bone' should so live
that if, after all, it is annihilation that finally awaits him,
that will be an injustice. 'What, then, is the new mission of
Don Quixote, today, in this world? To cry aloud, to cry
aloud in the wilderness.'

This is the quasi-religious philosophy of 'as if', and it is
a recurrent theme in the thought of our time. Whatever our
doubts, we should behave *as if* supernatural religion were
true. But Freud remembered a child of his who turned away
in disdain from fairy stories, and he commented: 'We may
expect that people will soon behave in a similar way towards
the fairy tales of religion, despite the advocacy of "as if".'[1]
Many thinkers less involved than Unamuno was in the
religious craving have agreed with Albert Camus that it is
necessary to think clearly and not to hope. They have drawn
a sadly clear distinction between the truth of traditional
religion's diagnosis of human need, its mapping of the
wilderness of life and the falsity of its offer to meet that need
and to make the wilderness blossom. Such sad sceptics
believe it to be wrong, however tempting, to embrace an
illusion for the sake of its comfort. They believe it to be
better to die on one's feet than to live on one's knees. Their
one hope is that much of the passion of religion may be
rescued from the 'death' of God and applied to our earthly
life, understood on an openly atheistic basis. Instead of
petitioning the supernatural, religion in their view should
inspire and consecrate human effort in this difficult and

[1] *The Future of an Illusion* (1927; revd. Eng. trans., London, 1962),
p. 25.

tragic world. So they seek a quasi-religion of humanity—not a tawdry glorification of Superman, but a quasi-religion for the time when the 'death' of God has really sunk into men's minds, a quasi-religion to give men some guidance and comfort as they enjoy a short day of frost and sun during the winter.

No writer in our time has expressed this attitude more powerfully than Bertrand Russell. He had a profoundly mystical or quasi-religious feeling for life. His *Autobiography*[1] made that clear, if it was ever obscure. The integrity of his devotion to truth shines through his self-revelation; and Russell was like another mathematical genius, Blaise Pascal, for it was the truth about man that concerned him most. He had plainly been moved to his depths by the finitude of man, by the mystery of man's brief existence in this universe, and by man's self-inflicted miseries. When Russell wrote of his compassion for humanity he clearly spoke the truth, and he further demonstrated that he did so by his passionate involvement in so many protests against injustice and war, against the subjection of women and against a woodenly unimaginative educational system. Here may have been the makings of our century's greatest religious leader. The unhappiness which he caused to others, specially to women, in the private life which he revealed so candidly, and the vanity and folly of many of his interventions in political or educational debates, should not be allowed to outweigh these signs of a great, quasi-religious prophet. But rightly or wrongly, Bertrand Russell allowed his youthful agnosticism and contempt for institutional religion to stay as the verdict of his maturity. He remained happily ignorant of most current movements in religion and theology. Religion seemed to him to be rightly concerned about the mysteries and miseries of our existence, but the falsity of the claims of all existing religions to supply information about the real world seemed so obvious that it did not appear to be worth a thinker's time to enquire more deeply into the mystery.

[1] 3 vols., London, 1967–9.

What will be the end of the secularism which Russell preached? In his 'Church Going'[1] the English poet, Philip Larkin, wondered

> *When churches fall completely out of use*
> *What we shall turn them into . . .*

For

> *. . . superstition, like belief, must die*
> *And what remains when disbelief has gone?*
> *Grass, weedy pavements, brambles, buttress, sky,*
> *A shape less recognisable every week,*
> *A purpose more obscure.*

Yet a church does mean something to this secularised humanist:

> *A serious house on serious earth it is,*
> *In whose blent air all our compulsions meet,*
> *Are recognised, and robed as destinies.*
> *And that much never can be obsolete,*
> *Since someone will forever be surprising*
> *A hunger in himself to be more serious . . .*

The probability is, however, that if secularisation completely empties the churches of worshippers—we think of many of the great churches of Soviet Russia, or of the Byzantine Hagia Sophia which is now a museum in the half-Muslim, half-secular city of Istanbul—men will choose other places in which to be 'serious' about their 'compulsions' and 'destinies', in quasi-religions uncontaminated by the supernatural ideas of the traditional religions. The English novelist, Kingsley Amis, has told us that the Russian poet, Yevgeny Yevtushenko, once asked him whether he was an atheist. 'Well, yes,' was the reply, 'but it's more that I hate him.' Yevtushenko seemed to understand what still troubled Amis about the death of God in England, but he himself voiced the more thoroughly

[1] In *The Less Deceived* (1955).

secular side of life in the Soviet Union. The Russian poet and the English novelist were conversing in King's College Chapel, Cambridge, and Amis tells us how in that great church Yevtushenko at this point delivered himself of a comprehensive verdict on the history of religion, after a friendly grin. ' "Me," he said, pointing to himself, then gesturing more vaguely towards the roof, the other people there, the Rubens, but also seeming to include the being I had just mentioned, "me . . . means nothing." '[1]

To sum up: the 'coming of age' of mankind, the sense that man is 'on his own now', may be seen from a religious angle in two ways. First, it is the sense, so widespread in our time, that men can do what previously was impossible; *men can celebrate the power and responsibility of adulthood*. Second, it is the sense, so noticeable in the smaller company of the sensitive, that men have to reconcile themselves with the fact that, because they cannot do everything, everything will not be done; *men must accept tragedy maturely*.

So the debate about the validity of religion in the modern world continues. It is a wider debate, and in places a deeper debate, than the nineteenth century or any previous century knew. At least we must say that the debate aroused by a secularism which is so cocksure sometimes, so poignant sometimes, has created a massive sense of uncertainty among religious believers. Will the future of religion lie in a humanism which will replace belief in a supernatural realm? Will the religion of tomorrow worship evolution or 'something larger' which is not God? Or can belief in, and worship of, the One who is eternal and divine survive the 'coming of age' of mankind—and even benefit from it? Has belief in God a stature sufficient to exceed the height of man's new powers, and a truth able to commend itself to the full exercise of man's free intelligence? Can belief in God flourish not at the frontiers of man's dominion and in the gaps of his knowledge, but at the very centre of his strength? Can its psychology be the psychology of maturity? Whatever answers it gives to such questions, religion over all the

[1] Martin Jarrett-Kerr, *The Secular Promise* (London, 1964), p. 48.

modern world is compelled to respond to the challenge of secularisation, which brings the impact of man's 'coming of age'.

One World

The second main feature which is new in the contemporary world, viewed from the angle of the student of religion, is its *unification*.

When the twentieth century dawned, railways and steam-ships had only begun the conquest of distance; and, re-flecting the great difficulties in secular communications, the age-old isolation of one religious tradition from another still prevailed to a large extent. Most of the tribes of Africa performed their ancestral rites. The masses of India were largely undisturbed in their Hinduism. China, an empire older than Rome, knew some excitements, but was in its depths stagnant. Buddhism, which seeks serenity, to a large extent knew it in 'the unchanging East'. Islam was funda-mentally one society, with one Prophet and one Law from the Atlantic to Indonesia and just as the Chinese traditionally distinguished between their 'Middle Kingdom' and the foreign barbarians, so the Muslims divided mankind into *dar-al-Islam* (the Household of Submission) and *dar-al-harb* (the Household of War). There were millions of Jews in Eastern Europe, and some elsewhere, who despite per-secution and temptation were proudly loyal to a timeless orthodoxy; they were the People of the God of Abraham, Isaac and Jacob.

Christianity was troubled by the alienation of many among the intellectuals and in the industrial cities, but few whose background was Christian doubted the superiority of their civilisation in Europe and America over all others. Many, perhaps most, Christians believed as late as 1900 in 'salvation' through the Church alone, or in 'justification' through faith alone, with the consequence that many, perhaps all, non-Christians would be punished everlastingly in hell. Moreover, the three main branches of the Christian Church were scarcely in communication with their critics or with each other. The Eastern Orthodox Churches maintained their hierarchies and recited their liturgies with a complacent traditionalism. The Roman Catholic Church was defiantly conservative. In the remarkably effective Papal thunder against French 'modernist' theology in 1907–10 may be heard an echo of Pius IX's solemn denunciation of the error that 'the Roman Pontiff can, and ought to, reconcile himself and come to terms with progress, liberalism and modern civilisation' (1864). Among Protestants, complacency took a different form. A more positive emphasis was placed on modern progress, but this was seen as 'building the Kingdom of God'. German Protestantism seemed to dominate the intellectual and cultural centre of the world; the American Churches were abounding with energy; the last of Britain's religious revivals swept Wales in 1904–5; and at this height of the British Empire an Archbishop of Canterbury, E. W. Benson, had declared that the Church of England was 'charged with the world's Christianity'. Among Protestant students a movement arose which would send from the colleges many thousands of missionaries pledged to 'the evangelization of the world in this generation' (to quote the watchword popularised by John R. Mott, an American Methodist who applied the energy of the YMCA to all the problems of churches and nations). Here was a movement which was more globally minded than any previous movement in religious history, but the World Missionary Conference in Edinburgh in 1910 demonstrated that the missionaries under Mott were not daunted by the variety to be found in the world. They were resolved to give to the world the benefit of their superior culture as well as of the final religion. In the very passage of their Conference Report in which they pleaded for sympathy with non-Christian religions, they declared: 'all these religions without exception disclose elemental needs of the human soul which Christianity alone can satisfy'. And in this Edinburgh conference on the world mission of Christianity, only seventeen non-westerners sat among the 1,200 delegates.

Today we see the religions plunged into the ferment of a revolutionary world.[1] Nowhere has the change been more conspicuous than in the recession of Christian missionary fervour. The survey by American laymen published in 1932 under the title *Rethinking Missions* rested on convictions that the heathen were not going to hell, and that Christians must learn to talk with them in a common search for truth. The chairman of that group was Professor W. E. Hocking, who argued that 'Christianity is not yet ready to serve as a world religion' and that 'our present Christianity does not include all that other religions have'. 'It is right, and indeed necessary, for the good of men, that the non-Christian religions should hold to their own, at least until they find themselves in fact understood, translated, and included in the growing power of a religion which, in achieving its own potentiality, achieves theirs also.'[2] Paul Tillich, one of the greatest theologians of the century, said openly that the aim of the Christian approach must now be conversation, not conversion.[3]

A dialogue between the religions is slowly beginning, and the fundamental cause of this new flexibility has been the common exposure of the religions to the challenge of secularisation. Is this challenge to be welcomed, so that all religions must be reshaped to serve a new age? Or is the challenge of the secular world to arouse a firmly negative reply, so that all religions must ally in the defence of God or of spiritual values? Or if our revolutionary world is more complex in its significance for the different religions, should we at least welcome the highly dramatic increases in communications, so that the religions can learn from one another? Such questions have been asked by many in our time. The comparison of religions has been developed as a science, and broadcasts or books have familiarised millions

[1] A comprehensive summary of the nineteenth and twentieth centuries, with bibliographies, was offered by K. S. Latourette, *Christianity in a Revolutionary Age*, 4 vols. (New York, 1951–62).

[2] *Living Religions and a World Faith* (New York, 1940), p. 262.

[3] *Christianity and the Encounter of the World's Religions* (New York, 1963).

with at least the outlines of other creeds. 'Dialogue in a plural world' has begun to be a *cliché*, at least among the sophisticated. Religions, like political creeds, learn to make the best of co-existence.[1]

Although this encounter of the world's religions has scarcely begun to influence the actual beliefs and customs of the masses, we can see more clearly the effect of the revolution in communications, and of the wider challenge of our time, in the simpler process of unifying each religion internally. In part, this process may be seen by studying the great religious conferences of the twentieth century. The Buddhist Congress in Rangoon, 1954–6, which was only the sixth in Buddhism's history, and which celebrated the 2,500th anniversary of the Buddha's entry into Nirvana, was by no means exceptional in its desire to unite all the adherents of a faith. Hinduism, Islam and Judaism have produced similar movements—most easily on the basis of charitable or political co-operation. Christianity, the most sharply divided religion in history, has now put its extraordinary energies into the cause of reconciliation. The ecumenical movement around the World Council of Churches, constituted in 1948, has involved Protestants, Orthodox and Anglicans in a strenuous process of reunion and renewal. The Second Vatican Council of 1962–5 showed against all previous expectation that the Roman Catholic Church was willing to participate in this new pilgrimage—even if as yet largely in its own way and in loyalty to its own doctrines. But more influential still in destroying the old isolationism of the religions, and of the denominations within them, has been the less organised movement of study, thought and discussion fed by education, broadcasting and writing. Many millions of individuals have attempted to relate their inherited scriptures and religious traditions to the scientific outlook and to life in a modern nation. The great religious conferences are thus part

[1] Professor Ninian Smart has provided two useful surveys: *The Religious Experience of Mankind* (London, 1971), and the more philosophical *The Phenomenon of Religion* (London, 1973).

of a much wider ferment of religious thought, responding to the secular challenge of the twentieth century.

Our mention of the revolution in communications has more significance than is exhausted by saying that delegates can now travel to international, interdenominational and interfaith meetings, while books reflecting these encounters can now be printed for distribution throughout the world. The real point is that all peoples of the world are now being drawn into a single stream of history. The age of the jet, succeeding to the age of the steamship, symbolises the Westernisation of the world, and the long-term trend to the West is not effectively halted when (in religion as in politics and economics) African, Asian or Latin American pride flings the arrogance of colonialism back in the West's teeth. By its own action or by arousing reaction, it is the West that sets the pace. Admittedly, East and West have not yet finally settled their accounts. Later chapters in this book will mention some aspects of the challenge or offer in the spiritual life now being made to the West by Africa and Asia. But the Westernisation of the world is a great and growing fact. Even at this stage of the transition we can already study much in this world-wide debate about religion if we approach it as an almost infinitely varied series of reactions to the 'coming of age' experienced by Western man in his scientific civilisation. Thus a treatment of the religions of the world does not make itself nonsensical, however inadequate it may be, if it concentrates on Christianity's own response to the scientific revolution which arose in a Europe which had been Christendom. If the impact of the secularisation brought about by Western science and technology is to result in a universal secularism, in 'no religion at all', it will be thanks mainly to Christianity's defeat in the West. And if a mature religion is recognised to be possible in the modern world, this place for belief may result from a conviction in the West that the essence of Christianity is credible by rational adults, more than from any other factor.

But perhaps we should try to avoid comparing the *religions* as such? Professor Cantwell Smith of Harvard, who is one of the world's leading experts in the comparison of religions, has pleaded that the word 'religion' should now be used as little as possible, because it is an idea which inclines men to attack or defend a set of other ideas associated with 'religion'. Cantwell Smith does indeed show that 'religion' in its modern sense is a product of the modern West. Other civilisations have had no exactly equivalent word in their languages: Ancient India did not, and Ancient Israel did not. The Latin *religio* did not have the full meaning of the modern 'religion', although it is the origin of our word. Many of the names of the 'other religions'—Buddhism, Hinduism, etc.—were developed by Westerners in the nineteenth century. We may add that it has been in dialogue with the West during the twentieth century that these 'other religions' have become more self-conscious and articulate than they were before the impact of the West. Muslim apologists commonly write with an eye on attacks by Christian missionaries and by Westernising secularists; world-wide Buddhism's first creed was written in 1945 by a convert who became an English judge, Christmas Humphreys;[1] and Hinduism has simplified its theology in order to reply to Christians in India, and in order to counter-attack through its own missions in the West. The idea of 'religion' has encouraged Christians themselves to defend 'Christianity' (and has encouraged secularists to attack it), although the Bible knows no such abstractions, preferring to speak about the whole of life being given direction through a covenant between God and man, or through a way of discipleship by which men can know and obey God. Cantwell Smith validly points out that this alleged necessity to attack or defend a whole religion such as 'Christianity' frequently distorts our understanding of real life, and hinders us from learning from each other as we share our visions of the mystery of man's place in the universe.

'It is what the Hindu is able to see, by being a Hindu, that is significant,' he writes. 'And we may be sure that, as he

[1] Christmas Humphreys, *Buddhism* (London, 1951; revd. edn., 1962), pp. 73–6.

looks around him, he does not see "Hinduism". Like the rest
of us, he sees his wife's death, his child's minor and major
aspirations, his moneylender's mercilessness, the calm of a
starlit evening, his own mortality. He sees these things
through coloured glasses, if one will, of a "Hindu" brand.
He sees also certain gods and institutions that may carry
this label, though the deeper and more sophisticated his
faith, the more he sees through these. His neighbour, also a
Hindu, sees the foreground differently; if their vision finally
converges, it is because both have been sufficiently penetrating to see through and beyond their foreground to a
reality that, if not altogether attributeless, is certainly quite
without the attribute of being in any sense *Hindu.*'[1]

This is the approach which more and more people are
coming to see is needed if man is to make religious progress
in the period into which he is now moving. It is unrealistic
to expect Christian missions, for example, to convert or even
to 'evangelise' in the world if their emphasis is on the propa-
gation of all the institutions and intellectual expressions of
present-day Christianity. The only realistic hope for
Christians is that, partly through the contribution of
missionaries but mainly through larger forces which have no
'Christian' label, the essential vision of man and of God
taught by what Jesus has been, said and done will be accepted
by more and more of those who are now—and who will
always in some sense remain—Hindus, Buddhists, Muslims,
etc. This development is unlikely unless those who are now
Christians strengthen their own grasp of that vision, if need
be letting go many of the outworn traditions of Christianity.
This 'reconception' of the religions (to use W. E. Hocking's
phrase) through the testing of abstractions by realities is a
development which may be heard as the music of the future.

However, the future is not the present, and the world is
not yet one. It is premature to ask men to forget about
'religion' or 'the religions' at a stage when (as we have
already noted) it is precisely the challenge of the new secular

---

[1] W. Cantwell Smith, *The Meaning and End of Religion* (New York,
1964), p. 127.

pressures that makes some of them more sharply aware of the questions raised for them personally by the religious tradition of an area. At present, the single stream of history into which the peoples of the world are being drawn is a single stream of questions, not of answers; and what unites the peoples is their common experience that their own societies are breaking up. What exists now is a supply of differently coloured spectacles through which the reality of God and the world may be viewed. Whether or not we regret this, what actually exists now is a plurality of religions. This has its parallel in the political sphere, where a world order including a world police force and some degree of world government is so clearly the long-term necessity, yet what exists now is a plurality of national states. To ask the religions to lose their self-consciousness in the face of secularisation is like asking the peoples to abandon their nationalisms while their pride still seems under challenge. The energy of what remains of the twentieth century will be absorbed by the relationships of the religions (and of the nations) to each other and to the pressure of the emerging future (spiritual and social). And in the religious as in the political sphere, it tests all of a commentator's intelligence to discern one pattern of response to these challenges in the separated parts of our world.

CHAPTER TWO

The Social Impact of the Secular Century

The Social Character of Religion

Before religion is thought of as a creed, it is offered as a prayer; and before it is offered as a prayer, it is experienced as a community. *Religio*, as the most probable interpretation of the Latin word suggests, is what 'binds' a group. *Religare* in Latin means 'to bind' (although some scholars dispute whether *religio* comes from *religare*).

It is necessary to set religion (and also irreligion) in this social context because believers (or unbelievers) sometimes suppose or pretend that their acceptance (or rejection) of religious belief was produced solely by personal meditation on the true, the beautiful and the good. An individual may indeed accept (or reject) his religious tradition in an intimately personal way—in extreme cases, in a mystical vision which leaves him confident that he knows the character of ultimate reality. But the individual is likely to reach a conclusion, or to receive a vision, which is directly related to the tradition of his community and to the whole pattern of his life. Within this century a number of Roman Catholics have claimed that the glory of heaven has been revealed to them, notably in the visions which three children saw of the Virgin Mary at Fatima in Portugal in 1917. We need not cast doubt on the sincerity of these visionaries, if we observe that the content of the visions and of the accompanying messages from heaven has corresponded with the expectations of the Church to whose members they occurred—or if we add that many non-Christians have received visions of the divine. Ramakrishna, for example, who died in 1886, and who is usually reckoned the greatest mystic of modern India, repeatedly entered *samadhi* (the bliss of enlightenment). In these trances he saw and talked with his 'Mother'. But his 'Mother' was the goddess Kali, who is usually imagined amid blood and skulls; she is the goddess of destruction, and must be worshipped as such (in the old days, by human sacrifice) before she will give the blessing of new life.

How are we to understand the connections and contrasts between the visions at Fatima and the visions of Ramakrishna? Many of the psychological experiences and effects of mysticism seem to be closely similar in Portugal and India. Nor need we confine our study to the stranger experiences of the acknowledged saints. Similar, although less dramatic, moments of vision are known by many religious believers—and by many others also. Mystical, or at least ecstatic, experiences have been reported by pantheists who worship nature, or who call nature God—and by atheists who remain atheists, and for whom mysticism may feed Sir Julian Huxley's secular 'religion' of humanism.[1] We are confronted here by *a basic religious sense* which seems to be innate in all (or almost all) people, whatever their theologies. This sense should not be reduced to an 'essence' consisting of morality (as the high-minded eighteenth-century Enlightenment maintained), or the herd-instinct or sex (as in the more cynical atheism of our own century). This religious sense seems to be the raw material both of believing religion and of the reverent unbelief which has been called 'religious atheism'; and if it is totally lacking —if an individual feels that in no sense does he belong in the world around him—then suicide may come. We may add that the connections between the religions at this level of man's basic religious sense are usually accepted by the

[1] In *Ecstasy* (London, 1961) an atheist, Marghanita Laski, collected memories of such experiences from many of her friends.

religions themselves. Thus the children of Fatima, had they known about Ramakrishna, would have been good Catholics if they had commented that Kali, if she was not an appearance of Satan, was an appearance of the Virgin distorted by Ramakrishna's heathen ignorance; and Ramakrishna, had he lived to hear about Fatima, would have displayed the Hindu respect for all the images under which the divine One appears or is conceived. And not all atheistic humanists would wish the Catholic visionaries or the Hindu saint to be certified as insane; they would respect the mystics' moments of human glory, amid the sad state of the economy in Portugal and India.[1]

But we shall not get very far in our assessment of religion if we confine ourselves to this basic agreement and exchange of compliments. The mystical ecstasies by themselves, stripped of all more contentious interpretations, seem to suggest no more than that the mind of man is related to the universe and can experience the universe intensely. Insanity or drug-taking can produce similar feelings. Any further interpretation immediately plunges us into disputes, for any further interpretation involves a very substantial and controversial element of choice or faith. It is important to remember this universal testimony of the mystics to 'something larger than ourselves' when we study the critics of religion, but it is also important to consider whether we may legitimately go beyond such a banal conclusion and say more about the significance of religious experience. 'Mysticism,' Bertrand Russell once wrote, 'is in its essence little more than a certain intensity and depth of feeling in regard to what is believed about the universe';[2] but many people want to insist that the phenomenon of religious experience in its total context should not be analysed *only* as insanity or drug-taking is analysed, for they attach great significance to what they believe about the universe. The trouble is that people's beliefs are so varied that, as we have already noted,

[1] See, e.g., W. T. Stace, *Mysticism and Philosophy* (New York, 1960).
[2] *Mysticism and Logic* (London, 1917), p. 3.

if we are to be realistic we have to speak not about man's *religion* but about the world's many religions and quasi-religions. The veneration of the Virgin Mary, and the worship of Kali, and Sir Julian Huxley's quasi-religion of evolution are (to put it mildly) different—for they arise not from the mystic experience themselves, but from the interpretations given to these experiences by the faiths of complex human beings.

Thus both the basically similar experiences and the different interpretations, both the ecstasies and the churches, both religion and the religions, should be given due weight in our assessment. On the one hand religious believers, and even religiously-minded atheists, do experience visions or ecstasies which are extremely hard to define or assess—and which it is unscientific to deny. Any student who acknowledges this fact must find much of the origin of religion at that fundamental level, in man's basic religious sense. On the other hand, the individual involved is not likely to be content with a vague feeling that he 'belongs' or that he is in touch with 'something larger'. He tries to interpret his experience more fully to himself and to others. And here is the point: when a person makes this attempt, when he undertakes one more crack at the riddle of the universe, *he does so almost entirely within the context provided by his community*. Catholicism suggests an interpretation in the shape of the Blessed Virgin; Hinduism suggests an interpretation in the shape of another Mother; modern secularism suggests a psychological explanation such as Sir Julian Huxley's (and perhaps the gentle charm of Harvard University suggests a religious moderation such as that of William James). The spectacles with which a religious believer (or an atheist) views reality are usually spectacles provided by his society.

This understanding of religion (and irreligion) as *an experience interpreted by the faith of a society* has come to be fairly widely shared by thoughtful people—with consequences which have not only influenced the academic study of religion, but which have also affected the position of the living religions in the modern world. On the one hand, the recognition of the reality of the mysticism behind religion has checked the confident dogmas of rationalism. It is now commonly acknowledged that a secularist who attempts to reduce religious experience to 'nothing but' this, that or the next 'essence' which can be fitted into his reasoning is not able to abolish the fundamental fact of man's religious sense—or the 'ecstatic reason' as Paul Tillich called it— but is simply offering one debatable interpretation of it, since any assessment of this strange and ambiguous pheno- menon in the experience of mankind will be an interpreta- tion linked with the observer's total response to the mystery of life. On the other hand, the recognition of what might be called the sociology of mysticism provides part of our cen- tury's challenge to religious belief, for nowadays only the naïve are willing to accept religious visions at their face values, without considering the total situation of the mystic.

Of course, the social context of a mystical vision or religious crisis is an extreme case to show the importance of a study of society in religious studies. A far more typical case would be provided by an individual whose religious con- victions were never fortified or displaced by a dramatic crisis but either matured gradually or vanished gradually. An immense amount of work has been done in this century to observe, classify and interpret religious behaviour with a scientific attempt at objectivity. Some of this work has been flavoured with hostility towards religion; such 'positivist' hostility, we may add, has marked 'sociology' as a self- consciously secular discipline ever since Auguste Comte, who invented the word in the nineteenth century. But some sociologists have been more sympathetic with the pheno- mena which they were examining, more modest about their competence to judge the truth of the beliefs involved, and thus better qualified to penetrate into the life of religion.[1]

---

[1] Peter Berger, *The Social Reality of Religion* (London, 1969), and Michael Hill, *A Sociology of Religion* (London, 1973), are distinguished by their authors' 'feel' for religion as well as by their sociological authority.

What is clear from these studies (and, of course, from personal observation also) is that in every case the community—the home, the school, the adult world or the religious group itself—deeply influences the individual's religion. The influence may be conveyed through formal instruction, through public or domestic ceremonies, through private conversations in families or among friends, or through behaviour which has little or no explicitly religious content. Religion is normally caught like a children's epidemic, in the tender years. It is often brought to a crisis by a conversion in adolescence, related to the crisis of sexual growth—but this religious decision is usually related closely to the experiences of childhood, and is taken at any age when the adolescent who gives his allegiance to a religion is not qualified to vote for a politician. When questioned in maturity, religious believers tend to base their answers on the faith of their fathers. They take their stand within a tradition. A Muslim, for example, is likely to intend to be loyal to Islam, however careless he may be in discharging the obligations of his religion, for the religion of Islam represents an important part of his heritage, and probably constitutes an important element in his identification of himself. Without this religion, he would feel cut off from his roots. Strongly as reformers in every generation regret this, it is inevitable that religion, where it flourishes, is usually conservative; for religion is usually associated with sentiments of gratitude to parents and teachers and with affection for the sights and sounds of childhood. If religious influences have been weak in childhood, or if the religion of childhood seems to have been defeated by stronger social forces, the acceptance of a religion is usually bound up with the desire of the adult to improve himself and to become a respectable member of a society which has a religious tradition accumulated over the centuries. If an individual is in revolt against his society, or against life in general, but adheres to a religious sect, one explanation can be that the individual has found his identity within the fellowship of that sect. He can now voice his protest through the sect's disapproval of society. A religious conversion, whatever else it may be, almost always includes the individual's acceptance of a social role proposed by a religious group.

The habits of irreligion in a society also deserve to be analysed sociologically. If a Muslim rejects the faith of his fathers, it is likely to be because of the attraction of the secular West through education and technology, not because of deep studies in philosophy or in 'comparative religion'. If a Frenchman is contemptuous of priests and churches, it is likely to be because his *milieu* is traditionally anti-clerical; for a map can be drawn of religious as of political electorates. Unbelief can be as irrational as any religious faith, because its social and psychological roots go just as deep; and, like a popular religious movement, atheism can be spread by a fashion.[1]

Both the power of religion and its eclipse therefore need to be studied in the context of the whole life of society. The ideas and the society need to be taken together. In passing we may observe that far too many theologians seem remote from the real world when they state their reasons why their particular religious theory has appealed or ought to appeal; and many secular humanists talk like shallow rationalists, naïvely over-emphasising the place of reason in human behaviour, as they state their reasons why religion has declined or ought to decline. Some of those theologians who have attempted to mediate between belief and unbelief have perhaps been the most absurdly intellectual of all. Their books sometimes seem to treat the contemporary society as a by-product of European philosophy or fiction, and seem to assume that the religious destinies of peoples hang on the lectures of theologians. Such intellectualist fancies will have to be abandoned if the serious study of religion is to make progress. David Hume once observed that 'reason is, and ought to be, the slave of the passions'. The famous saying applies with equal strength to religion—and to its rejection. Religion (or its rejection) is a psychological

[1] See Colin Campbell, *Toward a Sociology of Irreligion* (London, 1971).

phenomenon which shows with special clarity how man, although fundamentally mysterious specially in his basic religious sense, can be analysed with far-reaching success as a creature of circumstance, as a social animal, as the slave of the passions of the group into which he is thrown by the accidents of birth and upbringing. A realistic assessment of religion (or of atheism) must begin where people begin—not with ideas but with emotions, shaped as these have been by everyday experiences and by all the subtle influences of home and school, work and friends. Many definitions of religion have been proposed, but one of the best has been that put forward by the American sociologist, Dr. Gerhard Lenski: 'A system of beliefs about the nature of the force(s) ultimately shaping a man's destiny, and the practices associated therewith, shared by the members of a group.'[1]

What *are* the forces which ultimately shape our destinies? The sociologist, unfortunately, must himself make an act of belief in a social context if he attempts to answer this philosophical question. Here he is just like the rest of us; for the sociologist does not *know* in a scientific sense. 'Sociological theory must, by its own logic, view religion as a human projection, and by the same logic can have nothing to say about the possibility that this projection may refer to something other than the being of the projector. In other words, to say that religion is a human projection does not logically preclude the possibility that the projected meanings may have an ultimate status independent of man.'[2] What sociology can show is that the replacement of one religion by another may usually be interpreted as a shift in the psychological forces of society, encouraging a new belief about the ultimate forces of the universe; and sociology can also explain secularisation itself not as a mainly intellectual movement but as the process by which the beliefs and practices of all available religions are rejected by a group because they do not correspond with that group's present vision of its destiny. Religions, or secular substitutes for them, are

[1] *The Religious Factor* (New York, 1961; revd. edn., 1963), p. 331.
[2] Peter Berger, *The Social Reality of Religion*, pp. 180–1.

projections which groups think plausible. A particular
religion loses its grip on the hearts and minds of a society by
losing its plausibility or its power to symbolise that society's
corporate passions. We shall study the key area in modern
secularisation, which is Europe in the nineteenth century;
but first we may remind ourselves of the previous unification
of society through religion. Religious unity may be seen
most clearly in the life of primitive peoples, to which we now
turn.

Primitive Religion

Much attention has been given in this century to the study
of the role of religion in primitive societies, but confusion
has been caused because, mixed with the solid research and
sober interpretation, there has been a good deal of fanciful
speculation, inspired by one or more of three motives: (1) the
wish to recover the historical origins of religion, (2) the wish
to see the essence of religion in those origins and (3) the
wish to show that religion, having such origins and such an
essence, rests on an illusion. The speculation has been in
vain, because the origins and essence of the religious life of
mankind cannot be recovered by a strictly, scientifically
historical method. The evidence is far too obscure, and its
interpretation always demands the expression of a deeply
personal faith or of a deeply personal unbelief. Religious
experience cannot be *proved* to be illusory—any more than
it can be proved to reveal a supernatural reality.

Sir James Frazer's great study of primitive magic and
religion may be mentioned as a mixture of fact and fantasy typical of the brilliantly speculative generation of the
'arm-chair' anthropologists. *The Golden Bough* assembled
from all over the world, including the literature of Greece
and Rome, a mass of evidence about magicians and priests,
the deities of the hunt and the harvest, sacred kings and
scapegoats, sacraments and myths, taboos and festivals, and
it brought all these curious phenomena together in one
argument. 'We shall perhaps be disposed to conclude,'
wrote Frazer at the end of his work, 'that the movement of

higher thought, so far as we can trace it, has on the whole been from magic through religion to science. In magic man depends on his own strength to meet the difficulties and dangers that beset him on every side. He believes in a certain established order of nature on which he can surely count, and which he can manipulate for his own ends. When he discovers his mistake, he . . . throws himself humbly on the mercy of certain great invisible beings behind the veil of nature, to which he now ascribes all those far-reaching powers which he once arrogated to himself. But as time goes on this explanation in its turn proves to be unsatisfactory. For it assumes that the succession of natural events is not determined by immutable laws . . . Thus the keener minds . . . revert in a measure to the older standpoint of magic by postulating explicitly, what in magic had only been implicitly assumed, to wit, an inflexible regularity in the order of natural events which, if carefully observed, enables us to foresee their course with certainty and to act accordingly. In short, religion, regarded as an explanation of nature, is displaced by science.'[1]

That clear distinction between magic, religion and science has now been generally abandoned. It was part of the whole speculative approach. The basic trouble about Frazer's analysis was that he had no personal experience of 'savages' but, instead, relied on reading and on introspection to try and understand beliefs which he found very strange, so that he failed to do justice to the mixture of magical manipulation, religious awe and down-to-earth matter-of-factness which later anthropologists have found to be the actual mentality of primitive peoples still surviving. Frazer was too intellectualist in his emphasis on the theories of nature worked out by the 'keener minds'—and his intellectualism was dominated by the evolutionism of that age of Darwin.

A more promising approach was made by Emile Durkheim in his very influential discussion of *The Elementary*

---

[1] *The Golden Bough* (12 vols., London; 1900–15), abridged into one vol. (London, 1922), pp. 711–12.

Forms of the Religious Life.[1] Durkheim, like Frazer, was in religion an unbeliever, and his primary interest in anthropology seems to have been to expose the origins and essence of religion. He maintained that when a primitive group worshipped a god it was really worshipping itself, or at least its own traditional morality or collective conscience; it was building up its solidarity by its religious enthusiasm. He illustrated this theory by reports of the worship of totems by clans among the aborigines of Australia. However, Durkheim was another anthropologist who did no field-research among the primitive people whom he described. Had he done so, he would have discovered that the custom of totem-worship in Australia was not so simple as he thought, and that there was no evidence to show that this particular custom, in itself not very impressively religious, provided an explanation of all religious beliefs and practices. Durkheim's theory *may* be correct, but it cannot be demonstrated scientifically. In fact, the origins of primitive religion cannot be recovered, and any attempt to describe its essence needs to be treated cautiously, for beliefs and practices vary greatly from one group to another, from one period to another, from one individual temperament to another, and from one social situation to another.

It is true to say with Frazer that primitive man wishes to manipulate nature by magical rituals, and it is true to add with Durkheim that 'a religion is a unified system of beliefs and practices relative to sacred things, that is to say, things set apart and forbidden—beliefs and practices which unite, into one single moral community called a Church, all those who adhere to them'. But to add that these are the *only* origins of religion, and that all religion rests on the fantasies produced by these attempts of ignorant savages to do scientific and political jobs, so that 'the idea of society is the soul of religion', is merely to state one's own philosophy of life. The evidence is equally compatible with another suggestion: namely, that primitive men have responded to a reality which civilised men have also experienced—and to

[1] 1912; Eng. trans., New York, 1915.

which civilised men have responded in ways not radically different. Both in primitive and in civilised societies, 'the idea of society' and 'the soul of religion' may be viewed as two ways of establishing a society's total view of the world. This total view of the world comes before both the politics and the religion. 'It must be stressed very strongly,' writes one of the best of recent sociologists to discuss religion, 'that what is being said here does *not* imply a sociologically deterministic theory of religion. It is *not* implied that any particular religious system is nothing but the effect or 'reflection' of social processes. Rather, the point is that the *same* human activity that produces human society also produces religion, with the relation between the two products always being a dialectical one. Thus it is just as possible that, in a particular historical development, a social process is the effect of religious ideation, while in another development the reverse may be the case.'[1]

Many of the speculations of the 'arm-chair' anthropologists such as Frazer and Durkheim about primitive religion's origins and essence have been held up to deserved ridicule by Sir Edward Evans-Pritchard—an anthropologist whose own field work provided a model of humble study of the primitive peoples whose superstitious savagery the earlier theorists despised.[2] Through the work of such recent anthropologists a less highly coloured, but also more accurate, picture is emerging. In this picture, the valid part of Durkheim's analysis is preserved: namely, his suggestion that a religion, whatever may be its origins and essence in man's basic religious sense, is usually interpreted in a way which binds a group. Here we offer only a crude outline of current study of primitive religion, as this is relevant to the wider discussion of the role of religion in society.

In primitive religion is to be found not only the fear of the dead—which Frazer regarded as 'probably the most power-

[1] Peter Berger, *The Social Reality of Religion*, p. 48.
[2] See the essay on 'Religion and the Anthropologists' in E. E. Evans-Pritchard, *Essays in Social Anthropology* (London, 1962), and his *Theories of Primitive Religion* (Oxford, 1965).

ful force in the making of primitive religion'—but often also a glad communion with the dead. The present members of a village or tribe are united with their ancestors in a living fellowship. This communion symbolises and increases both their pride in membership of a society which goes back far into time, and also their ability to draw on the wisdom of the past for guidance in their problems. And it offers them this encouragement, that when they are dead, they will be remembered as they now remember. The inhabitants of a modern industrial city are indeed rootless in comparison. But communion with the past is not the only use of religion to primitive peoples. Regular participation in ceremonies such as dances immensely strengthens the solidarity of the living. Drinks or drugs may be used to intensify the group's experiences in these ceremonies, but the religion matters more in creating the party spirit. All the members of a tribe or a village have their parts to play, as actors or involved spectators, and the profound enjoyment with which they take part has often aroused the envy of their civilised, lonely guests. 'Savage religion,' in one anthropologist's famous phrase, 'is something not so much thought out as danced out.'[1]

Primitive religion has the further merit—in the eyes of observers who are most sensitive to their own civilisation's discontents—of putting each stage of the individual's life in a social, and even cosmic, setting. The ruler of the tribe of the village is a legitimate, and indeed sacred, ruler—almost one of the gods from whom he is expected to derive wisdom. The taboos of religion surround and safeguard (usually with hygienic consequences, if not motives) sexual intercourse, pregnancy, birth and weaning. The lore and rites of religion educate and initiate a young person into adult responsibilities. Daily work in the fields or at home is given significance and even holiness because religion provides both teachings about the duties involved, and customs which are vivid reminders of these teachings. Some rituals directly suggest moral duties, and even when what is specifically religious

[1] R. B. Marett, *The Threshold of Religion* (London, 1909), p. xxi.

seems to be unrelated to normal conduct, the rituals still have the function of expressing the group's life *as a group*— a life which in every primitive society leads to a more or less elaborate code about what is permitted and what is prohibited. When a tribe fights, its priests assure it that its gods fight with it. When a member of the group falls sick, religious belief either heals or consoles him. A dying person is told by religion where he is going, and religion helps the survivors both to express and to overcome their grief. Religion performs these services from the cradle to the grave not only by linking each crisis or duty with the total life of the group, but also by linking it with the whole of nature. Rocks or trees or other objects in nature are felt intensely, almost as if they were brothers. For primitive peoples nature is alive, extending punishment to those who defy it and friendship to those who live in obedience to its laws. What human beings do and think matters to the universe; man and nature are bound in a bundle. Here is one meaning of the stories of the world's creation, which at first strike a modern critic as mere legends. In primitive religion, the essential fact is the integration of man with himself and his environment, and 'myth, ritual and ethics are definitely but three facets of the same essential fact'.[1]

The primitive world-view is, paradoxically, more familiar to many in contemporary Europe and North America than is the rather similar world-view which was held during most of European history. This is because anthropological studies of primitive peoples have been supplemented for our civilisation by a popular fascination with Africa. When an African leader such as President Senghor of Senegal speaks about the deep meaning of *négritude*, Western people can understand something of his emotion, for they seek to share it through their own enthusiasm for primitive art, and above all for African music as this has been preserved from the pagan past and given new life by the (often deeply and actively religious) Negroes of the United States. Thus the

[1] Bronislaw Malinowski, *The Foundations of Faith and Morals* (London, 1936), p. 25.

sophisticates of New York turn for spiritual food to the remnants of African religion and the most progressive American colleges sponsor the separate development of 'black studies' and listen attentively to the advocates of 'black power'—at a time when in Africa's own cities the pagan survivals have been almost overwhelmed by the cultural impact of the West.

The paradox is great, but significant. *The West destroys primitive religion, but the West believes that it needs primitive religion.* Indeed, Africa, with its sense of the unity and meaningfulness of life, occupies in the imagination of the West in our time a status similar to the appeal of China to the eighteenth century, when by its order, rationality and elegance the more ancient civilisation fascinated a Europe emerging from the barbarities of the Wars of Religion. If so, the appeal of Africa is a sign of the West's growing awareness of the disintegration of its own culture, and it may be also a confession that the West seeks not only an injection of primitive vitality but also an initiation into the mysteries of religion.[1] The anthropologist Lucien Lévy-Bruhl used to speak about the *participation mystique* in nature and in society which is provided by primitive religion, and he would add that the need for participation remains more pressing, even in modern societies, than the need for knowledge or for conforming to logical exigencies, for it comes from the depths.[2] Many students and others who have to live in the West in the 1970s would echo that.

Christendom in Europe

For many Europeans in our time, special study and a scholarly imagination are needed in order to recapture something of the religious pattern which constituted Europe during the Byzantine Empire and during the Middle Ages

[1] See, e.g., John Taylor's moving introduction to African religion, *The Primal Vision* (London, 1963).

[2] See, e.g., his *The 'Soul' of the Primitive* (1927; Eng. trans., 1928). A good general introduction to *Social Anthropology* was provided by Godfrey Leinhardt (London, 1964).

in the West, although this pattern remained largely intact in the social conservatism of the mainstream of the Protestant Reformation and survived in a semi-secularised form into the recent past. One of Shakespeare's central themes was the importance of 'degree' if 'discord' was not to ruin society. The order of society—with rulers, barons, churchmen of various grades, merchants, craftsmen, apprentices, peasants and other groups all discharging their distinct duties—was upheld by the crown and by the feudal system, by civic guilds and by manorial courts; but at bottom it was upheld by religion. It was God who decreed the acceptance of the rights and duties of each grade in society. Indeed, a sacred order or a 'hierarchy' was thought to exist in the whole of God's creation, from the archangels to the dust out of which man had been created 'a little lower than the angels'. In the fourth century, under the Emperors Constantine and Theodosius, Christianity took over this insistence on order from the Roman state religion, connecting it with many teachings already to be found in the Bible. As the supernatural side of religion grew dimmer in the seventeenth and eighteenth centuries, this hierarchy of heaven and earth under God became a 'great chain of being', still keeping everything in the universe and in society in its proper place —a semi-secular version of St. Paul's 'the powers that be'.[1]

This hierarchical vision in Christendom and 'post-Christian' Europe has been so frequently described that it might seem redundant to offer even this brief reminder, had not influence recently been secured by a Dutch scholar, Professor Arend van Leeuwen, who in his book *Christianity in World History* (London, 1964) has maintained that the culture of Europe, based on the Bible, was essentially exempt from what he calls 'ontocracy'. He means by 'ontocracy' a rigidly ordered society, structured according to a religious understanding of 'Being', of the kind which he observed both in primitive paganism and in Islam while he was a missionary in Indonesia, and which he explored

---

[1] A. O. Lovejoy, *The Great Chain of Being* (New Haven, 1936), is one of the classics in the history of ideas.

further as he studied the religious cultures of India and China. *Christianity in World History* was a massively learned book, and the contrast which it drew between the message of the Bible and the normal type of religious society in history is of crucial significance. Christianity has been a faith restlessly and explosively dynamic, boldly and dangerously personal, and many in West and East have rebelled against their societies in the name of Christ, the divine outcast. Yet Professor van Leeuwen's readers will observe that a lack of understanding of medieval society indicates one of the few gaps in this Dutch Protestant's scholarly equipment. For medieval society *was* an 'ontocracy'. Radicals have been a small minority in most periods of Christian history, and in the Middle Ages few indeed were the Christians who offered a really radical opposition to their society. The great fact of the Middle Ages was the fact of a sacred society—a society which was unified almost as completely as the sacred societies of the East. It was the Christendom of the cathedrals and the crusades, and its aftermath lasted for a long time.

Frequently in the twentieth century Christian thinkers have expressed their hopes for Europe in a language about a recovery of Christendom. Many Lutherans have sought to recover the reality of the 'Folk Church'. A vocal group in the Church of England was called the 'Christendom' group (V. A. Demant, Maurice Reckitt, T. S. Eliot, etc.). More influential were Popes Pius XI and XII in repeated warnings against secularisation, and Roman Catholic writers such as G. K. Chesterton and Hilaire Belloc among the popularisers and Jacques Maritain and Christopher Dawson among the philosophers. Their vision of an England which was merry when it was Catholic, and their equation of Europe with the Faith, had many antecedents among Christians or romanticists of the nineteenth century, but in our age it has had this strong appeal, that sometimes the only alternative seemed to be Hitler or Stalin. Thus nostalgia for the Middle Ages has lingered on.

But the religious pattern of medieval Christendom could

not hold together. As it flew apart, each fragment tried to preserve religious uniformity and social hierarchy. The emergent nation states of Europe were Catholic or Protestant according to the ruler's choice; *cuius regio eius religio* ('he who controls the country, controls the religion') was the principle on which the Wars of Religion ended in Germany in 1648. German 'Culture-Protestantism' expressed the idea of a Christian society with a confident energy right up to 1918. In the Catholic countries of Europe the alliance of throne and altar was a powerful theme of the nineteenth century, with echoes into our own time through the sanctified dictatorships of Franco and Salazar. Still in 1900 the Church of England educated more schoolchildren than did the state; and Russia was Holy Russia until the Orthodox Church fell with the last of the Tsars in 1917. However, religious minorities obstinately survived, notably the English Nonconformists, and in the course of the nineteenth century the repeal of the 'tests' (religious qualifications for public office) indicated the gradual and partial erosion of the old identification of Church and State. Political and economic realities dictated first the practice and then the principle of religious pluralism and toleration, whether or not the National Church was formally disestablished. Four centuries after the Reformation, and three centuries after John Locke's great plea for toleration in England, the Roman Catholic Church conceded the principle of religious liberty at the Second Vatican Council in 1965. But even after tracing the rise of religious liberty in Europe, we have still not accounted for the most important cause of the end of the old identification of Church and State. For we have to remember that the Nonconformist religious bodies by no means included all the groups arising in society to disrupt its old patterns. In England they were only partially successful in their evangelism; on the Continent, they were often socially insignificant. The main attack on the religious establishment came from people whose hearts belonged to no church at all.

The Renaissance has often been regarded as the time when

the Middle Ages ended and 'humanism' began. Obviously, no one denies that there was a flowering of humanism then, but the Renaissance had its roots deep in the medieval culture—and, even more important, it did not produce many Machiavellis who entirely dismissed Christianity. All the tendency among recent historians is to see the end of the medieval religious pattern in the scientific revolution among intellectuals, and in the popular revulsion against the Wars of Religion, in the seventeenth century. But even this end of the medieval religious pattern was not the end of wide-spread Christian belief. The eighteenth century was the Age of Enlightenment in that most of the leading thinkers had by now rejected orthodox Catholicism or Protestantism, and in the parishes the flame of faith burned low. But the influence of the religious movement known as Pietism in Europe, the success of Methodism and Evangelicalism in England, and the Awakenings across the Atlantic, showed how much of Christianity was left, awaiting revival. Thus religious enthusiasm still could flare up. The religious establishments of Europe were still maintained in the official alliances of throne and altar, or of the manor house and the rectory, until the French Revolution; and although the Catholic Church in France suffered very severely through its identification with the monarchy and the *ancien régime*, the extreme anti-clericalism of the Revolution was shrewdly modified by Napoleon in his Concordat with the Papacy in 1802, for Napoleon knew that French unity could not be built on an anti-clerical basis. And the forces marshalled against the Revolution and Napoleon thought of themselves as defending religion. We may say that Europe was, in a real sense, a Christian continent into the nineteenth century.

Religion in the Industrial Revolution

The greatest defeat of modern Christianity was *its failure in the industrial revolution*. Pope Pius XI was right to call this the 'great scandal' of the nineteenth century, for the failure not only brought about the ruin of the Christian Church in the Europe which had been its home; it also provided a precedent for the decline of religion amid industrialisation elsewhere. And nowhere were this defeat and 'scandal' more evident than in England, the world's first industrial country. What was involved was more than shortages in the provision of church buildings and clergy in England's new industrial towns.

It was a defeat in theology. When the children sang their notorious hymn (first published in 1848) about

> *The rich man in his castle,*
> *The poor man at his gate,*
> *God made them high or lowly,*
> *And order'd their estate*

they were echoing the social philosophy of Christendom; but that philosophy infuriated the new industrial masses. For, whatever may have been the case with the feudal barons or the aristocratic landowners or the squires of the old agricultural society, the rich man in the new industrial society did *not* owe his wealth to his position in a timeless scheme of things. He owed it to his control of some financial capital, which he had increased by retaining profits instead of paying a just wage to the workers. The God who was the 'Lord of lords' among the gentry in the ordered countryside might be taken to town by the capitalists as their celestial mascot, who rewarded their thrift and energy with profits now and heaven hereafter; but in the factories and sordid tenements of the industrial age this God seemed a positive menace to the progress of the people. The social philosophy founded on the theology about this rural or capitalistic God taught that the division of rich and poor was inevitable, at a time when—precisely because of the novelty of industrial society—the masses were for the first time beginning to think that this might not always be the case. 'To the conservative,' wrote Horace Greely in 1868 in the midst of the industrialisation of the United States, 'Religion would often seem a part of the subordinate machinery of Police, having for its main object the instilling of proper humility into the abject, of contentment into the breasts of the down-trodden, and endowing with a sacred reverence for Property those who have no personal reason to think well of the distinction between Mine and Thine.'[1] Twenty years before, in *Politics for the People*, Charles Kingsley had told his English readers: 'We have used the Bible as if it were a mere special constable's handbook—an opium-dose for keeping beasts of burden patient while they were being overloaded—a mere book to keep the poor in order.' Similar quotations could be multiplied endlessly from the records of nineteenth-century English religion.

Society was mobile, but the social philosophy implied by official religion was not. Here was the basic defeat of re-ligion—a defeat for which there was no adequate com-pensation in the prestige rightly acquired by the philanthropic energy of the reforming zeal of many individual Christians. The working class in its day of need might accept charity or patronage or education from religious bodies, but it would not take doctrines from them and it would not give them its heart. This alienation of the working class from the churches, although normally producing a silent belief that religion was 'not for us', might easily explode into bitterness. Many capitalists who exploited the workers, or who were believed to exploit them, were regular churchgoers—as were many of the bourgeois who also profited out of the workers, or whose comfort aroused their envy. Some ecclesiastics (bishops in particular) seemed rich and reactionary; and ministers of religion without wealth could still be resented, as being hypocritical or stupid in their 'soft jobs'. Both the institutions and the personnel of religion became the targets of criticism and sometimes of abuse.

This spelt disaster for Christianity in an increasingly industrial Europe. And it was virtually a new problem. As Max Weber pointed out, 'Christianity began its course as a doctrine of itinerant artisan journeymen. During all periods of its mighty external and internal development it has been

[1] Quoted by H. J. Laski, *The American Democracy* (London, 1949), p. 271.

a quite specifically urban, and above all a civic, religion. This was true during Antiquity, during the Middle Ages and in Puritanism. The city of the Occident . . . has been the major theatre for Christianity.'[1] Weber quoted a point often made by the church historian Adolf von Harnack: the success of Christianity in any particular city in ancient times was in direct proportion to the size of that city, for it was in the city that old customs and castes were broken down and the ground prepared for a new brotherhood of faith. But in the nineteenth century the most genuine brotherhood in an industrial city was the brotherhood of the oppressed against their oppressors. The churches seemed to be lined up with the city's oppressors. So it is that in the twentieth century, Christianity's institutional failure is likely to vary with the size of the city: the bigger the city, the smaller the congregation. A visitor wishing to see the continuing strength of the ecclesiastical tradition should go to Herefordshire and not to Birmingham, to Brittany and not to Paris, to the Middle West and not to New York. And in its own social life, 'the city of the Occident' seems to have become the secular city.

That, in a rapid summary, is the story of the churches amid the industrial revolution. The summary is, of course, over-simplified. A fuller account would make us give more attention to the probability that the new industrial workers (or their parents) had not been enthusiastic churchgoers during their years in the countryside; and more attention, too, to the fact that many of the industrial workers were willing to use the churches as their allies in social and educational progress, while some people in industrial areas, usually in the class immediately above the proletariat, actually belonged to the churches—in England, specially to the Nonconformist chapels. The material position of many of the industrial workers can be shown to have been an improvement on their status in the agricultural society; and the numerical strength of the churches in the cities and

[1] *From Max Weber*, ed. H. H. Gerth and C. Wright Mills (London, 1947), p. 269.

towns can be shown to have been better than much anti-clerical propaganda or ecclesiastical lamentation would suggest. Yet the summary just given seems to be a true enough account of the basic psychological consequences of the shift from rural to industrial work. It was a crisis; and the churches were not the same, before and after that crisis. And more than nineteenth-century churchgoing suffered in the crisis. The African pagan lived in an enchanted forest. It was enchanted because its gods were honorary senior members of his tribe, because his rulers were the friends of those gods, because his whole life was ordered under the gods and the rulers, in a sacred society. Now in the industrial city, life was (to use one of Max Weber's favourite expressions) *disenchanted*. This was not only because the city was often very ugly, and often very unpleasant. The basic disenchantment came in the worker's realisation that society was a struggle, not an already ordered structure. In the city the rich exploited the poor, and all too often the poor had to compete with each other; and no gods controlled these battles.

Karl Marx used the term 'alienation' to describe the profound lack of satisfaction in his work and his society which the nineteenth-century industrial worker experienced. This 'alienation' could not be overcome except by a kind of religion—by a vision of man in society, past, present and future. But Marx believed that traditional religion was disastrous because it stressed the social hierarchy at the expense of human equality. In one of the supreme ironies of modern history, the founding prophet of Communism believed that the humanistic religion which was needed could be provided by his own understanding of human equality; and Marx proclaimed the coming of the Kingdom of Man.[1]

[1] See, e.g., Alisdair MacIntyre, *Secularization and Moral Change* (London, 1967).

Two Communist States: Russia and China

The writings of Karl Marx[1] still form a monument to the nineteenth-century revolt against religion, and the monument has cast its shadow over many houses of prayer in our time. Marx argued that all religion, like every other system of ideas or 'ideology', arises out of the economic structure of society. The religion which Marx knew was for him the 'opium of the people', because it was used by exploiters to drug the exploited into believing that their lot was inevitable, and that they must wait for the next world before seeking justice. Even for Marx, religion was also something deeper. Not for nothing was he the grandson of a Jewish rabbi. Religion was 'the cry of the oppressed, the heart of a heartless world'; as the comforting illusion that there was a God who cared for the poor, it was opium self-administered. He wrote in such terms about Hinduism as well as about Christianity. But this did not commend religion to Marx. On the contrary, he believed that 'all criticism begins with the criticism of religion'; and he was confident that when the poor came into their own economically, religion would be seen to be unnecessary as well as false. Marx hated the churches. As a political revolutionary, he hated them for their conservatism, one of the factors which disappointed the high hopes of 1848 in Germany. As an observer of the misery of the working class, specially in England, he hated them for their irrelevance to the social crisis. As an individual, he hated them because they were a particularly hollow and rotten part of the hypocrisy of unreformed society—as he had experienced when his Jewish father had thought it socially desirable to have the young Karl baptised a Christian.

This Marxist critique of religion has often seemed to belong to the very spirit of the twentieth century. Curiously enough, it has not had much influence on England, where it was largely formulated; English working-class anti-clericalism has found its own voices (Holyoake, Bradlaugh,

[1] The key texts were gathered in *K. Marx and F. Engels on Religion* (Moscow and London, 1957).

Bottomley, Blatchford). But elsewhere it has stimulated the whole modern movement analysing the social character of religion (for example, the challenge of Marx lay behind the analysis of the German 'history of religions' school, although Ernst Troeltsch, its leading exponent, subtly stressed the fact that religious ideas also influence social changes). And what is infinitely more important than any analysis: Marxism has changed the destinies of great countries. In these countries there was little industry and public opinion was conservatively religious; but an élite was determined to drag the masses into the modern world, forcing them by propaganda or political pressure to adopt the secular outlook of the Western European masses. Marx's posthumous career has indeed been astonishing. From the grave in Highgate Cemetery where he was buried in 1883 surrounded by crosses, Marx has by his philosophy changed the religious world. He has persecuted the Orthodox Church in Russia, he has discredited the three religions which had covered China for more than two millennia, and he has even overthrown the Lamaist palace-monasteries of Tibet. What Russia and China (and Tibet) shared in common with industrial Europe in the nineteenth century was the freezing of their official religions in rituals and doctrines which supported a social order doomed to disappear. Popular as such religion often was, it was incapable of internal reform on a scale large enough to meet the challenge of Westernisation.

In Russia, most of the Orthodox Church seemed completely identified with the stagnation of rural society, and with the Tsarist empire which was tyrannical and yet was unable to cope with modern challenges even before its wartime catastrophes. Priests were poor and ill-educated, their standards scarcely above those of the peasants among whom they lived. But this did not identify them with the people's cause, for they were under the detailed control of the bishops, and the bishops in their turn were controlled by the state-dominated Holy Synod. The Church's own central council had not been allowed to meet since 1721.

The system made churchmen, in Lenin's famous phrase, 'defenders of serfdom in cassocks'—as was shown by the hierarchy's reactions to the 1905 revolution. Some Christians in Russia saw the need of the people and struggled ineffectively to break out of the Church's disastrous position; and their vision of a Christian society honouring freedom and personality was developed later by the philosopher, Nicolas Berdyaev. But before the 1917 revolutions neither the hierarchy nor the bulk of the believers sympathised with the cause of radical change in this unjust society, and in the civil war to 1921 much of the Orthodox Church was openly identified with the White counter-revolution. The Christians of Russia have paid dearly for the social orientation of their leadership.

The Bolsheviks decreed the confiscation of all church property. During and after 1922 they imprisoned or shot many thousands of bishops and priests, they set up the 'Living Church' movement to gain control of the parishes, they closed down the seminaries, the church schools, the church hospitals and almost all the churches. Step by step they prohibited all forms of spreading religion, and they co-ordinated atheistic propaganda through the League of the Militant Godless. Intensified when Stalin came into full power and collectivised the peasants in 1928–9, this was probably the most savage and prolonged persecution ever faced by a large Christian community. Only the constitutional right to assemble for worship remained to church-people, and in practice this liberty was often denied. Sunday was abolished as a public holiday. In 1917 there were about 51,000 priests active in Russia; by 1939 there were only 5,000. A miracle was needed to save this remnant—and a miracle came, when Hitler invaded Russia and Stalin needed all the help he could get.

The persecution of the Russian Orthodox Church was called off by Stalin in 1943 in exchange for the bishops' support of the war effort. Religious liberty was also seen as a useful emphasis in Communist international propaganda and as a good basis for the Russian Church's attempt to become the leader of all Eastern Orthodoxy. The League of the Militant Godless was now dissolved. The key position of Patriarch of Moscow, which had been virtually in suspense since the arrest of Tikhon in 1921, was filled by Sergius (who, acting as *Locum Tenens* of the Patriarchate, had announced his loyalty to the Soviet government in 1927), and after his death by Alexis. Russian church leaders became prominent in the 'peace' campaigns. Within Russia a modest revival took place in church attendance. This revival seems to have alarmed those who took over after Stalin's death. Khrushchev's denunciation of Stalin in 1956 shook Marxist dogmatism to its foundations, but brought no blessing to the Orthodox Church (or to the smaller religious groups in the Soviet Union). From 1959 the anti-religious campaign grew hot again, although the methods used were now more subtle than before the war. The Russian Orthodox Church had been allowed to join the World Council of Churches, but what its future will be no one can tell.[1]

In China, the primary Confucianist virtue had always been filial piety, ritualised in ancestor worship; yet economic progress in China was impossible unless sons were to be educated above their fathers and were to be prepared to defy and even to abandon them. The stability of the family had been set in an empire which was stable because the emperor's ritual and moral behaviour was in accordance with the 'way of heaven'; yet the Manchu empire was unable to give efficient government to a country in desperate need of it, and the ancient examination system for civil servants, based entirely on the Confucian classics, was abolished in 1905. For all the attempts at renewal by Neo-Confucians and Neo-neo-Confucians, the last of the great reformers, Chu-hsi, had died 700 years before. The irrelevance of Confucian etiquette to the needs of the people had accounted for the rise of Buddhism—despite Buddhism's

[1] See J. S. Curtiss, *Church and State in Russia, 1900–17* (New York, 1944), and *The Russian Church and the Soviet State, 1917–50* (Boston, 1953).

other-worldliness, so uncongenial to the Chinese mind. The last of the Buddhist leaders with some hope of influencing China, Tai-hsu, died in 1947. Confucianism's failure had, however, mainly resulted in magic among the masses, as the peasants attempted to manipulate nature in the style of Sir James Frazer's primitive peoples. The less anxious élite in Chinese society turned to the nature mysticism of Taoism, with its philosophy of the simple life lived in accordance with nature's gentle decrees. Taoism certainly had its charm, and incidentally its enthusiasm for nature encouraged the early rise of Chinese science. But Taoism had a darker side also; the élite was encouraged to withdraw from all useful involvement in social life, and when Taoism reached the hungry masses what it produced was a further wave of magic (since nature, if it was unsatisfactory, might be adjusted). Thus by the nineteenth century A.D. none of China's religions—when pursued separately or (as was more usual) when fused together in a tolerant syncretism—possessed the dynamic power needed to unite, inspire, energise and transform the Chinese people. They were religions for gentlemen, and they provided the opium of magic for the masses.

There was a time when, in the search for a religious power to match China's time of crisis, Christianity seemed a live option. Protected (at least to some extent) by the extra-territorial privileges yielded to foreigners after the Opium War, missionaries poured into China. An unexpected result was the mixture of crusading Protestantism with popular Confucianism which inspired the Tai-ping rebellion in the 1850s. Christianity was never a popular movement after the crushing of that rebellion (by the devoutly Protestant General Gordon among others), but the Chinese élite did use the schools and colleges established by the missionaries. The result was another chance for Christianity: the Kuomintang when it emerged under Sun Yat-sen and Chiang Kai-shek, and founded the Chinese Republic in 1912, was to a considerable extent Christian in its leadership and inspiration. But the reliance of the Christians on

American and other foreign patrons was always a great embarrassment among a people so intensely patriotic as the Chinese. The Boxer Rebellion which was crushed by the Western powers and Japan in 1900, and followed by a crippling fine on the Chinese nation, was only the most violent of many protests against foreign interference symbolised by the hated missionaries; and actions such as those of the Roman Catholic hierarchy after the Rebellion did little to end the resentment. (The bishops used the compensation which was paid to them for murders of Roman Catholics to purchase land, adding to the Church's already conspicuous wealth and entanglement in the decaying social order.) When in 1919 the Western powers betrayed China in favour of Japan (over the claim to Shantung), anti-foreign feeling again flared up, and again turned against the missionaries, now known as the 'running dogs of capitalism'.

Nationalism, socialism and democracy were the great passions, and the main intellectual impact of the West on the élite of the Chinese Republic was through atheists such as Bertrand Russell, John Dewey and the Communists. Many Buddhist and Taoist temples were turned into secular schools. The moving spirit behind the 'Chinese Renaissance' in the 1920s and 1930s, Hu Shih, declared that 'the most important contribution that the religions of the world could make to modern societies in the world today would be to commit suicide'.[1] The 'Liberation' of 1947–9 clinched the answer to China's problem; but this answer had been probable since Sun Yat-sen's appeal to Soviet Russia for help in 1919. The religions, if they failed to commit suicide, would be slowly murdered, for only atheist Marxism provided a viable alternative to the corruption of the old society. Mao Tse-tung's 'long march' of 1934–5 went further than from Kiangsi to Yenan; it went from the old to the new. The constitution of 1954 provided for freedom of religious

---

[1] B. E. Meland, *The Secularization of Modern Cultures* (New York, 1966), p. 22. For the background, see Wing Tsit-chan, *Religious Trends in Modern China* (New York, 1954).

belief in the People's Republic, and for a time religious organisations and buildings enjoyed some patronage from the regime, on condition that they freed themselves from all foreign interference (the 'Three-Self Movement'). Missionaries were expelled, and Chinese who had collaborated with them were 're-educated', often violently. And then the pace of the march of secularism quickened. The Cultural Revolution of 1966 threw the Red Guards against all religion, closing almost all the temples and churches and humiliating such open believers as were left after two decades of Communism. Later the pace slackened—perhaps because little religion remained.

Three Lay Republics: France, Mexico, Turkey

Russia and China were two great peoples with essentially irrelevant, or even harmful, religions; their religions were broken, often brutally, by Marxism. But the twentieth century has provided many examples of countries where the grip of religion was ended by forces which were not Marxist in character. What these countries had in common with each other (and with the Marxist lands) was that in them all religion was identified with a doomed social order, and secularisation was the fruit of social protest.

France is the classic case. Through much of the nineteenth century the fate of the Catholic Church hung in the balance. Widespread intellectual rejection of Christianity was certainly an element in the danger which the Church faced. From Renan's *Vie de Jésus* in 1863 to the death of Anatole France in 1924 the current in French literary life was against religion, and the intellectual response of French Catholicism was inadequate. But in the history of French *laïcité* leading to open anti-clericalism, social factors mattered decisively. First the aristocracy returning after the Revolution and then the middle classes enriched by the new industries favoured the Church (with the American capitalist's blessing on religion as 'a part of the subordinate machinery of Police'); but when the Republicans triumphed in the elections of 1876 the doom of the Church was sealed with that of the monarchy which most vocal Catholics had supported. Specially through newspapers such as *L'Univers* or *La Croix*, churchmen openly and violently played at party politics, and the lower middle and the working-classes were out for vengeance. They were led by anti-clerical politicians of the stamp of Emile Combes. Combes had been trained for the priesthood but, after losing his faith, he was driven by the determination to take education out of the hands of priests and nuns and to transfer wealth from the maintenance of the religious hierarchy to the progress of the people. The political life of the Third Republic was dominated by religious issues, right up to the war of 1914; urgent social reforms were neglected because the overthrow and defence of Catholicism aroused the most ardent passions. The affair of Alfred Dreyfus, an army officer of Jewish descent who in 1894 was unjustly sentenced for selling secrets to Germany, was used to discredit the Church as well as the army. Religion was excluded from the State schools, and the Church's own schools were penalised. The religious orders were forbidden to do either teaching or pastoral work, and many religious houses were closed by the police. The government broke off diplomatic relations with the Papacy (under Leo XIII the Papacy had made some efforts to rally Catholics to compromise with the Republic, but under Pius X it was completely hostile). Finally in 1905 the separation of Church and State in France ended the large financial grants, the public privileges and the prestige which the Church had enjoyed since Napoleon's Concordat in 1802.

Much turned on the question of the use of the church buildings. Unlike the Russian Communists or the Red Guards in China, the French anti-clericals were not prepared simply to close all these down. But the position was dangerous for the French Church. Since 1790 the church buildings had been owned by the French State; the 1802 Concordat had left this arrangement intact, but the State had provided grants to the Church out of taxes, partly as a compensation for ownership of the buildings. Now the grants were abolished, other buildings might be used for a variety of purposes, and the churches themselves could be leased from the State for use in worship by *Associations Cultuelles*. For a time anti-clericals nursed the hope that Catholicism might split up in schisms, as isolated priests, wishing to use particular buildings, made their peace with the State without reference to the bishops. Such hopes were not realised. In a series of negotiations which were not concluded until 1943 the authorities of Church and State agreed to the use of almost all the buildings for religious purposes by leasing them to diocesan 'associations' formed under the bishops for the purpose, and Pope Pius XI accepted this principle in 1924. In its essentials, however, the 1905 separation of Church and State in France has proved permanent, despite many Papal thunders. It has been more than a matter of taking the crucifix out of the courtroom. The schools of France have taught ethics instead of any religious doctrine; there have been Catholic schools, there have been some Christian teachers in the State system, there have been many teachers who have been genuinely neutral in their attitude to religion, but there have also been many anti-clerical teachers who have taught, or at least implied, that all religious doctrines are false. In many French villages there was no longer a resident *curé* to take care of the parish church; and in these and many other villages a teacher who might be contemptuous of Christianity became the leading man. Between 1901 and 1913, both the number of ordinations and the proportion of ecclesiastical to civil marriages fell by about a half. Many of the parish clergy were reduced to poverty by the withdrawal of the State grants, and in the expanding industrial cities the shortage of clergy and of money in the Church meant that the working-class suburbs were virtually wildernesses in religious observance. Durkheim and many others wanted sociology with its anti-religious conclusions made a compulsory subject for the training of teachers in France's schools, but Durkheim's analysis of the centrality of religion in past societies had ceased to be true for his own country. The French Republic had turned to other totems.

The cause of religion in France has been damaged very severely not only by such frontal assaults but also by the mood of reaction which has gripped many who wished to defend Catholicism. The ending of the Concordat with the State meant it was now the Papacy that appointed all the bishops; Pius X favoured reactionaries and stopped the hierarchy from taking any concerted initiative. But the coldness in the intellectual atmosphere had causes more subtle than the bishops' dislike of anything which might be termed liberalism. The stark alternative of atheism or 'fideism' (the willingness to believe anything because it is taught by the Church) has been prominent in French intellectual life, with the Catholic believers in the minority. In 1907 Pius X violently condemned the 'modernism' of Alfred Loisy, Edouard Le Roy and a small circle around them. This was a group of French religious thinkers who, for all their liability to error, were at that stage intelligent and honest sons of the Church, prepared to accept the Church's teachings whatever interpretations they might put on them. Given time, such theologians might have worked out a modern Catholicism, but the Vatican announced that they erred in separating Church and State, as well as in separating faith and science. After the condemnation of 'modernism' there followed a virtual reign of terror among intellectual Catholics. For many years a tendency prevailed to avoid real thought lest it lead to heresy and condemnation. Many Catholics flirted with the militantly reactionary (although personally agnostic) Charles Maurras and his *Action Française*, at least until Pius XI condemned that semi-Fascist movement in 1926. When the experiment of the worker-priests going into factories was condemned by Pius XII, the scars of former conflicts still showed, for these priests had been driven to incur the wrath of the Vatican by their conviction that if they were to make contact with the dechristianised working class they must abandon most of the traditional discipline of a Catholic priest (not least his distinctive dress, the *soutane*) and must embrace the militant politics of the Left. All this took place in a France which had once been known as the 'eldest daughter' of the Catholic Church—and the canonisation of Joan of Arc as a saint in 1920 was a pointed reminder of that past. The diary of a country priest was now likely to be the record of a slow crucifixion, and the France of the 'Most Christian' monarchy had become, to use the title of Godin's book which shocked and excited Catholics when it appeared in 1943, *pays de mission*.[1]

A mission field France might be (Godin reckoned that only ten per cent of the population regularly practised their religion—but his statistics were criticised as unduly alarmist). However, Catholicism retained enough influence in France, and enough moderation, to prevent a complete conflict with the State. Across the Atlantic, Mexico provided an example of the Catholic Church in a duel to the death with a secular republic. For many years the bishops and clergy of Mexico had been denounced as the apostles of superstition and oppression; on the other hand, the churches were full, and the clergy controlled most of the schools and hospitals. Governments enacted anti-clerical laws (1874, 1917), and largely failed to enforce them. In 1923 there was ominous anger from the government when the bishops dedicated a huge monument to 'Christ, King of Mexico', and the explosion came when Plutarco Calles was elected President of Mexico in 1924. The old laws were now revived, and fresh restrictions added, with the declared intentions of cutting drastically the numbers of clergy (according to the wishes of the local authorities) and of restricting their work to the conduct of religious services. Religion was to be totally excluded from all schools, public and private. In retaliation the bishops forbade their priests to conduct any worship at all. Most of the bishops were exiled, and hundreds of priests and laymen shot. The

[1] Eng. trans. as *France Pagan?* (London, 1949). See Adrian Dansette, *Religious History of Modern France* (1948; Eng. trans., London, 1961).

Cristeros fought back, and the next President of Mexico, Obregón, was assassinated by a Catholic. A truce was patched up in 1929, but the anti-clerical legislation was retained. The government authorised under 200 priests to serve a Catholic population of 17 millions. The 1935–7 anti-clerical campaign under President Càrdenas drew from Pius XI the Papacy's first theological exposition of the subject's right to rebel (in the Encyclical *Nos es Muy*). It was only in 1940 that a President of Mexico, Avila Camacho, declared himself a believer. In the next two decades the Catholic Church recovered confidence with missionary help from the United States; but it could scarcely claim that Christ was still visibly King of Mexico, or the Virgin its Queen.[1]

We now pay a brief visit to a non-Christian country dramatically hit by secularisation in the 1920s.

The Turkish Empire had been ruled by the Ottoman Sultan who was also Caliph or Commander of the Faithful, thus symbolising in his own person the unity of politics and religion in the household of Islam. Turkey had governed its life according to the Prophet's holy book (the *Quran*) supplemented by the decisions taken as questions arose in the early years of Islam (the *Sunna*) and by the elaborate code of law worked out in the Middle Ages (the *Sharia*). Men had worn the brimless *fez* because it was suitable for prayers, to give one example of a religious regulation binding on all; and women had been veiled and separated into *purdah*, subject to divorce at the husband's will and without political rights. Memorising the *Quran* in the original Arabic had been the main task in education. But the modernisation of the young Turks and of Zia Gok Alp (a poet inspired by Auguste Comte) was given feet and fists by the passionate conviction of Kemal Ataturk and others that after its defeat in the world war Turkey must join Western civilisation at whatever cost. The Caliphate was abolished with the Sultanate, and since that historic year (1924) Islam has had no Commander of the Faithful. The *Sharia* was no longer

[1] See Graham Greene's novel *The Power and the Glory* (London, 1940)

part of the law of the land; instead, civil codes were adapted from Europe and decided such matters as divorce in secular courts. The *fez*, the veil and other time-hallowed customs were denounced in favour of Western dress. Women were given legal safeguards and political votes. No religious instruction was allowed in the new networks of schools set up by the State. The greatest mosque in Istanbul, which had been the greatest church of the city when it was the Christian Byzantium, was turned into a museum, and the use of Arabic for the call to prayer was made illegal; the *muezzin*, if he had to call, must call in Turkish. Subsequent Turkish regimes have not kept up Ataturk's secularising zeal, and the Muslim religion has retained much of its hold on the rural masses. The study of Islam has come back to schools and universities, and it is said that five thousand mosques were built in the decade 1950–60. But one reason why the Democratic Party was replaced in the military coup of 1960 was that it was alleged to favour religious reaction, and in its constitution, approved by a referendum in 1961, Turkey has remained a secular state on the French pattern—something undreamed of before Ataturk.[1]

The Dilemma of Islam

No other Islamic country has undergone changes as drastic as these in Turkey, partly because no other country is geographically so suitable for Westernisation (although also because no other country has had to deal with the Sultan-Caliph as the symbol of the old order). But in parts of Islam there already exists an intelligentsia moulded by an education which is Western in its ethos; the development of technology extends Western influences more subtly; and Western popular culture seeps through. It is possible to prophesy that other situations will develop towards an explosion or slow erosion which will do at least as much damage as was done in Turkey to the traditional fabric of

[1] See Nyazi Berkes, *The Development of Secularism in Turkey* (Toronto, 1964).

Islam, unless Islam can reform itself voluntarily. And 'Islam reformed', as Lord Cromer wrote when reporting on Egypt in 1908, 'is Islam no longer'.[1] Cromer's insult contains this truth: that when the *Quran*, the *Sunna* and the *Sharia* cease to regulate daily life, but instead criteria are applied which derive ultimately from the secularised West, then the unity of Islamic society has been disrupted, and a new chapter must open in Islamic history.

Islam is indeed in a dangerous position under this social impact of secularisation. Islamic society was the personal creation of the prophet Muhammed, who founded a single community, both political and religious, armed with the scimitar as well as with faith, so that a witty French sociologist could aptly describe Communism as the Islam of the twentieth century. As we have seen, Christianity developed such a religious-political society fairly quickly—indeed, at the first available opportunity. But what gives some justification to the argument that Christianity is not wedded to a static view of society is the fact that the founder of Christianity lived in circumstances far different from the circumstances of the founder of Islam. Muhammed entered a social vacuum in Arabia; to the West, his armies met no enduring opposition until they came to Tours and Vienna; to the East, the Caliphs of Baghdad and the Moghul Emperors of India ruled glorious civilisations in the name of Islam. Jesus and his first followers formed a small minority under the Roman empire and under the Hellenistic culture, so that they had no prospect of inaugurating their own society. St. John well understood Christ's rejection of the political hope of Jewish Messianism: 'My Kingdom is not of this world.' Christendom, when it was a united, sacred society in the European Middle Ages, was a mixture of Roman and Greek with specifically Christian elements; and always in the Christian tradition there remained many traces of the original separation of God and Caesar, religion and politics, Church and State. Now that the compromise called Christendom has disintegrated, the separation of Church and State in the West colours the whole modern word—and destroys the classic concept of Islamic unity.

It is not merely a question of the separation of Church and State in the future of Islam. The regulations governing the religious life of Muslims were largely untouched by the Turkish reforms—which is not surprising, since some of the most important of them have the authority of the Prophet himself. Muhammed, unlike Jesus, was a law-giver, and he set the style for the prolific legislation which has regulated the lives of Muslims.

Among the customs which he created were the Five Pillars of Religion: witness, prayer, almsgiving, fasting and pilgrimage. Each 'pillar' has been surrounded by vast discussions by Muslims and their critics during the twentieth century, but the relevance of each, as erected by the Prophet, is dubious if Islamic society is to be modernised. For *witness*, fundamentally a confession of Allah and his Prophet, was militantly aggressive and included the duty of the 'holy war' against infidels, understood as the defence of liberty to worship Allah. Can this now be interpreted solely as the duty of war against sin within? *Prayer* was regulated precisely in postures and words, and was to be in Arabic. Can this discipline be relaxed as Christianity has had to relax its equivalent disciplines in the West? (Only a sixth of the world's 300 million Muslims normally speak Arabic.) *Almsgiving* was defined so as to take a high and regular proportion of one's income. Can this be continued as a secular state provides education, social security and welfare services? *Fasting* included abstention from all food and drink during the daylight in the month of Ramadan. Is this possible in an industrial society? *Pilgrimage* was to Mecca, to which the daily prayers were directed. Can this Arabian city retain its sacred centrality when Arabia, under the rule of the puritanical Wahhabi movement since the eighteenth century, has become one of the most backward parts of Islam—despite its oil wells?

Such questions are typical of Islam's modern dilemmas, and it is not surprising that so many of Islam's teachers still give the fundamentalist answer. Islam, they proclaim, is what is laid down in the *Quran*, the *Sunna* and the *Sharia*, and it all stands or falls together. We may call this a totalitarian ideology if we wish, but we should understand that their religious law has been much more than a mere system to past generations of Muslims. It was the will of Allah, expressed without ambiguity or confusion. Muslims in controversy with Christians have constantly said that, despite all the merits of Jesus, Christianity suffers from being an otherworldly idealism; it does not give enough clear instructions for daily life. And now Muslims are being asked to refashion their faith so that it becomes as otherworldly as the Christianity which they saw in action in the crusaders of the Middle Ages, or more recently in the colonialists who seemed to rely more on the whisky bottle than on the Bible.

Yet, even in Islam, many voices today urge that religion must be separated from government; in a free society, it must be renewed as a spiritual faith helping modern people towards the eternal God, in the privacy of their own hearts and consciences. Ali Abd ar-Raziq wrote with this theme on *Islam and the Principles of Government* (Cairo, 1925). The controversy led to his expulsion from his teaching post at the Al Azhar mosque-university, but his modernist principles have been echoed and developed since in Egypt. The courts administering the *Sharia* have been abolished, and Al Azhar was itself modernised under the Nasser government. Syria, Jordan and Iraq have gone the same way. In the North African states, the Muslim traditionalism of the peasants and wandering *bedouin* was encouraged by the struggle with the French as Catholic colonisers; but Tunisia in 1957 took a momentous step when it prohibited polygamy on the ground that the Prophet had decreed that all a man's wives should be treated impartially—a thing said to be impossible in the circumstances of modern society. Even in Pakistan, created in 1947 as a national home for Indian Muslims (under the largely agnostic Jinnah), the description of the State as an Islamic Republic was abandoned in the revised constitution after the military coup of 1958, and no attempt has been made to enact for the nation all that the Islamic tradition prescribes. Pakistan's alliance with Red China against India was a fairly striking example of realism in power politics; and the civil war between West and East in Pakistan, eventually leading to two nations, was a reminder that Islam was no longer a powerful enough cement. The Arab League, founded in 1945, was modelled on Western political alliances and has never been thoroughly Islamic in the traditional sense—although many Arab leaders and conferences have declared that Arab culture depends on Muslim religion, and there have been resurgences of the powerful combination of anti-Israeli feelings with Muslim puritanism (as in Libya in the 1970s). 'Quranic Socialism' is sought by many in these Arab League countries, and is no more ridiculous in its aspirations than is Christian Socialism or Buddhist Socialism, but the *Quran* does contain much material which is difficult for a modern Socialist, exactly because the Prophet was more interested than the Christ or the Buddha was in the details of social justice in his time.

Because of the apparent irrelevance of Islam's traditional regulations in the modern world, only Saudi Arabia, Libya, Afghanistan and Yemen survive as states placed under Allah and Islamic law. To many millions of Muslims who still live in the Soviet Union, or in the constitutionally secular, largely Hindu, Republic of India, the separation of Church and State is basic to their hope that some form of Islam will survive to guide their children. Already in India some important Muslim thinkers have emerged, interpreting Islam as vision, not law.[1]

[1] Among the many recent studies of Islam by Western scholars may be mentioned: W. Cantwell Smith, *Islam in Modern History* (New York, 1957); Edwin Rosenthal, *Islam in the National State* (Cambridge, 1965); Clifford Geertz, *Islam Observed* (New Haven, 1968).

Pluralist Societies in Asia and America

Need this separation of Church and State be disastrous to religion? To a large extent it seems to have been in Russia and China, but the evidence from other countries shows that it need not be—so that religion may have a future within the 'pluralist' type of society in which various religions and secular bodies co-exist under the more or less neutral benevolence of the State.

We have already noted the religious recovery in secular Turkey. Today Islam makes its fastest progress (mainly through traders and other non-professional evangelists) precisely in an area where it must compete peacefully with paganism and Christianity for the allegiance of individuals or of small groups, and where it must tolerate a great many pagan customs surviving in its adherents' habits. Here Islam gives Muslims a pride in belonging to a great brotherhood, without the burden of attempting to regulate all the details of the life of any one society; it is, in other words, more a private religion than a comprehensive ideology. This area is tropical Africa.

At the other end of the Islamic world, Indonesia may be more typical than Pakistan as showing the trend of our time. Indonesia is overwhelmingly a Muslim country, and the education of its people still relies mainly on Muslim schools. Yet Islam only gradually conquered paganism in this vast archipelago, and never established a monopoly. Moreover, Christian missionaries under the Dutch colonialists succeeded in establishing many schools and churches including the powerful Battak Church, and when the Dutch were forced out this Christian element was sufficiently strong, and sufficiently indigenous, to survive. The result of this history is that in Indonesia Christian and other minorities are recognised in law (as in Pakistan) and definitely encouraged in practice (as they are not in Pakistan) because all available resources are needed for nation-building. This separation of Church and State in Indonesia flies in the face of the history of Islam, and is resented by many Muslims. But religion remains strong. Sukarno's regime had to put belief in God first among the principles of the Republic enunciated in 1945, and Sukarno's downfall twenty years later, amid the massacre of perhaps half a million, was due partly to Muslim reaction against his flirtation with the atheist Communists.

Although some Asian countries remain unified religiously (Thailand, Cambodia and Laos are examples of a traditional Buddhist monopoly), the separation of Church and State is practised in the different circumstances of other Asian countries without ruining religion.[1] In Japan, for example, the Shinto religion ceased to be the creed of a militant state and the Emperor renounced his divinity in 1946; yet the Japanese have always been interested in a syncretistic mixture drawn from different religions of Chinese origin (specially Confucianism and Buddhism), and in their own local experiments, while being, like the Chinese, most concerned with order and prosperity in the world. And Japan since 1946 has continued to be what the Emperor's brother called it: a 'laboratory' for religion.[2]

Greater examples of the separation of Church and State in the world today are provided by India and the United States. Those two gigantic countries are officially secular states. Historically, the main motive in choosing this status arose from the fact that both republics were from the beginning federations of states including citizens of many religious persuasions. Their governments are pledged by their constitutions to give no privileges to any religious body. Yet religious bodies of many kinds flourish in both countries; and this fact may indicate the style in which the social roles of religious bodies should be reshaped in the modern world.

Formed in 1947, the Republic of India prohibited all

[1] See *South Asian Politics and Religion*, ed. Donald F. Smith (Princeton, 1966), and *Religion and Change in Contemporary Asia*, ed. Robert F. Spencer (Minneapolis, 1971).
[2] See Raymond Hammer, *Japan's Religious Ferment* (London, 1961), and *Folk Religion in Japan: Community and Change*, ed. J. M. Kitagawa and A. L. Miller (Chicago, 1968).

discrimination on grounds of religion, race or caste in its constitution of 1950 and elected a Muslim President as the head of its secular state in 1967, yet Hinduism still accounts for more than three-quarters of its population. In the short run, Hinduism may be strong enough to use the machinery of the central government to suppress practices which are offensive to the Hindu conscience, such as 'cow-slaughter'; after all, it was a Hindu fanatic who in 1948 assassinated Gandhi in revenge on his liberalism. In the long run, Hinduism with its caste system and other outmoded social customs may not be flexible enough to accept the modernisation of the country, and China's solution may have to be India's. The corruption and inefficiency which spoil India in the 1970s, and the multiplication of wealth in the hands of the capitalists and landlords while the standard of living of the masses remains stationary or falls, are ominously like the defects in the Kuomintang in China in the 1940s—and the moral energy of Hinduism may not be enough to cure these diseases, despite the continuing strength of the Congress Party and the idealism of Gandhi's heirs. But even if the present Indian Republic fails, the idea of a secular state administering a largely religious India is unlikely to alter much during the twentieth century.

An English writer may be permitted to observe that the lessons of American religious history have not yet been taken with anything like adequate seriousness in discussion about the future of religion. Even American thinkers have allowed themselves to be mesmerised by European patterns. For example, European religious history suggested to Max Weber that the National Churches and the small splinter-groups were almost completely different in atmosphere; the 'church-type' must be distinguished from the 'sect-type'. American thinkers copied this approach. Above all, modern European secularisation was interpreted by a host of intellectuals whose influence was large in the United States; if God was dead in Europe, it seemed to follow that he was dead in America. But in fact the religious histories of Europe and of the United States have been surprisingly different.

Religious pluralism became the American destiny because when the thirteen colonies federated in the course of their rebellion against George III no single National Church could be contemplated. Many of the American colonies had their own Established Churches (the last to be disestablished was that of Massachusetts in 1833), but amid this variety a federal government could not make a religious option. Anyway, religion was not popular in the American Revolution; scriptures more influential than the Bible were Tom Paine's *Rights of Man* and *The Age of Reason*, and thinkers more influential than any churchman were the sceptical philosophers Benjamin Franklin and Thomas Jefferson. However, it was a largely unexpected consequence of this crisis for American religion that the churches were now exempted from the dilemma of being either 'church-type' (i.e. identified with King George III or with some other reactionary force) or 'sect-type' (i.e. narrow, ignorant and bitter). So gradually a new type of church emerged: a free church. Most of the early settlers who had crossed the Atlantic in search of religious liberty and material opportunity had thought that their dream of the Kingdom of God in America must involve something like the European pattern of a communal religion, although on a different basis; only so could a godly commonwealth be built in the wilderness. What now remained from the colonial period in American history was the recurrent American dream that the way to Paradise could be reopened by the sweat of Adam's brow; but the godly commonwealth, in so far as it has been built in the history of the New World, has been founded on the basis of real liberty, involving pluralism.

In the infant United States, the number of regularly attending church members seems to have been very low, according to one estimate about five per cent of the population; but surveys suggest that nowadays well over half of the United States goes to church regularly.[1] The 'Great

---

[1] Guy Swanson in *The Religious Situation: 1968*, ed. D. R. Cutler (Boston, 1968), pp. 811–13, summed up the surveys as suggesting that

Awakenings' of the eighteenth century, with their focus in the theology of Jonathan Edwards, began the rebirth of Protestantism in the life of America, but four great crises may be seen in the subsequent story of the churches. One crisis came at the Frontier: as the American people moved West, the preachers moved with them. In Sunday schools or in revival camps, or during uncountable hours of homely talk, the preachers won the hearts of many of the pioneers. Another crisis was the immigrant flood: as the millions poured in from Ireland or Continental Europe, they found or brought with them the churches which could serve as familiar landmarks in America, preserving their languages and customs. The third crisis came with Americanisation: even when the use of English and pride in being American became dominant in the second and third generation after immigration, the American churches have still been valued as a means of preserving or gaining some identity in this mobile society by recalling ethnic and cultural roots, and by reaffirming the idealism of the American dream. And the fourth crisis came with industrialisation: as the cities grew the churches were weakened, but the weakening seems to have been less in America than in Europe, partly owing to heroic efforts by American churchmen to reach and serve the urban masses. Thus American religion has flourished through identifying itself with the people after the most fruitful crisis for the churches in the whole of their history in the New World—the First Amendment to the Constitution of the United States in 1791, enacting that 'Congress shall make no law respecting an establishment of religion, or prohibiting the free exercise thereof'.[1]

approximately sixty-eight per cent of the adult population attended religious services in any given four-week period, while seventy-nine per cent claimed church membership.

[1] See, e.g., Franklin Littell, *From State Church to Pluralism* (New York, 1962).

The Social Reality of American Religion

The peculiarities of the American religious scene are often misrepresented abroad, in the belief that the religious overtones given to the 'manifest destiny' of 'America the Beautiful' are humbug, for at heart the American is at least as godless as the European. Thus decisions of the Supreme Court, sharply separating Church and State and culminating in the 1962 prohibition of even the simplest of prayers in public schools, have been cited as proof that secularism is the real creed of America.

Confusion in the assessment of American religion as a social phenomenon is often increased by observers whose discussion of it proceeds after an unreasonably narrow definition of the word 'religion'. Thus we find a British sociologist, Dr. Bryan Wilson, writing that 'belonging to a faith in America becomes unconnected with distinctive belief to an extent quite unparalleled in Europe'.[1] What he means is that many American Protestants change their denomination because a particular church is more convenient to their home or because a particular congregation includes more of the kind of people they would like to be identified with in friendship or at least in prestige-giving association. But it does not follow that these mobile Americans hold *no* 'distinctive belief'. By tradition Americans believe in progress and togetherness, and the 'protest movement' erupting in the 1960s was a demand for faster progress and more togetherness. These American characteristics are usually connected with a kind of religion. This is a layman's attitude, although shared by many leaders of American religious thought. It can lead to truly dreadful banalities, as in the speeches of American politicians, but it can also lead to the appeal to God which was the central theme of the Gettysburg Address—and it is not secularism. 'We shall overcome . . .' is, after all, a hymn; for in America protest itself has a flavour of religious faith. The piety of the United States has by no means been confined to the

[1] *Religion in Secular Society* (London, 1966), p. 94.

'silent majority' which has voted for Eisenhower and Nixon against radicalism. It was no accident that a Baptist pastor such as Martin Luther King and a Jesuit such as Daniel Berrigan became such heroes among the anti-racism, anti-war radicals.

To be sure, the American churches in the cosy atmosphere of their 'suburban captivity' have often been fairly remote from the harsher realities of twentieth-century life. But dilution of earnestness seems to be absolutely inevitable once churchgoing becomes a large-scale social phenomenon; and critics are often grossly unfair to the surviving hard centre of American church life. For what do the American millions meet, when they escape into their churches? They meet there the endorsement of their own prejudices and illusions, to a considerable extent—but unless the preacher has completely diluted the religion which he has been commissioned to proclaim, the millions are also liable to meet ideas which are dangerous. Almost all American churches expose their ministers and congregations to the reading of the Bible, to the singing of hymns which embody historic Christianity and to the practice of worshipping a transcendent God. Much of American religion remains theologically conservative. American Catholicism, for example, is dominated by its clergy, and the clergy are dominated by an Irish respect for religious (although not for social or political) authority. Among the Protestants, much Fundamentalism survives; great denominations such as the Southern Baptists and many (especially 'Missouri Synod') Lutheran congregations are solidly conservative; and even the avowedly liberal churches, even the 'community churches' which do not belong to a particular denomination, are not without roots in historic Christianity. Although Unitarianism is more successful in America than in Britain, attempts to found churches which should be liberal rather than distinctively Christian have had remarkably little success. The 'Jesus movement' arising in the early 1970s has not taken its young members far from the historic faith; indeed, it sometimes looks like Funda-

mentalism in jeans. The enthusiasts in the more adult
Pentecostal or 'charismatic' movement have quite often
remained within the historic churches, including the Roman
Catholic Church.

It can be said that both the civil religion of contemporary
America (i.e. the watered-down 'democratic' faith which
pleases the millions by confirming what they believe already)
and the less compromising and more challenging 'old-time'
religion in its various forms are at bottom religions of
escape—for, it can be said, none of this religiosity is
allowed to argue with the crude materialism which dominates American life; and (as we shall see in the next chapter)
there are certainly some signs that such a verdict on American religion may be gaining validity as the psychological
impact of secularisation increases. Many Americans are
quick to deride any claim that their civilisation is in any
real sense Christian, or in any real sense civilised; there has
been a colossal failure of nerve, shown not least by the
envy which many sensitive Americans feel for the superior
spirituality of poverty-stricken India. Yet such anti-
Americanism seems unnecessarily harsh. The truth appears
to be that in the United States the religious communities are
powerful and exercise a considerable influence on the daily
lives of their members. The society as a whole is pluralist,
and no particular variety of religion dominates it, but the
religious life of this pluralist society is *communal*—which,
sociologically speaking, means that it is strong. In this
respect the United States may be compared again with
India.

The caste system has been of the essence of Hinduism, and
its power still largely survives although the State has put its
legislation and its influence behind some major reforms (the
abolition of untouchability, the permission of marriages
between members of different castes, etc.). Almost every
Hindu born before 1945 has experienced his membership
of a caste as an important factor in his psychology, and
almost every Hindu has expressed this membership by
participation in religious ceremonies presided over by a

member of the Brahmin caste. Recently the necessities of 'communal' development in independent India have compelled the government and other agencies to classify all citizens of the Republic in neighbourhoods, without regard to their castes. There has been a stream of anti-caste legislation since 1955, and influential spokesmen such as K. M. Panikkar have prophesied that the caste system must, and will, be transformed in the modernisation of India. Already in the cities and industries of India, caste divisions begin to lose their significance for fellow-workers who jostle each other in the crowded public transport or on the factory floor. Many in the younger generation of the élite share Gandhi's contempt for caste. But the overwhelming majority of Indians is still to be found in the villages, engaged in the work of subsistence agriculture and in domestic duties, with a few modern amenities but mainly in a timelessly conservative atmosphere. Here, in the village and the home, lies the strength of Hinduism. Here its rituals are almost always compulsory, indeed almost always unquestioned and beloved, symbols of the identity of the family and its kin (the 'extended' family). The future of Hinduism seems to be bound up with the question of the future of this group life at the parched grass roots of Indian society. At present the withering away of the 'extended' family in the Indian village is too remote for its consequences to be foreseen. A more immediate prospect, to the discussion of which we shall return, is that the Hindu stress on kinship will survive, and the Hindu ritual will survive, more strongly than the supernatural element in the Hindu religion.

The communal sense of American Christianity is also strong, for communalism survives in urban America, however different its forms may be from those of rural India. (Indeed, in view of the divisions between White Anglo-Saxon Protestants, Catholics, Jews and Negroes, some observers go so far as to speak of an American caste system.) One great difference between American and Indian communalism is that in the United States the religious bodies to a considerable extent *create* the social communities.

Studies of Roman Catholic parish life have painted, in the style of academic sociology, a picture of the 'nuclear group' at the heart of a parish, around its priests.[1] The influence of this group is extended to a much wider circle of Catholics, mainly through regular pastoral visitation by parish priests. It has often been stated that such parish life depends on the discipline, and also on the relative poverty and educational backwardness, of American Catholics, many of whom are of Irish or Polish stock; and it has been added that the priests' lack of influence on the major worldly concerns of Catholic parishioners—on their family life, politics, attitudes at work, etc.—shows that secularisation is already eroding the authority exercised by the religious group and its representatives. We may agree that as the sophistication of American Catholics increases, their solidarity is likely to decrease. Much will depend on the clergy's handling of the laity's current revolt against the official teaching on birth control. But the social cohesion of American Catholicism is still very strong. It depends in part on the national network of parochial (i.e. denominational) schools built and maintained at enormous cost, and the present rumblings of Catholic critics against this education system as divisive and wasteful do not seem likely to lead to a major reversal of the policy.

Moreover, even if American Catholicism becomes more like American Protestantism, it will still not lose all sense of community. The sociologist Gerhard Lenski has investigated the attitudes of Protestants and Jews, as well as of Catholics, in the great urban area of Detroit. He concentrated not on doctrinal problems but on attitudes to work, politics, family life and education—and he found that the religious factor was stronger than he had expected. 'From our evidence,' he wrote,[2] 'it is clear that religion in various ways is constantly influencing the daily lives of the masses of men and women in the modern American metropolis . . .

---

[1] See, e.g., J. H. Fichter, *Social Relations in an Urban Parish* (Chicago, 1954).
[2] *The Religious Factor*, p. 320.

Depending on the socio-religious group to which a person belongs, the probabilities are increased or decreased that he will enjoy his occupation, indulge in installment buying, save to achieve objectives far in the future, believe in the American Dream, vote Republican, favor the welfare state, take a liberal view on the issue of freedom of speech, oppose racial integration in the schools, migrate to another community, maintain close ties with his family, develop a commitment to the principle of intellectual autonomy, have a large family, complete a given unit of education, or rise in the class system. These are only a few of the consequences which we have observed to be associated with differences in socio-religious group membership, and the position of individuals in these groups.'

The picture here presented is not a simple one of orthodox religion controlling personal and social behaviour; the interaction of religion and life is much more subtle than that. Nor is it a picture likely to give joy to all religious leaders— for many of the attitudes revealed have little to do with the Christian Gospel, and sometimes have not much to do with the leaders' official teaching (on social issues, religious leaders tend to be more liberal than their followers). But it is a picture of religion linked with the whole of the life of a community within Detroit. Since the emphasis of the German sociologist Ferdinand Tonnies on the intimate, organic community (*Gemeinschaft*) as contrasted with the looser, more functional society or organisation (*Gesellschaft*), many analysts of our culture have taught that, for better or for worse, the day of the real community is over in modern society. But in American cities, communalism—and religious communalism at that—survives.

Despite the failure of nerve among American Christians (as among their fellow-citizens), few definite signs have yet emerged of any dramatic decrease in the influence of these religious communities. 'Most of the changes now occurring in the structure of American society,' Professor Lenski concluded,[1] 'are weakening and reducing in relative size

[1] On p. 319.

those elements in the population least involved in the churches (e.g. first-generation immigrants and members of the working class), and strengthening and enlarging those elements most involved in the churches (e.g. third-generation immigrants and members of the middle classes).' The reference to immigrants indicates a development vital to the churches' strength. We have already mentioned that in the past, in the absence of secular agencies, the churches played an important role in the process of integration. They provided communities where the immigrant would feel at home (and often would be able to speak his native language); and these communities gradually and painlessly Americanised themselves (e.g. by adopting the English language for public services). The evidence suggests that this has been a role of diminishing effectiveness, as immigrants—or at least, their children—have become embarrassed with churches which might be reckoned backward-looking, and have turned instead to the more secular institutions of America (schools, trade unions, etc.) where the old European cultures are submerged (through ceremonies honouring the Federal United States flag, etc.). But the *third* generation is often the one which values the churches most, finding in them now convenient places for meeting friends and spouses without embarrassment. The churches are now thoroughly American and thoroughly respectable—but are valued because they are carriers of what seems attractive in a European group's culture which has lost most of its political and secular expressions.

Professor Lenski's reference to the decline of the anticlerical working class, as capitalism progresses into a general prosperity not expected by Marx, is an even more important sociological observation. In the United States, many of the religious prophecies of Marx seem to have been falsified along with many of his economic predictions. The vast and growing middle classes of America tend to associate churchgoing with respectability, leisure and culture. As the days of struggle by the various ethnic groups have receded into history, the symbol of the American dream has become not the revolutionary barricade, but the 'friendly' church—the coffee-stained heart of the long weekend in the affluent suburb. And middle-aged parents are criticised by teenage rebels not for indulging in escapism but for not being religious enough—if we take 'religion' in a very broad sense to mean the protest of the spirit against materialism.

It is important that critics should in fairness acknowledge that the strength of these American religious communities is connected with a moral consensus in the whole nation. In affluent America as in poor India, the religious communities may be valued by society chiefly as means of expressing and increasing that moral consensus. In India, the vitality of Hinduism (and of the minority groups of Muslims, Christians, Jains, Parsis, etc.) is due in part to the widespread Indian agreement that while the economic tasks of nation-building are urgent in order to avert famine, economic advance should not be bought at the price of denying the importance of the individual's spiritual life. In the United States, where economic progress is accorded a far higher priority, there survives a strong belief in certain values which the churches promote—those values of togetherness, helpfulness and enthusiasm for culture which (in older or younger styles) add dignity to 'the American way of life'. Most Indian leaders constantly stress the importance of religion in the life of the country, and it was symbolic of much that Nehru's wish that there should be no religious ceremonies at his funeral was set aside by his heirs in deference to public sentiment. The Supreme Court of the United States, precisely in the years when it was driving religious worship and instruction out of the public educational system, was insisting that that system should be integrated racially. As many voices from the American churches have proclaimed, racial integration is one of the hardest possible ways of saying that America has a moral consensus, expressed in the formula that it is 'one nation under God, indivisible, with liberty and justice for all'.

It seems clear that in the United States as in the Republic

of India, *the 'secular' state governs a people which is still profoundly religious.* One of the most distinguished of American sociologists has, indeed, described the United States as 'the new modern version of the Christian society'. 'By most of the standards of our dominant tradition of liberal Protestantism,' he added, 'it is a society that must be said to have advanced far along the road of institutionalising the basic moral precepts of its religious base, however far it falls short of the desired level of perfection.'[1] Whether or not we agree with that assessment, we may certainly conclude with a Victorian Englishman: 'so far from suffering from want of State support, religion seems in the United States to stand all the firmer because, standing alone, she is seen to stand by her own strength'.[2]

Is Sweden Inevitable?

When we return to the Europe where the modern form of secularisation began, and when we ask what may be the significance for Europeans of the twentieth-century revival of religion in the United States, the correct answer seems to be complicated—for in American religion various elements are fused which cannot be expected to come together in exactly the same way elsewhere. The present uncertainty in Europe may be seen by asking briefly *whether the United States or Sweden is likely to provide the best clue to the future of English religion.*

In England during the first half of this century, the figures for weekly church attendance slumped from nearly a quarter of the population to nearly a tenth. York, for example, is the seat of one of the Church of England's two archbishops, and is dominated architecturally by York Minster. But in York on a Sunday in 1948 only one citizen in twenty-one attended Anglican worship, whereas in 1901

---

[1] Talcott Parsons in *America and the Future of Theology*, ed. W. A. Beardslee (Philadelphia, 1967), p. 153.
[2] James Bryce, *The American Commonwealth* (revd. edn., London, 1891), vol. ii, p. 584.

it had been one in seven.[1] Since a considerable prosperity and education came to England between 1900 and 1950, such figures suggest that the 'withdrawing roar' of religious faith may have been speeded by material and intellectual progress. But the puzzle is how to interpret this trend.

The York statistics may represent some of the delayed effects of the nineteenth-century alienation between the churches and the industrial democracy. Trends in religious observance frequently register a delay before they reflect trends in social and cultural life, and it would not be surprising if the English churches in the twentieth century were paying for the sins of their Victorian fathers. If this is the correct analysis, future trends may show an upward swing in religious observance, so that England resembles the United States in its piety as well as in more mundane matters. On the other hand, the flourishing American churches may reflect the influence of some special factors in American social history, and these factors may prove to be temporary even in America. In that case, the moral and religious inspiration of 'the American way of life' will be replaced by the irreligion and the immorality which hostile critics inside and outside the United States already attribute to the American people. Amid the general collapse of religion, the model for the religious future of England (and of many other countries) would be Sweden.

In Stockholm, statistics showing the regularly church-going element in the population hover around three per cent. The Director of the Institute of Religious Sociology in Stockholm has reckoned that over the country as a whole, including all denominations, the figure is about six per cent.[2] Yet more than most countries Sweden was once a religious unity, and this past is recalled by the fact that only two per cent of Swedes have exercised their legal right to contract out of contributing to the upkeep of the

[1] See B. S. Rowntree and B. R. Lavers, *English Life and Leisure* (London, 1951), and Kenneth Slack, *The British Churches Today* (revd. edn., London, 1970).

[2] In *The Scandinavian Churches*, ed. L. S. Hunter (London, 1965), p. 50.

(Lutheran) 'Folk Church'. Not many more refrain from having their children baptised, their daughters married and themselves buried in church; and most Swedes are still solemnly confirmed in order that they may receive Holy Communion. The Swedish Church possesses many beautiful buildings which seem to belong to the landscape; its organisations and finance are directly under the control of the State; and its well-paid clergy act as civil servants, collecting the statistics of births, marriages and deaths. What, then, has ruined the religion of Sweden? The history of the period approximately 1875–1925 records the alienation of the essentially authoritarian and rural Folk Church from the new industrial workers, but since Sweden's brand of Socialism has now secured both social justice and economic prosperity what matters even more than that legacy of working-class bitterness is the alienation of the middle classes. And what matters even more than the anti-Christian character of many of the effective trends in public opinion is the lack of vigour in the Christian response to the secular challenge. Swedish Christians do much good work, of course, but there seems to be a prevailing complacency. Thus we find the Christian sociologist just cited writing about Sweden: 'There is no need for concern over a supposed retreat from Christian moral standards; what is happening rather is that the norms of Christian morality are now being accepted, not because they are imposed by society and regarded as authoritative from the first, but because personal experience of life has shown them to be true.'[1]

In an account of a stay in Sweden, Miss Kathleen Nott expressed a good many reservations about that country, 'the most comfortable and least cosy in the world'. When she went to Sweden her mind was full of its social problems. 'The Swedes are so accustomed to being asked about their high suicide rate that officials get it in first . . . The best counter seemed to be, "Well, no, it's the drunkenness I've called about"—or the divorce rate—or the lunacy—

[1] p. 53.

or the homosexuality.'[1] She left the country feeling that its human problems have reached their present proportions precisely because Sweden is a society which does not interfere in people's private lives unless people misbehave in such an anti-social way as to demand the attention of the social workers and even of the prisons. Here we have a welfare state which has explicitly left its citizen's morality to their free choices. Here we have, too, what a Swede has called 'a standardised mass-culture distributed through broadcasting, newspapers, etc., which imposes a superficial uniformity but is basically a-ethical: the image of man is presented without his deeper motivations; themes such as sin, guilt, responsibility, anxiety, aging, sorrow and death are being eliminated; and we are left with a superficial description of happiness and prestige'.[2]

This withdrawal of the State from concern for people's morals or motives may be part of what being a secular country means, if secularisation is taken in a more radical sense than in India or the United States; and it contrasts with the strong pressure of public opinion on private behaviour under the regimes of Communism's quasi-religion. On the whole, Miss Nott seems to have thought the prize of individual freedom worth the cost of moral disorder in Sweden—for, as she says, a free society must come to terms with the fact that its citizens will have some anti-social tendencies. Sweden apparently no longer needs a Folk Church, or even a quasi-religion as a substitute for its Lutheran past. Its moral unity is apparently only of pride in being affluent and tolerant. Its religion has apparently been overwhelmed by the impact of our secular century.

The Churches in a Pluralist Society

The example of the United States shows that a society genuinely open to religion as well as to other convictions

---

[1] *A Clean, Well-Lighted Place* (London, 1961), p. 26.
[2] H. Aronson in *Christian Social Ethics in a Changing World*, ed. J. C. Bennett (New York, 1966), p. 265.

may be built on the basis of the separation of Church and State. And this may be all that many secularists demand; for example, H. J. Blackham, the Director of the British Humanist Association, urges not the abolition of religion but the end of any pretence that it should have the monopoly. 'Religious faith,' Mr. Blackham writes, 'belongs along with all ultimates of interpretation, choice, aim, dedication, aspiration, worship. Because these cannot be required or sanctioned by a society without losing their authenticity, they are not therefore without profound effect upon society.'[1] If this is to be the pattern of the future, many religious believers will welcome the challenge. They believe that a secular state can leave sufficient opportunity for 'religion' in its more limited sense, according to the nineteenth-century ideal of 'a free church in a free state', but above all they believe that a secular state can be built on the moral unity given by the general acceptance, by religious believers and agnostics alike, of some 'self-evident' truths of Natural Law, or at least of the duty to secure liberty, dignity and justice for all through the tasks of nation-building. Thus for broadly social as well as for narrowly religious reasons we find that a social analyst who is perhaps the shrewdest thinker among Indian Christians, M. M. Thomas, is an advocate—although also a careful definer—of the secular state;[2] as was the leading intellectual among Catholics in the United States, John Courteney Murray.[3]

The debate in modern England has its special interest. J. N. Figgis in *The Churches in the Modern State* (London, 1913) advocated a position not far from the pluralism of Thomas and Murray. But the formal establishment of the Church of England has remained, and during the first quarter of the century Nonconformists resented the privileges involved. In the second quarter their cry for dis-

[1] *Religion in a Modern Society* (London, 1966), p. 129.
[2] *The Christian Response to the Asian Revolution* (London, 1966).
[3] *We Hold These Truths: Catholic Reflections on the American Proposition* (New York, 1960).

establishment diminished, partly because the Established Church's privileges had decreased, but a wish to liberate the Church from the Crown's nomination of the bishops, Parliament's veto over changes in worship, etc., has remained. The probable solution of this problem looks like being the re-establishment of the Church of England (particularly in connection with its reunion with the Methodist Church) according to the pattern provided by the established (and Presbyterian) Church of Scotland. The Church of Scotland is a National Church in the sense that it accepts an obligation to serve the whole nation, and is honoured by the nation as such; but the State has no control over its government. Such an arrangement applied to England might secure many of the advantages of 'a free church in a free state' while avoiding the disadvantages for the churches which exist in the American form of the separation of Church and State. The advantages would be that both Church and State would secure their integrity; and the disadvantages which could be avoided would be the difficulties of the American churches in relating religion to government at the national and local levels, and to the State-sponsored schools. The possibility arises of a National Church which may offer the contributions of religion to public life (as symbolised at the coronation of the monarch) without confusing religion with politics.

In recent years the debate in England has shifted away from the more formal aspects of establishing a church to the more substantial question, whether it is right to give religion privileges in the educational, broadcasting and television systems of the nation. When comparatively few Englishmen regularly go to church, such privileges seem anomalies. However, surveys of public opinion show that the privileges are not in fact widely resented. The great majority of English parents seem to want religious worship and instruction in schools, and religious broadcasts have large audiences. It seems probable that improvements in the communicating power of religious broadcasting and education will take place in the context of continuing privileges for religion.

Much attention has also been given to the relationship of law and morality. Until recently many British laws attempted to force an old-fashioned version of Christian morality on to a public which rejected the doctrinal basis of that ethic, and a healthy distinction between crime and sin is only beginning to emerge in current legal reforms. But it is unlikely that British (or other) law will ever be entirely without moral content. Some evidence that the British people wishes to observe high standards of decency and compassion comes in its acceptance of the legal prohibition of public prostitution and racial discrimination.[1]

This confused situation has resulted in a contrast between two thoughtful books by distinguished lay members of the Church of England. In *The Idea of a Christian Society* (London, 1939), T. S. Eliot argued that although only the community of believing churchmen could be expected to reach the highest standards, the whole of society could be expected to conform with Christianity to the extent, for example, of accepting public regulation of private morality. In *The Idea of a Secular Society* (Oxford, 1963), D. L. Munby rejected this argument in favour of a society without a common philosophy and without official images, but with a deep respect for the variety of individuals and for the importance of facts. Many in England would probably feel that, while the rejection of T. S. Eliot's nostalgia for the sacred society of Christendom was inevitable, Mr. Munby was unrealistic in his minimising of the role of public opinion with its images and agencies. The moral pressure exercised by society is still a great reality; and perhaps what Mr. Munby meant to defend was not the 'secular society' but the 'pluralist' or 'open' society. On Mr. Munby's showing the *State*, not the society, needs to be secular. And if the society is genuinely 'pluralist' it may not be necessary to enforce a complete separation of the religion in that society from the work of the state. Religious bodies, like general charities, may—and to a certain extent must—have

[1] See, e.g., Basil Mitchell, *Law, Morality and Religion in a Secular Society* (London, 1967).

dealings with a secular state. It may be possible to work out an arrangement for safeguarding the freedoms of all citizens in a pluralist society, while relating the agencies of religion to the public agencies.

It may be significant that church members in Britain and Western Europe have been willing in recent years to give more money to support their churches, whether or not they attend church, as often as was the former pattern. When Tom Harrisson revisited the English 'Worktown' (it was actually Bolton) after an absence of twenty years, his new survey noted that although attendance at the local churches had declined, their income had increased. This seemed 'in part a product of the affluent society; in part a deepening sense of responsibility towards religious institutions by those who remain concerned. This sort of change is difficult to measure . . . It is not the sort of feeling that can be expressed by an ordinary Briton holding it—sometimes only vaguely and far down in private opinion—when asked by a stranger, however subtly questioning.'[1] For the future of the Church of England, the sixty-six per cent of the total population who are baptised members of the Church may matter less than the six per cent who receive Holy Communion at Easter.[2]

Active churches which depend on popular support do still exist in the modern world—whatever Marx thought. And it does not seem to be finally disastrous if the support comes mainly from the middle classes—whatever Marxists now say. Christianity when domesticated in its 'suburban captivity' in the United States is plainly open to much criticism; but such a Christianity, however unromantic, may have lessons to teach. Economic trends seem likely to falsify Marxist predictions, and make almost all North America and almost all Europe middle class. What will that mean to the churches? Will the spread of suburbia over the face of Europe bring into new prominence that important American

---

[1] *Britain Revisited* (London, 1961), p. 85.
[2] See Trevor Beeson, *The Church of England in Crisis* (London, 1972).

phenomenon: the keen support of voluntary associations including the suburban family church? At present in England only about twenty per cent of the population identifies itself as middle class, and of the present bulk of the remainder it is true to say that 'one aspect of working-class styles especially important for participation in church life is the widespread resistance to *any* kind of major involvement in voluntary associations, trade unions included. With every step up the status scale active participation in voluntary associations of every kind increases.'[1]

The twentieth century has certainly witnessed in Europe a surprising recovery by some churches which have, at least to some extent, overcome their alienation from their own people. This can be seen in France. We noted that the identification of the French Catholic Church with the *ancien régime* of the eighteenth century and with the monarchies of the nineteenth century brought about its downfall early in the twentieth century. A few Christian democrats such as Marc Sagnier, and a few Christian socialists such as Charles Péguy, made lonely protests, but the Church's identification with the enemies of the Republic was effectively questioned only when priests and laymen fought and suffered in the trenches of 1914–18. Over 4,500 priests were among the million French casualties. That suffering by its Church for *la patrie* was repeated under the German occupation, 1940–4, when Catholics and Protestants worked together in the Resistance and Catholic priests went voluntarily to minister among the working people deported to Germany (although it was also true that many Catholics supported the Pétain regime). Frenchmen grew bored with anti-clericalism. Diplomatic relations with the Vatican were resumed in 1921; and both the reactionary bishops and the anti-clerical politician Edouard Herriot failed to sabotage the Catholic Church's agreement with the Republic. After the second war modest state subsidies to church schools became possible. And so French religion slowly came to

[1] David Martin, *A Sociology of English Religion*, p. 105. See also his essays on *The Religious and the Secular* (London, 1969).

have a spiritual integrity which was more than the spirit which had fought to preserve the visible integrity of all Catholic institutions and doctrines; and the new religion was humble, charitable, outgoing. The desire to form specifically Christian fellowships within the secular environment led not to a Catholic Party but to Catholic Action's 'apostolate of the laity'. Catholic Action applied to France the maxim of Pius XI, the Pope who encouraged it in the 1920s and 1930s: the Christians in a particular group or class must spread their faith among their own companions, much as the Church in Asia or Africa must be rooted in the local life, must become a 'native mission'. In 1941 the *Mission de France* opened its seminary at Lisieux, to train priests not for the comfortable routine of a *bourgeois* parish but for an unprecedented mission within the de-christianised areas. A map of the religious geography of France, and a crucifix, looked down on the students during their meals. The *Mission de Paris*, founded by Cardinal Suhard in 1944 for the industrial proletariat alienated from the parish churches, led to the experiment of the worker-priests.

The tragic drama of these worker-priests—crushed as they were between Communism and other anti-clericalism in the working-class, and indifference or hostility in the bulk of the Church—emphasised the continuing problem of the Church's alienation from the people.[1] So did the refusal to be baptised, made by one of the century's most brilliant and saintly converts, Simone Weil. She hated the idea of separation from the mass of her fellow-countrymen. That made her refuse to eat extra food in her illness, and brought her to her death in 1943; it also made her refuse to become a member of the Catholic Church. 'I love God, Christ and the Catholic faith,' she wrote, 'but I have not the slightest love for the Church . . . What frightens me is the Church as a social structure.'[2]

---

[1] See, e.g., Gregor Siefer, *The Church and Industrial Society* (1960; Eng. trans., London, 1964).
[2] See her letters and papers, *Waiting on God* (1950; Eng. trans., London, 1951), specially Letters I and II.

Yet the inner recovery of French Catholicism could not be crushed. It has been expressed in the vision of intellectuals such as the philosopher Jacques Maritain or the novelist François Mauriac, men of integrity concerned to relate the traditional faith to the realities of the twentieth century. The Catholic review *Esprit*, founded by Emmanuel Mounier, has been since 1932 a focus for a 'personalism' which has claimed freedom and fulfilment for humanity instead of privilege for the Church. As if anticipating such a movement, the French philosopher Henri Bergson in his last book, in 1932, distinguished between *Two Sources of Religion and Morality*. One source was static; that kind of religion conserved the moral conventions of the group, as Durkheim had said. But there was another source, both more mysterious and more commendable, which produced a dynamic and adventurous religion and an 'open' morality of human dignity and growth. To that religion, born in the human spirit, Bergson at the end gave his allegiance.

Of course, philosophy is not enough. What of practical religion? The French worker-priests were disciplined, and some left the Church. At the same time, the leading French theologians with liberal views were exiled from Paris and silenced. There seemed some prospect of a return of the 'black terror' of 1907. But when Pius XII died, the French cardinals played a leading part in the election of the more liberal John XXIII, and French churchmen (including theologians disgraced in the 1950s) were among the spiritual masters of the Second Vatican Council. With many of its insights now preserved in that Council's decrees, no Church in the world has done more than the French Catholic Church to embody the spirit of Christian renewal, reaching out to the people in the people's language. (The sociological researches sponsored by the Church have been inspired by this motive.) And in 1965 a symbolic gesture came to mark the new mood: permission came from Rome for the revival of the experiment of priests in full-time industrial work, under slightly different conditions and with no publicity. The working class to which the priests returned was more prosperous, and there was some likelihood that a militant proletariat preferring Communism to Catholicism would be a diminishing factor among the French Church's problems. The dechristianisation of France has, of course, not been reversed, but with its four million regular communicants the Church of the 1970s is in better heart than was the Church of the 1900s.

In France, then, such reconciliation as has been achieved between the clergy and the people has been helped by the Church's patriotism: a patriotism of the trenches and also a patriotism of 'open' love. But Catholic nationalism is a wider phenomenon, for the Catholic Church has been supported in other European countries by peoples who, in a time of a national crisis, have found in the Church the great sanctuary of national memories and hopes. Cardinal Mercier of Malines, who from 1914 to 1918 was with King Albert the symbol of Belgian courage under German occupation, has had an unexpected number of successors. The greatest example of Catholic nationalism is, of course, Irish Catholicism. The Catholic Church virtually *was* Ireland when the country was exploited and Irish culture derided by English Protestants; when political independence was won in 1922 the Catholic Church received no establishment or endowment, but also needed none, in order to be the Church of the Irish people. The majority of the Irish people is now dispersed outside Ireland—and everywhere gives strength to the Catholic Church.

The national spirit has sustained Catholicism even under Communism. The Catholic Church has been the heart and soul of Poland through the centuries when the country has been poised precariously between Protestant or Nazi Germany and Orthodox or Communist Russia. Independent Poland after 1918 gave a privileged position to Catholicism. Although the German and Russian occupations from 1939 executed or deported thousands of bishops and priests as the leaders of Polish patriotism, the revolt of 1956, while not changing the Communist character of the government, freed Cardinal Wysynski from gaol, instilled a respect for popular religion into the State authorities, and even (for a time) restored religion to the State schools. The Polish Communists organised a mostly abortive movement of 'patriotic priests' to work with them, but it was precisely by being the symbol of remembered independence, proudly patriotic in the latest phase of Poland's sufferings, that the Polish priests loyal to their own tradition have achieved and retained their popular following. The failure of the 1956 revolt in Hungary to secure similar concessions was due partly to the Hungarian churches' record of support for Nicholas Horthy's pro-Nazi regime (1920–45); but the partial liberalisation of Hungary since 1956 has included more freedom for the religion which still survives fairly strongly, as the controversial figure of Cardinal Mindszenty recedes into history. In another country under Communist rule, Czechoslovakia, religion, although severely handicapped, has gained both in internal morale and in the respect of the people, in comparison with the inter-war atmosphere of French-style anti-clericalism. We are not claiming that the future of the Catholic Church in Eastern Europe is assured. Thousands of bishops and priests—perhaps as many as 10,000—were executed or exiled in the decade 1945–55, and the Church which has survived carries many wounds. Control by the Vatican, which to many has belonged to the essence of Catholicism, has become tenuous, although only in China have the links with Rome been broken completely. All that is being claimed is that under Communism the Catholic Church has become a carrier of national culture rather than a supporter of social reaction. Marx could not foresee this social process which has made it possible that the Church will outlive the Communist Party in the hearts of the people.

At the other end of the political spectrum, the Catholic Church in Spain and Portugal has owed much of its hold on the people to the fact that the old religion—the religion which blessed the crusade against the Moors in Spain and the discovery and colonisation of America and the East, the religion which kept its glamour while the country grew

old and poor—has remained the symbol of national pride.
The Spanish laws of 1938–9, re-establishing religion in the
schools and State grants for the clergy, said so very plainly:
'Catholicism is the very marrow of the history of Spain.'
More recently strong elements in Spanish and Portuguese
Catholicism have been identified with the hopes of the
workers and peasants rather than with the Franco and
Salazar dictatorships—which may well turn out to be a
shrewd investment in the future. And in many parts of
Western Europe since 1945, the leadership of Catholics has
been conspicuous among the Christian Democrats who have
led national reconstruction; for after the collapse of Hitler
and Mussolini, as after the fall of the ancient Roman
Empire, the Catholic Church has in the eyes of Europe
appeared as the City of God against which 'the gates of
hell shall not prevail'.

We have also to remember the patriotic pride of Russians
and others in their Orthodox Churches. Quite apart from
other evidence, the novels of Boris Pasternak and Alexander
Solzhenitsyn are enough to show how the spiritual tradition
of the Orthodox Church is still being used by Russians to
interpret areas of life to which Marxism has nothing to say
—half a century after the Revolution. If we ask why the
Greek Orthodox Church, despite great problems and scandals, retains such a grip on the affections of the Greek
people, we receive a similar answer: it was the Church which
was the shelter of the Greek spirit while the country was
under Turkish occupation until 1829, and the memories of
that past have not perished. The sufferings of the two
World Wars brought Church and people still closer together, and an Archbishop of Athens, the great Damas-
kinos, was called to lead his country as regent when the
alternative after the Second World War was Communism.
More recently, Europe has seen Archbishop Makarios acting
as the leader of Greek nationalism against the British, and
emerging as the President of independent Cyprus. The
Romanian and Bulgarian Churches are other Orthodox
Churches with popular followings, although the Com-

munist regimes have been too efficient to allow their bishops to play a role as nationalist 'ethnarchs' in the style of Makarios.

Protestantism also has gained from patriotism. Protestants have been involved in many of the religious situations just mentioned. In Norway under German occupation, Bishop Berggrav became the symbol of patriotism—and that was only one part of the toughening of religion in those stern years. In Germany itself the standing temptation of Christians has been to be *too* patriotic, and at more than one point in this book we shall have to observe the tragic compromises involved. But the defiance of the 'Confessing' Church against Hitler, symbolised in the great names of Martin Niemöller and Dietrich Bonhoeffer, turned out to be the true patriotism, and since 1945 in West Germany that group has been significant as a source of moral integrity and self-respect. Its survivors have carried a Christian contribution into new questions confronting society; and the memory of its courage has shown that the *Acts of the Apostles* can be continued into our own time. In very few places since 1945 has the relationship between an old religion and a new society been worked out more impressively than it has been by the Protestants of East Germany—Lutheranism's birthplace. Warned and even strengthened by their experience under Hitler, these Christians have maintained much of their integrity under Communism, but equally significant has been the determination of many of them to love their people and to co-operate with their government within the limits of conscience. Such Christians in a Marxist land have avoided an 'inner flight' to the capitalist West, and under a barrage of atheist propaganda many East Germans have been surprisingly loyal to the Church remaining in their midst.

CHAPTER THREE

The Psychological Impact of the Secular Century

Gods High and Near

Both belief and unbelief are likely to protest if our analysis is confined to describing religion's functions in society. Man's basic religious sense may be interpreted largely through the faith of the surrounding society; yet it is, after all, the individual who makes the interpretation, and—specially when his society is disintegrated—the individual is liable to be concerned with questions which go deeper than his place in society. What about religion's claim to be the means of unifying a personality more precious than many societies? What about religion's claim to confront the soul with God? Does the statement that man's heart is restless until it rests in God indicate man's true destiny, or does it merely indicate a disease which must be cured if a person is to be healthily himself? It is in such questions that the psychological impact of our largely secular century comes home, challenging in a period of much self-consciousness and individualism the interpretations of the religious sense which the old societies decreed.

When we were studying the religious implications of the disintegration of modern society, we compared this with the social unity which was supported by primitive religion; and now that we are to be more personal, we may begin again by taking a brief look at the psychology of primitive religion. Immediately we may note that among primitive peoples there often seem to be two levels of divinity, which exist simultaneously (the one does not arise out of the other, as the evolutionary theorists of religion used to maintain). These two levels in primitive religion have often been pictured as the realms of the Sky Father and the Earth Mother—the God above being sometimes as remotely benevolent as the light of the sun, sometimes as terrifying in his wrath as a sudden storm, and the goddess beneath always the warm, loving provider of life, comfort and food. A religion flourishes when sky and earth, Father and Mother, are kept in one vision. Above is the 'high God' who created the world by the exercise of his mysterious will, and who has now withdrawn into his eternal blessedness, but who remains in some sense ruler and judge over all. Below are the gods or goddesses or spirits whose benevolence or anger may be experienced in particular times and places, and who need the friendship of mortals. Practical religion concentrates on worship at the lower level, and therefore on sacrifices and ceremonies likely to please the spirits. It may be analysed as polytheistic (believing in many gods) and even as magical. But primitive religion also keeps alive the memory of the 'high God' through the proverbs of the folk, and sometimes also through the private meditations of the few who are gifted with special insight. Primitive religion may therefore also be analysed as monotheistic (believing in one God) and spiritual. The truth seems to be that both these levels, 'higher' and 'lower', should be remembered for both belong to the experience of the primitive worshipper, who feels his religion as a single whole.

The Western religious tradition has also included the two levels, 'high' and 'near'. It did so in ancient Greece, where the abstract speculations of the philosophers were accompanied by the friendly superstitions of the people, and where the 'mystery' religions met a need because, by promising an initiation into the mysteries of life and death, they offered to fuse the two elements. It did so in Islam, where the austere obedience of the Prophet to the one God was accompanied by the enthusiasm of the Sufi movement for the God who dwells within the human heart—and by the cult of martyrs and mediators between God and man, among the Sufis or in the Shia sect. And Catholicism, taking the European civilisation over from Greece and Rome, continued to operate at both the high and the human levels. Most of the philosophy of the Middle Ages sought to be rational in arguments leading from the order in nature to the existence of one perfect God, and some of the mysticism would enter the eternal darkness beyond the personality of this God, but most of the real life of the medieval Church lay in the heartfelt adoration of Christ, the Virgin and the saints for favours received as part of God's providential ordering of life. The God of Catholicism was thus both high and near; the God of the Catholic philosophers was also the God of the peasants.

But in Africa and India we can already witness the beginnings of the disintegration of this religious world-view, as of the religious society which sustained it; and in Europe the disintegration has gone far. Essentially, what has happened has been that *the 'high God' has seemed to get higher and higher*, more and more remote from the lives and thoughts of men, more and more hostile to them; while the stories of Christ, the Virgin and the saints have seemed less and less adequate as descriptions of life as it is or can be.

Already this was the psychological crisis in the Reformation and Counter-Reformation of the sixteenth century. Like many in the waning of the Middle Ages and in the Renaissance, Luther and Calvin both regarded God as hostile to most of the human race, the implacable Judge. However, God was real for almost all in the sixteenth century, and the Reformers and Counter-Reformers who regarded him as terrible succeeded in overcoming their sense of estrangement from God because their sense of deliverance from damnation through the mediation of Christ (and for the Catholics, also of the Virgin and the saints) was so strong. It was, in fact, Martin Luther's stupendous achievement to wrest out of his own spiritual crisis an experience of the overwhelming goodness and grace of the near God, in the lovable person of Christ. That experience, more than anything else, awoke Germany, Sweden and other parts of Europe into the new religious vitality of Protestantism—and awoke the Catholic world also. New systems of Protestant or Catholic thought and devotion were then constructed. But neither the Reformation nor the Counter-Reformation looks very flourishing today, 450 years after Luther's great protest. For many in Europe who have a Christian background, the shape of God has become a vague blur in the back of that background, while the religious objects in the foreground—the conventional portrait of Jesus, and churches with their images of saints—although more real are viewed with little interest, because they also do not seem to belong to the everyday world. God, if there is a God, is the unknown God, and the world, which clearly exists, is best described and used in a secular way.

Freud as a Witness to Secularisation

Sigmund Freud, who died a refugee from Hitler in London in 1939, was the greatest witness to the psychological consequences of this collapse of religion in nineteenth-century Europe. He was able to make his witness with extraordinary power partly because of his genius which combined scientific integrity with imaginative and literary capacities of a high order, and partly because of his social background, which was a group which might be expected to register religion's collapse at least as fully as any other group in the world—the intellectual Jews of Vienna. The Vienna where Freud came to his maturity was famous both for the heights of its cultural life and for the depths to which anti-semitism sank among those who resented the outstanding abilities of many of its Jews. This resentment against the Jews in both the top and the bottom sections of society had a Catholic flavour. Until 1918 Vienna was the capital of the Hapsburg empire with its throne-and-altar alliance, and the Austrian Republic which emerged after the fall of the Hapsburgs was controlled by Christian Democrats who looked to the Catholic clergy for inspiration. But the resentful at the bottom of society were also Catholics. Adolf Hitler was brought up in nearby Linz and spent five bitter years as an unemployed 'artist' in Vienna; he despised the Catholic Church almost as greatly as he hated the Jews; but he had been baptised and confirmed and that, tragically, meant something—for he was never excommunicated. When Hitler took over Austria in 1938, the Cardinal Archbishop of Vienna had to be rebuked by the Vatican for welcoming the invasion. This Catholic anti-semitism was, of course, not exclusively Austrian. In its 1933 Concordat with Hitler, the Vatican attempted to secure privileges for the Catholic Church in Germany when the Nazis' anti-semitism was already published and demonstrated. And even if the Austrian and German Catholics of the 1930s had been more sensitive to the iniquity which was to lead to the murder of six million Jews, Freud and others of his race would have experienced the terrible legacy of Christian hatred for the Jews who had 'killed God'—a hatred continuous for centuries and only made worse by Luther.

In his early years Freud was taken to church services by a Catholic nursemaid (who was old and ugly and was subsequently dismissed for stealing), and as a schoolboy and medical student Freud faced Catholic anti-semitism. He was not given a religious upbringing, for his parents had rejected the orthodox Rabbinic Judaism which seemed the only religious alternative to conversion to the oppressive Catholicism, but he and his family were acutely conscious and proud of being Jewish by race. When after many difficult years as a student and teacher of orthodox medicine, Freud gradually emerged as a hypnotist and psychoanalyst, most of his patients were other Jews who were also without any personal religion. Religion therefore to him meant primarily the authoritarian, corrupt, anti-semitic Catholicism of Vienna. That was what caused him to identify himself with the crusading Protestant, Oliver Cromwell (after whom he named a son), and with the ancient Semite, Hannibal, in his crossing of the Alps in the march on Rome. That was what made Rome a frequent subject of his dreams. That was what aroused the consuming fire of denunciation in his secularist tract of 1927, *The Future of an Illusion*. Only once, in his last book, *Moses and Monotheism* (London, 1939), written while he was dying of cancer, did he make public a major presentation of a higher variety of religion. There he described the religion of Moses, a manly belief in an all-powerful, all-loving God leading worshippers not to fear or to ritual but to strength and purity of intelligence and life. But as if to show that such a religion could not really belong to the real world, Freud indulged himself in the speculation that Moses was an Egyptian who had acquired this faith from Pharaoh Iknhaton, and who for his pains was murdered by the Hebrews in the wilderness. From this early Jewish experience, Freud taught, there survived a guilt about the murder of Moses, accounting for the Jewish feeling of inferiority; but there also survived an integrity in rejecting all idols (as Moses did), accounting in the twentieth century for the courage of those Jews who were open atheists. As Freud in *Moses and Monotheism* described the lush, foolish, degrading religion into which most of the Jews fell after their Lawgiver's death, it is not hard to see what he was thinking about: Catholic Vienna. And as he described Moses the heroic prophet of truth, it is not hard to see whom he really had in mind: himself.

In Freud's reaction to Catholic Vienna, we may therefore see the final phase of that nineteenth-century rebellion against Christendom which we watched at an earlier stage in the analysis of the English industrial cities made by Karl Marx. The idea of God was associated with a social order which was hated. God seemed repulsive and frightening, and his hostile character could be seen clearly on those rare occasions when God's nearness was experienced by unhappy people; or God was simply remote, ineffective, unreal. In all this, the God of Catholic Vienna was rather like the Church of industrial England. The symbols of religion meant little or nothing to Freud and his patients, much as the details of the new Gothic churches built in the industrial cities meant little or nothing to Marx and his workers. Society was breaking up around Freud as around Marx, and each thinker used a particular aspect of the disintegrating social system to describe the disintegrating religious situation. Freud found the key in the alienation of children from their oppressive parents—as Marx found it in the alienation of the proletariat from their industrial work under the capitalists. Here Freud offered a brilliantly imaginative reconstruction of man's psychological history—just as Marx built a fascinating interpretation of social history around the theme of the class war. For both Marx and Freud religion was an illusion which dangerously prolonged the helplessness of childhood's need for protection and guidance in face of the difficulties of the external world. For Freud, what mattered was the childhood of the individual; for Marx, the childhood of the race. Both men gave their lives in order that their fellow-men might 'come of age'.

If we proceed on the principle which Freud himself taught us, we must trace Freud's doctrines about childhood and its psychic dramas to his own childhood. The evidence is not as plentiful as we might wish. Unfortunately Freud was never psychoanalysed. The standard biography was written by an Englishman, Ernest Jones, who was Freud's only highly distinguished pupil who did not break away from the master; and while making some important points to show that Freud could be analysed in Freudian terms, Jones revealed less than the irreverently curious would wish about the secret life.[1] But enough evidence survives for our purposes.

The Interpretation of Dreams, which appeared in 1900 as the first great work of psychoanalysis, included many of Freud's own dreams which he decided to analyse after the shock of his father's death in 1896, and something is revealed also in the glimpses of an intense and neurotic young man provided by surviving letters. What we know is that, even allowing for the special relationship between mothers and sons in Jewish homes, Freud's mother was more than usually devoted to him. She was not twenty years

[1] Revd. edn., New York, 1961.

old when he was born. Her husband had married her when he was aged forty and already the father of two sons older than she was. Moreover, her only other son, Sigmund's younger brother, died in infancy, and Sigmund had been fiercely jealous of this brother. Sigmund's wish that the little rival should die had been fulfilled, and (although sisters arrived) 'for the rest of his life he felt guilty, for the rest of his life he felt he deserved to die, and so he wished death to come and dreaded its possible approach throughout his life'.[1] Freud's conscious relationship with his father was less unusual, and superficially we might say that all was well. Despite the special complexities of the double family and the tensions which belong to all growing up, Freud lived at home until he was aged twenty-six. But it is not claimed that there was the deep understanding between Freud and his father that there was between Freud and his mother. As Ernest Jones notes, Freud's childhood left him with deep needs both to love and to hate. In adulthood Freud passionately turned for help to male friends, and as passionately quarrelled with them; he published for the world to see views about fatherhood, which, on his own showing, must reflect his childish hatred of his own father.

The representation of the 'high God' as 'Father' is common to many religions, but is specially prominent in Christianity. Basically, it symbolises the strong love which God has for men. Freud came to believe that God was called 'Father' because children invented him as the invisible personification of their fathers, whom they basically disliked as being cruelly authoritarian, etc. The event which particularly called forth this dislike and its supernatural projection was the passion of a boy between three and five years old to possess his mother sexually (the Oedipus Complex). The wish was frustrated by a threat of castration believed to come from the father, and the son felt guilty as well as defeated. This guilt was the basis of the formation of the conscience or 'super-ego', a kind of internal father exuding disapproval—and it was also the origin in the individual's

[1] Gregory Zilboorg, *Freud and Religion* (Boston, 1958), p. 57.

life of the idea of God the heavenly Father. The origin of the idea in the life of society was traced back by Freud to an actual murder. In guessing about the life of 'the primitive horde' soon after the emergence of *homo sapiens*, Freud picked up some remarks made by Darwin and some speculations offered by the early anthropologists. The young men in the primitive horde decided to kill their leader in order to have the young women whom he controlled. They did this, but were overcome by guilt. They then represented their murdered leader or father-substitute in a symbol; this was Frazer's and Durkheim's totem. This totem, a sacred animal normally not to be hunted or touched, could be eaten in a sacrificial feast. Later the totem was believed to be supernatural, and so religion began. The fate of Moses among the Israelites repeated that primitive drama, but even without such repetitions in 'history' its influence was passed on through the unconscious mind by which the human race's collective experience was silently taught to each human infant.

Since neither five-year-old boys nor the men of the primitive horde were available to speak clearly about these incestuous and murderous desires, Freud based his theories on his own memories, on what he was told by his patients and particularly on what his patients told him about their dream-life, that 'royal road to the unconscious'. For some years, he tells us, Freud listened to his women patients recalling how their fathers had raped them, and to equivalent confessions about their mothers from men—until he came to see that these were the wish-fulfilments of the reality which was the Oedipus Complex in boys and the equivalent Electra Complex in girls. The conclusions which Freud formed as a result of these experiences were applied to the human race in his amateur anthropology, notably in his 1913 book on primitive religion, *Totem and Taboo*. In his *Moses and Monotheism*, he was unrepentant in the face of criticisms of *Totem and Taboo* made by professional anthropologists—criticisms which were specially directed against his reliance on the pioneering British anthropologist,

Robertson Smith. 'I am not an ethnologist but a psycho-analyst,' he wrote. 'It was my good right to select from ethnological data what would serve me for my analytic work. The writings of the highly gifted Robertson Smith provided me with valuable points of contact with the psychological material of analysis and suggestions for the use of it.' Freud liked to present his work as purely scientific, and in reality it was founded on his deeply impressive carefulness in countless hours of listening to patients and of introspection; nor should we forget that he spent nine years in the study of chemistry, zoology and physiology, before turning to neurology (and so, through hypnosis, to psychoanalysis), so that he had good reasons to claim that he understood the scientific attitude and method. But very few, if any, anthropologists can now be found who take seriously Freud's selection from the evidence about primitive religion; and greatly as all are indebted to the many flashes of genius by which his writings have illuminated all subsequent work for mental health, almost as few qualified and experienced practitioners in psychological medicine take literally Freud's descriptions of the child's unconscious mind.

Driven by a passionately experienced unhappiness which we cannot now completely recover, Freud became not primarily a scientist but a poet for the age of science. He was a researcher, but he was also a great maker of myths. As he listened to his memories and to his patients, he drew from their sordid mess of trivialities some grand, unifying ideas. Nothing was in its depths what it seemed to be superficially—apart, to be sure, from the sexual appetites. All human behaviour was determined by a few simple origins; even accidents, even slips of the tongue, could be traced to their causes in the *libido*, and mostly to sex. In order to express these ideas about origins and causes Freud turned to the tragic drama of ancient Athens, for the figures of Oedipus and Electra. When the real, public tragedies of 1914–18 made so much fresh psychological material available for study (specially the cases of battle-shocked soldiers), and as his own experience and reflection matured, Freud

turned to the Greek language in order to express other
unifying, interpretative ideas. *Eros* was now the word for
the force of life and love, and *Thanatos* the name of the
resisting force of death, for which men secretly longed.
When in 1923 he came to present his doctrine systematically,
es, *ich* and *uberich* appeared as a mythological trinity, and
they could be expressed also in the Latin more familiar to
readers of English translations of Freud's work: *id*, *ego*,
superego. These ideas clearly are myths, although (as tends
to happen with myths) they may be given a life of their
own, so that we are liable to see an Oedipus as the central
figure in the story of every man, a battle between *Eros* and
Thanatos in an everyday decision, and a geographical division into three in every personality. But more subtly
influential than such myth-making was the imaginative
power of Freud's personal vision of life. This vision, more
than any other, has become the corporate myth of twentieth-
century intellectuals.

Attitudes to God and society were summed up for Freud
in the son's wish to murder the father. Here in Freud was
the vision of the man of life and love, the man of intelligence
and integrity, alienated from religion and from society,
and pitted against them to the death. While the masses
have turned to other myths, the sensitive few have been in
a basic sense Freudians. Freud did not cause their vision;
it was caused by the rapid change in their society. For a
middle-class intellectual, it was the equivalent of the
worker's alienation as seen by Marx. Nor did Freud begin
this way of looking at life; it has a long history into the
nineteenth century and beyond. But Freud was the greatest
teacher of this vision to our time.

The Challenge of Freud

In his *Civilisation and its Discontents*,[1] Freud saw civilisation
as the enemy of happiness. Public opinion, reinforced if
necessary by the police, prevented people from giving free

[1] 1929; Eng. trans., London, 1930.

expression to their sexual and aggressive instincts or 'drives'. Freud, who thought that most people were too stupid for it to be safe to allow them to run their own lives, on the whole approved of this repression of the turbulent masses, but he was preoccupied by the control exercised by a civilised society over the discontents of its more intellectual members—a control not through the policeman but through the superego. This control, forcing down the vital drives, resulted in neurosis. Many symptoms showing the danger of this repression were quoted by Freud, and they included a prevailing sense of guilt. The First World War was interpreted as the explosion of aggressive drives which civilisation had attempted to repress, but even more dangerous was the cost of civilisation in terms of personal happiness. Freud seems to have experienced (either in himself or through the reminiscences of his patients and friends) the disappointments of civilised, *bourgeois* marriage. He had no high opinion of the intellectual capacities of women (although his daughter Anna became an exceptionally able psychoanalyst). He thought that as a sex they lacked strong personalities (because having had no fear of castration they could not develop a formidable superego, but could only envy men for their superior sexual organs). Even sexual satisfaction was doubtful in marriage; and what restrained a man from seeking it elsewhere was not his love for his wife but his fear of his superego as the forbidding voice of civilisation. It is not surprising that many of Freud's followers have taken his researches to justify a more thorough rebellion than he advocated against the conventions of civilisation.

In assessing this revolt which has taken the name of Freud, we cannot forget that even apart from the menace of anti-semitism Freud and his patients found the moral atmosphere of Vienna stifling. Many marriages had boredom at their heart, and prudery about sex—a prudery which scarcely corresponded with the adults' secret thoughts—menaced the healthy development of young people. Such a society, binding its members by conventions rather than convictions, was already fundamentally disintegrated, and Freud performed a service by digging its grave. Freud continued to analyse hysterical women, when his senior colleague Josef Breuer withdrew because of the sexuality which was being brought to the surface; and that quiet decision of 1894 may be reckoned as one of the decisive turning points in the progress of mankind towards a saner and happier future. But Freud suggested that the whole of civilisation was as sick as these women, and if this was true of the society around him the analysis throws light on that society rather than on all human history. In integrated, healthy groups individuals have drawn much of their happiness, and indeed most of their identity, from their social environment. For all the tensions involved between corporate and individual wishes, society has not seemed the enemy; and so far from society being viewed as *Thanatos*, many people have believed that they have lived most fully as participants in the group-life. The work which they have done in teams, or as individuals working for markets, has meant for them pleasure as well as toil. They have been proud to belong to a village, a tribe, a city or a nation (Freud, an estranged Jew to the end, analysed all this in terms of dependence on mothers and fathers). They have been specially proud of their society's literature, art and religion (to Freud, despite his love of literature and art, these were all at bottom symptoms of neurosis). They have believed that this cultural activity was what lifted man above the animals (and so did Freud, but it was easy for some of his followers to reduce the total content of culture to the psychological factors which Freud had seen at its roots). They have been proud to rear children (Freud, an excellent father, thought that parental love rested on sexual self-love or narcissism). In particular, society has been thanked for making available partners in sexual happiness. Such partners have sometimes been temporary, 'for the fun of it', and society has not taken too heavy a view of such fun; but the main source of sexual fulfilment for civilised mankind has been marriage, in a lifelong loyalty based on joy. Although these things are the platitudes of the history of man, it is difficult to remember them if we separate Freud's books from his exemplary style of life. Freud's position has often been misrepresented, but we must observe that many of those who have been most capable of doing justice to the Freudian analysis of man have in the end judged it to be inadequate.

Freud's excessively biological approach to the study of man in society has been the principal cause for the rebellions against his authority by psychologists who are indebted to his genius. Alfred Adler broke with his teacher in 1911 because he put sexual drives in the wider context of 'life-cycles'. Adler's chief scientific contribution was a study of psychological compensations for physical inferiorities (small men being argumentative, etc.). When he came to present a general philosophy of life, he taught that what most people desired was power or at least significance—a place in society—and he explored the consequences of a child's place in the family as the training-ground for this life-style in society. Adler may have been as unscientific in his general observations as most members of the medical profession now think he was, yet his insistence that life was not all sex was rightly welcomed by the public, was a stimulus to a more subtle analysis by the professionals and was to some extent accepted by Freud himself.

In the United States, a school of 'Neo-Freudian' and semi-Marxist analysts has arisen (H. S. Sullivan, Karen Horney, etc.), developing some of the insights of Adler and stressing both the duties and the delights of 'social adjustments'. Their analysis of man may seem to be shallow in comparison with Freud's; from the point of view of Christian theology Reinhold Niebuhr has urged that the individual's drives to pleasure as described by Freud present a problem which cannot be cured by happier homes or a better arranged society, for what Freud described was the fact which in theology is termed 'original sin'.[1] The Neo-Freudians' pur-

---

[1] *Freud and the Twentieth Century*, ed. B. Nelson (New York, 1957), chapter 15. This volume gathered assessments in connection with the 1956 centenary of Freud's birth and included a bibliography.

pose may even be sinister in comparison with Freud's, for the individual's adjustment to society may easily degenerate into conformity. Voices have been raised to protest that conformity is the plague of American life—the man becomes the 'organisation man', bought by a business corporation body and soul, the woman becomes dependent on the approval of her suburban neighbours—and such voices have added that the use of psychology in order to select 'integrated' executives, suggest the sexual appeal of an automobile or advertise a breakfast cereal on the basis of motivational research, is a gross betrayal both of Freud the scientist and Freud the prophet. Fortunately it is not our task to adjudicate in such disputes, where many subjective as well as many scientific elements are involved and are as yet imperfectly assessed. What is clear is that, whatever mistakes may have been made by these Neo-Freudians, the progress of psychology since Freud has involved a very widespread recognition of the inadequacy of his understanding of human nature. To give only one example: it is generally agreed that the infant's dependence on the mother for food, comfort and affection is the first great experience through which both boys and girls learn to relate to others, and infant sexuality, while it is not denied, is subordinated. Such a recognition of the social as containing the sexual but not dominated by it may be found in the great majority of contemporary practitioners of psychological medicine.[1]

Bound up with this recognition of man as a social animal has come much agreement that man is more deeply religious than Freud granted. Adler, for one, often emphasised religion. C. G. Jung broke with Freud in 1912 largely because Freud so disliked the mystical and psychical phenomena which were becoming Jung's chief interest in life, and Jung's words have become famous: 'Among my patients in the second half of life—that is to say, over 35—there has not been one whose problem in the last resort was

[1] See J. A. C. Brown, *Freud and the Post-Freudians* (London, 1961).

not one of finding a religious outlook on life.'[1] Jung explored the connections and the roots of the great symbols of the world's religions in the 'collective unconscious' of humanity, and his emphasis on the wisdom preserved in the history of the religions has naturally commended him as an ally to religious believers, specially to Roman Catholics.[2] Erich Fromm, a Neo-Freudian writer without Jung's passion for the mystical, has included the more sexually active and generally aggressive under-thirty-fives in the religious world, arguing that there is no one without a religious need to have 'a frame of orientation and an object of devotion'.[3] Philosophical writers such as Jung and Fromm are usually reckoned by medical professionals to have abandoned the scientific method, and they are clearly open to criticism; but they are only the two most prominent examples of the prevailing view that Freud himself was unscientific in his angry dismissal of religion. Religion to Freud was essentially the fear of a hostile authority, and it has not needed much reflection among his followers to see that, although this element is present in religion and can easily lead to neurosis, both history and observation show that religion is a much more richly varied phenomenon, as wide as life.

Some psychiatrists have given to such religion a respect which is more whole-hearted than that of Jung and Fromm. Dr. David Stafford-Clark, for example, has described the popular theory that religion is wish-fulfilment ('believing because it is more comfortable to believe, because such a belief implies a promise of pie in the sky when you die') as 'peculiarly superficial'. 'It entirely ignores the fact that the central idea of religion is not a projection of gratification, but a quest: a quest for the purpose of life, and for the individual's place in this purpose; a quest for a relationship in which men give rather than receive. Worship, not reward, is

[1] *Modern Man in Search of a Soul* (1931; Eng. trans., London, 1933), p. 264.
[2] See Victor White, *God and the Unconscious* (London, 1952).
[3] *Man for Himself* (New York, 1947) and *Psychoanalysis and Religion* (New Haven, 1950).

the consistent feature of the great religions of the world.'[1]
In *The Individual and his Religion*, Professor Gordon Allport
agreed with Freud that much religion is infantile or neurotic
or fear-ridden or an 'escape from freedom'; but examination of actual examples of religions and behaviour (much in
the tradition of his predecessor at Harvard University,
William James) convinced Allport that much religion is
mature. While Freud had left the impression from the
examples he used that religion was either primitive or patho-
logical, Allport affirmed that 'many personalities attain
a religious view of life without suffering arrested development and without self-deception. Indeed, it is by virtue of
their religious outlook on life—expanding as experience
expands—that they are able to build up a mature and well-
integrated edifice of personality. The conclusions they reach
and the sentiments they hold are various, as unique as is
personality itself.'[2]

Allport said clearly: 'I make no assumptions and no
denials regarding the claims of revealed religion. Writing
as a scientist, I am not entitled to do either.' This limitation
of the scope of psychology is crucial, whether or not
psychologists reach opinions which favour religion. Even
Freud in *The Future of an Illusion* had acknowledged the
limitations of science and had explained that he used the
word 'illusion' in a special sense, without prejudging the
question whether or not the religious emotion might be in
touch with a supernatural reality—but Freud had been so
obviously and so passionately convinced of the basic falsity
of religion that he had in practice forgotten this restriction,
and had conveyed to the average reader the impression that
religion was illusory in the everyday sense of the word.
Allport's greater modesty seems more compatible with the
scientist's role, for as L. W. Grensted pointed out, 'whether
the reality inherent in the holy is the reality of God, or the
reality of the father, or simply the reality of the experience,

---

[1] *Christian Essays in Psychiatry*, ed. Philip Mairet (London, 1956),
p. 15.
[2] *Personality* (New York, 1951), p. xi.

is not within the province of psychology to decide'. Freudianism cannot give any account, or make any conclusive denial, of 'the reality of the God to whom by the process of projection the characters of the father-image, together with characters drawn from other sources, come to be transferred. No argument is possible from the reality of the process to the reality of the things, entities or persons concerned in the process, for the word reality is used in two different senses in the two halves of any such argument.'[1] This limitation on the philosophical significance of the psychologist's explorations applies equally to non-Freudian descriptions of the mechanism of religion in the 'subliminal self' or 'collective unconscious'. The reality of God (or of the Buddhist *Nirvana*), of whom (or which) children, men and women conceive more or less satisfactory images, cannot be determined scientifically; only the images can be studied by psychology, although psychology can certainly help us to see which images are more (or less) healthy, because they correspond (or fail to correspond) with human mental health, and which images are more (or less) compatible with the results of experience outside religion. Grensted concluded his survey of *The Psychology of Religion*: 'The findings of psychology are of less importance theoretically and of more importance practically than is commonly supposed to be the case. The ultimate interpretations of cult and creed, in terms of their worth and their correspondence with what is really true of the being and purposes of God and of the being, obligation and destiny of man, are very little affected by psychological theory and analysis.'

After comments such as those just quoted from Stafford-Clark, Allport and Grensted, either favouring religion or restricting the psychologist's right to condemn it, many religious writers have jumped to the conclusion that the challenge of Freud may now be dismissed. However, the right conclusion seems to be that, while Freud's attacks on

[1] L. W. Grensted, *The Psychology of Religion* (London, 1952), pp. 159, 160.

religion were projections from his own psychology rather
than the unanswerable verdicts of psychological science,
both they and the reception given to them were very
important indications of the temper of our time. The corruption of Viennese Catholicism, and in particular its
virulent anti-semitism, lay behind the whole Freudian
onslaught, and the Roman Catholic Church has begun to
confess openly that these have indeed been its sins. Much in
Protestantism, specially its anti-sexual puritanism and its
anti-intellectual Fundamentalism, would have given Freud
similar material for prophecy, had he experienced it at first
hand in his formative years (he was acquainted with it through
reading and travel); and it may be as well for the composure
of Christians that Freud never analysed Eastern Orthodoxy.
The condition of orthodox Judaism may be assessed from
the fact that Freud, for all his Jewishness, never considered
embracing its faith, and we are entitled to doubt whether
other religions would have looked better under the search-
light of that honesty. It seems reasonable to conclude that
religion in Freud's day was in need of a radical reformation.

Clear evidence of the inadequacy of organised religion in
Freud's world is provided by the influence of his idea that
the psychoanalyst would be the new secular priest. Before
Freud, doctors cultivated a heartily cheerful, but often also
arrogantly impersonal, manner in order to do what they
thought best to their patients' bodies. Freud may be said to
have discovered the patient. The chief part of the therapy
which he offered consisted of listening to his patients, and a
single patient might absorb the attention of the analyst for
fifty minutes a day on five days a week for two or three years
or more. Ideally, Freud thought, an analysis should never
be terminated. He wanted to preserve the impersonal
dignity of the medical profession as far as possible, but he
came to expect his patients to transfer their deepest emotions
to him as a substitute-father; on the whole, the men hated
him and the women loved him, and each sex presented its
problems for him as a fellow-human. He believed that a cure
would probably come if only the patient could talk long

enough and frankly enough. The memories which festered like wounds in the unconscious, and which poisoned the patient's whole life, would be healed by being remembered and understood. Brought into the open air and the sunshine, these wounds would become scars on a body which could again be active along life's paths. The analyst might help the patient to understand these memories, but his main role was simply to listen.

The obvious disadvantages about this method of healing were its demands on the patient's time and money; only leisured and well-off people were likely to be able to afford a Freudian analysis. But the demands made of the analyst were scarcely less great, and Freud's acceptance of these demands may be regarded as his greatest victory. Only a few thousands of people in the world have been able to claim that they were 'cured' by a Freudian analysis, but millions have sensed that this was an approach to their misery by a man who had disciplined his high intelligence to serve in compassion, and the example of Freud has transformed the Western world's understanding of what care means. Even outside the ranks of professional psychiatry many thousands of 'medical' and 'social' workers have been, as they would put it, 'client-centred'. This means that they have become pastors whose care of people has followed the example of love, and that their love has again and again been therapeutic.

Outside the ranks of all these pastors, public opinion as a whole in the West has been profoundly influenced. The 'child-centred' approach to education, which only a few extreme progressives advocated in the nineteenth century, has become the philosophy of twentieth-century teachers. The child himself, no longer viewed as an angel or a devil, has become the fascinating battleground of the superego and the id, and adults, offering respectful sympathy, have learned that they are themselves the child's chief problems. The self-consciousness of modern adults, in this era of rapid change, would have been massive without Freud, but Freud has taught the West that the dramas of the self matter more than the dramas of society in bringing happiness or misery; Freud has taught the West that the self's most important dramas occur in the unconscious, at a level deeper than the reason or the conscience—at an emotional level which is not revealed by public speech, by intimate confidences, or even by a person's habitual self-knowledge, but which may be explored if only man will have the courage and the patience needed for the conquest of his own inner space; and Freud has taught the West that people, who are all driven by dark, irrational forces and wounded to the heart by memories of events they never desired, should learn to be gentle with each other and even with themselves. In the Freudian description of the self we recognise the stuff of the modern novel, of the modern drama, and of much in modern life. Freud has become, in the words of W. H. Auden, a 'climate of opinion' rather than a name, because it is Freud who has taught us that, if we are to love one another, love, instead of being blind to realities, must do what another great modern poet saw was necessary:

> *Players and painted stage took all my love,*
> *And not those things that they were emblems of.*
> *. . . Now that my ladder's gone,*
> *I must lie down where all the ladders start,*
> *In the foul rag-and-bone shop of the heart.*[1]

Specially in the United States the Protestant minister has reconceived his role as a pastoral counsellor in this light, and the Roman Catholic priest is now far less inclined than he was when hearing penitents' confessions to regard himself as a judge. But the corruption of religion cannot be expressed more powerfully than it is in the answer which follows the question: *why was this love of man, as man actually is, left to the secular Freud?*

The question of the reality of God remains after all that Freud said; but the strength of the welcome given to Freud's attack on religion demonstrated the strength of Freud's case

[1] W. B. Yeats, 'The Circus-Animals' Desertion', in his *Last Poems, 1936–39* (London, 1939).

against the God of his disintegrating but still viciously powerful society. Whatever may be the validity of his assessment of religion as an illusion, the God whom Freud described was recognised as their God by many millions, and many millions have been happy to use Freud's authority in the rejection of this God. It may or may not be wise to make sex the chief topic of a civilisation, and to regard any mention of God as bad taste, but the truth about our century is revealed in the strength of the agreement to do so. It may or may not be possible to build a religion without God, but the religious crisis is demonstrated by the popularity of the attempt. It may or may not be the case that belief in God arises from a three-year-old boy's wish to marry his mother and to murder his father, thus repeating the great murder of the father by the primitive horde, but it is a noteworthy comment on our time that so many have believed that such were the origins and essence of man's quest for God.[1]

A Suicidal Defence of Religion

We have noted that many of Freud's successors in the psychological field have taken more trouble than he did to understand religion. But here we must briefly add that many sympathetic discussions of the role of religion in modern society may in the long run prove no less dangerous to religion than was Freud's all-out attack. For many psychologists have basically accepted Freud's essential point that the whole of religion rests on an illusion. Their disagreement has been on the question, how seriously this illusion was to be taken; and the degree of seriousness with which they have taken the religious phenomenon may be closer to Freud's position than the defenders of religion would wish. Alfred Adler, for example, who often praised religion's contri-

---

[1] Among the many books on Freud may be mentioned: R. S. Lee, *Freud and Christianity* (London, 1948); Philip Rieff, *Freud: The Mind of the Moralist* (New York, 1959); Paul Ricoeur, *Freud and Philosophy* (New York, 1970).

bution to a 'life-style', was personally unable to accept religious doctrines.[1]

Freud himself acknowledged that many neuroses had been absorbed in most generations by the myths and rituals of religion. He definitely admired the psychological value of the religion of ancient Israel, for example, or the confident Catholicism of the Middle Ages. He also came near to the theory which his ex-disciple, Jung, developed about the 'collective unconscious' as the storage place for the great human neuroses and for the great religious symbols which correspond with them. However, Freud noted that even in the days of its strength religion was unable to take care of all neuroses. Like many others, he drew special attention to the abominable cruelty with which medieval Catholics had tormented the wretches whom they accused of witchcraft, and of course he had constantly in mind the neurotic character of the Christians' hatred of the Jews. Above all, Freud emphasised the guilt and fear associated in all believers' minds with the idea of God as pure and powerful, and he believed that even the Egyptian religion of Moses was neurotic in this basic sense. He therefore considered that the atheism which he always assumed to be true was in its psychological effects healthier ever than the best religion. He saw science as the alternative to religion, and although he appreciated the difficulty of educating the masses in the scientific method, he nursed the hope that, just as the neuroses of an individual patient could be cured (however painfully) if exposed to the truth, so religion, the 'universal neurosis' of humanity, could be cured by exposure to science over a considerable period of time.

Erich Fromm, despite his teaching that every man needs a religion, follows Freud when he adds that the religious belief in a God who stands outside man and outside nature is an escape from man's proper responsibility for his own future. It is part of the 'fear of freedom' which Fromm analyses as the central temptation of twentieth-century man; here Fromm apparently sees no essential difference between

[1] See Lewis Way, *Alfred Adler* (London, 1956).

submission to God and submission to Hitler or Stalin. The religion which Fromm praises therefore resembles the religion which Sir Julian Huxley advocates. Psychologically it is a religion without the celestial father-figure, and philosophically it is a religion without a transcendent God.

Carl Jung took a much more favourable view than Freud or Fromm when he assessed the psychological effects of traditional religion, but he was always unwilling to affirm that the religious symbols which he valued corresponded with any supernatural reality. Sometimes he wrote that this was due to a wish to preserve the objectivity of science within the limits of science, but at other times he seemed to indicate that his personal attitude was one of disbelief in eternity. His posthumously published autobiography showed him as a man with a thoroughly religious outlook on life, and with many religious, or at least psychic, experiences; but the undiscriminating gusto of his religious enthusiasm must raise the question whether, by the standards of the rational tradition of the West, he was interested in religious truth.[1] Such a defence of religion may be accepted for a time as encouraging participation in religious observances when the alternative is more degrading to man (as it was under Hitler or Stalin, or as it often was in the spiritually empty Western Europe where Jung listened to his patients with their religious nostalgia). In the long run, since the religion which Jung defended contained so much which was irrational, those who put a high value on the human reason are likely to renounce religion, and will be encouraged to do so by the availability of an alternative more attractive than Hitler, Stalin or the West of the 1930s. To give one example: the Roman Catholic dogma of the physical assumption of the Virgin Mary into heaven was defended by Jung on the ground that it was a symbol for the glory of womanhood. Jung rightly thought that Western Europe in his time was excessively masculine in the toughness of its industrial, commercial and political life, and he

[1] Carl Jung, *Memories, Dreams and Reflections* (1964; Eng. trans., London, 1965).

rightly suspected that masculinity was not enough even for a man, since every man had a feminine side to him. But the Vatican itself has often rejected such help for its doctrines from those who view them as only symbolic, and in this the Vatican seems to be shrewd. It may well be the verdict of the future that the feminine element in human life can be recognised in a simpler and more rational way than through the Roman Catholic dogma of the assumption (or Jung's own jargon about the *anima*, etc.). Thus religion, if it adopts Jung's suggestions for its defence, may find that it has blundered into a suicide no less final than the murder which the angry Father suffered at the hands of Freud; and Freud may be proved right when he expressed for the Jungian defence of religion a contempt more profound than his great dislike of faith in God.

There are, indeed, signs that the presentation of religion as natural rather than supernatural, of the Church as attractive rather than persuasive, and of the idea of God as useful rather than true, may be appealing quite widely to religion's professional defenders. While the century was still young, liberal Protestants and modernist Catholics were accused of holding such views ('immanentism'), and in some cases the accusation was just. The (often excessive) reaction of orthodoxy in Protestantism, and above all in Catholicism, was for a time thought to have discredited these views, but as the second half of the century opened it could be seen that 'immanentism', however heretical, was far from dead.

Albert Schweitzer

The power and appeal of a religion ultimately without God may be seen by a brief study of the thought of one of the twentieth century's greatest and most attractive figures: Dr. Albert Schweitzer.

In the English-speaking world remarkably little controversy surrounded Schweitzer's theology after the initial excitement when his *Von Reimarus zu Wrede* (1906) was translated as *The Quest of the Historical Jesus* (London,

1910). His earlier and fuller explanation of his own view, published in German in 1901, did not become available in English until *The Mystery of the Kingdom of God* appeared in 1925, and by then the 'jungle doctor' was widely believed to have turned his back on his youthful indiscretions. By the 1920s (the period of his greatest influence), the public was attracted to Schweitzer's discovery of the ethical principle of 'reverence for life'. The implications of this phrase, which occurred to him in 1915, were worked out in profound books on the problems of civilisation, in public warnings against the suicidal folly of war which continued until his death in 1965, in his most attractive love for music and for animals, and supremely in his heroic work in the hospital at Lambaréné. Many would describe him as the greatest Christian of the century; and sneers at him in his old age, alleging that his approach to the African was out of date, did little more than to show that when he had abandoned his mastery of the culture of Europe in order to establish his hospital in equatorial Africa in 1913, he had been a pioneer.[1]

Schweitzer was, then, a disciple of Jesus. *But who for him was Jesus?* In his brilliant history of German New Testament scholarship up to his day, he demonstrated that almost all accounts of the psychology of Jesus have rested largely on speculation and thus on the scholar's own psychology. The gospels, although our only evidence for the life of Jesus apart from a few fragments elsewhere, are not modern biographies; and detailed reconstructions of the life of Jesus remind us of the man who peered to the bottom of a deep well, and saw his own face reflected. But Schweitzer observed truly that, amid much that is unknowable about Jesus, some things are clear. To Jesus, God is 'a dynamic Power for good, a mysterious Will, distinct from the world, and superior to the world. To Him we yield our will; to Him we leave the

[1] Many books have been written about him, of which the best remain George Seaver, *Albert Schweitzer: The Man and his Mind* (London, 1947), and Henry Clark, *The Philosophy of Albert Schweitzer* (London, 1964).

future of the world.' And in the thought of Jesus, 'the ethical activity of man is only like a powerful prayer to God, that He may cause the Kingdom to appear without delay'.[1]

This Kingdom of God was an idea which Jesus, being a first-century Jew, expressed in the language of his time, and the 'apocalyptic' literature which has survived from that time shows us that many of his contemporaries thought of a Kingdom which would be introduced miraculously, by God sending his angels, raising the dead, etc. Yet the message of Jesus was not completely identical with such crude hopes, which were doomed to disappointment; and the ethic of Jesus was not merely for the 'interim'. 'Jesus spiritualised the conception of the Kingdom of God, in that He brings it into subjection to His ideal and ethic of love. In due time this transforms the conception of the Kingdom.'[2] On the basis of our limited but reasonably secure knowledge of the historical Jesus, it would have been possible for Schweitzer to interpret the message of the Kingdom of God for our time as a faith that the ethical activity of man was in harmony with the will and power of God to transform our wills and to improve the world, so that at some future date hidden from us the reality and rule of God would be acknowledged in the love for each other and for him of all the children of God. Such a presentation of the everlasting Gospel of Jesus, reinforced by a personal example of heroic sanctity, might have had a profound influence in the world-wide Church and throughout the world. For as Schweitzer himself wrote: 'A religion possesses just so much of an understanding of the historical Jesus as it possesses of a strong, passionate faith in the Kingdom of God . . . The only thing that matters is this: that the significance of the concept of the Kingdom of God for our world-view is the same as it was for Him.'[3]

[1] *Christianity and the Religions of the World* (London, 1923), pp. 15–17.
[2] This admission, included in his Preface to the 1954 edition of his *Quest*, seems to have been first made clearly by Schweitzer in E. N. Mosley, *The Theology of Albert Schweitzer* (London, 1950), p. 105.
[3] Quoted in Henry Clark, *The Philosophy of Albert Schweitzer*, p. 201.

As it was, however, the psychological impact of our secular century almost overwhelmed Schweitzer as it has almost overwhelmed millions of lesser Christians. The weak point in his own psychology seems to have been his pride. This pride, founded on the possession of extraordinary natural gifts, with an extraordinary energy of mind and body, was disciplined by a life of extraordinary self-sacrifice; but it was typical of Western intellectuals in our time. His pride was noticed by his detractors in his latter years when they commented on his patronising attitude towards the 'natives', whom he always treated as children, as the 'children of nature'. But in taking this attitude, Schweitzer only belonged to his period; the key point is that he regarded his own labours and sufferings in Africa as a sacrifice, an atonement, offered in memory of the many sins committed by Europeans against Africans. More significant was his habit, reflected in many books, of regarding as mistaken all his predecessors in the attempt to understand Jesus, with the partial exceptions of St. Paul and Luther. His intellectual self-confidence led him to a psychiatric analysis of Jesus; he wrote at length about this in a book of 1913, which grew out of his study for a medical doctorate before going to Africa.[1] Not surprisingly, the Jesus whom Schweitzer discovered at the end of his quest, was a hero of elemental spiritual power, a rebel against everything which was merely conventional, and a prophet who was determined to bring in the Kingdom of God; but he was a Jesus who had to be defended against the charge of madness (and not all Schweitzer's readers would consider Schweitzer's defence convincing). Since the Kingdom delayed during the single year which was the total extent of Jesus's public ministry 'from seed-time to harvest', Jesus grew convinced that his death was necessary to God, as a sacrifice or atonement for the sins of his people, and that his death would immediately result in the harvest of the miraculous Kingdom on earth. Jesus was, therefore, fundamentally mistaken about his mission (although not insane), and our acknowledgment

[1] *The Psychiatric Study of Jesus* (Eng. trans., Boston, 1948).

of his spiritual authority over our wills ought to be accompanied by our rejection of his view of the world. As Schweitzer wrote: 'There is silence all around. The Baptist appears, and cries: "Repent, for the Kingdom of heaven is at hand." Soon after that comes Jesus, and in the knowledge that He is the coming Son of Man lays hold of the wheel of the world to set it moving on that last revolution, which is to bring all ordinary history to a close. It refuses to turn, and He throws Himself upon it. Then it does turn; and crushes Him . . . The wheel rolls onward, and the mangled body of the one immeasurably great Man, who was strong enough to think of Himself as the spiritual ruler of mankind and to bend history to His purpose, is hanging upon it still. That is His victory, and His reign.'[1]

Schweitzer's Jesus, who sought to conquer God's delay by his own courage, was thus close to Nietzsche's Superman, who sought to take over after God's death. And the consequence of this strange interpretation of the gospels—which on Schweitzer's own admission discarded all those sayings in which Jesus anticipated an interval, long or short, between his death and the consummation of the Kingdom—was that, for all the religious heroism of his life, Schweitzer's view of the world was essentially secular. Schweitzer did not share the Christian belief that love is 'the last word about life'. He believed passionately that it ought to be, and he lived passionately so that love was the meaning of his life and his gift to those who suffered around him; but he often expressed his conviction that life as a whole remained an enigma. He, like his Jesus, was a Prometheus, heroic in his defiance; but in the end also a doomed Sisphus.

Schweitzer taught that 'the spirit of Jesus' could lead any man who would follow along the road of love in faith; but he added that knowledge of the objective world was another matter, for knowledge of the world could be reached only through thought, and thinking yielded no light on any ethical purpose existing or emerging in nature. Values should be created by men; they could not be discovered in the

[1] *The Quest of the Historical Jesus*, pp. 368–9.

universe. This tragic view of reality was reinforced by Schweitzer's own experience of the pain of Africa and the ruthlessness of the jungle, but it is clear from his autobiographical writings that already as a youth in Europe his compassion was based on his pessimism, and as a young theologian he developed the separation of values from reality which is found, although in a less extreme form, in nineteenth-century religious thinkers.[1] 'My knowledge is pessimistic,' Schweitzer wrote, 'but my willing and hoping are optimistic. I am pessimistic in that I experience in its full weight what we conceive to be the absence of purpose in the course of world-happenings. Only at quite rare moments have I felt really glad to be alive . . . But however much concerned I was at the problem of the misery of the world, I never let myself get lost in brooding over it; I always held firmly to the thought that each one of us can do a little to bring some portion of it to an end.'[2]

It is also clear that Schweitzer's ethic of reverence for life was not based on the Jewish and Christian belief that the world was created essentially good (although not perfect) by the perfect God. On the contrary, 'ethics consists in this, that I experience the necessity of practising the same reverence of life towards all will-of-life, as towards my own. It is good to maintain and cherish life; it is evil to destroy and check life'. This was the religion of the Jains in India, who would not take the life even of an insect; but it is difficult to believe with Schweitzer that 'the ethic of reverence for life is the ethic of Jesus brought to philosophical expression, extended into cosmical form, and conceived as intellectually necessary'.[3] For Jesus believed in a God who ruled the

---

[1] The German Protestant theologians' reinterpretation of Christianity as a religion of feelings or values is associated particularly with the great names of Schleiermacher and Ritschl. It was a response to the breakdown both of dogmatic Lutheran orthodoxy and of a philosophical tendency to base religion on reason or ethics. This great debate has set both the standard and the terms of much theology. For an outline, see James Richmond, *Faith and Philosophy* (London, 1966).

[2] *Out of my Life and Thought* (1931; Eng. trans., London, 1933), pp. 279–80.

[3] *Civilisation and Ethics* (London, 1923), p. 258.

world. But Schweitzer did not. 'Without understanding the meaning of the world I act from an inner necessity of my being . . . I fulfil the will of the universal will-to-life which reveals itself in me. I live my life in God, in the mysterious ethical divine personality which I cannot discover in the world, but only experience in myself as a mysterious impulse.'[1] Here is the Gethsemane or Calvary part of Christianity, and it would be impertinent and useless to speculate about how much of the Christians' God he did experience in himself—but it is ominous that Schweitzer placed so little emphasis in his teaching (or, apparently in his own life) on what had been the heart of the religion of Jesus: petitionary prayer to God as Father. He was an agnostic about the possibility of eternal life. Indeed, in his last years Schweitzer would agree with inquiries that he had used the word 'God' in order to communicate with conventional Christians.[2]

Three Books of the 1960s

It is a striking fact that three religious best-sellers of the 1960s, written by professional theologians who wished to define the true essence of Christianity, and to preserve it, did not hesitate to express a basic acceptance of secularisation. All three books were unprofessionally confused. But psychologically they were important.

Paul van Buren's *The Secular Meaning of the Gospel* (New York, 1963) argued that since assertions about God are meaningless—a philosophical claim which he assumed had been demonstrated beyond the possibility of a convincing contradiction—Christianity should be expressed afresh as solely a message about the significance and power of human freedom and love. Professor van Buren's book was an

---

[1] *Civilisation and Ethics*, p. xvi.
[2] This was brought out in a book on *Albert Schweitzer* written with his approval by a Norwegian, Gabriel Langfeldt, who warmly approved his rejection of the traditional Christian understanding of God (1958; Eng. trans., 1960).

interesting revival of Kant's plea in the eighteenth century for a religion of freedom and morality 'within the limits of reason alone'. It was followed by others more emotionally charged and more confused, which have proclaimed the 'death' of God as the fact with which a new theology must begin its reconstruction of the significance of Jesus for real life. It was not entirely clear what such books meant by picking up Nietzsche's 'death of God' and using it in thought which aimed at being Christian. Believers have been able to point out that if God ever existed he is not mortal, so that what looks like his death is his apparent eclipse. Sometimes these books have seemed to be saying as a minimum that the reality of God has been eclipsed in our time by the more obvious reality of science-based technology, and that talk about God has become extremely difficult to fit into the common language.[1]

In *The Secular City* (New York, 1965) Professor Harvey Cox urged that the work of the Church must be replanned on the basis of an acceptance of many elements in that secularisation of American life which has been influenced largely by its urbanisation. He argued that 'secularisation arises in large measure from the formative influence of biblical faith on the world, an influence mediated first by the Christian Church and later by movements deriving partly from it'. These arguments were scarcely more convincing than Professor van Buren's. Whereas van Buren had assumed that the collapse of biblical Christianity must follow the decline of the religious world-view, Cox seemed to be saying that the decline had actually been caused by the Bible's triumph; and much more discussion of the subtle issues involved would be needed to convince those not inclined to accept the authoritarian preaching style of these secular theologians. Indeed, both van Buren and Cox, being honest men, did not let much time pass before announcing that they were no longer convinced themselves— and were once again on pilgrimage. But more important than such arguments was the tone of these books, and of the

[1] See also Paul van Buren, *The Edges of Language* (New York, 1972).

welcome for them. The tone indicated that the American return to the God of heavenly peace, the return to the little church in the peaceful village or the suburb, was over.[1]

It has been argued that Dr. John Robinson, then Bishop of Woolwich, who became world-famous as the author of *Honest to God* (London, 1963), was toying with the idea of a Christianity without God—although in a style more confused than Professor van Buren's or Professor Cox's. In his more recent writings, particularly his *Exploration into God* (London, 1967), Robinson has shown that this was far from his intention, but the letters and reviews printed in *The Honest to God Debate* do record the wish of many in Britain, as elsewhere in the Western world, to develop a godless creed. If that is one lesson to be learned from the most widespread theological debate to be held in twentieth-century England, we may rest assured that the identification of God with the more beautiful side of nature and with man's own advancing mind is by no means as dead as orthodox theologians would like it to be. Over half a century before *Honest to God*, R. J. Campbell's electrifying *The New Theology* (London, 1907) had included amid much enthusiasm for pure religion and social progress some loose expressions suggesting that 'Jesus was and is God, but so are we'. Campbell himself had been warned off heresy by the replies to him, and had died a blameless canon of Chichester Cathedral, but the 'new theology' has remained powerful in that world which theologians do not normally approach. Alasdair MacIntyre may have been right in his summary of the creed of the English: 'The difficulty lies in the combination of atheism in the practice of the life of the vast majority, with the profession of either superstition or theism by that same majority. The creed of the English is that there is no God and that it is wise to pray to him from time to time.'[2]

Perhaps the chief significance of *Honest to God* lay in its ambiguity. (Thus *Honest to God*, like *The New Theology*

---

[1] See also Harvey Cox, *The Feast of Fools* (Cambridge, Mass., 1969).
[2] *The Honest to God Debate*, ed. David L. Edwards (London, 1963), p. 228.

before it, refuted the suggestion that only what is clear, neat and slick can excite the public.) Robinson was aware of this ambiguity in his position when in his Preface he confessed that the line between the 'lay' world and 'the traditional orthodox supernaturalism in which our Faith has been framed' was a line which 'runs right through the middle of myself'. The spectacle which fascinated was, as a London newspaper put it, 'an agonising and unusual spectacle—a bishop groping for truth, admitting that he does not know all the answers'. *Honest to God* could, indeed, be read in two different ways, so as to leave impressions of two radically different books, and so as to supply both sides in the controversy with ammunition.

On the one side of the dividing line between the defence of the Gospel and its betrayal was an *Honest to God* which was unconventional but basically orthodox. The missionary bishop who wrote this book was descended from a line of distinguished clergymen, could not remember a time when he had not wished to be ordained, was a lecturer at Cambridge University in New Testament studies, was enthusiastic about making the Holy Communion a more corporate service of worship, was dedicated to pastoral work in the unrewarding area of South London, normally preached sermons which (he said) did not get 'within remote range' of revolutionary ideas about God, and had studied the philosophy of religion deeply enough to be aware that the images of God which seemed inadequate were images only and need not be taken literally. For this man, the theological revolution which he had in mind was 'a reluctant' revolution. He was in love with the Christian tradition; and the revolution could be seen as a turning back to the first source of the Christian tradition, to the Bible itself. It was not really the end of theism, i.e. of belief in God, for he insisted that the revolutionary image of God was only a different 'projection' (as on a map) to depict essentially the same faith as traditional theism. It was an effort to show that true religion arises out of real life, and in particular that God is met and loved 'in and through' one's neighbour, so that, in Bonhoeffer's phrase, 'God is the "beyond" in our midst.' God in *Honest to God* remained 'beyond', for 'the eternal *Thou* is not to be equated with the finite *Thou*, nor God with man or nature'. Christ remained 'the bearer of the final revelation and the embodiment of God's decisive act', for 'it is in Jesus, and Jesus alone, that there is nothing of self to be seen, but solely the ultimate, unconditional love of God'. The love embodied in Jesus evoked Robinson's courageous faith. 'The Christian affirmation is not simply that love *ought* to be the last word about life, but that, despite all appearances, it *is* . . . And that takes an almost impossible amount of believing. It is frankly incredible *unless* the love revealed in Jesus is indeed the nature of ultimate reality, unless he is a window through the surface of things into *God*.' Thus Bishop John Robinson endorsed the affirmation of St. John, which was not that 'love is God' but that 'God is love'. Another way of expressing this faith was to say that 'love is *of* God', so that 'our convictions about love and its ultimacy are not projections from human love; but rather, our sense of the sacredness of love derives from the fact that in this relationship as nowhere else there is disclosed and laid bare the divine Ground of all our being'.

On the other hand, Robinson showed that he was deeply sympathetic with atheism, so that in some moods for him 'the Ground of our being' could be (but these crude words are not his) not the inexhaustible source and support of human life, but merely the bottom bit of it. He was prepared to question 'the thought of God as a personal being, wholly other to man, dwelling in majesty', although R. W. Hepburn, from whom he quoted that phrase, rightly saw that 'to sacrifice it seems at once to take one quite outside Christianity'.[1] He was prepared to say that when such a theologian as Paul Tillich speaks of God as being experienced in the depths of human life (instead of 'up there' or 'out there') 'he is not speaking of another Being *at all*. He is speaking of "the infinite and inexhaustible depth and

[1] *Christianity and Paradox* (London, 1958), p. 193.

ground of all being", of what we take seriously without reservation.' In that comment on Tillich, Robinson did not emphasise the 'infinite and inexhaustible' mystery which Tillich used to call 'Being-itself'; instead, he seemed to equate God with anything anyone might take seriously, and to present God as 'the ground of *our* being', as in the title of Chapter 3. On this showing theology might well be reduced to anthropology, for 'a statement is "theological" not because it relates to a particular Being called "God", but because it asks *ultimate* questions about the meaning of existence' and 'statements about God are acknowledgments of the transcendent, unconditional element in all our relationships'. Transcendence could now be interpreted as simply the experience of meeting a 'thou' who is different from 'I', and Jesus himself could be seen not so much as 'the man for God' as 'the man for others', 'the one in whom Love has completely taken over, the one who is utterly open to, and united with, the Ground of his being'. What was the significance of those capital letters in Love and Ground? Instead of explaining this philosophically, Robinson showed himself as at heart a pastor, for he pressed on to interpret holiness as 'the depths of the common', prayer as 'to open oneself to another *unconditionally* in love', deep love as the one guide in morality, and the service of the world as the charter of the Church. These were all causes which could amount to the dismissal of God from practical Christianity, although they could also encourage the renewal of the sense of the presence of God in daily life.

What was apparent in *Honest to God* was the necessity of some degree of 'secularisation' in Christianity, for the biblical message must be stated with fresh power if it is to reach secular man. But *Honest to God* also made clear the danger, for the restatement can easily leave the impression that the three letters G, O and D when combined are no more than an old way of saying 'love' or 'Love'. Here the challenge of our secular century was seized, but its psychological impact seemed on some pages of *Honest to God* likely to overthrow one of the Church of England's most

gifted sons.[1] And where Robinson tottered, some other
Christians have been happy to fall, in the conviction that
only by joining the world of honest thought and feeling,
and consequently abandoning belief in God, could Christian
faith of any kind at all be made possible for future generations.[2]

Judaism and Islam

But not only have Christian theologians been confused by
the psychological impact of our time. We may turn briefly
to two religions which are associated with two deeply
divided sides in Middle Eastern politics, but which have the
common experience of facing the challenge of secularisation.

What, we must ask, is the future of *Judaism*? Many Jews
in their Dispersion have been thoroughly assimilated into a
secular society, and have abandoned the beliefs and almost
all the practices taught by their religion. But perhaps equally
significant as evidence of the pervasive secularisation has
been the uncertainty of many of those who, although
'emancipated', have wished to keep alive their distinctive
and beautiful traditions in religion. In the dilemma of
these Jews we see the drama of the question whether
secularisation must lead to secularism.

From the first Zionist Congress in 1897 to the victory of
Israel in 1967, political Zionism often seemed the solution
to the problem of Jewish identity. However, the orthodox
Jews who aroused enthusiasm for the return to the land of
Israel—Shapira, Gordon, Cook, Bruer—have not been
able to persuade the people to return to their ancestral
faith. Theodor Herzl, who more than anyone else was the
founder of Zionism, was secular like Freud (and also from
Vienna). The writer Ahad Ha-am and the statesman Chaim
Weizmann also stressed the cultural rather than the religious
elements in the Jewish heritage. As a result of these mixed

[1] See also John A. T. Robinson, *The Human Face of God* (London,
1973).
[2] See, e.g., Alistair Kee, *The Way of Transcendence* (London, 1971).

origins of the modern state of Israel, orthodox rabbinic regulations are prominent in the national life, and the Hebrew language has been revived for daily use, but visitors estimate that the overwhelming majority of the Israelis is indifferent to religion.

Among Jews outside Israel, an orthodoxy scarcely altered since the Middle Ages has similarly invited a response which capitulates to secularisation. The orthodox rabbis are so sharply in conflict with the modern spirit that they insist that the first five books of the Old Testament were dictated by God to Moses and are permanently authoritative. For questioning such beliefs, one of the most learned of the English rabbis, Louis Jacobs, was expelled during 1964.[1] This reactionary spirit is supported, at least nominally, by many Jewish laymen who wish to be loyal to the faith of their fathers in a century which has seen the massacre of six million Jews by nominal Christians and which has not yet seen the end of anti-semitic prejudice and worse. It is understandable that the Jews of Soviet Russia (for example) should often see the religious situation in terms of loyalty to the God of Israel *versus* the latest persecution by the godless. But Conservative and Reform movements also exist among the twelve or thirteen million Jews surviving, particularly among the American Jews; and these movements have adjusted Judaism to the challenge of the nineteenth and twentieth centuries.

In another Jewish movement, the adjustment to modernity has gone very far indeed. The 'reconstructionism' or 'greater Judaism' advocated by Mordecai Kaplan retains most of the traditional observances in 'synagogue-centres' for Jewish communities in the United States, but has abandoned all belief in a personal God. 'For the Jews there can be no higher purpose than that of exemplifying the art of so living individually and collectively as to contribute to the intellectual, moral and spiritual progress of mankind.'[2]

[1] See Louis Jacobs, *Principles of the Jewish Faith* (London, 1964).
[2] *The Purpose and Meaning of Jewish Existence* (Philadelphia, 1964), p. 294.

Professor Joseph Blau, an authoritative commentator on *Modern Varieties of Judaism*, believes that this open abandonment of the supernatural is, 'despite its grounding in a non-rational philosophy, a reasonable faith for reasonable men', with great potentialities for the future.[1]

These more liberal movements in contemporary Judaism have an optimistic streak in them (reminding us that they have been nourished amid the prosperity of the United States), but Richard Rubenstein, a Conservative rabbi who was chaplain to all Jewish students in the great university of Pittsburgh, has outlined a Jewish philosophy which rejects hope, consciously echoing Albert Camus.[2] Harvey Cox's *Secular City* is denounced as being too hopeful. Rubenstein urges men to give up waiting for the Messiah—even for a secular one. His own reconstruction of Judaism is based on the two greatest events for the Jews in the twentieth century: the destruction of Central European Jewry, and the building of the modern nation of Israel. For Rubenstein, the first event poses the problem: if God had existed as Lord of History, in accordance with the Judaism inherited from the Old Testament, he would not have permitted this evil. The second event provides the answer: the God of the tradition does not exist, but the earth exists, and modern Jews must escape from the tradition by cultivating the earth as normal human beings. For Rubenstein, any talk of the Jews as the Chosen People separates the Jews from the normal human lot, and therefore runs the risk of bringing on them another Auschwitz—a disaster which might be made worse, if its horror could be deepened, by the thought that this might be a punishment by God for his People's sins (as Father Panelou interpreted the plague in the novel by Camus).[3] But it is not right to try to forget that one was born a Jew; there must be a deliberate, mature, life-affirming acceptance of the death of the God of Judaism, and apparently this is

[1] (New York, 1964), p. 184.

[2] *After Auschwitz* (New York, 1966).

[3] E.g. in Arthur Cohen, *The Natural and the Supernatural Jew* (New York, 1963).

the task to which Rubenstein feels called as a rabbi. 'What then of Judaism? It is the way we Jews share our lives in an unfeeling and silent cosmos . . . Ultimately as with all things, it will pass away, for omnipotent Nothingness is Lord of All Creation.'[1]

So we may turn to *Islam*. Islam has been less exposed than Judaism to the acids of modernity, but here again the riddle of theological modernism is whether in the long run it will restore, or ruin, faith in God. Nothing is more disconcerting in Islam as observed by its learned friends[2] than the contemporary lack of basic theology. What Muslims need is an intellectual debate of the quality of that waged eight hundred years ago by rational philosophers of the stature of Avicenna and Averroes, and by that great philosophical sceptic and theological mystic, al-Ghazali. The great Sufi movement of saints and brotherhoods dedicated to the service and enjoyment of God reconciled that debate between reason and revelation by claiming that their mystic experience brought the high Allah near, to dwell in the human heart, thus clothing in vivid emotions a faith which was essentially the orthodoxy of the *Quran*. But today the old debates are largely irrelevant to the new challenges, and in many places the Sufi movement is largely exhausted as a popular enthusiasm based on a genuine mysticism. Now is, therefore, a time for a fresh theology.

The best book of twentieth-century Muslim theology is Sir Mohammad Iqbal's *The Reconstruction of Religious Thought in Islam* (Lahore, 1930). The reconstruction which it attempted was based on the method taught by another Indian Muslim, Muh Abduh, who had found the culture which he knew before his death in 1905 already present, embryonically but authoritatively, in the *Quran*. Iqbal in his day argued in terms of the evolutionary life-force which great Western names including Henri Bergson had recently propagated, but which has been abandoned by most

---

[1] *After Auschwitz*, p. 225.
[2] Such as Kenneth Cragg, *Counsels in Contemporary Islam* (Edinburgh, 1965).

Western philosophers. The snag was that this life-force had to be reconciled with the *Quran*'s essential insight into the otherness of God. Looking back on Iqbal's attempt, some questions must be asked. Is it true to say with Iqbal that 'the birth of Islam is the birth of inductive intellect' and that 'in Islam, prophecy reaches its perfection in discovering the need of its own abolition'?[1] Is it true that in physics the *Quran* anticipated the science of the twentieth century, and in politics had 'spiritual democracy' as its ultimate aim?[2] What becomes of the great slogan which was so familiar to generations of Muslims and is emblazoned on the uniforms of the Indonesian youth movement Ansar: 'There is no law or authority except in Allah'?

A book such as Iqbal's *Reconstruction* cries aloud for sequels, and indeed there have been sequels, but none on the necessary scale; and it is significant that in his poems collected as *The Ardent Pilgrim* (London, 1951) Iqbal condemned all Muslim theological debates. The nature of Islam has been discussed endlessly by the experts—but not the nature of Allah. There have been some moving testimonies by Muslim laymen to the power which still comes from the Prophet's personality and poetry: a power which makes for personal integrity and social justice on the foundation of belief in the reality and righteousness of God. There have been books of prayers and interpretation showing that Muslim devotion to Allah is still alive in the hearts of millions—that the call of the minaret to prayer is still heard. But are even these things enough, as the expressions of a living religion? It is meaningless to generalise, for Islam is so vast today, and its destiny awaits tomorrow. But many Muslims and others voice a profound disquiet, for as the regulated unity of Islamic society is eroded by Westernisation and pluralism its fundamental faith in God will have to be very strong to act as the basis of a new kind of Islam; and on present evidence it is doubtful what will remain when the foundations have been shaken. As Iqbal

[1] p. 176.
[2] pp. 110–11, etc.

warned: 'During the last five hundred years religious thought in Islam has been practically stationary . . . The most remarkable phenomenon in modern history is the enormous rapidity with which the world of Islam is spiritually moving towards the West.'[1]

Dr. Fazlur Rahman, Director of the Islamic Research Institute in Karachi, has recently issued a very grave warning to his fellow-Muslims. His conclusion after a survey of the last seven hundred years is that 'it would hardly be an exaggeration to say that the actual force and efficacy of Islam in practical terms (beyond the political sphere) was reduced to a collection of superstitious beliefs and practices generated by the Sufi movement'. Dr. Rahman sees that the task of integrating the genuine inner life of the heart—the *élan* of Sufism—with the social code of the *Sharia* must be achieved on the basis of a reconstructed orthodoxy, and he says: 'If a correct vision is not forthcoming of what is needed—and, judging from the overall performance of both the conservatives and the modernists to date, one cannot help questioning whether this vision has yet fully developed —irreparable damage might be done.'[2]

The Survival of Religion

Thus Freud has fellow-witnesses to the psychological power of secularisation even among the theologians. In Christianity, Islam and Judaism, much of the contemporary scene is bleak for those who expect religious leaders to talk convincingly about God; and this failure of nerve among the professionals only reflects the confusion of the public.

However, this is by no means the whole truth about religion in the twentieth century. In a pluralist society, *the individual himself is often plural*, believing one thing with one part of his mind and another with another; and in our largely secular society, many individuals do retain an affection for religion. It is this fact, rather than any theo-

[1] *Reconstruction*, p. 9.
[2] Fazlur Rahman, *Islam* (London, 1966), pp. 246, 250-1.

retical refutation of Freud's *The Future of an Illusion*, which compels us to say that the future of religion is still an open question.

There may be a future in the religious sentiment and community-sense—in the mystical experience of 'something larger' and in the clan's worship of the totem as its collective conscience. This emotion may be valued for its psychological wisdom as Jung claimed, and it may be freed from its dependence on a supernatural God as many have suggested. (We shall examine this possibility further in later chapters.) But the more traditional supernatural religion does survive, in at least part of the mind of the man who may be 'coming of age'. We have already noted that the passion of faith survives in millions of Muslims, and it would be unfair to conclude our pessimistic view of Islamic theology at the present day without emphasising that most Muslim thinkers—even the most critical of them such as Fazlur Rahman—believe that its difficulties can be overcome. And it is not only faith within Islam that has preserved into our time the sense of the overwhelming power and glory of a transcendent God. Judaism has kept some of its essential heritage of belief, in the midst of this age of Freud.

Will Herberg, who has studied the popularity of American churches and synagogues so ruthlessly in his sociological writings, is a Jew who by no means endorses Kaplan's 'reconstructionism' as the best solution to the problem of Judaism in the twentieth century. On the contrary, he was led back to a Bible-based faith (through Reinhold Niebuhr's influence), and he has written his personal testimony to the living significance of his ancestors' worship of God.[1] Even the tragedy of Auschwitz has not signified to all the death of the God of the Jews. A book entitled *The Face of God after Auschwitz* has presented the great tragedy as man-made; in it, the Jews once again suffered because of

[1] See Will Herberg, *Protestant, Catholic, Jew* (New York, 1955; revd. edn., 1960), and *Judaism and Modern Man* (New York, 1951). Other books in the same field include Abraham Heschel, *God in Search of Man* (New York, 1955), and Eugene B. Borowitz, *A New Jewish Theology in the Making* (Philadelphia, 1969).

the sins of the world; and after it, the face of God could again be seen in blessing. The author of this presentation of Auschwitz has also offered an interpretation of the state of Israel. He points out that a medieval orthodoxy is honoured in Israel because the European Jewry which was destroyed in the gas chambers held such a faith; and he hopes that when time has done its healing work a stronger, more personal and more progressive faith will emerge in Israel.[1] And in other literature one may already see what such a Judaism, traditional but fresh, would look like; for few books contain more personal religion than the small, seminal *I and Thou* by one of the spiritual fathers of modern Israel, Martin Buber.[2]

Buber distilled the thought of a brilliant generation of German Jews (Franz Rosenweig, etc.) and, behind them, of the Hasidic mystics of Jewish history—although he also liberated himself from the need to observe the Jewish ritual laws. He moved beyond the rootless individualism of the 'assimilated' Jews in the Dispersion. He saw that we are social beings, made by our relationships with others, and that a living faith must issue in better relationships (for Buber, after the horrors of the 1940s, specially in the *kibbutzim* of Israel). He saw that all our increased understanding of the subtleties of the person in community is most valuable when it leads us to see what occurs between man and man is a preparation for, and a part of, the relationship which the personal God has chosen to open with us and sustain with us. Although this relationship does not yield information of the kind that is included in scientific knowledge, nevertheless through it we can know about a reality which is greater than all the objects known to science, a reality which is not a dead *It*, but a living, active *Thou*. Buber learned from, but contradicted, Feuerbach's claim in *The Philosophy of the Future* (1841) that 'man with man,

---

[1] Ignaz Maybaum, *The Face of God after Auschwitz*, was published for the Reform Synagogues of Great Britain (Amsterdam, 1965).

[2] 1923; Eng. trans., Edinburgh, 1937. See Maurice Friedman, *Martin Buber: The Life of Dialogue* (revd. edn., New York, 1960).

the unity of *I* and *Thou*, is God'. He included, but transcended, the kind of religion of nature which William James had in mind when he wrote: 'The universe is no longer a mere *It* to us, but a *Thou*, if we are religious.'[1] And so the great German-American Christian philosopher, Paul Tillich, used to say that it was the awareness of the presence of the personal God, conveyed by Martin Buber, that enabled him to preach at all. Knowing that in our time it is not enough to preach to the converted, Tillich added this comment: 'God could never become an "object" in Martin Buber's presence. The certainty of God always preceded the certainty of himself and his world. God, for him, was not an object of doubt, but the presupposition—even of doubt. That is the only way, I believe, which makes a dialogue with those who doubt and even those who deny God, possible.'[2]

As the century opened a number of those Christians who were most sensitive to the problems of faith had already turned to study and to teach the central importance of mysticism and other religious experience. In his Bampton Lectures at Oxford in 1899 on *Christian Mysticism*, W. R. Inge, later Dean of St. Paul's, had made this appeal, and he pursued it until his death in 1954. Dean Inge once described the Roman Catholic scholar, Baron Friedrich von Hügel, as 'our greatest theologian'. Like the Dean, the Baron combined an emphasis on the experience of God with a wide awareness of the intellectual and cultural life of the age; but more than Inge, von Hügel was specifically Christian in his mysticism, and—perhaps in consequence—was a saint. (Inge's great love was for the Greek philosopher Plotinus, and he was reluctant to see differences between Plotinus and Jesus.) Von Hügel's two volumes on *The Mystical Element in Religion* (London, 1908), based on a study of St. Catherine of Genoa who had died four centuries before, enabled him and others to survive the crisis of faith brought about by the Papal condemnation of the Catholic

[1] *The Will to Believe* (New York, 1897), p. 27.
[2] *A Reader in Contemporary Theology*, ed. John Bowden and James Richmond (London, 1967), p. 55.

'modernists'. The modernists had appealed to the realities of Catholic experience, rather than to the intellectual formulations of Catholic dogma. In a more balanced way, von Hügel sustained that appeal.[1]

However, neither Inge's Greek philosophers nor von Hügel's Catholic mystics have been the most successful Western group to communicate to the twentieth century the sheer reality and excitement of religious faith. A thread which runs through much of the theology addressed to our time is the influence of a Dane who died a few months before the birth of Freud, Sören Kierkegaard. As a character, Kierkegaard was infinitely less admirable than Inge or von Hügel. He was, indeed, approximately as neurotic as his anti-Christian opposite number in the history of nineteenth-century thought, Nietzsche; and Freud would have made fascinating case-histories out of both men. But this melancholy Dane had one thing to say, and he said it with a haunting eloquence. Kierkegaard's 'one thesis' was, he said, that 'Christianity does not exist'. He did not mean that one could not be a 'knight of faith'. He meant that one could not be born a Christian, that one could not be enrolled automatically in a Christian society, that one could not drift into faith. Prophetically discerning the break-up of the Christian society of Europe, Kierkegaard with a sharp and ever-memorable passion expressed his conviction that *a man must choose*. Christian faith was not submission to Christendom (represented for him by the doctrines and conventions of the Danish State Church); it was the leap of personal trust into submission to the self-revelation of the Wholly Other, the mysterious, transcendent, divine Person. For Kierkegaard 'truth is subjectivity', not in the sense that since truth is unattainable the subjective experience is what matters, but in the sense that the all-demanding experience of personal religion (rather than impersonal study or routine acceptance of authority) leads the worshipper into the knowledge of the God whose reality has an 'infinite quali-

[1] See Adam Fox, *Dean Inge* (London, 1960), and Joseph P. Whelan, *The Spirituality of Friedrich von Hügel* (London, 1971).

tative difference' from the worshipper's own anxiety-filled existence and from the existence of the world. Kierkegaard knew a God more actively personal than the God of Plotinus, and even harder to reach than the God of the Catholic mystical tradition. Above all, Kierkegaard knew a God who, instead of claiming to be beyond contradiction (and both Inge and von Hügel did seek to raise mysticism above all philosophical doubts or theological controversies), called on each solitary individual to choose for himself.[1]

For many, therefore, God is still a live option, however difficult the choice may be after all the psychological impact of our time. Despite the secularisation of Sweden, one whom many would judge to be the embodiment of what is best in that nation's character, Dag Hammarskjöld, while Secretary-General of the United Nations, found God in a lonely mysticism.

His concentration on suffering and death amid great worldly success may be psychoanalysed in terms of unhealthy self-love, self-dramatising, narcissism, masochism, etc., but W. H. Auden, introducing his spiritual notes after his death, has effectively replied to suggestions that this is the only analysis appropriate to such holiness. Hammarskjöld's fascination with the tremendous mystery of God did for long encourage his self-absorption, because he probed himself and the writings of the mystics tirelessly in order that his intellect might come to terms with his religious sense (thus supplementing Albert Schweitzer's ethic, which impressed his boyhood). But the God whom he slowly found in the deep silence was a God who was revealed in every 'thou' and supremely in the active self-sacrifice of Christ (when he died, *The Imitation of Christ* by St. Thomas à Kempis was in his pocket). A return to the world was implied after years of a private life of loneliness and despair when he wrote the apparently conventional meditation for the New Year, 1953: 'For all that has been—Thanks! To all

[1] See John Macquarrie, *Twentieth-Century Religious Thought* (New York, 1963). The last section of this comprehensive survey sums up the impact of existentialism on religion.

that shall be—Yes!' If Hammarskjöld's sense of impending death was the last self-indulgence of a self-dramatising narcissist or masochist, this was an indulgence which was other than the suicide to which he had been tempted previously. It was self-indulgence of a kind which would fulfil the self's life by rescuing the Congo and the world from disaster. When he spoke about Christ's cross to the World Council of Churches in 1954, he saw in it the symbol of the Christian's stretching out to the world. He said 'Yes' not to a reflection of himself but to a demanding reality; and so instead of suicide, he met death in the course of duty. In Hammarskjöld's own phrase, his road to holiness passed 'through' action for the sake of others.[1]

Such men prove nothing—except that the mystery of God still has the power to fascinate adults who are thoroughly the children of the twentieth century, a time of scepticism, and who do not escape from that century's tensions. At the time of his death Dag Hammarskjöld was working on a Swedish translation of *I and Thou* by Martin Buber; and this chapter may be concluded with a passage from another book by Buber. The passage recalls that one summer's morning in Germany, Martin Buber was asked by a friend why he continued to use the word 'God' to describe the reality about which he was attempting to speak. For this friend, the evil which had been done in the name of 'God' had ruined the word.

'Yes'—so Buber reconstructed the reply he then gave spontaneously to his critic—'it is the most heavy-laden of all human words. None has become so soiled, so mutilated. Just for this reason I may not abandon it. Generations of men have laid the burden of their anxious lives upon this word and weighed it to the ground; it lies in the dust and bears their whole burden. The races of men with their religious factions have torn the word to pieces; they have

---

[1] See his *Markings* (1963; Eng. trans., New York, 1964), the biography by Henry P. van Dusen (New York, 1967) and the commentary by Gustaf Aulen, *Dag Hammarskjöld's White Book* (Philadelphia, 1969).

killed for it and died for it, and it bears their finger-marks and their blood. Where might I find a word like it to describe the highest? If I took the purest, most sparkling concept from the inner treasure-chamber of the philosopher, I could only capture thereby an unbinding product of thought. I could not capture the presence of Him whom the generations of men have honoured and degraded with their awesome living and dying. I do indeed mean Him whom the hell-tormented and heaven-storming generations of men mean. Certainly, they draw caricatures and write "God" underneath; they murder one another and say "in God's name". But when all madness and delusion fall to dust, when they stand over against Him in the loneliest darkness and no longer say "He, He", but rather sigh "Thou", shout "Thou", all of them the one word, and when they then add "God", is it not the real God whom they implore, the One Living God, the God of the children of men? Is it not He who *hears* them? And just for this reason is it not the word "God", the word of appeal, the word which has become a *name*, consecrated in all human tongues for all times? We must esteem those who interdict it because they rebel against the injustice and wrong which are so readily referred to "God" for authorization. But we may not give it up. How understandable it is that some suggest that we should remain silent about the "last things" for a time in order that the misused words may be redeemed! But they are not to be redeemed *thus*. We cannot cleanse the word "God" and we cannot make it whole; but defiled and mutilated as it is, we can raise it from the ground and set over it an hour of great care.'[1]

[1] Martin Buber, *The Eclipse of God* (New York, 1952), pp. 7–8.

CHAPTER FOUR

The Decline and Fall of Christian Dogmatism

The Old Coherence

Our analysis of the religious situation ought not to be *only* sociological or psychological. Obviously enough, education has often been a powerful factor in the communication of a society's beliefs and values, and education has some intellectual content. A more technical society must be a more educated one, so that the number of citizens active intellectually is liable to grow; already modern developments in broadcasting, serious journalism and book publishing have increased the size of the intellectual community and the quantity of its debate on a scale which has created a new cultural (and religious) situation. Already many educated citizens claim that the intellectual objections to religious belief are paramount, whatever may have been the actual causes of their choice of unbelief. Altogether, then, we may say that a considerable intellectual challenge has been presented to the theologians.

We have already discussed, however briefly, the theology of Judaism and Islam in the twentieth century, and in our next chapter we shall turn to Hinduism and Buddhism. In this chapter we can, therefore, spend a little more space on the intellectual challenge to Christian dogmatism—a subject which has given to our century many millions of agitated words.

The *Oxford English Dictionary* reminds us that the meaning of 'dogmatism' slides from 'positiveness in the assertion of opinion' to 'a way of thinking based upon principles which have not been tested by reflection', so that to 'dogmatise' can mean to 'speak authoritatively or imperiously without reference to argument or evidence'. In religion, we may add, the essence of dogmatism is the attitude which regards as obvious something which in fact is received only as a matter of faith. A religious dogma is held to be obviously true, 'without reference to argument or evidence', because it forms part of a faith which seems to be obviously true. The system of beliefs to which this dogma belongs is more or less compulsory; for it is a whole society's philosophy.

A society's religion, thus accepted uncritically, has commonly been thought to possess a uniform texture, uniting its moral injunctions (for example) with its myths about the world's creation, and suggesting the dependence of the former on the literal truth of the latter. This is because all (or almost all) of the contents of a religion have apparently been embodied in one revelation, which was to be accepted or rejected as a whole. We can see this in the attitude of most Christians to their traditions—and specially in the attitude of Fundamentalism, where the dogmatism of a society is expressed more imperiously than ever before because that society is challenged by an alien way of life and thought. As a sociologist expresses it: 'The less firm the plausibility structure becomes, the more acute will be the need for world-maintaining legitimations.'[1]

The 'Fundamentalists' at the peak of their power in the United States were not ashamed to be so called, because they thought that they were defending the very foundations of the Christian faith. The series of books on *The Fundamentals: A Testimony to the Truth*, launched in 1909, and the World's Christian Fundamentals Association, founded ten years later, prepared the way for attacks on many 'liberal' or 'modernist' preachers. As a climax in 1925 came the prosecution of a schoolteacher in Dayton, Tennessee, for teaching that man was descended from the lower

[1] Peter Berger, *The Social Reality of Religion*, p. 47.

animals. In this 'monkey trial' William Jennings Bryan, a former Secretary of State and Presidential candidate, secured the condemnation of the teacher (and of Charles Darwin) by arguing that all American piety would be in danger if the literal authority of *Genesis* were to be sacrificed. His argument was not entirely ridiculous—after all, his opponent in the court was Clarence Darrow, a well-known agnostic who (honourably) practised law in the Chicago of the gangsters. And Bryan, in the monkey trial, had on his side much support from the Christian Church through the centuries—although before the rise of modern science questions of historical truth in the Bible were seldom posed so sharply as to produce Fundamentalism in reaction.

The popular Catholicism which these Protestant Fundamentalists so hated has been very similar in its absence of intellectual flexibility. Among the faithful millions, this absence of flexibility in 'the Faith' has, no doubt, been due largely to an absence of thought; but among the intellectuals, great sophistication has been exercised on the development of a rationalism which at every important point has been subordinate to the traditional faith. Probably the most authoritative proclamations of the power of the Christian traditions in this century were the two Papal Encyclicals, *Pascendi Dominici Gregis* from Pius X in 1907 and *Humani Generis* from Pius XII in 1950. Both documents were directed mainly against French Catholic intellectuals who had made concessions to the knowledge and spirit of the day; and both denounced such concessions with a confident dogmatism. Catholicism was a system, these Encyclicals declared; and this system must be defended as an integral whole.

Not only Rome has maintained this conservative view of Catholic Christianity. Charles Gore, the Anglican leader who died in 1932, loved to emphasise what he called the 'coherence' of Christian doctrine, founded on the authority of Holy Scripture and the Catholic tradition. He thought that the necessity of bishops was part of this doctrine, and as a bishop he very energetically defended parts of the Church of England's traditional faith and organisation which modernisers were prepared to abandon. He saw this basic conservatism as the only possible answer to the many perils of his time—and already in the first hours of the twentieth century he was warning his congregation in Westminster Abbey of the decay in civilisation and of the evils in store for the Church.[1] Many conservative Lutherans or Calvinists have occupied roughly the same position as Gore, although without his passion for bishops, sacraments and other elements retained by the Church of England from the Catholic tradition.

Conservatives of this kind have not been complete Fundamentalists, for they have been prepared to make some concessions when minor points in the religious traditions were proved wrong by modern knowledge. Pius XII, for example, encouraged biblical scholars to study 'the modes of expression of ancient peoples' in his Encyclical *Divino Afflante Spiritu* (1943). Charles Gore alienated his more conservative friends by his acceptance of many of the results of scholarly work on the Bible and by his abandonment of some traditional beliefs such as that Jesus was omniscient. But essentially, the old system was good in the eyes of Pope Pius, Bishop Gore and many thousands of lesser teachers of Christian conservatism. Theirs was a refined version of the faith of the millions, for what mattered more than their minor concessions to modern knowledge was their burning conviction that the teaching authority of the Bible and the Church could be preserved substantially intact. Whether the Bible was interpreted with a simple Fundamentalism or with a more sophisticated conservatism, whether the Church was thought to be the guardian of the unchanging 'deposit of faith' (handed on from the apostles to our time) or was thought to be the teacher of a doctrine which included some developments of the apostolic faith, the Bible or the Church (and preferably both) could be trusted. This meant that when a problem was raised, Christians assumed that the answer to

[1] See my *Leaders of the Church of England, 1828–1944* (London, 1971), pp. 257–72.

it could be derived authoritatively from teaching which already existed in a sacred book or in a sacred community.

The Authority of the Bible

During the twentieth century this dogmatism is being shattered by the impact of criticism on the material previously regarded as sacrosanct. In the nineteenth century biblical criticism spread from Protestant Germany and proceeded from an analysis of the literary history of the Old Testament (and even of the New) to the higher criticism which expressed and tackled larger questions about the truth of the Bible. The 'higher critics' sought to recover the true history of the events which were portrayed in the Bible beneath a thick varnish of comments and legends, and to discern the real authorship and authority of commandments associated by the Bible with Moses, Jesus, Paul, etc. In the twentieth century biblical criticism has widened its popularity, being taught now in schools and even sometimes in pulpits, as well as in universities and the more advanced theological seminaries. Biblical criticism has also made its attack on the authority of the biblical tradition more thorough in our time. Criticism has been bold to assess the early books of the Bible as folk-tales, to discriminate between the Old Testament prophets for their religious and ethical values, to reject miracles including the resurrection of Jesus, to assert that neither of the two spiritual giants of the primitive Church, Paul or John, correctly interpreted Jesus, and even to question freely the authority of the teaching ascribed to Jesus in the synoptic (the first three) gospels. Some of this teaching has been traced by the critics to the editorial or inventive abilities of the early Christians, and some parts were attributed to the limitations or mistakes natural to a first-century Jew such as Jesus. In particular, the historical Jesus was presented by Albert Schweitzer and other critics as being apocalyptic and remote from modern standards of rational thought or ethical behaviour.

Conservative Christians have made some effective

counter-attacks on biblical criticism, and have caught the critics out in many exaggerations or mistakes. Discoveries in biblical archaeology, for example, have suggested that some biblical narratives reflect the historical circumstances of the relevant time more accurately than some critics supposed; and increased knowledge of the peoples surrounding Palestine has increased appreciation of the uniqueness of the religious ideas with which the Jews interpreted their unique history. The originality of Jesus within this stream of Jewish history has been stressed; Jesus has been contrasted as well as connected with the Essenes who wrote the recently recovered Dead Sea Scrolls, or with the Christians themselves in their second-generation timidity. The destructive atmosphere which made most of the history in the Bible seem mythical, and which attributed most of its theology to Near Eastern or Greek pagans, has therefore been dispelled—at least to some extent, and at least among those who have taken the trouble to study the Bible in depth. But the claims of some theologians that biblical students can now revert to dogmatism in a 'post-critical' age are dangerously misleading, for the scholarly counter-attacks on the excesses of the sceptics cannot restore the old authority of the Bible. Criticism has prevented honest and thoughtful students from occupying their fathers' positions on a host of questions. Both among careful students and among the general public it is agreed that, while the extremes of destructive scepticism need not be accepted, the simple appeal to biblical texts to provide an unquestionable authority in support of Christian doctrine cannot be restored. A human element, liable to error, is present everywhere in the Bible.[1]

Indeed, it may be doubted whether the full force of the revolution in biblical studies has even now been experienced by the Christian churches. The teaching of the Orthodox churches has scarely been touched by the critical spirit. The biblical movement in Roman Catholicism advocates more thorough study among scholars, the laity's access to the

[1] See, e.g., Stephen Neill, *The Interpretation of the New Testament, 1861–1961* (London, 1964).

Bible in modern translations, and greater prominence for Scripture in worship and preaching. In theology this biblical movement scored its greatest victory with the movement of the Second Vatican Council towards the belief that Scripture is the sole source of the Church's tradition. But the biblical movement has been acceptable within the Roman Catholic system because it has largely dissociated itself from the 'negative' or 'modernist' approach of Protestant critical scholarship; it has submitted itself instead in full loyalty to the teaching authority (the *magisterium*) of the Church. Pope Pius XII, while encouraging biblical scholars, reminded them that they must assume that Adam and Eve were actual individuals who 'fell', and that the whole human race was descended from these two parents; and this note of caution is typical of a certain ambiguity which remains in the Roman Catholic Church's welcome to modern knowledge. Much sound scholarship has been produced in these circumstances, but also a great flood of pious speculation arising under ecclesiastical inspiration from an uncritical meditation on the text. The intellectual weakness may be seen most plainly in the writings about the Virgin Mary. Only a few hundred words may be found in the Bible about the Virgin, there is no other evidence, and during its first few centuries the Church knew no real Marian doctrine; but in 1959 the published titles relating to this subject by Roman Catholic biblical students were estimated at about 100,000.[1] A few signs have begun to appear that such use of the Bible for such dogmatic purposes no longer satisfies. But the impact of the critical approach on the entire system of Roman Catholic doctrine, and on the whole Roman Catholic understanding of authority, cannot be for ever delayed, and when it comes, it is bound to cause pain and confusion.

Even among Protestants, the regular teaching of the churches will be challenged and shocked as the critical approach makes its full impact. D. E. Nineham has well described the theological heritage: 'It has often been thought

[1] Hans von Campenhausen, *The Virgin Birth in the Theology of the Ancient Church* (1962; Eng. trans., London, 1964), p. 8.

in the past that being a Christian means holding a certain series of beliefs and behaving, or refraining from behaving, in certain specific ways. Along with this has gone an understanding of the Bible as a source-book from which Christians derive their characteristic beliefs and ways of behaving—a collection of inerrant propositions and irreformable demands and prohibitions, guaranteed by their direct divine origin as timelessly valid and universally binding.' 'I should like to emphasize,' Nineham continued, 'how long-lived this attitude was and how deep-seated it has become . . . Anyone who takes part in the meetings of the synods of the various Churches as they attempt to lay down the "biblical norms" of orthodox Christian behaviour must be aware that such views are very much alive. And is not each one of us aware of it . . . ? When we read of doubt being cast on the accuracy of some biblical statement, do we not secretly feel that another nail has been knocked into the coffin of biblical inspiration?' So conservatism lingers on, even while, as Nineham has noted, scholars today agree with surprising unanimity that instead of the old view of biblical authority Christianity should be defined in some such terms as 'putting your whole trust in God for life and for salvation'.[1]

If this is the situation among scholars and ecclesiastical leaders, in the parishes conservatism is still thought to be the only practical method for pastoral purposes. In many pulpits —perhaps in most—what 'the Bible says' is still quoted in order to clinch an appeal without further argument. In most pulpits the substantial accuracy of the passage being preached about is assumed without troubling the congregation with 'scholarly questions'. This seems to be true even in Germany, where the divorce between the universities and the parishes is long established. Most Protestant preachers in the twentieth century have, therefore, still to face the problem posed by the fact that most of the material in the Bible has been filtered through the preaching or story telling of the community of ancient Israel or the early Church before assuming its present form.

[1] *The Church's Use of the Bible*, pp. 147–8.

What we possess in the Bible, according to most of the scholars, is what was told around the camp fires or when the day's farming was done or over tables in Jerusalem or in meetings for worship in the early Christians' homes. It is often possible to pierce through this form by 'form-criticism', and to suggest with a reasonable confidence what was originally said or what originally happened, and in some parts of the Bible—as in the court history of King David, or in the authentic letters of St. Paul—it is possible to have direct access to the real history. But the bulk of the Bible was shaped by the theology of the chroniclers or evangelists, whose motives were different from those of modern historians. The appeal to the Bible today is, therefore, only in part an appeal to the actual words of Jesus, his forerunners and his apostles; it is also in large part an appeal to the experience of the Hebrews and the Christians. The Old Testament, for example, incorporates many fragments from early days, but the historical narratives no less than the laws and prophecies in it were edited to strengthen a community's faith. St. John's gospel contains some history, but its main substance seems to be the meditations of its unknown author on what the Church had learned towards the end of the first century A.D. The theology of St. Mark, St. Matthew and St. Luke (in the gospel and in *Acts*) must be considered along with the historical value of the sayings and incidents preserved in the tradition of the local church behind the evangelist. The form in which we have the evidence about Jesus is now seen to be the form given to that evidence by the early Church. This is the reason why in Rudolf Bultmann's *The Theology of the New Testament* the discussion of 'The Message of Jesus' occupies less than thirty pages out of almost 600.[1]

If this assessment of the Bible is correct, it follows that preachers will one day have to adopt a new approach. They will have to accept their task of presenting the Bible as a library written by men and by churches for their purposes, not as a book dictated by the Holy Spirit solely for the

[1] 2 vols., 1948–51 (Eng. trans., New York, 1951–5).

purposes of God; and when that day comes, popular reaction to the authority of the experiences and convictions of the Hebrews or the first Christians is likely to be a very different matter from the old popular reaction to the Bible as the Word of God. People will be confronted by the Word of God *as mediated by the People of God*; and unless they ascribe infallibility to ancient Israel or to the early Church, people will be forced to make up their own minds, point by point, about the truth or error of the Scriptures which those Hebrews or Christians wrote. The question must arise: 'If the truth about God's revelation . . . be such that those men saw it and wrote of it like that, what must it be for us?'[1] A theology can be built on the Bible thus understood, but the old appeal to the authority of the Bible cannot be sustained among those who are intellectually free.

The Authority of the Church

If biblical criticism has thus questioned the authority of the Bible, the authority of the Church has been eroded in a parallel process which may be called doctrinal criticism.

In the Eastern Orthodox and Roman Catholic Churches, the twentieth century has preserved the image of a teaching Church, infallible on its most solemn occasions and authoritative in the daily guidance of the flock by bishops and priests. As we look more closely at Eastern Orthodoxy, however, we find that, while the liturgy has indeed preserved with fairly trivial modifications under the control of the hierarchy, the thought of these Churches has usually developed, where it has developed, through laymen such as the theologians in the Greek universities. Among these, the one genius to win wide attention in the West—not in the Orthodox world—was the turbulently eloquent Nicholas Berdyaev, but he was a philosopher in rebellion against most of the prevailing trends in his Church. If the Communist revolution had not exiled him to Berlin and Paris, the ecclesiastical

[1] Leonard Hodgson, *For Faith and Freedom*, vol. i (Oxford, 1956), p. 88.

authorities would almost certainly have arranged for him to go to Siberia.[1] Eastern Orthodox theology in our time has usually sought to remain loyal to the tradition inherited from ancient days, but its cohesiveness has been expressed in that untranslatable Russian word *sobornost*—a spiritual togetherness in worship and life, resting intellectually on the seven 'ecumenical' councils of the Church (of which the last was held in the year 787), by no means identifiable with the argued coherence of Catholic or Protestant doctrine. Whether this kind of conservatism can for ever withstand the impact of our secular century remains to be seen. Partly because the largest Orthodox Church has been forced into a spiritual ghetto by the Russian state, Eastern Orthodoxy has never experienced the Reformation or the scientific movement; and for the most part the Orthodox Churches in the West have been nostalgic exiles in a strange land. But there are some hopeful signs of renewal: in the participation of the Orthodox in the World Council of Churches, in the *Zoe* (or Life) Movement in Greece, and in the slow emergence of religious unity and vigorous theology among the three million immigrants from Orthodox traditions in the United States.[2]

The Roman Catholic Church is, of course, dogmatic. This characteristic can be seen in a lack of theological vitality in the twentieth century—a lack noticeable when one considers that Church's vast resources. Some writers have been creative theologically—such as Baron von Hügel, or the French philosophers Jacques Maritain, Etienne Gilson and Gabriel Marcel, or Karl Adam and Romano Guardini who exercised a wide and liberal influence in Catholic Germany. There have been some major contributions from priests in the French religious orders (Henri de Lubac, Yves Congar and Teilhard de Chardin) and in the post-war German universities (Bernard Haring, Karl Rahner and Hans Küng).

---

[1] See Donald Lowrie, *Rebellious Prophet* (New York, 1960), and for the background Nicholas Zernov, *The Russian Religious Renaissance* (London, 1965).
[2] See, e.g., Timothy Ware, *The Orthodox Church* (London, 1963).

These are intellectual circles which are relatively free from the interference of the Vatican and the bishops—although the three great Frenchmen just mentioned all knew periods of disgrace, and the German professors have not been without their highly placed critics. Many more Roman Catholic scholars could be listed; but the whole of English-speaking Catholicism has not produced a major theologian since Newman's death in 1890, and throughout the Church the half-century after the 'modernist' crisis in the 1900s was marked by the crippling effects of the ecclesiastical authorities' censorship and control. Over French theological vitality, the Vatican exercised a close and suspicious watch; towards Latin American superstition its attitude was relaxed. This era culminated in two actions by Pius XII in the second half of 1950. One was his Encyclical *Humani Generis*, already mentioned; the other was his 'infallible' proclamation of the dogma that 'the Immaculate Mother of God, the ever-Virgin Mary, having completed the course of her earthly life, was assumed body and soul into heavenly glory'. This doctrine of the assumption was desired by popular devotion, but was confessedly unsupported by historical evidence, so that its proclamation was the strongest possible illustration of the Roman Catholic hierarchy's dogmatism.

But the evidence seems to show that religious dogmatism has no long future in the modern West—not even when dogmatism is so splendid and triumphant as it has seemed at Rome. Within fifteen years of 1950 the Roman Catholic hierarchy, without changing any doctrine, had modified its rejection of the modern world. The Second Vatican Council made several significant concessions. It acknowledged the Bible as the one source for Christian doctrine, as we have mentioned. In the crucial question how the Bible was to be interpreted, the Council adopted several positions which might lead to a less rigidly dogmatic attitude in the years ahead. The Council stressed the 'collegial' (corporate) nature of the teaching authority of the bishops under the Pope; it invited criticism from, through dialogue with, fellow-Christians of other Churches and even total unbelievers;

and, while abandoning no doctrine, it pointedly refrained from additions. It now seems improbable that any other dogma will be defined through the exercise of Papal infallibility. Moreover, in the 1960s the rumblings of the clergy against the law of celibacy, of the laity against the prohibition of contraceptives and of the left wing against the political attitudes of reactionary bishops, developed into open criticism of the whole authoritarian style and legal structure of Roman Catholic moral teaching. A new emphasis is emerging on the primacy of love in ethics and of freedom in the conscience of the individual. It now seems probable that a severe questioning of the hierarchy's code of discipline as the content of Catholic morality—particularly in the intimately emotional matter of birth control—will lead to doubts being thrown publicly on the hierarchy's past teaching as the criterion of Catholic doctrine. The Roman Catholic Church may be on the eve of a period of self-criticism no less dangerous than the Reformation of the sixteenth century and no less drastic than the debating which has eroded Protestant orthodoxy. 'A knowledge of the past seems to indicate almost nothing of the future of Roman Catholicism,' wrote an American scholar John L. McKenzie, in his candid and able survey of *The Roman Catholic Church* (New York, 1969).

In the Protestant world the collapse of dogmatism became evident during the nineteenth century. The Reformation of the sixteenth century exalted the Reformers against the Popes, and was in that strictly limited sense a triumph for individualism, but seldom before the nineteenth century did the Protestant churches frankly abandon their struggle for uniformity in their ranks. Over the last hundred years the view has prevailed widely that Jesus did not entrust his authority to any Church, except perhaps to the invisible fellowship of those who obey his moral teachings. Theological fashion has since the 1920s moved away from the teachers of that low view of the Church, but such liberal Protestantism has remained the simple creed of many millions of Protestant laymen. Many of these have, indeed, maintained that to be a Christian it is not necessary to 'go to church' at all. When the corporate expression of Christianity has been honoured, the Church has been understood as a fellowship of laymen trying to live decent lives with help from stories about Jesus and from such worship as has appealed to individual temperaments or congregations. On this liberal, democratic basis an authoritarian teaching could not be successfully erected. Some theologians have attempted to substitute the professor or the preacher for the old-style bishop or priest, but the great Protestant principle has remained: the true Church is essentially not an institution but an event, the event which happens when a Christian obeys Christ.

As a consequence of this low view of the Church's authority, conservative leaders of the Protestant churches have not been allowed to control men's thoughts. The historic doctrinal statements (the Lutheran Augsburg Confession, the Anglican Thirty-nine Articles or the Presbyterian Westminster Confession) are now regarded so ambiguously that it has become virtually impossible to punish preachers who have disagreed with them. An English theologian who died in 1967, J. S. Bezzant, outlined the traditional Christian 'scheme of salvation' (based on the verbally inspired Scripture, the rebellion of Satan, the fall of Adam, the substitutionary sacrifice of Jesus to appease God's wrath, the predestination of the elect among the true believers in the Church to the resurrection of their bodies, the endless torment of the rest of mankind in hell, etc.), and added: 'This outline has been so shattered that bare recital of it has the aspect of a malicious travesty.'[1] Even the creeds of the ancient Church, while regarded as binding in many theories about the basis of church life, have in practice often not been treated as decisive. The so-called 'Athanasian' Creed has become a document of history for theologians, and the Nicene and Apostles' Creeds have been commonly viewed as containing some statements about Christ which need not be

[1] *Objections to Christian Belief*, ed. A. R. Vidler (London, 1963), p. 84.

taken literally—the descent into Hell or the ascent to the right hand of the Father, and for many also Christ's virginal conception and physical resurrection.

Protestantism from Harnack to Bultmann

It is obvious that great confusion has been caused in modern Protestantism by the debates among the theologians after this collapse of ecclesiastical authority.[1] The fear of open confusion inspired many Roman Catholic boasts that certainty was to be found only in submission to Rome—until the bishops went to Rome for their Council, and so moved nearer to joining the debates. A similar fear made many Protestant churchmen in the English-speaking world glad that the faithful were not exposed to the theological agitations in the German universities—until broadcasts and paperbacks placed radical theology within reach of the millions. Today, an element of confusion is being accepted by more and more Christians as the only possible alternative to a dead or doomed dogmatism. But even now the impossibility of a new dogmatic *system* has probably not been fully appreciated; for many Christians seem to hope that faith which will emerge from the current confusion will be a new kind of dogmatism.

The simplest kind of new dogmatism would be that which was associated with many of the liberal Protestants in the days of their battles with the Fundamentalists. By the removal of miracles or of harsh sayings which were 'unworthy' of Jesus and were thought to be the inventions of the early Christians, the liberals wanted to reduce drastically the dogmatic element in Christianity, but they still maintained that the original teaching of Jesus was true in a fairly obvious way, and they were optimistic that modern men of intelligence and good will would accept it. Adolf von Harnack's eloquent lectures on 'the essence of Christianity', delivered in the University of Berlin as the century began,

---

[1] But William Nicholls, *Systematic and Philosophical Theology* (London, 1969), is a good guide.

presented this reduced Gospel about 'God the Father and the infinite value of the human soul', a Gospel resulting in 'the higher righteousness and the commandment of love'.[1]

Here we need not pause to attempt a full criticism of the theology of Harnack and other 'liberals', but we shall simply consider the claim that this creed was a fairly obvious set of truths, well authenticated by the teaching and life of Jesus. Nor need we deal here with Albert Schweitzer's point, already mentioned, that the truly historical Jesus had preached no such message—that (unlike Harnack) the historical Jesus would not have been a popular professor amid all the civilisation of pre-war Berlin. The question we must raise is closer to the criticism offered by Alfred Loisy in his book on *The Gospel and the Church*,[2] for Loisy argued against Harnack's whole attempt to define the original essence of Christianity and to condemn the Church from its own experience. At that stage of his career Loisy was prepared to defend Christianity as developed dogmatically by the Roman Catholic Church. Jesus, having been an apocalyptic dreamer, was (Loisy hinted) not very relevant as the sole arbiter of religion in subsequent centuries, but the Church had been more successful—'Jesus expected the Kingdom, and it is the Church that has come'. But here was not the essential point made in the criticism of Harnack. What was most significant for the future of Christian theology was the stress on the *contemporary* essence of Christianity. Christianity, Loisy urged, deserves to be judged as it is today, not as it was in the beginning. No event in the past, however authoritative—not even the teaching and life of Jesus himself, if that could be recovered in detail—can make sure that the Gospel will be accepted; the hearer must be prepared to open his eyes and ears to the Gospel's strangeness, and to change his life in response to its revolutionary demand. Essentially, this would still be the case even

---

[1] Translated as *What is Christianity?* (London, 1901). For a collection of extracts with an Introduction, see *Liberal Protestantism*, ed. B. M. G. Reardon (London, 1968).
[2] 1902; Eng. trans., London, 1903.

if the Jesus of history was nearer to the Jesus of Harnack than he was to the Jesus of Schweitzer and Loisy. For the Christian critics of Harnack, the Gospel-character of the Gospel depends on the hearer accepting it as good news *for him*, with a personal faith; and this Gospel about God cannot be heard unless the hearer has first faced a profoundly disturbing question about the character and meaning of *his own life*. No doubt this 'subjective' element in Christianity has always been present, but in Liberal Protestantism (as in Protestant Fundamentalism and conservative Catholicism) the emphasis had been on the 'objective' revelation, and the necessity of a personal choice had been obscured.

In tracing the revolution in Protestant theology since Harnack, we may mention first Karl Barth with his famous attack on the whole notion that the Fatherhood of God is obvious. Barth protested that the God who was obvious was likely to be a false God, for the real God had to reveal himself before he could be known at all. Harnack replied that Barth (his former pupil) was being irrational, and was thus a traitor to the great tradition of German theology. But Barth has continued to prefer the description of the living God given in the atheist Feuerbach's *Essence of Christianity* to Harnack's 'essence' some sixty years later. Feuerbach, Barth thinks, got to the heart of the matter; and Barth, taking the great God whom Feuerbach presented and denied, simply said: that God is real.[1] No doubt the pendulum of living theology would have swung from Harnack's position if Barth had never been born; optimism died in the trenches of 1914–18, and even in neutral Sweden the urge to take up again the sterner themes of Christian doctrine prevailed. But it was the genius of Karl Barth that gave a storm centre to the new theology of crisis.

As a young pastor in Switzerland from 1909, Barth preached the 'Culture-Protestantism' which he had learned in Marburg from his liberal teacher Wilhelm Herrmann (and through him from Albrecht Ritschl), and was drawn to the

[1] See Karl Barth's Introduction to the Harper Torchbooks edition of Feuerbach's *Essence of Christianity* (New York, 1957).

'Religious Socialism' propagated by the Blumhardts from Bad Boll. Thus Barth was the heir to the whole nineteenth-century reconciliation of Christianity and culture, and has never abandoned his broad cultural interests (his devotion to the music of Mozart is famous). But he found that this liberal message of reform and progress did not wear well in his pulpit at Safenwil, and could scarcely be reconciled with the wartime newspapers. Two events of 1914 seemed particularly ominous. Ernst Troeltsch, who studied Christian theology as a department of the scientific study of the history of religion, resigned as Professor of Theology and became Professor of Philosophy; and ninety-three German intellectuals, supporting their Kaiser's war in a manifesto, included to Barth's horror 'the names of nearly all my theological teachers . . . I perceived that I should not be able any longer to accept their ethics and dogmatics, their biblical exegesis, their interpretation of history, and that at least for me the theology of the nineteenth century had no future'.[1] So Barth turned to an intensive study of St. Paul's Epistle to the Romans. In agony of mind he wrote one commentary (1919) and then rewrote it for a second edition (1921). That second edition was the book which burst like a bomb in the playground of the German theologians—although it was not translated into English until 1933.

Barth proclaimed Christian faith as decision after the moment of crisis, in which God miraculously addresses man; and he showed Christian life to be no crown of culture, but a resurrection from the dead. Abandoning the quest for 'points of contact' between Christianity and culture, he became a humble pilgrim to the 'strange new world' of the Bible. Called unexpectedly into German academic life, Barth continued to develop this stark theology of crisis, making one beginning with *Christian Dogmatics*, only to scrap it and to begin the great *Church Dogmatics*. His booklet *Nein!* (1934) rebuked his fellow-theologian Emil Brunner for continuing to toy with the idea that there might be some

[1] Karl Barth, *God, Grace and Gospel* (1957; Eng. trans., Edinburgh 1959), p. 57.

revelation of God outside the Bible. Expelled from his professorial chair in Bonn in 1935, Barth moved back to Switzerland to teach (at Basle) and delivered Gifford Lectures in Scotland (at Aberdeen) with a destructive zest. Entitled *The Knowledge of God and the Service of God* (London, 1938), they were based defiantly on the Scottish Confession of John Knox and his fellow-Calvinists of 1560, and they made clear Barth's conviction that, in the twentieth century as in the sixteenth, no genuine knowledge of God is available without obedient faith in the Word of God, who is Jesus Christ. Without the eye of faith, even 'Christians' who see Jesus as the Rabbi of Nazareth see only the *incognito* which conceals God.

Barth's negative view of Liberal Protestant dogmatism has largely prevailed. To say this is not to say that the Barth of the 1920s and 1930s was unanswerable; indeed he was answered to some extent by the Barth of the 1950s and 1960s, who confessed that his earlier onslaught against the natural reason had been exaggerated. While still denying 'natural' theology as a way from man to God, Barth was increasingly overwhelmed by the sheer joy of the Gospel which he has served, by the humanism of the God who has chosen to be human for ever in Jesus Christ; and the humanity thus blessed by God has been praised by his servant Karl Barth also. Partly because of this shift of emphasis, Communism was never been denounced by Barth as Nazism was; indeed, he called on Protestants in Eastern Europe to accept it. Barth's fierce hostility to religion outside Jesus Christ must be understood as part of his prophetic indignation against the 'German Christians' who, merging piety with patriotism and worship of evolutionary progress with adoration of the Aryan blonde beast, supported first the Kaiser's war, and then the greater evil of Nazism. His booklet on *Theological Existence Today* was a ringing call for faithfulness to the Gospel in 1933, and in May 1934 he wrote all but one sentence of the Barmen Declaration of the anti-Nazi 'Confessing' Church, with its proclamation: 'Jesus Christ, as he is attested to us in Holy Scripture, is the one Word of God, whom we have to hear and whom we have to trust and obey in life and in death. We condemn the false doctrine that the Church can and must recognise as God's revelation other events and powers, forms and truths, apart from and along-side this one Word of God.'

Karl Barth's proclamation of Jesus Christ as the Word of God was far less comprehensively dogmatic than the older Protestant orthodoxies; nevertheless the system set out in Barth's *Church Dogmatics* was dogmatic and ecclesiastical of set purpose, and its imperfect contact with a modern, critical approach to the Bible and to Christian tradition and language explains why Barthianism already belonged to history when Barth died in 1968.[1] And if we ask what has effectively replaced the theology of Harnack among reflective Protestants, we must turn to the thought of the Marburg Professor, Rudolf Bultmann. Bultmann regards himself as continuing Barth's work in 'dialectical' or 'crisis' theology. Essentially, what he has done is to show that the ambiguity which Barth found in nature and in history as a whole is present also in the events which to Barth so clearly revealed the Christians' God.

Bultmann's programme for 'demythologising' the New Testament was first outlined in an article of 1941.[2] The controversy caused by that short document has been im-mense, passionate, profound and bitter—partly because so many unsatisfactory elements in traditional Christianity are (somewhat confusingly) joined together by Bultmann under the one word 'myth'. But as the discussion begins to settle down after a quarter of a century, the effect of the impact of Bultmann's challenge begins to be seen. The 'demythologis-ing' programme includes not only an insistence that the spatial imagery of traditional religious talk ('he ascended into heaven', etc.) cannot be taken literally, and not only an emphasis that the traditional symbols in the religious world-view mean little to modern man, and not only a consistent

[1] See, e.g., John Bowden, *Karl Barth* (London, 1971).
[2] Reprinted with a variety of replies in *Kerygma and Myth*, ed. H. W. Bartsch (London, 1953).

rejection of all anti-natural miracles (the physical resurrection of Jesus, etc.), and not only a drastic criticism of the gospels as history, but also something which we do not find in previous German critics—or in the English-speaking modernists who had for long been voicing roughly similar opinions on those points.

Bultmann's 'demythologising' programme arises from a great scepticism about whether *any* event can by itself reveal God. For him, even a non-miraculous, solidly historical event does not show God's nature and activity at all obviously. Bultmann advances an interesting reason for this emphasis that God is not revealed through events without a personal response. He maintains that the God who is not mythical cannot be reduced to the level of particular events and made an object among other objects. The real difficulty of the religious language in which Christianity has been expressed since New Testament times has been, for Bultmann, its tendency to present God as a god who appears among men like the gods in the Greek or Hindu myths. This, he thinks, is what has made Christianity incredible in our time, despite the eloquence of theologians such as Barth. Bultmann's solution to this whole problem of the inadequacy of 'objective' events to reveal God is to stress the 'existential' character of faith. By this he means that Christian faith arises out of the depths of a person's own existence, and declares what an event means to that person. For example, the myth of the physical resurrection of Jesus represents (and may obscure) the fact that the apostles' own faith rose at Easter. This faith involves a new self-understanding, and a new style of personal life ('authentic existence'). The faith is, in part, a response to past events, but the significance of those events is seen in terms of their interpretation which transforms personal existence. This faith is what makes an event 'eschatological', i.e. a disclosure of ultimate reality, for that person. In the event its potential 'eschatological' significance slumbers until that person's faith can 'awaken' it.[1] For example, the apostles' faith rose at Easter as an

[1] *History and Eschatology* (Edinburgh, 1957), p. 155.

interpretation of the solidly historical death of Jesus as the 'eschatological' event. In a famous sentence, Bultmann laid bare his existentialist view of faith by writing: 'The question of God and the question of myself are identical.'[1]

We do not have far to look if we ask what influences have contributed to the urgency of this teaching that *faith* must interpret history, and so lead to 'authentic existence'. Bultmann has told us that his 'demythologising' programme was sparked off by a plea for help with their preaching from some of his pupils who serving as chaplains in Hitler's army. In Bultmann's lifetime Europe was made, smashed and remade by political forces which owed their psychological power to their ability to interpret the whole of European history in the light of a central idea. The textbooks in the schools had to be written and rewritten. Christianity, if it was to survive, could not be understood as a faith with less power over history; yet Christianity was plainly unable to do battle with the political forces on their own ground. The power of Christian faith could be presented only as power over *personal* history; its drama could be read not in the newspapers but in people's hearts. Nor should we wonder why history to Bultmann is usually disastrous and dead (the symbol of this for him is the judgment which the crucifixion of Jesus pronounced in all human hopes)—until the Christian faith, the Easter faith, imposes a new interpretation on it (by seeing in one bit of this tragic history, the cross, the place where the glorious future of man is made manifest to faith). For Bultmann and his fellow-Germans, the history of the first half of the twentieth century brought little but disaster and death. Therefore for him, faith, and only faith, is what gives hope to history. 'Man,' as he once wrote, 'can never jump out of time, but has only to choose whether his present is to be determined by the past or the future.'[2]

In the 'demythologising' of Rudolf Bultmann, we witness, therefore, the abandonment of the appeal by Protestant

---

[1] *Jesus Christ and Mythology* (New York, 1958), p. 53. This book remains the best short presentation of Bultmann's thought.

[2] R. Gregor Smith, *Secular Christianity*, p. 135.

theology to past events or past teachings which of themselves would authenticate an 'orthodox', 'liberal' or 'neo-orthodox' creed. The whole dogmatic attitude is discredited. The society which laid down the dogma has disintegrated. A *personal* faith is seen to be vital. Each man for himself has to decide how his experience is to be interpreted. He must choose one past event which will enable him to escape from the burden of the remainder of the past. He must place his faith on a bit of history which will lead him beyond ordinary, tragic history into authentic existence.

Natural Religion and the Necessity of Faith

Barth and Bultmann in their different ways have shown Christian theologians the absolute necessity of faith. The truth of the Gospel was not so obvious as the happier generation of liberal 'Culture-Protestantism' had liked to suppose; on the contrary, Barth in relation to 'natural' theology and Bultmann in relation to 'revealed' theology repeated the cry of Martin Luther that a Christian could know nothing and could be nothing without a personal, radical faith responding to the 'free gift' of the gracious God. Thus both Barth and Bultmann restated for our time the essential insight of the sixteenth-century Reformation, 'justification by grace through faith'. However, as we trace the decline and fall of Christian dogmatism, we have to move outside the world of theology proper in order to consider the fate of a dogmatism which was vaguer than anything preached by the liberal theologians of 'Culture-Protestantism'.

Essentially dogmatic because convinced that all men should recognise its truth, 'natural' religion has often been thought likely to lead to the universal acceptance of a watered-down version of Christianity. In the eighteenth century the Deists (and many who sympathised with them) abandoned the traditional religion because its authority seemed to depend on an incredible system of miracles and prophecies, and because its central dogma, the Atonement of God and man through the sacrifice of Christ, repelled their intelligence and morality. They turned instead to a Christianity 'not mysterious', to a Christianity 'as old as the creation'. They quietly accepted and taught a calm and clear belief in a Supreme Being or Author of Nature, who had created the universe, who had left it to operate according to rational laws, and who had placed in it, as its masters, rational human beings with a moral law already written in their hearts. In this belief, Jesus became a teacher with a happy gift as a story-teller, illustrating a religious philosophy which almost all men accepted anyway. At the end of the eighteenth century William Wordsworth arose as another teacher, rebelling against the philosopher's description of nature as a lifeless machine (as others had done before him), but still essentially concerned to experience and to communicate the God of nature without reference to the books and sermons of the specifically Christian appeal to revelation. Here was the God of many of the enlightened in Britain and Europe, and here was the God mentioned in the Constitution of the infant United States. Here was, in short, 'natural' religion, the religion of all sensible men (even of the mocking Voltaire). Because its doctrines seemed obvious commonplaces needing only a poetic touch to become the universal religion, such a philosophy was able to unite a whole society; and because its happiness about the divine benevolence owed much to the Christian joy in the God of love, it was able to help in a return to a more traditional faith for many (as for Wordsworth himself).

As the twentieth century has gone its way that acceptance of a well-ordered universe, that praise for Jesus and for other poets of the obvious, and that appeal to the God of nature as the modestly retiring author of reason and of happiness, have not been the public philosophy. On the contrary, Albert Schweitzer's presentation of the conclusion of thought about the natural world has been typical of the general attitude. The malignant power of evil in the human heart and in society has been experienced by our time against a background of a disordered nature without purpose or meaning. Religious belief has seemed to be not agreement with the inevitable but a decision to defy the appearances of nature and of human nature in the name of a God who is mysteriously transcendent over, and victorious over, the evil and disorder. For the thoughtful, worship has increasingly become either an impossibility or a leap of faith, and it has been more difficult to study theology in the way laid down by Lord Gifford when he founded the Gifford Lectures in the Scottish universities: 'as a strictly natural science, the greatest of all possible sciences, indeed, in one sense, the only science, that of Infinite Being without reference to or reliance upon any supposed special, exceptional or so-called miraculous revelation'.

We may be able to express some of the difficulties which many feel with 'natural' religion in our time, if we consider one or two recent books by religiously minded scientists. The contemplation of nature as known to modern science often produces an attitude of awe in the face of the indescribable greatness, majesty, beauty and order of the universe. Many a scientist reverently ponders the process by which matter, organised in ever greater complexity, gives rise to the life of fish, birds, animals and men. He takes very seriously the 'phenomenon of man' (to use the title of Teilhard de Chardin's book which, when published in France in 1955 after its author's death, fascinated so many). He believes that to a considerable extent man can now understand his own place in nature, and can control his future evolution, which will be mainly mental and cultural, with untold glories to come. Thus along the 'living stream' of evolution there is carried the 'divine flame' in man, to use the titles of the Gifford Lectures which an eminent zoologist, Sir Alister Hardy, delivered in Aberdeen twenty years after Karl Barth.[1]

But the God of the Bible cannot be found clearly in all this evolutionary panorama. Teilhard de Chardin and his many Christian admirers have been reluctant to admit this, but the point was made with admirable clarity by Sir Julian Huxley when he introduced *The Phenomenon of Man* to the English-speaking world (London, 1959). Teilhard's vision of Christ

[1] 2 vols., London, 1965–6.

as the fulfilment of evolution, as the incandescent centre of a universe aflame, and of God as the *point Omega* towards which the whole immense process of evolution moves, was described more brutally by another scientist, Sir Peter Medawar, as 'tipsy, euphoric prose-poetry'.[1] Teilhard's superiors in the Jesuit Order, who decreed that his books could not be published during his lifetime, had for all their tragic clumsiness grasped the truth that the science being described was not necessarily as Christian as Teilhard thought it was.

Sir Alister Hardy's *The Divine Flame* may be studied as a learned, honest and clear presentation of a natural theology conceived with reference to the latest science. Hardy's chief purpose was to emphasise that science had produced no valid evidence against the transcendent God of theism being true, and to plead for scientific research into religious experience, in the hope that such research would throw light on the nature of the divine. But Hardy did offer some suggestions of his own, and the negative character of these should be enough to remind us how unlikely it is that scientific research will ever positively demonstrate the existence of God.

Hardy rejected crude doctrines on the Atonement ('that the appalling death of Jesus was a sacrifice in the eyes of God for the sins of the whole world, or that God, in the shape of his son, tortured himself for our redemption'—ideas which are 'among the least attractive in the whole of anthropology'),[2] and he also rejected the tendency to take the image of the Sky Father literally ('the reality must be something very different').[3] Was he, then, able to accept for himself the transcendent God of the theists? He wrote as a 'theistic humanist', but the understanding of God which he felt able to state in his book was in parts barely compatible with what the theistic tradition has regarded as the heart of the matter. Thus he quoted the Marxist biologist, J. B. S. Haldane, about what Auguste Comte called the 'Great Being' above men: 'To my mind the teaching of science is

[1] In a review reprinted in his *The Art of the Soluble* (London, 1967).
[2] *The Divine Flame*, p. 218.
[3] p. 242.

very emphatic that such a Great Being may be a fact as real as the individual human consciousness . . . and it seems to me that everywhere ethical experience testifies to a super-individual reality of some kind.' But the same quotation showed what the Great Being was to Comte and Haldane: 'If the co-operation of some thousands of millions of cells in our brain can produce our consciousness, the idea becomes vastly more plausible that the co-operation of humanity, or of some sections of it, may determine the Great Being. Just as, according to the teachings of physiology, the unity of the body is not due to a soul superadded to the life of the cells, so the superhuman, if it existed, would be nothing external to man, or even existing apart from human co-operation.'[1] Hardy's suggestions about prayer were such as to crystallise the uneasiness of most theists.[2] 'Instead of supposing that one great personal-like Deity is thinking out simultaneously the detailed answers to millions of different problems of all the individuals in the world, is it not more reasonable to suppose that some action is set in motion by prayer which draws the particular solution for each one of us from our own subconscious minds?'

If the God of the Bible cannot be found clearly through 'natural' theology, it is also sadly true that no meaning at all in the total pattern of nature may be demonstrated with scientific certainty. The sheer size of the universe deters most scientists from attributing a meaning to it; the silent immensity of these infinite spaces frightens them, as it did Pascal. Copernicus and Galileo did more damage to the religious world-view than is commonly granted by religious believers, for they began the modern astronomy which has treated this planet as a speck in a universe which is crowded with uncountable galaxies, stars and satellites—and which is growing at a speed faster than the speed of light. We on earth know simply nothing about the purposes of our planet's companions. We do not know if there is life elsewhere in the universe—life which may be far superior to our own. Even on this planet, the facts discovered by science seem larger

[1] p. 230.   [2] p. 236.

than the values cherished by men, much as the life on the bed of the Atlantic Ocean is larger than the life on the ships which pass above. *Homo sapiens* knows very little about any purposes fulfilled by any other species thrown up by evolution.

Can man see a purpose behind his own evolution? The answer is far more difficult for science than a 'natural' religion finds comfortable. The twentieth century's great advances in biochemistry, molecular biology and genetics have prevented many scientifically minded people from endorsing 'natural' religion's sense of the uniqueness and grandeur of human life. That sense remained strong for many even after Darwin's demonstration of man's descent from other animals, and the new scientific revolution has not made nearly so great an impact on public opinion as did the dramatic controversy around Darwin. But in at least two ways the knowledge has placed a question against the idea that evolution led up to man (by a natural tendency if not by a divine design).

First, the physical basis of life is now much less of a mystery than it was for all previous human generations. A scientist has defined life as 'a partial, continuous, progressive, multiform and conditionally inter-active self-realisation of the potentialities of atomic electron states'. At first sight that definition may not seem to have dethroned man or God, but the scientist who offers it assures us that 'the study of the origin of life is likely to prove a greater solvent of old ideas and attitudes than any branch of science has been in the past'. In particular, old religious beliefs will, Professor Bernal assumes, 'become essentially unintelligible if not ridiculous'.[1]

Second, recent advances in genetics have shown in astonishing detail how the evolution of every species, including our own, is the result of genetic mutations which occur at random, without reference to the biological needs of the

[1] J. D. Bernal, *The Origin of Life* (London, 1967), pp. 166, 168, 182. See also J. Z. Young, *An Introduction to the Study of Man* (Oxford, 1972).

animal. Evolution does, in fact, depend on a vast lottery. These mutations are almost always harmful and recessive—a shorter neck may emerge when the species needs a longer one. Mutations which contribute to evolutionary progress do so because members of the species without them are more liable to perish or to be killed without producing offspring, and therefore over great tracts of time the descendants of the original winners in the lottery survive through their superior adaptation to their environment. It is a way of advance which is wasteful, risky and slow beyond anything we could have planned. Huxley, Hardy, Teilhard de Chardin and many other distinguished scientists emphasise the parts played in evolution by the inquisitive, adventuring spirit of many animals, by the formation of habits in a species, by the slow influence of those habits on an animal's physical development, and by the transmission of information and skills by parents and by groups; and these aspects which may be described as purposive, or at least as psychic, do deserve to be pondered by those who would see evolution as a whole. Starvation and death at the hands of rival predators are not the only, and may not be main, instruments of 'natural selection'. But unless we are to subscribe to the clearly false teaching of Lamarck (who died in 1829), revived in our time by the Russian Lysenko, that acquired characters can be inherited genetically, we have always to come back to the random nature of the genetic mutations which are the raw material of evolution. The mechanism of genetic inheritance appears to be completely independent of any effects arising from mental or moral progress, or even from the use or disuse of physical organs. The genes which an organism will pass on are not influenced by its experiences. The result may be progress, but it is progress in which the selection by machine-like laws of material provided by sheer chance plays an alarming part. God may be emerging or even in control, but, if so, he emerges out of, or he allows, a process which few, if any, lesser potentates would have chosen as a method of working.

The possibility of an ultimate absence of meaning in

nature, the possibility that nature may be a mere survival-machine which sorts out the genetic lottery, has haunted the scientific conscience in this century—just as the pointlessness of daily existence has haunted the artistic imagination. For many it has amounted to the death of the God of 'natural' religion. T. H. Huxley used to tell Victorian England that evolution had no more connection with theism or atheism than geometry had. Sir Alister Hardy himself states clearly that the 'natural theology' which he commends contains no hard facts about the divine power which are demonstrable with scientific certainty. 'The most important issue for a natural theology' is recognised as the question: 'do these forces which play so important a part in man's religious life belong only to his sub-conscious mind or do they indicate some extra-sensory contact with some Power beyond the self?' And although future experiments may help, Hardy states that 'natural' theology provides no answer to this question at present. 'It would be folly to speculate and pretend at this stage that we have any idea as to the true nature of this power,' he writes, adding: 'it is for natural theology of the future to tell us more.'[1]

In this situation of scientific uncertainty, Hardy recognises that 'natural' theology is optional; in other words, that *it is a religious faith*—just as much as Christian orthodoxy is. 'Our view of life is no doubt coloured by our temperament,' he has written. 'One person sees evolution simply as the result of changes brought about by random chemical mutations being selected in different ways by the ever-changing physical environment; another sees it essentially as the manifestation of a living process selecting (unconsciously) the changing chemical units, and pushing itself by creative novelty into every position that will hold it.'[2] In 1916, Teilhard de Chardin wrote to a friend about his vocation: 'To tear away the mask of atheism from these new currents of thought and expose them as Christian—that is my great hope.' But shortly before his death in 1955 he asked himself: 'How is it,

[1] *The Divine Flame*, pp. 101, 230–1.
[2] In *Biology and Personality*, ed. I. T. Ramsey (Oxford, 1965), p. 78.

then, that I find myself in a class alone, as it were? Alone in having *seen*? . . . May I not be, after all, at the mercy of a mirage within me? I often wonder.' The conclusion which we draw from the biographies of Teilhard is that he would not have 'seen' Christ as the flaming heart of the universe if he had not first accepted Catholic devotions to the 'sacred heart' of Jesus and to Jesus in the bread at Mass.[1]

It is only right to add after such criticisms that the religious understanding of the universe chosen by Teilhard and Hardy is clearly a live option for well informed, deeply thoughtful and thoroughly honest scientists, although it cannot be supported with scientific proof. As long as it is presented *as one option* among a number of possibilities, it appears to be intellectually respectable. Indeed, this attitude has had a long and distinguished history in our century.

Many philosophers, while wishing to reject any religion which was opposed to science, have hymned the evolutionary process as favouring man's noblest values, and religious believers have found support in that vision. As a young man Teilhard de Chardin was thrilled by Henri Bergson's *Creative Evolution*.[2] Teilhard's English equivalent, Charles Raven, had his own debt to Conwy Lloyd Morgan, Professor successively of Zoology and of Philosophy.[3] If a God of order could not be proved from the design of nature, at least a God of goodness (or values which were more or less a substitute for such a God) could be glimpsed emerging in nature's broad tendency. British philosophers wrote Gifford Lectures which now survive in large volumes, like granite monuments to that era of cosmic optimism. Statesmen contributed also,

[1] Robert Speaight, *Teilhard de Chardin* (London, 1967), pp. 75, 329.
[2] *Creative Evolution* (1907; Eng. trans., London, 1911) did not argue for belief in a transcendent God, but with its emphasis on an instinctive intuition into the dynamic life of the universe, it was one of the first books to counteract the crude materialism of the French anti-clericals.
[3] Charles Raven, *The Creator Spirit* (London, 1927), and *Science and Religion and Experience and Interpretation* (Cambridge, 1953), showed the enduring influence of Lloyd Morgan's Gifford Lectures on *Emergent Evolution* and *Life, Mind and Spirit* (London, 1923–6).

such as Field Marshal Smuts, who turned from his leadership of the Union of South Africa and the new British Commonwealth to explain the natural tendency of the universe to greater and greater wholes.[1] Scientists of the eminence of Sir James Jeans interpreted the latest physics to show how 'the universe begins to look more like a great thought than like a great machine. Mind no longer appears as an accidental intruder into the realm of matter; we are beginning to suspect that we ought rather to hail it as the creator and governor of the realm of matter—not of course our individual minds but the mind in which the atoms out of which our individual minds have grown exist as thoughts.'[2] Sir Arthur Eddington also taught that 'the idea of a universal Mind or *Logos* would be a fairly plausible inference from the present state of scientific theory'.[3]

Yet for all the distinction of such philosophers and scientists with their 'natural' religion, the tradition represented by them always had its sceptical critics within the philosophy of science. What matters even more to the student of science as a social force is that somehow that kind of philosophy became unfashionable. After the mid-1930s, fewer philosophers and scientists could be found talking about the universe as anything other than a problem to be solved by astronomy. In part, this change of mood among the intellectuals was due to the new coldness in the atmosphere of the society around them, but in part, it was due to a more sophisticated understanding of the nature and limits of scientific knowledge. That the depression in the social climate should contribute to such a notable lowering of philosophers' temperatures shows clearly that the ardour of successive Gifford Lecturers for natural religion always had to compete with a chill at the heart of natural science. To change the metaphor: many in our time, although they have tried to be as sensitive as their predecessors were to the glory of the flower of human genius and love, have found their

---

[1] *Holism and Evolution* (London, 1926).
[2] *The Mysterious Universe* (Cambridge, 1930), p. 148.
[3] *The Nature of the Physical World* (Cambridge, 1928), p. 338.

minds drawn more and more to the sordid roots of the flower, and to the apparently accidental planting.

Martin Heidegger's *Being and Time* (1927; Eng. trans., London, 1962) was a grand metaphysical construction in the high tradition of German philosophy. Heidegger then saw man as thrown into an 'inauthentic' existence which serves no external purpose, and which must be dominated by anxiety as the inexorable move to death brings home the threat of nothingness. As an alternative to despair Heidegger for a time sympathised with Nazism; later he retreated to even more obscure philosophical activities instead of completing the projected second volume of the great metaphysical work. Perhaps the upshot of it all was best put by a Glasgow philosopher. In his deeply impressive Gifford Lectures, W. McNeile Dixon declared: 'The first and last of all life's complicated circumstances, the presiding fact, utterly astonishing, even stupefying, is that we are utterly in the dark about everything.'[1]

This chilly attitude—the philosophical equivalent of T. S. Eliot's poetry of the 'waste land'—may pass, as the preceding optimism passed. But what will remain with us for a long time is the memory of the chill, teaching us once more that it is dangerous to be dogmatic on the basis of 'natural' religion. The God of nature is in fact *not* obvious, once 'natural' religion is tested by reflection. A choice is involved; and this choice must be made by the person who is confronted by the mystery.

This is why many recent religious thinkers have confessed that the twentieth century is truly for them also the age of history in which the certainty of God has been eclipsed, or has died—and in which the atheist's counter-attack on God, mounted in reply to the aggression of traditional religion, has ceased to be relevant to life's real experience. Faith, if it is to arise now, must arise on the ruins of certainty, and must always have doubt as one of its ingredients. Here—or so these thinkers claim—is religious adulthood. Children see things in black or white: 'it is' or 'it isn't', 'it's true' or 'it's

[1] *The Human Situation* (London, 1937), p. 199.

a fairy tale'. The adult is not so certain. Many an old story, authoritative when we were children, may turn out to be like a fairy tale; but in the fairy tale may be hidden a vision which is more important than all science. So God is not assumed calmly, or denied confidently; the idea of God has become a mystery, to be grasped by faith—or not to be grasped at all.

'An increasing number of people,' a German theologian wrote in 1965, 'are so gripped by this experience that they can no longer reconcile it either with theism or with atheism because these two positions alike betray a naïve, undisturbed ideological confidence. No attempt to relate the new experience to such settled positions does justice to the reality of the mind's oscillation between them, to its inability either to answer or to drop the question concerning the meaning of existence and the purpose and goal of history . . . In this continuing reflection—a process which is not so much articulated as experienced—the only constant factor is the uncertainty itself, which it is impossible to ignore since it is felt to be rooted in the conscience. The phrase "the death of God" is meant to give theological expression to these changed psychosocial conditions.'[1]

A Transition—to What?

The limitations of the appeal by Christians both to revelation and to nature can be seen in the theological work of William Temple, Archbishop of York and of Canterbury. Temple's mind was formed at Oxford University by 'idealist' philosophers who taught that 'spirit' and 'value' were supreme in nature. They preserved a Christian atmosphere even if they had doctrinal doubts, and they made it easy for their pupils to hold that life had a spiritual purpose. In this tradition, Temple gave expression to a philosophical faith in many articles and books, most permanently in his Gifford Lectures on *Nature, Man and God* (London, 1934). It was, at

[1] Dorothee Solle, *Christ the Representative* (1965; Eng. trans., London, 1967), pp. 11–12.

its heart, a serene faith; indeed, a dogmatic one. But in at least two respects Temple's theological insight summed up the problems discussed in this chapter.

First, Temple renounced the old appeal to an authoritative revelation. He was not basically critical of the old tradition; not many years after his ordination his lingering doubts about the virgin birth of Jesus were dispelled during a symphony concert, and his best known devotional writing was based on a conservative view of the authorship and historicity of St. John's gospel.[1] But Temple's knowledge of the scholars' criticism of the Bible led him to the conclusion that God does not 'speak' in the sense of uttering propositions which are repeated by prophets or church leaders and thus become binding on all who would be reckoned as believers. It is in the *event* that God's revelation is discerned, supremely in the events to which Christians refer when they think of Jesus; and the interpretation comes after the event, although until the event has been interpreted, the revelation is not complete. For Temple, revelation was therefore 'the coincidence of divinely controlled event and mind divinely illumined to read it aright'.[2] St. John's gospel, for example, was for him 'valid history so far as its record of events is concerned', but the discourses attributed to Jesus in it might be partly the interpretation of the events by St. John. He believed that most of the Bible's witness to events, and almost all the undivided Church's interpretation of them, was correct, but this distinction between event and interpretation (which was clearer than Barth's idea of revelation through the Word of God) could be used by others taking a more sceptical view of the ability of the Bible and the Church to record or to interpret events aright.

Second, Temple renounced the old appeal to 'natural' religion. Although he regarded himself as a philosopher, he was fundamentally a Christian prophet and church leader who owed his self-assurance to his glad acceptance of almost

---

[1] *Readings in St. John's Gospel* (2 vols., London, 1939–40).
[2] *Revelation: A Symposium*, ed. John Baillie and Hugh Martin (London, 1937), p. 107.

the whole traditional faith. In his philosophical books a basic confusion lurks beneath many passages because Temple repeatedly presented as the conclusion of 'philosophy' positions which he did in fact adopt because he was a Christian; as Emil Brunner wrote to him, 'your natural theology is natural only in appearance, whilst it is in truth Christian'.[1] Already in those books Temple was tending to speak of a 'general revelation' granted by God outside the Bible rather than of the 'knowledge' alleged to be reached in a purely 'natural' religion, and his sympathy with the younger generation of theologians arising in Britain after the completion of his *Nature, Man and God* led him to see that man's faith in God, and particularly the Christian's faith in God through Christ, should be distinguished far more sharply from knowledge about nature than had been the custom in the intellectual circles to which he had belonged in his early years.

In 1937, writing the Preface to a Report on *Doctrine in the Church of England*, Temple confessed that as he reviewed 'the result of our fourteen years of labour, I am conscious of a certain transition in our minds, as in the minds of theologians all over the world'. This was the transition from a 'Christocentric metaphysic' to a 'theology of Redemption'. A theology of Redemption, Temple explained, 'tends rather to sound the prophetic note; it is more ready to admit that much in this evil world is irrational and strictly unintelligible; and it looks to the coming of the Kingdom as a necessary preliminary to the comprehension of much that now is'. In the journal *Theology* in November 1939 Temple wrote that 'our task with this world is not to explain it but to convert it. Its need can be met . . . only by the shattering impact upon its self-sufficiency and arrogance of the Son of God, crucified, risen and ascended, pouring forth that explosive and disruptive energy which is the Holy Ghost.'

Many, observing the collapse of the old Christian appeal to authority, have drawn other conclusions from the spectacle. The rejection of revelation and redemption as unreal

[1] F. A. Iremonger, *William Temple* (London, 1948), pp. 531–2.

ideas is now taken for granted among most Western intellectuals, and it is today inconceivable that a philosopher of Temple's power would be as impervious as he was to the force of secularist attacks on the basic structure of Christian belief. It is recorded that Temple's flow of eloquence, which normally was unfailing whether the subject was doctrinal, devotional, ecclesiastical, social, philosophical or literary, and which shied away neither from the problems of the nature of Christ nor from the reform of the banking system, did on one occasion falter. It was at a conference of students, and the subject was 'Why I Believe in God'. Temple's talk to the students was 'almost a complete flop', and afterwards he explained to a friend: 'You see, I have never known what it is to doubt the existence of God.'[1] Had William Temple's mind been formed in a slightly later epoch of English intellectual history, there might have been many more occasions when nothing could have been said authoritatively in the sphere of religion, even by him.

The secularised agnosticism of so many educated people in our time has been expressed philosophically by the linguistic analysis which has dismissed all religious statements (and all the 'idealist' metaphysics which may be regarded as a semi-secularised form of theology) as meaningless apart from any incidental light which such statements may throw on ethics and psychology. The 'empirical' approach in philosophy is primarily British in origin. It is at least as old as David Hume, who died in 1776; it made its most dramatic advances through the work of three philosophers of Cambridge University in the twentieth century, G. E. Moore, Bertrand Russell and Ludwig Wittgenstein.

The attack on religion from this philosophical movement is recorded most eloquently in Professor A. J. Ayer's *Language, Truth and Logic* (London, 1936). This was a youthful and passionate, and therefore over-simplified, manifesto for 'logical positivism' (and its author lived to modify its demands), but it nevertheless expressed a very widespread impatience with metaphysical speculations. Apart from the

[1] F. A. Iremonger, *William Temple*, p. 379.

necessary truths of mathematical logic, the only reliable propositions have seemed to be those capable of verification by scientific experiments. Historical, aesthetic and ethical statements might have to be fitted in; room might have to be found on which to rest the validity of philosophical arguments such as this 'verification principle' itself. It might be too much to demand that all meaningful statements should be capable of verification; a looser test might be enough, asking what their opposite would mean or how they might be falsified. A particular statement might be legitimate, although it defied philosophical analysis, if it was a useful contribution to a larger proposition which was meaningful; it might be part of the 'game' of the language appropriate to a particular approach to reality. But however subtly the first enthusiasm for logical positivism might need to be redefined, the contempt for attempts to interpret life in the universe as a whole has remained prominent. Natural religion and Heidegger-type metaphysics have been attacked or ignored, no less than historic theism. Some European philosophers, such as Karl Jaspers,[1] have insisted on keeping the metaphysical tradition alive, and in the 1960s some metaphysical activity resumed in the English-speaking world; but this broadening of empiricism in a return to the old questions (if not to the old answers) did not amount to a change, or to the immediate prospect of change, in the general intellectual climate of the age of science.

In an essay on 'Gods',[2] Professor John Wisdom told a parable about two people returning to their long neglected garden, and finding that to some extent the garden is still in order. One says that a gardener has been at work, and he persists in this belief although no one has recently seen a gardener, and no tests can prove his activity. The other person says that no gardener comes. In 1944 Wisdom told that parable in order to stress the ambiguity of nature, the impossibility of proving religious belief correct, and yet the

---

[1] See, e.g., his *Philosophical Faith and Revelation* (1962; Eng. trans., New York, 1967).
[2] Reprinted in his *Philosophy and Psychoanalysis* (Oxford, 1953).

obstinate endurance of faith's interpretation of the patterns in the facts. Some years later Professor Antony Flew 'developed' this parable. Here the parable has been adjusted, we might almost say twisted, in order to stress the folly of the person who believes in the activity of the gardener. Flew argues that the force of a religious assertion may be dissipated completely by the admission that the evidence is against it, although the believer continues to make the assertion; 'a fine brash hypothesis may thus be killed by inches, the death by a thousand qualifications'. In Flew's parable we can see what can happen to 'liberal' or 'natural' religion when the mind of man no longer feeds in worship on the authority of the Bible or the Church or on the revelation in the event or the experience. Here is the full intellectual impact of our secular century. For in this parable the sceptic at last turns on the believer and demands: 'Just how does what you call an invisible, intangible, eternally elusive gardener differ from an imaginary gardener or even from no gardener at all?[1]

[1] *New Essays in Philosophical Theology*, ed. A. Flew and A. MacIntyre (London, 1955), p. 96. See also Antony Flew, *God and Philosophy* (London, 1966).

CHAPTER FIVE

Light from the East?

The Challenge to Christianity

One of the most striking paradoxes in our time is that Western society is so powerful economically and culturally that its influence covers the face of the earth, yet it finds its own inherited religion so hard to believe that it is poor—many would say bankrupt—in the things of the spirit which are still held in deep respect by Africa and the East. Inevitably in this situation, many suggestions have come from East and West alike to the effect that secularisation is a just punishment on the arrogance of the Christian Churches. Christianity's best policy is, it is said, to learn humbly from other religions, so that the spiritual resources of the West may be renewed. The small numbers of missionaries from the East to the West, and of Western converts to Eastern faiths, by no means exhaust the significance of this challenge.

The modern Western interest in Eastern religion can be traced back into the nineteenth century. Sir Edwin Arnold's long poem *The Light of Asia* popularised Gautama the Buddha; and Orientalists such as the Oxford scholar, Max Müller, translated the sacred books of Hinduism and Buddhism, incidentally giving to the East the benefit of chronologically ordered scriptures. A World Parliament of Religions was held in connection with the Chicago World Fair in 1893, and the young Hindu, Swami Vivekananda, there spoke with electrifying force about India's spiritual gifts now on offer to the West. The World Congress of

Faiths has sponsored a dialogue between the religions since 1936, and during this period the centre of discussion has shifted from the intellectually disreputable 'theosophy' (founded in 1875 and dominated by collectors of religious curiosities such as Madame Blavatsky and Mrs. Besant) to a more thorough study of the historic theologies and spiritualities.

Many of these communings between West and East, like many other good things, were encouraged by the imperial connection, but the end of empire in two revolutionary decades, 1947–67, has fully released the bitterness of the East and the guilt of the West. This was symbolised by the popularity of K. M. Panikkar's book on *Asia and Western Dominance* (London, 1953) with its triumphant announcements that the Vasco da Gama epoch in Asian history had ended and that the Christian missionary effort had failed. All over Asia, and now all over Africa also, the anti-colonialist revolt has had its religious implications.

The branding of Christianity as colonialist was partly unfair to the subtle relationships between missionaries and governments; most missionaries had purely religious motives, and few governments welcomed their potentially trouble-making initiatives and criticisms.[1] Yet in practice missionary pioneering had often stimulated both Western commerce, with its tendency to exploit, and the extension of Western political rule. Missionaries had whipped up domestic interest in Asia and Africa; missionaries in difficulties had been given the protection of Western consuls and soldiers, specially in China; and missionaries in educational and medical work, or their assistants such as teacher-catechists and hospital staff, had received subsidies from colonial governments. Westerners abroad for commercial, political or military purposes had been regarded as Christians by people whose religious and social identities were still unified, and the Christian religion had been judged wherever there had been objectionable behaviour. Both

---

[1] A judicious survey was provided by Stephen Neill, *Colonialism and Christian Missions* (London, 1966).

missionaries and lay Westerners had in fact entangled Christianity with colonialism, and it was too much to hope that the separation of these ideas—although vital if the indigenous Church was to flourish in days of national independence—could proceed smoothly.

Although national independence has been secured, the legacy of colonialism in Christian history is still not exhausted. All over Asia and Africa Christianity is now seen as the white man's religion, and many in the non-Christian world link this with their fears of American and European economic and cultural imperialism. Although the white man's military interventions have grown more spasmodic, Algeria in the 1950s and Vietnam in the 1960s have remained symbols of what the white man can still do. 'Quiet' Americans have promoted 'Coca-colonisation'; and gentlemanly British and civilised Europeans, without leaving their own shores, have inflicted terrible damage on young nations by refusing to pay good prices for the raw materials which they have imported from Asia and Africa. Much of the Afro-Asian anger may be unfair to the good intentions behind interventions or aid from the United States, Britain and Europe, but it is foolish for Westerners ever to forget the fact of the continuing bitterness of many Asians and Africans (to say nothing of the bitterness of Latin Americans against North American capitalists).

This identification with colonialism or neo-colonialism has been one of the greatest obstacles to the spread of Christianity in the contemporary world. Many Latin Americans have rejected both the Catholicism which looks to the Spanish or Portuguese past and the Protestantism which looks to North America, and they have turned instead to a home-grown Spiritualism, to more intoxicating local religions or—more commonly—to secularism. In his book on *The Religions of the Oppressed*[1] Vittorio Lanternari has studied the spiritual revolt which has come where the 'natives' replied to the white man's exploitation by reviving a primitive paganism and combining it with a messianic

[1] 1960; Eng. trans., New York, 1963.

expectation derived from Christianity itself. Dr. Lanternari presents examples from Latin America and the Carribbean islands, from the South Sea islands of Melanesia and Polynesia, and from the Red Indian tribes within the United States. Similar patterns may be found in the thousands of Christian or semi-Christian 'independent' churches in Africa, united only in their dislike of missionaries[1]—or in the many new religions which have arisen in Japan since Christians dropped the atomic bombs.[2] The same revolt against the spiritual dominance of the West largely explains why Islam makes greater progress than Christianity in Africa—and why some American Negroes have become Black Muslims. The revival of Hinduism in the 1940s and 1950s was an anti-Western, anti-Christian baptism for the newly born independent nation of India. When B. R. Ambedkar led the Indian 'untouchables' into Buddhism in the 1950s, he not only restored Buddhism to its native India; because the Christian Church was still identified with power and privilege, he also ended the missionaries' hope of an imminent mass-movement into Christianity. When U Nu built his World Peace Pagoda near Rangoon in the 1950s, it did not seem to be a move likely to replace St. Peter's, Rome, as the centre of the world's religious hopes for peace; yet in the 1960s the world depended on the Buddhist tranquillity and compassion of another Burmese statesman, U Thant, Hammarskjöld's successor as Secretary-General of the United Nations. Those nations whose past has included both Christianity and colonialism have often seemed morally inferior to such Eastern peace-makers. And in many parts of Asia the continuing power of Buddhism in the life of the people is shown by the continuing participation of its monks in national politics.

So the rejection of Christianity as colonialist dominates many discussions about religion in our time. But some specifically religious criticisms of Christian arrogance have

[1] See David Barrett, *Schism and Renewal in Africa* (Nairobi and London, 1968).
[2] See Harry Thomsen, *The New Religions of Japan* (Tokyo, 1963).

been made widely in Asia and Africa—and find a ready echo in Christianity's homelands. The Eastern counter-attack, so little expected in the flood tide of the West's civilising mission, now often looks like winning. One of the current objections is that Christianity has been organised hierarchically, and its priests and preachers have dominated society with a thoroughness unknown to non-Christians. Judaism and Islam, and to a slightly lesser extent other religions such as Hinduism in its regulations for its different castes, have had elaborate codes of conduct based on religious law. It has been a very serious, and almost unheard-of, step for an individual to defy the code. Yet for all the strength of their codes and their castes, none of these religions has developed a tyranny over the individual as thorough as the Inquisition in Catholic Europe or the Puritan theocracies in Geneva or Scotland or New England. The basic reason seems to be that only Christianity has given such prominence to its clergy, separating them into a full-time profession, making their ministry of the Word and Sacraments some kind of essential mediation of the Divine grace, entrusting them with disciplinary powers and matching their work with the divisions of civil society so that in each parish the priest or preacher might be a judge, and in each diocese the bishop might be a lord. The clergy of other religions may have been honoured as being uncanny or wise or powerful, but they have seldom enjoyed such power as these envoys of the Carpenter of Nazareth.

It is, therefore, not surprising that there exists a widespread revolt in the West against the fussy, domineering officials of the Church, and a widespread sympathy with the East's alternative ideal for the religious leader: the *guru*, the holy man who is holy not because he has been appointed and paid by an institution and trained to preach that institution's doctrines, but because he has peace in his heart, the peace of his vision of eternity. And it is also no accident that the psychological and intellectual impact of our time has made specially fierce attacks on Christian doctrine.

More than any other religion, Christianity has attempted

to systematise and to enforce the use of images and ideas expressing the divine. Christianity has not been the most monolithic of the great religions; Islam has been that, but Islam has been united by its elaborate law, the *Sharia*, while its theology, for all its sophistication in medieval times, has been based on only a few ideas about the transcendence of Allah and on the one image of the Prophet and his Book. Christianity has not been the most fertile of the religions in its teachings; Hinduism has been that, followed by the Northern or *Mahayana* Buddhism, but these other religions have proliferated their mythologies in order to suit devotional needs or tastes without attempting to reconcile one myth with another (as we have noted, their very scriptures were in confusion until Western scholars set them in order). What has been unique to Christianity has been the zeal with which its hierarchy has used its powers of discipline in the attempt to impose a single, vast system of beliefs and values on all who wished to be saved. No other religion has a record of theology reducing the greatest metaphysical mysteries about God, about man and about the unique 'God-manhood' of Jesus Christ to simple-seeming sentences which could be adopted by a council or other authoritative body and made compulsory on all believers by anathematising the slightest disagreement as heresy most foul; and in no other religion has intellectual discipline been accompanied by such a strenuous effort to make worship elaborate yet also uniform. Christianity has produced a wealth of symbols, in stones or glass, statues or icons, sermons or hymns, and has often regarded one set of these symbols as essential to the portrayal of the divine. Admittedly, Christianity has been divided in its theologies and its symbolisms, yet within each tradition—Catholic, Orthodox or Protestant —there has been much the same attempt at uniformity. Admittedly, Christianity has nurtured mystics and moralists who in their different ways have discounted doctrine and organisation, yet the doctrine and the organisation have been forces which have meant religion to the common people. Since the fourth century A.D. the history of Christianity has been dominated by the combination of Roman law with Greek philosophy, improbable as such a future would have seemed in Nazareth or Jerusalem; and the discipline which conquered the Roman empire and the intellectual confidence which closed the schools of Athens have largely accounted for the power of Christianity in Europe and the world. It has been the power of a system. Too much of the history of Christianity has been a history of uniformity, achieved or attempted.

This fateful legacy from Rome and Greece may now prove to be Christianity's undoing, for almost the whole world—East and West alike—now rejects this idea of religion as uniformity. When we ask why some aspects of the life of an impoverished country such as India have appealed so deeply to many sensitive spirits in the affluent West in our time, we have to answer that the West acknowledges the wisdom of the Hindu insistence that the ultimate is 'not that, not that' (*neti, neti*). Here, too, is one secret of the popular appeal of Zen Buddhism, in its origins a military (or at least aristocratic) cult in China and Japan: Zen does not intellectualise. Professor Arnold Toynbee speaks for many of his contemporaries when, in the concluding pages of his great *Study of History* and in other books, he uses the continuing yet gentle power of Eastern religion to hammer home the truth of the anti-Christian protest of the Roman pagan, Q. Aurelius Symmachus, that 'the heart of so great a mystery cannot be reached by one road only'.[1]

God in East and West

Many of these criticisms of Christianity would be echoed by many Christians. Since Dostoevsky depicted the Grand Inquisitor in *The Brothers Karamazov*, many Christians

[1] The position of Arnold Toynbee is summarised in his Gifford Lectures on *An Historian's Approach to Religion* (London, 1956), and in his *Christianity among the Religions of the World* (London, 1957). See also his *Change and Habit* (London, 1966). For Asian reactions, see e.g., Thomas Ohm, *Asia Looks at Western Christianity* (New York, 1959).

have known who is the real enemy of Christ: the discip-
linarian who crushes human freedom in the name of Christ.
The Inquisition is now over. A new humility leading to a
new flexibility is seen to be indispensable to a new shape for
the Christian Church, and to a new statement of Christian
belief, without which Christianity seems unlikely to survive
on any large scale. But the heart of the religious debate is,
of course, *the question of God.* We must turn now to the
onslaughts which have been delivered in the name of Eastern
religion against the West's identification of religion with the
worship of one supernatural God.

This Eastern attack on the Western idea of God is not so
simple as we might wish for the purposes of exposition, since
Eastern religion is itself a very large and complex phenomenon, giving rise to a bewildering variety of beliefs and to
an equally great variety of Western reactions to those beliefs.
A religion in the East is not so much a road (a Westerner
cannot help feeling) as a traffic junction without a policeman.
Indeed, many in East and West alike have refused to agree
that Eastern religion can be summed up so as to suggest a
radical contrast between the Eastern and Western conceptions of God. Under the influence of Judaism and Christianity, the West—it is acknowledged—does mean by the
word 'God' the eternal and holy Other; but the East also—
or so it is claimed—worships the same God, although in
many different ways.

While Director of the Centre for the Study of World
Religions at Harvard, R. L. Slater sought to counteract
the prevailing sense of a deep contrast between the Eastern
and Western religious worlds. He quoted Dr. Friedrich
Heiler's address to the Ninth International Congress for the
History of Religions in Tokyo in 1958, in which that
eminent scholar saw seven principal areas of unity mani-
fested by all the higher religions: (1) the reality of the
transcendent, the holy, the divine; (2) the immanence of
this transcendent reality in human hearts; (3) the identification of this reality with 'the highest good' for man; (4) its
identification with 'ultimate love'; (5) the way of man to

God as a way of sacrifice, renunciation, resignation, prayer; (6) the way of love, uniting man to man; (7) the way of love as 'a most superior way to God'.[1]

Such a synthesis of the higher religions would clearly be relevant to the religious problems of the West, for it would represent much in the West's own vision of God, with the way of love substituted for the Inquisition. *But does such a synthesis really do justice to the religion of the East?* Here we must set aside the religion of Islam; Islam, of course, belongs to the Afro-Asian world geographically, but it belongs to the same spiritual family as the Christianity and Judaism of the West—and it has been discussed, however unsatisfactorily, earlier in this book. Hinduism and Buddhism will be sufficient varieties of Eastern religion for us to consider at this stage.

In Hinduism, *bhaki* or devotion to a personal God has been taught by a succession of philosophers, of whom the greatest was Ramanuja (in the eleventh and twelfth centuries A.D.). This religion of human love responding to the divine grace has produced many noble lives, remembered particularly in the tradition of devotional hymns. Kabir, the Punjabi hymnologist, and Nanak, the first of the Sikh *gurus*, bridged the gulf between Hindu and Muslim by the purity of their love of God. And it is not only this *bhakti* version of Hinduism that has affinities with the Western idea of God. In the descriptions of ultimate reality by many Hindu philosophers we find a tone which is near to the tone which theists adopt when they state their belief in God. In the philosophy of the ninth-century Sankara, for example, the unity or 'non-dualism' between the ultimate reality (*Brahman*) and the self (*Atman*) is stressed—yet the *Brahman* enjoys Being, Consciousness and Bliss (*Sat, Chit, Ananda*), and from it all existence, awareness and happiness derive; and the Self which is one with it is somehow a deeper, purer self than is the 'I' of everyday personal experience (the 'empirical ego' of Western philosophy). Thus the Hindu idea

[1] R. L. Slater, *World Religions and World Community* (New York, 1963), p. 38.

of the identity of the *Brahman* and the *Atman* can be presented as resembling the Western idea of the identity of God in the universe with God in the soul (in Dr. Heiler's words, 'the immanence of this transcendent reality in human hearts'). Holding such a view of Ramanuja's *bhakti* Hinduism and even of Sankara's more wide-spread 'non-dualism', many Western observers of Hinduism have been glad to welcome India's closeness to the West in a sense of 'the reality of the transcendent, the holy, the divine'. Thus it was possible for a Protestant missionary such as J. N. Farquhar to argue that Christ fulfils the highest aspirations of Hinduism.[1] C. F. Andrews, the friend of Gandhi and probably the greatest of twentieth-century missionaries in India, could declare that he saw the light of Christ in the eyes of Hindus, and the same generous assessment of Indian religion has been expressed more philosophically by a Roman Catholic theologian with a Hindu father.[2]

Buddhism, like Hinduism, can be assessed by Westerners as a religion continuous with the type of religion which has prevailed in the West. Thus Gautama the Buddha can be understood as the One who reveals ultimate reality—as a prophet, but also as more than a prophet, as the incomparable man who attaches to himself the kind of worship which Christians give to Jesus. Gautama the Buddha taught that man would be absorbed into *Nirvana*, and at first sight this revelation seems to have little to do with the claims about God made by the prophets of Israel, by Jesus and by Muhammed. But what is *Nirvana*? The *Mayahana* variety of Buddhism finds a positive glory in *Nirvana*, and the conception of *Nirvana* as a mere Nothingness is rejected passionately. The most popular sect of *Mayahana* Buddhism teaches about a 'Pure Land' which is like the Christian's heaven; and it believes that entry can be secured by faith in the name of Amitabha, a saviour or *bodhisattva* who made

---

[1] *The Crown of Hinduism* (London, 1912).
[2] See B. Chaturvedi and M. Sykes, *Charles Freer Andrews* (London, 1949), and Raymond Panikkar, *The Unknown Christ of Hinduism* (London, 1964).

a vow to liberate all sentient beings before he would himself enter the supreme bliss, and who in his infinite compassion is willing to suffer for their sakes. *Mahayana* Buddhism prays to the Eternal Buddha in deep devotion, but it believes that the Buddha-nature can be found in many people and animals, on the path to liberation. Its doctrine of the 'three bodies' of the Buddha—eternal, incarnate in a person, and generalised—sounds very like the Christian's belief in God as Father, Son and Holy Spirit. Kyan-yin, a female *bodhisattva*, has played a role in Chinese Buddhism approximately similar to the role of the Blessed Virgin Mary in Roman Catholicism. It is not surprising that some Christian thinkers have found some of the teaching of Christ foreshadowed in the teaching of Guatama, who had compassion on all who were ignorant of their eternal destiny.[1] Nor is it surprising that Professor Arnold Toynbee, for example, has often argued that *Mahayana* Buddhism should be regarded as Christianity's greatest ally in the modern world.

But there is, of course, another tradition at work in religious contacts between East and West. This is a far more controversial tradition. It declares that *Judaism, Christianity and Islam are basically incompatible with Hinduism and Buddhism, so that the religion of the East is not likely to purify the religion of the West. Instead, the spiritual triumph of the East would mean the end of the faith of the West.* This insistence on a radical difference can itself take two forms. First, it can take the form of a denunciation of the 'polytheism' (*worship of many gods*) of Asia. The average Muslim's contempt for the average Hindu's piety has had this justification. When Christians first went to the East from Europe, most of them were horrified by the 'pagans' who sacrificed to 'devils'. Sacrifices in Hindu temples can seem to visitors a very squalid and evil debasement of humanity in front of repulsive idols, into our own day, and many modern Hindus would agree with such Western critics in wishing to cleanse

[1] For two sympathetic Christians' assessments of Buddhism, see George Appleton, *On the Eightfold Path* (London, 1961), and W. L. King, *Christianity and Buddhism* (Philadelphia, 1962).

the temples, to change the caste system drastically, to abolish the untouchability of the lower castes in practice as well as in law (as the burning of widows at funerals was abolished by the British a century ago), and to reform Hinduism in other ways. Buddhism has seldom aroused this moral repulsion, but in practice it does incorporate a great deal of primitive religion or 'animism', and in our own time the Westernisation of China has involved a fierce attack on Buddhist 'superstition'.

Probably this contrast between polytheism and monotheism should not be considered the major religious issue now at stake. Every religion, when it has to cater for great numbers of people, in practice has to tolerate (however uneasily) local superstitions about the powers of local spirits. We may be reminded of this by the Roman Catholic Church's hospitality to the cults of local Virgins and saints, or by the worship at tombs or the rites to placate the spirits or *Djin* in Islam. But 'higher' religion always sees these images of God as images only—rather like the national flags to be found in the sanctuaries of liberal Protestantism. They are to be used, and perhaps to be worshipped, if that helps the popular mind, but they are not to be regarded by the thoughtful as in themselves ultimate. For higher religion, the ultimate remains the One—the 'One without a second'. If the divine exists, it must be basically unified: that seems to be demanded once men think strenuously and clearly. This is taught in the first of the Hindu Upanishads, and very few Eastern philosophers dispute the point. Polytheism is not the real issue. The real issue is this: *in the last analysis, does the divine exist in distinction from the human?*

Religion in the West has been so heavily influenced by monotheism that since the end of Caesar-worship in the Roman empire the confusion of the human and the divine has been inconceivable for almost all religious thinkers—apart from the unique case of Jesus (where, indeed, it was one purpose of the official Chalcedonian Christology to teach that the divine and human natures were *not* confused). The God of Western religion stands distinct from, and above, all nature, including human nature. Man is regarded as sinful and mortal. The God who of his own will choose to bestow the gift of life on a man may choose to bestow on that man the further gift of eternal glory; but even in eternal glory a man will always be in an important sense distinct from God, like a fish swimming in the ocean of God. Such is the legacy of the prophets of Israel, among whom the prophet from Nazareth should be reckoned; and Christianity, for all its Trinitarianism and Mariology, has remained monotheistic except in its corruptions. And ever since the wrath of the prophet Muhammed against the idols of Arabia and against the blasphemies which he saw, or thought he saw, in a corrupt Christianity, *shirk* (the association of any creature with God) has been the supreme sin in Islam. Moreover, Judaism, Christianity and Islam have shared a suspicion of mysticism (although also an ability to breed mystics)—because the distinction between the Creator and the creature can be blurred so easily when interpreting the mystical experience of unity. But the religion of the East has not been dominated by the austerity of this worship of the One God. The classical philosophy of Hinduism and Buddhism is clear about the ultimate identity of man with ultimate reality. Moreover, it is clear that man has both the duty and the capacity to see this identity through meditating about himself. Once man sees this, he is liberated from the limitations of human life and from the sufferings which come with these limitations. 'That art thou' (*tat tuam asi*)—the words with which Uddalaka taught his son Svetaketu that he was one with the true Being, the Cosmic Power, as salt was one with water in salt water—are deeply sacred words in Hinduism, and their refusal to admit any ultimate duality between the *Atman* and the *Brahman* has coloured the whole of Indian thought.[1] And these words are developed by Gautama's teaching that the one salvation lies in *Nirvana*, which is compared with the blowing out of the flame of a candle. The original teaching of Guatama

[1] See Ninian Smart, *Doctrine and Argument in Indian Philosophy* (London, 1964).

has been recovered by Western scholars over the last hundred years, and on the whole it justifies the Southern school of *Theravada* (the Doctrine of the Elders) against the *Mahayana* Buddhism of the North. Gautama did not regard himself as in any sense divine, he did not offer any help except his teaching, he did not express any belief in God or gods, and the essence of his message was the impermanence of the self. Individuality was at present held together by a temporary combination of elements in those doomed to live; but in *Nirvana* all traces of it would disappear. The *Nirvana* of Gautama certainly seems closer to the Western idea of Nothingness than it does to the Western idea of heaven. Gautama taught, as Uddalaka did, that the salt must merge with the water—that man must merge with the ultimate; but, unlike Uddalaka, Guatama refused to say anything positive about the ultimate, the salt water.

If in its main emphasis Eastern religion does deny that there is any reality higher than man, then it cannot complain if many Westerners regard it as incompatible with the worship of God. Among the most recent and best informed Western students of Hinduism and Buddhism, we therefore find a tendency to say that the East's basic theme is not the 'prophetic' insistence on the otherness of the transcendent, the holy, the divine, but is the 'mystical' identification of the human heart with the ultimate reality in the universe. The contrast between 'prophetic' and 'mystic' forms of prayer has been emphasised,[1] and the Swedish scholar, Archbishop Nathan Söderblom, made this the theme of his Gifford Lectures on the 'basal' forms of personal religion in West and East.[2]

This strong contrast between the 'prophetic' and the 'mystical' was put with tremendous emphasis and prolonged effect by Dr. Hendrik Kraemer in his *The Christian Message in a Non-Christian World* (London, 1938). Kraemer wrote that book for the Tambaram Conference of the Inter-

[1] Especially in Friedrich Heiler, *Prayer* (1918; Eng. trans., New York, 1932).
[2] *The Living God* (London, 1933).

national Missionary Council, and in it he stressed that the Christian message was the proclamation of the Word of God in the Bible—a message for which there was little or no preparation in non-Christian religions. The realisation of the identity of man with the ultimate reality of the universe was the goal of religion in Asia, this Dutch scholar declared; *but precisely this was the supreme blasphemy to Christians, for it put man in God's place.* Here was the application of Karl Barth's theological revolution to the world-wide missionary strategy of the Christian Church; and Dr. Kraemer always insisted on its truth—although he lived to modify some details of his polemical presentation of 1938, and to witness an ever-growing resistance to this clear division between the Christian and the non-Christian.[1] Our own analysis would suggest that Kraemer, by a process not unknown elsewhere in the history of thought, was correct in what he affirmed and mistaken in what he denied. He was correct to describe Christianity as unique; he was also correct to say that a religion usually works, and usually deserves to be judged, as a whole; but he was mistaken in his denial of a substantial continuity between many elements in Christianity and many elements in other religions. This unwillingness led him to adopt an unsympathetic attitude to every non-Christian religion as a whole. The kind of 'no' which Christians have rightly given to degrading superstitions in Western or Eastern paganism—for example, Nazism—was wrongly extended by Kraemer and his circle to include elements in the religions of the East which Christians ought to welcome and revere.

A more balanced presentation of the continuity and discontinuity is found in the writings of the Oxford scholar, R. C. Zaehner. While deeply versed in the scriptures of the Eastern religions, and while sympathetically aware of the similarities between some of their teachings and mono-

---

[1] His later writings afforded impressive evidence of the width and continuing liveliness of his mind. See his *Religion and the Christian Faith* (London, 1956), and *World Cultures and World Religions: The Coming Dialogue* (London, 1960).

theism, Professor Zaehner does not hesitate to stress the radical contrast between their 'wisdom', exalting man, and the monotheistic 'prophecy' about God, the prophecy which has become the religious heritage of the West.[1]

Western scholars may be thought prejudiced in such an assessment of the significance of Eastern religion. But we should note that the rejection of a transcendent God is a common theme in the missionary literature of Hinduism, for example in the California-based 'Vedanta for the West' movement of Aldous Huxley, Christopher Isherwood, Alan Watts, etc.[2] In the earlier writings of Alan Watts, the 'supreme identity' among the world's mystics turned out to be the Supreme Identity between the Self and Ultimate Reality, but more recently Mr. Watts has recognised an obstinate incompatibility between Christian (and other) faith in God and this Supreme Identity which he wishes to commend. 'If the Christian view of the world is true,' he now says, 'the Hindu cannot be true. On the other hand, if the Hindu view is true, the Christian can also be true—in the sense that the situation of seeming to be a soul other than God and in peril of damnation could be one of the most extreme and adventurous roles of the Self.'[3] An even more clearly non-theistic philosophy (rather than the *Mahayana* religion of salvation) has been stressed by D. T. Suzuki and by many other Buddhist evangelists in the West.[4]

Since Eastern religion is so vast and so ambiguous, it is impossible to prophesy accurately what will be its future development. Hinduism and Buddhism could develop internally in the direction of a stronger, simpler and purer belief in 'the reality of the transcendent, the holy, the divine'. In that case, a religious alliance based on Dr. Heiler's seven areas of unity might well become the dominating factor in

[1] See the *Concise Encyclopaedia of Living Faiths*, which he edited with an Introduction and Conclusion (London, 1959).

[2] See *Vedanta for the Western World*, ed. C. Isherwood (New York, 1948).

[3] *Beyond Theology* (New York, 1964), p. 205. Compare his earlier book, *Supreme Identity* (New York, 1950).

[4] Examples of the teaching given to British inquirers may be found in Christmas Humphreys, *Zen Comes West* (London, 1960).

the religious situation of the world; and many worshippers of God, in East and West, now long to see that day. On the other hand, Hinduism and Buddhism could develop in such a way that the secular humanists of the West would greet the emergence of a common consensus *on the basis of atheism*; and already in some Western reactions to the spirituality of the East there are some signs showing how a universal atheism might look. When meditation is recommended by Eastern religious philosophy as the way of attaining such knowledge, Western man may be willing to hear the call from the many distractions of getting and spending to the contemplation of a deeper level of existence through the love of nature, through art, through music and through silence. When Eastern mysticism discards all images, Western man may feel vindicated in his sense that the symbols of religion have failed. And—here comes the crunch—when the 'non-dualist' Hindu says that the *Atman* is the *Brahman* (Uddalaka's salt water), Western man may be willing to translate it into his own language as 'Glory to man in the highest'. When Gautama teaches about *Nirvana*, Western man may be willing to see here the brave and glad acceptance of the loftiest destiny which is compatible with the truth that everyone must die, never to rise again.[1]

How will the choice be made between these two possible impacts of Eastern religion on the West, for or against belief in God? Here we must revert to a point previously made in this book. In religion, a choice for belief or unbelief is not likely to be primarily a result of a coldly rational examination of all relevant arguments; in religion, a choice is much more likely to reflect a whole person's involvement in a whole situation in a whole society. Social and psychological factors will powerfully influence the West's future attitude to the spirituality of the East. An equally important, and connected, point is that while the West changes the East will

[1] The idea of the meeting of Eastern and Western religions in repudiation of the supernatural has attracted a number of recent writers. Its fullest statement was perhaps F. S. C. Northrop, *The Meeting of East and West* (New York, 1946).

not remain a static society. Eastern religion should not be assessed primarily as an affair recorded in libraries. It is a living reality—and to live is to change.

Western thought presses remorselessly on Eastern religion as on every other area of Eastern life, through the East's need to import science and technology. Even if the East never develops as an industrial society comparable with the nineteenth- and twentieth-century West, its style of life and thought must change profoundly. Even if the political and cultural influence of the West in Asia decreases, the multiplying population of Asia will make the avoidance of famine the central concern of Asian politics. The East will demand, and will be ready to pay any price for, efficiency in the government and progress in the economy. This crisis, already grave enough, seems likely to deepen, and with it will grow the prospects of a social revolution on something like the Chinese pattern, seeking to modernise every corner of the national life. Eastern religion has too often been considered in isolation from this social context. We cannot be sure what will be the fate of religion in the Asia of the future, but the examples of China and Japan offer grim warnings to those who foretell the wider and wider adoption of the kind of synthesis for which Dr. Heiler spoke in Tokyo.

China, Tibet and Japan, traditionally the heartlands of the *Mahayana* Buddhism, have been modernised in a systematic attempt to bring them into the same category as post-Christian Europe; and so far Buddhism does not seem to have displayed anything like the resilience under attack to be found in European Christianity. In China (and perhaps in Tibet also) the millions have found enlightenment—or have obediently echoed slogans proclaiming that they have —in dialectical materialism, not in the Buddhist renunciation of all desire. In post-war Japan, Buddhism has indeed survived, but amid the astonishing economic boom it has not been nearly so active as the 'new religions' which are concerned more about progress in this life than about ultimate reality.

Secularisation may come even in India. It is ominous for

the future that Gandhi, who embodied so much of theistic Hinduism that the masses believed him to be an *avatar* or incarnation of God, consistently opposed industrialisation and many other aspects of the modernisation of India— and that his successor Nehru felt compelled to reject Gandhi's religion as well as his social conservatism. It may be that M. N. Roy, the atheist who used to argue that Nehru's compromises with Hinduism, although limited, were a tragic betrayal of the social revolution, will be proved right in the march of history. Devotional Hinduism has a very deep appeal for the Indian soul at present, but the drama of the evolution of Indian society is by no means concluded.[1] The twenty-first century may see India a secular state in social reality as well as in constitutional law, thus giving a new force to something which Dr. Radhakrishnan wrote in 1927: 'Hinduism is more a way of life than a form of thought. While it gives absolute liberty in the world of thought it enjoins a strict code of practice. The theist and the atheist, the sceptic and the agnostic may all be Hindus if they accept the Hindu culture and life. Hinduism insists not on religious conformity, but on a spiritual and ethical outlook on life.'[2] The examples of India's neighbours, Ceylon and Burma, are relevant. The struggle against British colonialism was accompanied by a high enthusiasm for 'Buddhist Socialism'—the attempt to build a social order on the specifically Buddhist alternative to selfishness, an attempt greatly helped by the charismatic appeal of U Nu to the peasants. But the early enthusiasm in independent Ceylon and Burma has not lasted, any more than the early idea of an Islamic Republic lasted in Pakistan. All over Asia the coming pattern may be shaped by regimes which pay little more than lip service to a supernatural religion.[3]

[1] For a Christian assessment, see William Stewart, *India's Religious Frontier* (London, 1964).
[2] *The Hindu View of Life* (London, 1927), p. 77.
[3] An experiment of 'Buddhist Socialism' was studied by Donald E. Smith in *Religion and Politics in Burma* (Princeton, 1965). A sensitive English visitor to Burma, Dr. Trevor Ling, recorded his impressions in

Some religion there is sure to be in the East of the near future, for the masses cannot be expected to accept a quick and complete abandonment of the religious traditions which have given them some sense of identity and purpose through thousands of years. Even in China the anti-religious bias of the Communist regime may have to be modified before the regime achieves stability, and of all Eastern countries China has for many centuries been regarded as the least other-worldly. In pluralist societies elsewhere in Asia, many of the familiar rituals and myths may be continued to form the religion of the people. After all, few nationalist leaders have yet had the courage to break with the religious past, for they know too well how the masses still feel. But beneath the continuity of ritual and myth in popular religion, the doctrinal content of the East's future religion may well be based on the ultimacy of man rather than on belief in the supernatural.

If this is likely to be the future of Eastern religion, then its message for the West must become more problematic than Hindu or Buddhist evangelists now like to admit. *For if the ultimacy of man is to be the final conclusion of religion in a secular society, why should the West learn this from the East?* The West's home-grown atheism, post-Jewish, post-Christian or post-Islamic, seems to be a tradition which is vigorous enough to need no strengthening from the secularisation of the Hindu *Brahman* or the Buddhist *Nirvana*; and there are advantages to be preserved by the West in keeping to its own tradition, as we shall now see.

Religion and the Dynamism of the West

The real objection to the West's adoption of the Eastern world-view lies in the static character of the East which gave rise to that world-view. The West is dynamic, and for it to adopt a static philosophy would be for it to turn its back on

Buddha, Marx and God (London, 1966). See also W. H. Wriggens, *Ceylon: Dilemmas of a New Nation* (Princeton, 1960).

all that has made modern Western society. For all the errors of the West, its dynamic energy has thrust towards the transformation of the world; and despite the defeat of colonialism, the nineteenth and twentieth centuries have been the period when this thrust has awakened the East. And Western religion has been a key factor in this energy. The very faults of the Western churches bear witness to this. The churches are rightly criticised as being too talkative, too highly organised, too authoritarian, not meditative or mystical enough. Yet religion as 'the flight of the alone to the Alone'—the kind of religion which was desired by the Buddha, by Sankara and by many other great teachers of India—has, as a matter of history, often left history behind, condemning it as unimportant. 'Neither Hinduism nor Buddhism, in its classical formulation,' writes R. C. Zaehner, 'pays the slightest attention to what goes on in this world.'[1] We need not ignore the great charitable and cultural achievements which are a glory of Eastern religion to reach the conclusion that Eastern religion, when regarded as essentially an escape from the miseries of this earth, has been more harmful to man's progress on earth than all the dogmatism of Western religion. The Christian Church's aggressive entanglement with colonialism, and its arrogant dismissal of the 'heathen' East, are scandals; yet the Church has at least been vigorous. By the cohesiveness of its theological and liturgical life, and by its network of officials and congregations, the Church has developed and safeguarded a remarkable energy, whatever vices it may have displayed in the process. This vigorous energy has made Christianity the first world-wide religion in history. In the world today, although in many nations the Church is a small minority, in some its representation is minimal and in some (e.g. Tibet) no Christian congregation is known to exist, members of every race are to be found among the Christians.

There must, it seems, be far-reaching consequences for the spiritual future of mankind in the historical fact that the scientific revolution which has created modern civilisation,

[1] *The Convergent Spirit* (London, 1963), p. 36.

Western and Eastern, occurred in the West, not in the East; in the society whose Chosen People was Israel, not in the far larger society whose Chosen People was India. We need scarcely emphasise the obvious point that this fact of history does not by itself prove that the traditional religion of the West is destined to overthrow the traditional religion of the East. The traditional religion of the West may be overthrown and replaced within the West. What is suggested by history is only this: that the dynamic character of Western religion is likely to be preserved in whatever may come in the West, and is likely to influence the East in coming centuries. The more static religion of the East—despite its many merits and despite its great contemporary appeal in East and West—is unlikely to have such a strong future as the scientific revolution takes its course.

Much turns on the question: *why did Christendom give birth to modern science?* Both India and China were civilised while Europe was barbaric, and China in particular has a magnificent record of scientific inventions. But it was Europe that was the birthplace of the scientific revolution, and Europe at that time was a continent saturated by centuries of Christian teaching. Recent studies may perhaps now be summarised so as to suggest an honest (although very sketchy) account of the rise of Western science in relation to its religious background.[1]

Too much should not be claimed by religious believers. The explosion of science in the West seems to have resulted from a complicated combination of factors including a fusion of its religious tradition with a rationalism derived from the philosophy of pagan Greece. Just as rationalism by itself was not enough, as we are reminded by the failure of Ancient Greece to exploit the experimental method, so religion by itself was not enough to produce a scientific civilisation, as we are reminded by the technological

---

[1] See Herbert Butterfield, *The Origins of Modern Science 1300–1800* (London, 1949); E. A. Burtt, *The Metaphysical Foundations of Modern Physical Science* (London, 1951); C. F. von Weizsäcker, *The Relevance of Science* (London, 1964).

incompetence of the men of the Old Testament. And if religion did encourage science, Christianity did not have a monopoly here. Jews have played a large role in the advancement of knowledge and in the application of science to life, while Islamic culture by reviving the mathematical and philosophical legacy of the Greeks gave birth to its own brilliant period of intellectual life and was the teacher of medieval Christendom. The religious tradition of Europe was, of course, dominated by the figure of Jesus, the prophet of God's love for the world, the poet who saw reflections of that divine love in the processes of nature and in the lives of men; yet Jesus and the early Christians were consumed by their love of God more than by their love of the world, and their vision was of God speedily bringing in his Kingdom to replace the present age of the world. This might be interpreted (as by Rudolf Bultmann) as a warning against the subjection of the authentically human by the merely material—or it might lead to a withdrawal into otherworldliness. Thus Max Weber, as if warning us in advance against much shallow talk about the secular Jesus, summed up his impression as a sociologist studying the origins of the Christian religion: 'Jesus held in general that what is most decisive for salvation is an absolute indifference to the world and its concerns.'[1] It is evident that the contribution we are looking for was not absolutely unique to Christianity, and took some time to make itself clear in that religion.

A. N. Whitehead believed that the modern scientific spirit had its origin in the medieval Christian insistence on the *orderliness* of the Creator. The vision of God in St. Thomas Aquinas, 'conceived as with the personal energy of Jehovah and with the rationality of a Greek philosopher', was contrasted by Whitehead with the Asian conceptions of a God who was 'either too arbitrary or too impersonal'.[2] Another English philosopher, Michael Foster, put the emphasis on the freedom of the Creator in the thought of the Middle Ages (as compared with, for example, Plato). God with his energy

[1] *Sociology of Religion* (1922; Eng. trans., Boston, 1963), p. 273.
[2] *Science and the Modern World* (Cambridge, 1926), p. 14.

and rationality was free to create this, that or the next universe *ex nihilo* ('out of nothing'); only a close observation of 'the wisdom of God in creation' could tell what had been his choice. The book of nature, as well as the book of Scripture, must be studied reverently. But perhaps these philosophers did not sufficiently bring out the historical complexity of this unique phenomenon, the rise of science in Christendom. In the Middle Ages there were men who in various ways anticipated the seventeenth century's enthusiasm for scientific experiments, but the prevailing tendency was one of reliance on the authorities of the ancient world, specially Aristotle. Indeed, an extremely important characteristic of the rise of modern science was its willingness and ability to ignore, and if need be to defy, the pronouncements on scientific matters of the official custodians of the philosophical traditions, so that the names of Galileo and Darwin must stand for ever so reminders of the warfare of science with theology, of experiment with dogma, of progress with reaction.

We must observe also that the personal religion of scientists and of philosophers of science has sometimes encouraged them to adopt attitudes which subsequent researchers and thinkers have had to abandon in the name of truth. An example may be found in that brilliant company of Christians who led the scientific revolution in seventeenth-century Europe—men whose faith went deep, although often it did not coincide with that of the ecclesiastical leadership. Names such as those of Galileo himself, Copernicus, Kepler, Pascal, Descartes, Boyle, Locke and Newton are rightly held in honour wherever science is honoured, and many (if not all) of them were devout believers, but running through much of their thought was the philosophy of 'mechanism'. This had two essential themes. First, nature was like a machine. God was needed to construct the machine, to start it working and to correct its mistakes, but otherwise he did not come into the picture. Second, the mind of man was like a ghost in this machine. It was essentially different from the matter which constituted the bulk of the universe, partly because it was by his mind that man could know the God of nature. Both these ideas in the philosophy of 'mechanism' were remnants of the Christian philosophy of the Middle Ages, and they remind us of how the pioneers of the modern scientific movement were also partly dogmatists, sleep-walking into their new world. Such ideas have had to be abandoned, as scientists and philosophers have pressed on to examine all nature as a continuous whole without reference to a Creator and without any complete discontinuity between the inorganic and the organic, between matter and mind.[1]

We must, therefore, express the Christian contribution to the rise of modern science in a quite complicated and guarded way. But after recognising the complications, we may reasonably attribute to the Christian Bible, which was recovered for the Protestant laity in the sixteenth century, two ideas which have been crucially significant for the scientific civilisation, as this civilisation has spread from the seventeenth-century West to dominate the twentieth-century world. We may fairly interpret the two key ideas of 'mechanism', which we have just outlined and rejected, as debased versions of the two ideas now to be expounded; and we may fairly claim that when the influence of these ideas on the modern West is contrasted with the religious philosophy most characteristic of the East, the scientific civilisation is seen to be post-biblical rather than anti-biblical.

Nature and History

The first of these ideas concerns *nature*. For the Bible, nature from beginning to end is the creation of God. Its existence derives from his will. This means that nature itself is not divine, nor does it contain gods. Nature is a mere creation, and therefore men can investigate nature without fear, even without an inhibiting reverence. Men have been created superior to the rest of nature; in them, rather than in stars or mountains or waters or groves or cows, is the 'image of God'. Men have been given the dominion over

[1] See, e.g., L. Charles Birch, *Nature and God* (London, 1965).

nature; in the *Genesis* myth, Adam names the animals and cultivates the earth with a power which is not taken away from him after his sin. On the other hand, nature, while not divine, is sacred, because the God who created it made it 'very good', in the words of *Genesis*. God has given to his whole creation much of the beauty and order which belong in their perfect purity to his own nature and which can be seen specially in God's noblest work, man. Despite some appearances to the contrary, the God of Western monotheism is fundamentally reasonable and responsible, and the goodness of his creation is demonstrated by the fact that normally he rules according to his law in nature, not by extraordinary miracles. Everything he did, God did on purpose; and with the help which comes from his inspiration, men may detect this purpose by using their minds on his work. Scientists humbly studying the handiwork of God therefore find themselves 'thinking God's thoughts after him'. Wherever they look in nature, through the telescope or down the microscope, they can expect to find an order existing or emerging; an order which ultimately they will understand. This is the presupposition of modern science, but it arises before science, in religion.

The second religious idea behind the rise of Western science concerns *history*. Here again there has been an extensive recent discussion.[1] To Western monotheism, history from beginning to end is under the control of God, for the divine will which initiated and sustains the whole of creation is being worked out with a special energy through the doings of men. Every event can therefore be traced to the will of God, or at least no event occurs without the permission of God. This belief can inhibit the scientific method, when events are ascribed to God and the study of secondary causes is dismissed as trivial. The Hebrew scriptures, Christian medieval chronicles and the history of Islam are full of examples of this. But the belief in God's control over history is in the long run of crucial significance for modern

[1] See Alan Richardson, *History, Sacred and Profane* (London, 1964), for a discussion and a comprehensive bibliography.

intellectual activity because it leads to the belief that events hold an important meaning which should be extracted from them. They are not in the last analysis either accidental or illusory. Within the general revelation of God's purpose in history, a special revelation is received through particular events. Reading the 'signs of the times', and discerning in current events urgent proclamations of God's will, has been the most prominent activity of religious prophets, from Moses (or earlier) to the present day. Key events have been linked together by the prophetic tradition as conveying a disclosure of God sufficient to arouse a saving faith in men; here in these sacred events is the history of our salvation, for here in a unique sense the Creator has acted. All history should be interpreted in the light which shines through these events, and what we see here, announced and effectively inaugurated, is the purpose of God to establish his kingdom on earth as in heaven, ultimately bringing all events entirely under his sovereignty. The whole of history is thus progressive, for the clue to all history is the coming of the Kingdom of God in history, to embrace all history. Even Albert Schweitzer, who emphasised (and exaggerated) the supernatural, apocalyptic elements in Jesus's understanding of the Kingdom of God, had to admit that Jesus's denunciation of life as it is before the Kingdom comes does *not* lead to a withdrawal from the world. 'It is characteristic of the unique type of the world and life negation of Jesus,' he wrote, 'that his ethics are not confined within the bounds of that conception. He does not preach the inactive ethic of perfecting the self alone, but active, enthusiastic love of one's neighbour. It is because his ethic contains the principle of activity that it has affinity with world and life affirmation.'[1] Great cultural consequences have flowed from the significance attached by Jews to the Exodus of Israel from Egypt, or by Muslims to the conquest of Medina and Mecca; but the most important result of the historical nature of Western monotheism has naturally been connected with Christianity,

[1] Albert Schweitzer, *Indian Thought and its Development* (London, 1936), p. 4.

which is the faith most deeply involved in particular events. The dating of years from the birth of Christ was the beginning of modern chronology, and modern historical scholarship as it flowered in nineteenth-century Germany had its roots in critical methods first used in biblical studies.

Such ideas have influenced far more than the intellectual life of the West. Since Max Weber's *Protestant Ethic and the Spirit of Capitalism*[1] drew the attention of historians and sociologists to the role which religion had played in the rise of the modern Western economy, there has been a prolonged debate which has modified Weber's argument in details. But the main contention stands: Christianity, which already in medieval Europe had consecrated the growing prosperity of the towns (through guilds, etc.), has since the sixteenth century placed an increasing emphasis on the duty of the individual to improve himself and the world in this life, on and thrift.[2] This amounts to modernisation. One of the best informed recent discussions of *Religion and Progress in Modern Asia* points out that 'today's Asia shares with the age of the Protestant Reformation the problems of the first emergence of historic society and historic religion into the modern world', and that, mainly for this reason, 'Christianity, through missionaries and local convents, has had an influence on cultural modernisation in Asia out of all proportion to the small number of people involved . . . Although there is great variability from country to country, Christianity and Christian institutions, especially schools, have been important catalysts for change.'[3]

The same scholar faces the challenge to the religions of the East. 'Let us consider . . . what a religion of historic type must do if it is to contribute maximally to modernization. It must be able to rephrase its religious symbol system to give meaning to cultural creativity in worldly pursuits. It must

[1] 1920; Eng. trans., London, 1930. See R. H. Tawney, *Religion and the Rise of Capitalism* (London, 1936).
[2] See Robert Theobald in *Economic Growth in World Perspective*, ed. Denys Munby (New York, 1966), pp. 155–72.
[3] Robert N. Bellah in the symposium which he edited on *Religion and Progress in Modern Asia* (New York, 1965), pp. 198, 203.

be able to channel motivation disciplined through religious obligation into worldly occupations. It must contribute to the development of a solidary and integrated national community, which it seeks neither to dominate nor to divide . . . It must give positive meaning to the long-term process of social development . . . It must be able to accept its own role as a private voluntary association and recognise that this role is not incompatible with its role as bearer of the society's ultimate values.'[1] We saw in Chapter 2 that no historic religion has yet completely transformed itself in this way (Filipino Catholicism, the deepest rooted large Christian community in Asia, is scarcely modern on this showing); and we must emphasise that it is not impossible for any religion to undergo 'modernisation'. But it has in fact been Christianity that has come nearest to playing such a role, and some of the most constructive comment on the role of religion in contemporary Asia has come out of the East Asia Christian Conference and the Institutes on Religion and Society which are linked with it.

We must add that in Christianity lie many of the origins of the modern democratic idea, for all the influence of the secularising French Revolution. Ancient Israel was plainly not a modern democracy, for its God, Yahweh, ruled through judges or prophets or kings; essentially, it was a theocracy. Yet Israel was closer to equality than was Ancient Athens, for while the religion of Israel was a religion extolling brotherhood under Yahweh the civilisation of Greece rested on a mass of slavery. The early Church had no clear theory about society, and the medieval Church reflected the inequalities of feudal society (to the extent that bishops and monasteries owned serfs), but even then Christians taught that a person's relations with the personal God were the most important thing in life, and that Christ had died for all; and the thrust towards human equality which marked the seventeenth century did receive a powerful impetus from Protestant Christianity. For all its endorsement of the medieval picture of an ordered, hierarchical society, main-

[1] p. 202.

stream Protestantism, through the active life of its local congregations, trained countless numbers of the lower middle classes in the democratic arts of free speech and corporate decision making, and so equipped them to rise in society. About the elect in these congregations, if not yet about the broad mass of humanity, Protestantism declared: their consciences are inviolable, for God speaks to their consciences in secrecy and silence, and their souls are invaluable, for God sent his Son to die for them. A sense of the sacredness of the individual was thus one of the great contributions of Protestantism to the world, and it appealed to biblical authority. In the nineteenth and twentieth centuries Protestantism, a more democratic Catholicism, and a non-theological Protestant ethic have all been forces making for the social progress of the masses; and all these forces—while owing much to economic and political factors—have appealed to the Christian Bible as a manifesto of man's dignity and fundamental equality. Through the missionary movement, and through the wider dissemination of Christian and post-Christian values in the whole impact of the West on other societies, these values have contributed greatly to the recent awakening of Asia and Africa. The charitable works of the missionaries, serving those whom the other societies despised and rejected, have conveyed, more effectively than many words, what it is that Christianity believes about every individual. The Hindu imitation of these acts of charity is perhaps the highest tribute which the East has ever paid to the West. But the whole modern rise of democracy is indebted to European Christianity's estimate of the individual.

These ideas about nature and history, and about the dignity of man at work and in politics, can be paralleled roughly in parts of Eastern religion. But they are not so basically characteristic there as they are in Western monotheism; and they have not been so widely influential in society. On the contrary, the basic attitude to nature in the East has been one of awe, whether this be the fear which the villager has for the spirits dwelling in local objects, or the desire of the philosopher to devote his whole being to the contemplation of nature so as to be absorbed into harmony with it. In the East men have not *used* nature as they have in the West, for while desiring to escape from many of its manifestations they have given to its essence the worship which is reserved in the West for God alone. This seems to be the fundamental reason why the many inventions which came earlier in China or India than in Europe did not lead to the thorough application of technology as the means of taming nature. One of the most curious facts in cultural history is that the law of *karma*, stressing that rewards or punishments inevitably follow thoughts and actions, did not lead to a development of an understanding of scientific causality (despite the efforts of some recent Hindu and Buddhist apologies to claim this), whereas in history the Jewish-Christian view of nature, shot through as it was with the miraculous, did produce the ideas of natural law and natural science. The explanation seems to be that the Jewish-Christian view interpreted the occasional miracle as the revelation of the permanently true nature of things— and was convinced that the true nature of things included the mastery of man over nature, symbolised in the Israelites' miraculous crossing of the Red Sea and in Christ's miraculous resurrection from the dead.

If the East has not used nature as nature has been used in the West, neither has the East valued history as history has been valued in the West. At its centre, Eastern religious philosophy concerns not the interpretation of history nor its transformation, but its abolition in timelessness. Mythologically, history may be described as *lila*, the play of the gods; more philosophically, as *maya* or cloudiness. History consists of one life after another, one cycle of events after another, and does not move towards a goal. The *Bhagavad Gita* has in India become 'the scripture of the new age, the main foundation on which its ethic, its social doctrines and even its political action depend. Its message is carried daily to the common man in a thousand new popular versions'. So K. M. Panikkar points out, explaining that the basic contribution to the 'Hindu Reformation' of two of India's greatest spiritual teachers, Bal Gangadhar and Tilakard Sri Aurobindo, was to exalt the ideal of the person of equable mind, without selfish desire, working for the welfare of the world. To this noble ideal Gandhi added the doctrine of *ahimsa* or non-violence.[1] We can well understand how the beautiful *Bhagavad Gita* has come to be soo deeply loved, and why so many have been inspired by it towards an activism suited to India's present needs but calmly spiritual and truly civilised. Yet we cannot help asking whether this will be the final scripture of India's new age. For when we read the *Bhagavad Gita* without a modern commentary, what do we find is its story? The divine Krishna, incarnate in a charioteer, tells the prince Arjuna to take part in a civil war, for that is his destiny as a warrior—and it does not really matter who will die in the battle, for all will be reborn anyway. Another relevant point is that although the incarnation of Krishna in the *Bhagavad Gita* is a beautiful story, like so much else in Eastern religion this revelation of the insignificance of human life is expressed with a revealing absence of reference to real history. It does not matter to Indian spirituality whether or not an actual charioteer ever spoke to an actual prince before an actual battle.

All interpretations of existence use some mythical language, but whereas the mythological elements in Western monotheism have grown around the historical events (for example, the crucifixion of Jesus), which are believed to hold the key to the riddle of life, in Hinduism and Buddhism mythologies flourish without any anchorage in events. Incarnations of the divine such as the Hindu *avatar*, or perfections of human nature such as the Buddhist *bodhisattva*, arouse the devotion of the masses but not the assent of historians. Legends have clustered around the story of Jesus—but if the quest of the historical Jesus is difficult, the quest of the historical Rama, Krishna or Amitabha is impossible. It is no accident that vast tracts of

[1] K. M. Panikkar, *The Foundations of New India* (London, 1963), pp. 36–46.

Eastern history are, in comparison with the care of Western chronology, dateless. Oscar Cullmann has written of the 'linear time' of Christians, in contrast with the 'eternal recurrence' in the East's 'cyclical' time. In other words, all time in the Christian West had a centre in Christ and moved towards an end, the victory of Christ, but time in the East had no general meaning, the only pattern being one made by events repeating each other.[1] The widespread beliefs of the West that history had been short, and that the future would be shorter still, did handicap acceptance of the nineteenth-century discoveries of the immense vistas of evolutionary time, and it is interesting that Hinduism and Buddhism presented no obstacles to the scientific world-view on that score; but if we ask whether the Western or the Eastern vision of time is more harmonious with the scientific world-view, only one answer is possible. As Dr. Joseph Needham points out, in the West 'the Enlightenment secularised Judaeo-Christian time in the interests of the belief in progress which is still with us, so that although today when "humanists" or Marxists dispute with theologians they wear coats of different colours, the coats (to an Indian spectator, at least) are actually the same coats, worn inside out'.[2]

Of course the attitude towards nature and history which we have just attributed to Eastern religion is very far from the whole truth about the many thousands of millions of human beings who have lived in the vast area thus vaguely described. In particular, the high culture of the great Chinese Empire was closer than India was to the West (as Dr. Joseph Needham has shown). Taoism did lead to an intense interest in nature, and Confucianism revered the history of the family and the State. In Buddhism itself, there has been some glorious art to tell the Buddha's story, and culture has arisen on the basis of Buddhist compassion for the transitory life of men and animals, as in the empire of Asoka in India. In

---

[1] See Oscar Cullmann, *Christ and Time* (1946; Eng. trans., Philadelphia, 1951).

[2] *Time and Eastern Man* (London, 1964), p. 50.

Hinduism there has been much healthy emphasis on the duties of the lover and the householder before the stage of life comes when one should wander off in poverty to seek peace of soul; and the erotic sculptures which adorn some Hindu temples exceed Western railway station bookstalls in their delighted portrayals of the lusts of the human animal. But we need not indulge in Christian propaganda about the 'escapism' of Eastern religion, or in the ignorance of Western contempt for the 'timeless Orient', if we repeat that, taking the society concerned as a whole over a long period, there has been a basic difference between the destinies of East and West. In its broad outline, the contrast in their histories, as these histories have been inherited by our own time, is clear. China, for all its past glories, was so backward when the twentieth century began that heroic surgery was needed if the disease was not to be fatal, and the surgery has eventually taken the form of a wholesale rejection of the ancient culture. Although India has not yet been desperate enough to seek Westernisation at that price, many modern Indians experience a growing alienation from their traditions, which now become to them outmoded superstitions.[1] The same tension—apparently inescapable once modernity has been experienced—may be seen in the literature of Western disillusionment with Indian spirituality. Rejecting both the religion and the materialism of their own civilisation, sensitive Westerners have been attracted by books about the wisdom of India, and have found themselves against their own wishes disgusted by the sights which they have found at the end of their pilgrimage.[2] Such literature could be paralleled by many Asian (and African) records of disillusionment with the 'Christian' West, but other literature by Indians themselves drive home the contrast between East and West.

These Indians warn the West about the consequences of

[1] See, e.g., Agehanda Bharati, 'Hinduism and Modernisation', in *Religion and Change in Contemporary Asia*, pp. 67–104.
[2] See, e.g., Arthur Koestler, *The Lotus and the Robot* (London, 1960).

a doctrine of God. At first sight the West would be inclined to shrug off such talk as metaphysical and meaningless. Some reflection might persuade the West to welcome the warning, because as we have seen the intolerant dogmatism of the West's religious past is now a source of shame. But if the West goes deeper still into the warning from India, it will see that what is at stake is nothing less than the question whether personality is a mere 'appearance'. The scientists of the West have increasingly revealed to the wonder of men a universe infinitely more mysterious than 'common sense' sees, and superficially the latest Western physics resembles the East's ancient doctrine that 'all our differentiations merge into a unified cosmic Oneness',[1] but the main appeal of science to the West has been its differentiation of personality from nature and its subjection of nature to personality. And the theologians of the West have always known that the personal must be transcended in the eternal if 'the eternal' is real, but they have almost always believed that personal power and personal love, the keys to the improvement of man's earthly circumstances, are also the best categories by means of which man may begin to understand and obey the ultimate reality.

India's warning against the personal was put clearly in a recent book by the head of the Vedanta Society of Southern California. 'Devotion to the *Ishwara*, the personal God, may lead a man very far along the path of spirituality; it may even make him into a saint. But by itself it does not give the ultimate knowledge. To be completely enlightened is to go beyond the *Ishwara*, to know the impersonal Reality behind the personal divine Appearance. We become *Brahman*, since *Brahman* is present in us always. But we can never become *Ishwara*, because *Ishwara* is above and distinct from our human personalities. It follows, therefore, that we can never become rulers of the universe. To rule it is *Ishwara*'s function, and the desire to rule it is the ultimate

[1] As is argued in, e.g., Ruth Reyna, *The Concept of Maya* (London, 1962).

madness of the ego.'[1] Yet to rule the world has become the desire of man 'come of age' in the West, and he learned this desire when he believed that his Father was the personal God.

Religion and Suffering

Sarvapelli Radhakrishnan, the philosopher who became President of India, has painted a noble and deeply attractive picture of India's religious tradition. 'This figure of Siva, the great Yogi,' Dr. Radhakrishnan wrote in a typical passage, 'has been here for five or six millennia dominating the spiritual landscape of India, indicating that perfection can be achieved only through self-conquest, through courage and austerity, through unity and brotherhood in life. This ideal is to be met with in the seer of the Upanishads rapt in communion with the Eternal, in the calm and compassion of the Buddha victorious over ignorance and ill-will, in the ecstasy of the saint who, through his heart's surrender, becomes one with Universal love, and in the servant of God, who, lifted above selfish desire, carries out on earth the will of the Transcendent Supreme.'[2] But such a picture is the equivalent of writing a history of Christianity with no realism about its psychological and social roots. We need not deny the splendour of the ideal, if we ask what have been the deep roots of Eastern religion in Eastern society. And if we ask that question, we discover the one fact which dominates all others in religion's significance for the East: *the fact of suffering*. We discover also that Eastern religion does not transform suffering; it seeks detachment from it.

In Hinduism and Buddhism alike, an estimate of man which seems superbly optimistic has in fact arisen from a bleak pessimism, and what looks like humanism turns out to be the annihilation of man. For the basic teaching of these religions is that to be a man is to be miserable, and that a

[1] Swami Prabhavananda, *The Spiritual Heritage of India* (New York, 1962), pp. 289–90.
[2] *East and West: Some Reflections* (London, 1955), p. 20.

man cannot enter bliss and remain human. If he is to escape from his misery, an individual must be *absorbed* into the divine, or into nature, or into nothingness. Only a tiny minority in any one generation attains the enlightenment which leads to this absorption; and in the lives of this minority, only a few moments are ecstatic because enlightened. This is why Hinduism has placed so much emphasis on the Brahmin caste as the only full recognised status group; and why Buddhism—where a spiritual genius who belonged to the *kshatriya* or warrior caste led a revolt against the caste system—has taught that for an aspirant really to 'take refuge in the *Dharma*' (Buddha's Doctrine) he must also 'take refuge in the *Sangha*' (the Buddhist Order of contemplative, mendicant monks). If we ask why Buddhism virtually disappeared in its native India, the answer is simple: its monasteries were destroyed by Muslim conquerors. The superior status of the Brahmin caste or the Buddhist *Sangha* is the Eastern equivalent of Christianity's clericalism; although the Hindu pundits and the Buddhist monks do not have the disciplinary powers of Christian priests or ministers, in fact their status represents a more severe verdict on the common people than has been characteristic of Christianity. Traditionally Hinduism has taught that one's place in the caste system indicates one's moral and spiritual worth, for it shows what was one's behaviour in previous incarnations. For both Hinduism and Buddhism, ordinary people's lives are significant only in so far as the virtue in them accumulates into merit which is rewarded by enlightenment in another incarnation (for Hinduism, in another caste); and since an inconceivably vast number of reincarnations in animal or human lives will be necessary before all who are capable of enlightenment attain it, the significance of an individual existence is small. Human life, which has so little meaning bestowed on it by these religions, consists largely of suffering. The 'Four Noble Truths', which were the original essence of Buddhism, state clearly that to live is to suffer, and that therefore the supreme problem for man is to avoid being reborn by eliminating the desire to live. The common way of accounting for the presence of so much evil in the world is to say that it is a punishment for misdeeds in previous incarnations, according to the iron law of *karma*. We need not deny the humanitarianism of many Hindus and Buddhists in the past and present if we observe that the main impression left by these religions is that most of the evil in the world cannot be reformed away, and probably ought not to be, for without it the justice of *karma* could not operate. Thus fatalism has been encouraged, whatever the modernisers of these religions may say. Indian religion has been based on the negation of life, as Albert Schweitzer saw so clearly—Schweitzer, who saw also that the message of Jesus was not the simple, cheerful life-affirmation of liberal Culture-Protestantism. And Schweitzer, who was so critical of Western civilisation's decay, saw that essentially what was missing in Indian religion, at least until the renewal of Hinduism under the impact of the message of Jesus, was a unifying principle teaching the active love of the neighbour based on obedience to the mysterious God who as 'ethical Will' is greater than all the world's forces. Compassion was taught by the Buddha, but it was not a compassion which drove Buddhists to attempt to heal mankind's sores; it was the compassion which interpreted all life as suffering, and which therefore bestowed as its greatest blessing the secret of escape from life.[1]

The history of deviations from the official religions shows the contrast between the forms taken by protest in the West and in the East. In the West, the religious sects, protesting against the established churches and social customs of the time, have sometimes abandoned hope for this life, but for the most part they have sustained themselves by the faith that the God to whom they turned would bring in his kingdom of justice and love. Until this kingdom came, the sects have done their best to improve their lot on earth. But in the East, the sects have sought escape through the absorption of

[1] See Albert Schweitzer, *Christianity and the Religions of the World* (London, 1923).

the individual into the object of worship, with few consequences for everyday life. Max Weber put it with his
formidable jargon: 'The Occidental sects of the religious
virtuosos have fermented the methodical rationalisation of
conduct, including economic conduct. These sects have not
constituted values for the longing to escape from the
senselessness of work in this world, as did the Asiatic
communities of the ecstatics: contemplative, orgiastic or
apathetic'[1]

The Hindu and Buddhist world-view arises from a profound and prolonged human experience of suffering. Suffering, it says, cannot be ended except by the end of man. In
the conditions of life which we know, such a view can never
be completely falsified, for the burden and mystery of evil
can never be completely removed. But in the West, and
increasingly in the East, a more optimistic view is taken of
the capacity of the human intellect to lessen human suffering
by active love and by the application of the natural and
social sciences. The humanity which holds this hope and
faith is, in its own eyes, sharply distinguished from the
animals, many of which it tames or eats, and from the rest
of nature, which it confidently uses. It accepts the gift of life
with joy. In this humanism lies the challenge to religion of
'man's coming of age', and it is clear that the religious
pessimism which has dominated Hinduism and Buddhism
cannot for long survive the challenge. This is clear not only
as a point of philosophy; it is being demonstrated day by
day in the transformation of Eastern society and its religion
under the impact of the West.

Dr. M. M. Thomas, the Director of the Christian Institute
for the Study of Religion and Society at Bangalore, has
recently pointed out that the newly independent nations of
Asia are searching for new spiritual foundations in order to
prosper in the modern world. Their technology demands
that nature should be taken seriously. Their democracy
demands that the person acting in history should be taken
with an equal seriousness. Their religious traditions do not

[1] *From Max Weber*, p. 291.

view nature or the person in this way, and therefore their religious traditions are on trial. Thomas writes: 'The recognition of the reality of nature and the manipulation and conquest of nature by man have been very necessary for Asia to develop the concept of man as distinctly standing out of nature. In this sense science and technology have contributcd to Asia's spiritual awakening of the personal.'[1]

Thomas quotes from a recent booklet called *The Christ We Adore* by Swami Ranganathanandan of the Ramakrishna Mission, which calls for the 'detribilisation' of Christianity. He comments: 'What the Swami calls dogmas of Semitic tribalism are those of the prophetic tradition which saw God acting in history for the judgment and salvation of mankind, and made the drama of historic existence a movement of ultimate spiritual significance. There is no doubt that Jesus himself shared this framework and saw his messianic vocation within that setting. Furthermore, it is this prophetic spirituality which has made its impact through Western secularism and Christianity on Asian peoples and cultures in modern times and awakened them to what I have called the personal dimension of human existence. Therefore any rejection of the prophetic tradition as tribalism is a denial of the fact of Jesus as he is presented in the gospels, and is also detrimental to the spiritual quest behind the new Asian awakening.'[2]

As an Indian Christian, Thomas believes that Israel's prophetic tradition, summed up by Jesus, will eventually be acknowledged as the answer to Asia's spiritual quest.[3] This may well be the future in the long term, but it seems likely that before Christianity can be acknowledged as the light of Asia many decades, and even centuries, must pass during which it will still be branded as colonialist—and during which Eastern religion will be transformed internally by pressures in its own evolution, pressures which may take it

---

[1] *The Christian Response to the Asian Revolution,* p. 68.
[2] p. 119.
[3] See his *The Acknowledged Christ of the Indian Renaissance* (London, 1969).

further from belief in the God of monotheistic prophecy. If the suffering of Asia through famine increases tragically, and if Asia does not accept this with its traditional fatalism, it is probable that the political and economic way of escape will be thought to involve not Christianity but a Marxist or other version of Christianity's secularised child, Socialism. Meanwhile we may leave the matter with the modest and clear words of the English secular humanist, H. J. Blackham: 'In Europe it has reasonably been said that Christianity made a major contribution to the development of both science and democracy, and is therefore at home in modern culture. In the East modern culture is an import or an imposition and may therefore be harder to reconcile with traditional religion. In both cases the open society offers the best way and the best hope.'[1]

Since the impact of the West on the East is not likely to diminish (even if Western *religion* continues to be rejected by the East), much of the future of the whole world will depend on what the West makes of its own religious heritage. It is ominous that the mechanistic view of God's relation to nature, which we saw to be characteristic of Christian scientists in seventeenth-century Europe, lapsed before long into open Deism (the belief that God is so remote from nature and man that for practical purposes he does not matter); for Deism turned out to be the road to agnosticism and scepticism. We must discuss the relations of religion and science in the West further (in Chapter 8), but we can see now that the move from Deism to agnosticism may be typical of a wider process in the life of the post-Christian West. The historian traces modern civilisation to its origins in European Christendom, and, contrasting post-Christian lands with others, he may conclude that secularisation is in some sense the fruit of the Christian Gospel. But that does not prevent secularisation from developing its own drive, whatever its origins may have been; nor does it prevent secularisation from acting as the enemy of the Gospel now that the help which Christianity provided is no

[1] *Religion in a Modern Society*, p. 169.

longer needed. As a Christian historian has put it, in a discussion of religious liberty: 'A Christian civilisation by its very nature has to develop towards what its most faithful servants feel to be its own undoing. Once civilisation has so far advanced, freedom of conscience becomes the first requisite for a Christian order of things, even if the result is a kind of world in which it is harder to be a Christian.'[1] Another historian has made this simple comment on the complicated truth about the origins of modern science: 'The sixteenth and seventeenth centuries were Christian in orientation and conception . . . The great scientists were consciously Christian, and they were certainly unaware that they stood on philosophical grounds which were destined to threaten and, for some, to undermine Christian thought . . . Hence, they could not understand why churchmen should be at all opposed to their discoveries . . . The theologians were only too afraid that the direction taken by the new science would destroy Christianity, and promote atheism as they understood it. They were remarkably right.'[2]

What we have so far suggested may be summed up like this. *Any religion dominating the West is likely to be dynamic, unless its society ceases to be dynamic. In the past, this energy came mainly from the religious belief of monotheism; the spiritual legacy of Christianity, Judaism and Islam did much to inspire the scientific civilisation; and it is difficult to imagine that the dynamism will be inspired in the future by the religion of the East.* But we must turn now to examine suggestions that Western man in the age of science should worship neither his traditional God nor himself, but some external force which is a secular substitute for the God of Christianity.

[1] Herbert Butterfield, *Christianity in European History* (London, 1951), p. 35.
[2] John Dillenberger, *Protestant Thought and Natural Science* (New York, 1960), pp. 186–7.

CHAPTER SIX

A New Religion for the Secular West?

'Modern man appears to suffer acutely from his loss of emotional reassurance,' a sociologist, Dr. Bryan Wilson, reminds us, in a study of the consequences of secularisation.[1] This anxiety-making result of the 'death' of God, so familiar in the West, has led to many attempts to fill the vacuum by a religion similar in some ways to historic Christianity but substantially new. These new religions, or quasi-religions, have differed in the elements which they have adopted from the old faith, and corresponding with these differences of theological content have been differences of social appeal. All such substitutes for Christianity are worth considering with respect and sympathy. Certainly the orthodox Christian churches are in no position to sneer at them, for had it not been for the churches' failure these new religions, or quasi-religions, would not have been necessary. But as the last quarter of the twentieth century approaches, we observe the failure of the new movements to replace Christianity in the hearts of the Western millions.

Aware of this failure, secular humanism is increasingly taking the line that there is no need to replace Christianity by any substitute on terms dictated by the religious tradition, for (it is suggested) modernisation gradually results in the disappearance of the need for 'emotional reassurance', the need to which the old religions ministered; Dr. Bryan Wilson is among the humanists who offer speculations to

[1] *Religion in Secular Society*, p. xviii.

this effect. Some evidence supports this conclusion, for Western man now seems to have less need of religion than he had before, as science has taken over many of the productive or medical jobs which were traditionally allocated to God or the gods. That is why theologians such as Bonhoeffer have joined in the chorus affirming that man who is 'coming of age' may be becoming 'religionless'. That is why it was possible and necessary to write the first chapter of this book. But a total dismissal of the religious quest must rest on the speculation that at some date in the future man's basic religious sense, hitherto one of the most obvious facts about human nature, will be found to have disappeared. When and if that phenomenon arises, it will call for consideration. All that is certain in the 1970s is that Christianity has not been replaced so far in the mind of the West. Western man is still shopping for a religion, and all the philosophies about the human condition need to be brought into relation with this fact.

The Religion of the Life Force

While Aldous Huxley promoted Western appreciation of the timeless ecstasy in Eastern mysticism, his brother Julian was campaigning for a new religion based on the dynamism of evolution.[1] He was convinced that 'religion in some form is a universal function of man in society, the organ for dealing with the problems of destiny, the destiny of individual men and women, of societies, and nations, and of the human species as a whole ... A humanist, evolution-centred religion too needs divinity, but divinity without God. It must strip the divine of the theistic qualities which man has anthropomorphically projected into it, search for its habitations in every aspect of existence, elicit it, and establish fruitful contact with its manifestations. Divinity is the chief raw material out of which gods have been

[1] Notably in his *Religion without Revelation* (London, 1927) and *Evolution in Action* (London, 1953).

fashioned. Today we must melt down the gods and refashion the material into new and effective organs of religion.'[1]

Sir Julian Huxley's suggestion clearly deserves a careful hearing, for it deals with psychological and social problems to which many other humanists are curiously insensitive. These other humanists put forward a system of values as an alternative to moral anarchy after the collapse of religion. Free thought, free speech, freedom for physical and cultural pleasure, enjoyable friendships—these are usually found high among the values propounded as 'humanism'. Such values, if more widely held sacred, would indeed make the world a happier place; yet the vision and style of life urged by many modern humanists often seem luxuriously unrelated to the real priorities of actual existence in the world as most people experience this. This gentle humanism reckons too little both with the grandeur and with the misery of man; with the passions, despairs, loves, self-sacrifice and dutifulness of the millions. European atheists, after the tragic experience of their continent, often know better than Anglo-American humanists what is the size of the task confronting a movement which would replace the Christian vision of human destiny.[2]

Sir Julian Huxley's quasi-religion of evolution is connected with the Gospel of the 'Life Force' preached by George Bernard Shaw.[3] Huxley takes up the theme that

[1] Julian Huxley, *Essays of a Humanist* (London, 1964), Pelican edn., pp. 224–7.

[2] Examples of British attempts to work out an ethical code backed by a world-view are J. B. Coates, *A Challenge to Christianity: The Task of Humanism in Contemporary Society* (London, 1958); Reuben Osborn, *Humanism and Moral Theory* (London, 1959); Robert Robinson, *An Atheist's Values* (Oxford, 1964); H. J. Blackham, *Humanism* (London, 1968); *The Humanist Outlook* ed. A. J. Ayer (London, 1968). Gerhard Szczesny, *The Future of Unbelief* (1958; Eng. trans., New York, 1961), reflected the situation in West Germany, where 'after the failure of recent substitute religions, Christianity again seems like the unassailable treasure house of all human values' (p. 11. *A Humanist View*, ed. Ian Edwards (Sydney and London, 1969), came from Australia).

[3] See *Shaw and Religion*, an anthology ed. W. S. Smith (London, 1966); and for the background, W. S. Smith, *The London Heretics* (London, 1967).

science demands new attitudes in ethics and politics—
another theme with a long history in our time. Evolution
is clearly an idea whose time has come, and the divinity in
it—the creative mystery which is the setting of the destiny
of the individual and the race—may well be revered as
almost God-sized. The stream of life can be pictured as
flowing from sources fantastically improbable and remote
into a future which will be as superior to our own time as
our time is to these origins. *Homo sapiens* has, we are told,
eight thousand years of civilisation behind him, but he
emerged about a hundred thousand years ago. *Homo erectus*
may have emerged a million years ago; life, three thousand
million; the earth, four to five thousand million. Another
two thousand million years may pass before the earth
becomes uninhabitable; and in the history of the immeasur-
able universe, what will that matter? The stream of life
on which man voyages is inseparable from the rest of nature,
however unique life and mind may be reckoned. For mind
itself is but matter organised in an astounding complexity,
and all matter can be studied as one stream of energy, with
its source in the dance of its elementary particles. The stream
of energy and the stream of life seem to be rivers more
sacred than Ganges or Jordan.

Moreover, Sir Julian Huxley and other evolutionists are
able to preach that a great purpose may now be seen in
evolution. This purpose may be compared in some respects
with the will of the traditional God, although in fact it has
emerged out of the educational and cultural transmission of
human values and skills, the basis of evolution being for
Huxley the natural selection of random mutations. This
purpose (if we may express it with an unscientific crudity) is
the survival and progress of *homo sapiens* by the overcoming of the aggressive instincts which man has inherited
from the animals. An individual who instead of either
resting or fighting tries out a bold, new attempt to wrest a
better life out of nature is, whether he be a bird or a scientist, progressive; a family which rears its infants well con-
tributes to the progress of the species; and a nation which

subordinates its selfish interests to the interests of the human race is building up the peaceful world order which becomes essential to the survival of civilisation in the age of expanding, hungry populations and of nuclear armaments. In man's history evolution begins to be 'conscious of itself', and man can to a large extent control his own evolution now—whether or not he becomes able to determine his future by the manipulation of the genes transmitted in the creation of new human life, thus entering the paradise of eugenics.[1]

However, when all that can be said in favour of evolutionary ethics has been said (and it may be a great deal more than many sceptical philosophers grant), there remains a basic difference between 'is' and 'ought', as the philosopher G. E. Moore emphasised in his exposure of the 'naturalistic fallacy' at the beginning of this century.[2] This difficulty damages Sir Julian Huxley's evolutionary ethics, for it is impossible to be sure that the evolutionary process ('is') does in fact encourage all the forms of ethical behaviour which we admire ('ought'). Although the feeling that we ought to do what is right may be regarded as an instinct planted in us originally by the individual's or the group's urge to survive, and although many forms of ethical behaviour are clearly advantageous in an evolutionary perspective, this is not a complete account of ethics. Some acts of self-sacrifice which we admire as highly ethical are only remotely advantageous to either the individual or the group, and many less heroic choices which we have to make in everyday ethical decisions are hard to relate to what seems to be evolution's sole criterion: survival through fitness in adaptation to environment. Indeed, T. H. Huxley (Sir Julian's grandfather, who coined the word 'agnostic') in his Romanes Lecture of 1893 declared that 'the ethical progress

[1] See C. H. Waddington, *The Ethical Animal* (London, 1960); W. H. Thorpe, *Science, Man and Morals* (London, 1965); Konrad Lorenz, *On Aggression* (London, 1966); Alex Comfort, *Nature and Human Nature* (London, 1966).
[2] G. E. Moore, *Principia Ethica* (Cambridge, 1903).

of society depends not on imitating the cosmic process, still less in running away from it, but in combating it'.[1]

What T. H. Huxley had in mind when he called on the moral Victorians to 'combat' evolution was an ethical evolutionism very different from Sir Julian's. T. H. Huxley was attacking the ethics of Herbert Spencer, according to whom the science of evolution taught a gladiatorial view of life, in which free competition must weed out the unfit. Spencer, on this basis, opposed welfare or education for the poor. The harsh vigour of American capitalism was justified on the same 'scientific' basis: 'Competition is a law of nature'.[2] Yet Karl Marx seriously thought of dedicating *Das Kapital* to Darwin, and Engels wrote much about the material basis of life as revealed by Victorian biology. Evolution has, in fact, meant many things to many people in the emotional life of society in the first century after Darwin;[3] and evolutionary ethics is an idea which is so ambiguous that we can see why, with very few exceptions, contemporary philosophers either ignore it or denounce it. Thus A. M. Quinton writes of Sir Julian's attempts in this direction: 'Huxley realises that there are many possible lines of future evolutionary development . . . Huxley makes his selection by reference to higher values of a wholly extra-biological kind. An ethical theory that requires this sort of reinforcement, however much evolutionary material it makes use of, is not really an evolutionary ethic at all.'[4]

We can see why many hold that it is far more useful to the causes both of science and of religion to be more or less sceptical about evolutionary ethics. Dr. David Lack, for example, concluded that 'natural selection is amoral, so cannot have produced man's moral or spiritual character-istics'. About the origin of some of the most important of moral or spiritual characteristics, all men are, in Dr. Lack's words, 'in the dark'; and they will remain in the dark unless

---

[1] See T. H. and Julian Huxley, *Evolution and Ethics* (Oxford, 1947).
[2] See Richard Hofstader, *Social Darwinism in American Thought* (Philadelphia, 1944).
[3] See J. W. Burrow, *Evolution and Society* (Cambridge, 1960).
[4] *Biology and Personality*, ed. I. T. Ramsey, p. 119.

the darkness is illuminated by religious faith. Only religious faith dares to suggest that man has these moral or spiritual characteristics because, while descended from other animals, while analysable by biology, physics and chemistry, man is also the child of God and in these characteristics is Godlike. Without religious faith, much of the moral and spiritual life of man must remain a puzzling episode, so that we repeat McNeile Dixon: 'we are utterly in the dark . . .'[1]

However, the shakiness of its intellectual foundations may be of concern only to a minority of those to whom the evolutionists address their new religion. What concerns us more here is the question whether the new religion based on evolution is likely to give enough satisfaction to enough people psychologically. Here a large doubt must be expressed. The evolutionary process is magnificent, but the divinity in it is not God, and if human nature continues to want an object at all like the God of traditional religion, then evolution as the object of worship will not give an emotional reassurance at all like traditional religion at its greatest. At first sight the size of evolution may not seem to handicap it religiously. After all, Western monotheism has insisted that God is infinite. But whereas the infinite God, being purely spiritual, had to be expressed for men in a definite symbolism, law, revelation or incarnation—in some object to which people could give their worship—evolution is a theory about a very great number of objects; and it is difficult for a worshipper to relate himself to a process which is as long as time and as large as the universe. The spectacle of evolution does not in fact easily arouse *worship*; wonder and fear are common reactions to it, but not religious worship. This is the equivalent in psychology of the philosophical objection that no amount of scientific facts, arranged by the theory of evolution, can produce *ethics*. The science of evolution is too complicated to be the basis of a new religion, if the religion is to serve even approximately the purposes which Sir Julian Huxley sees fulfilled in the old religions.

[1] David Lack, *Evolutionary Theory and Christian Belief: The Unresolved Conflict* (London, 1957), p. 108.

Indeed, it is very doubtful whether the quasi-religion prophesied by Huxley will allow room for any worship. In the essay already cited he grants that 'what precise form these new agencies of religious thought will take it is impossible to say in this period of violent transition', but he does exclude from his picture much of what man has usually thought essential to religious worship. 'In place of eternity we shall have to think in terms of enduring process; in place of salvation in terms of attaining the satisfying states of inner being which combine energy and peace. There will be no room for petitionary prayer, but much value in prayer involving aspiration and self-exploration.' Huxley further grants that 'Christianity is a universalist and monotheist religion of salvation. Its consolidation and explosive spread, achieved through a long period of discussion and zealous ferment, released vast human forces which have largely shaped the Western world as we know it.' But he believes that 'an evolutionary and humanist religion of fulfilment could be more truly universal and could release even vaster spiritual forces'.[1] We need not doubt that if more people agreed with Huxley's evolutionist philosophy mankind would be more co-operative and happier than it is now. However, we must be clear that, as a quasi-religion, evolutionism is no substitute for old belief in God. It gives us no reality which is really ultimate, despite Huxley's brave talk about an 'enduring' process, for in evolution everything changes and everything in the end decays to death. Evolution cannot be trusted as the eternal God has been trusted. Evolutionism also gives us no purpose which really cares for us, despite Huxley's talk about a 'satisfying' peace of mind, for in evolution no human life is significant except through its contribution to the progress of the species, in a vast time-scale. Tennyson's poem *In Memoriam*, published nine years before Darwin's *Origin of Species*, cannot after all be faulted as a vision of the ruthless cruelty of nature to the individual according to evolutionary theory. Evolution cannot be loved as the saving God has been loved. That is

[1] *Essays of a Humanist*, Pelican edn., pp. 227–9.

why H. G. Wells found no help from the religion of evolution when he came to the place where the old religion was at its strongest, where man's mind is at the 'end of its tether'. And that is why the religion of evolution has so far not caught on widely as a 'religion without revelation'. It is precisely the revelation of ultimate reality, of almighty grace, that is desired in the West's traditional religion; and no major artist, sensitive to the human condition in our time and serious in utter integrity (Bernard Shaw cannot be included in such a category), has found in evolutionism the answer to the anxiety of man now that this desire for revelation is thought to be a desire for an illusion. The only divinity that really matters to man's religious sense remains 'dead' even if evolution is highly impressive, and the existence of the individual—which is what matters supremely to every individual—remains, as Sartre and Camus said, 'absurd'. Here are severe handicaps in the struggle to create a new religion centred on evolution—which may explain why the quasi-church of this quasi-religion has faced problems in attracting adequate popular support.

The Religion of Nature

'It is not enough to formulate honest and high ideals,' one British atheist confessed recently. 'We must also create the ceremonies and the atmosphere that will hold them before us at all times. I have no conception how to do this; but I believe it will be done if we try.'[1] Many people in our time also have 'no conception' about how to create a new religion —but they also have no belief that they could do it if they did try. They feel that a 'Catholicism without Christianity' (T. H. Huxley's description of Auguste Comte's 'religion of humanity') needs something more than earnest trying if it is to replace Christianity. There are, however, many people of the highest intelligence and sensitivity who, while avoiding these artificial attempts to create a new religion without God, still seek to meet the needs of human nature's surviving

[1] Robert Robinson, *An Atheist's Values*, p. 157.

religious sense within the categories of secularism. It is the hope of such people that *nature may be able to take the place of God*. Several things may be meant by the serious cry for a religious return to nature, and a few aids to reflection—maddeningly superficial as they must be—may not be irrelevant.

For a few, the religious value of nature may be mediated through *natural science*. Clearly, there is an element reminiscent of traditional religion at its best in science's laboriously truthful observation of the world, in the comradeship of scientists who are thus pledged to truth, in the dismissal of prejudices and passions and in the moments of ecstatic discovery. Science can certainly teach and sustain honest and high ideals. But as a quasi-religion, science has this important disadvantage: the public profoundly devoted to its cause is a minority composed of intellectuals.

It is significant that Dr. Jacob Bronowski's widely read exposition of *Science ond Human Values* (New York, 1958) never got round to answering the question with which it began: was the atomic bomb of 1945 the 'baby' of modern science? The destruction of Hiroshima and Nagasaki was, of course, a monstrous misuse of the physics of the age of Einstein, Rutherford and Bohr; and of course if the spirit of the laboratory could spread into the world we should no longer be in the position we at present occupy—when, in Bronowski's words, 'the body of technical science burdens and threatens us because we are trying to employ the body without the spirit'. But the problem of how to employ modern science is caused by the fact that most people are not motivated by purely intellectual passions. Unless a totally new society arises, the passions to which people are in fact subject will not be trained by making them pure intellectuals; they will be tamed only by a wisdom which is relevant to them. Traditionally it has been the task of religion to nourish this wisdom, and it is a measure of the corruption of contemporary religion that Dr. Bronowski in his book nowhere envisaged a role for religion in a scientific society as anything but the enemy of truth. 'All science,' he wrote, 'is the search for unity in hidden likenesses,' and that is a fine description of the creative scientific mind as it contemplates and penetrates the surface of things; but all the religious vision is also a search for unity. Religion seeks the integration of the person in union with the true sum of all things. In the light of Hiroshima and Nagasaki, and of the years since their horror, we may say—as so many, from Albert Einstein downwards, have already said—that unless the wisdom of religion can be reborn for the age of science the possibility of misusing science on a catastrophic scale will remain.[1]

For some, *the use of science* in technical advance can provide the fascination. At earlier times in this book we have reminded ourselves of this fascination, and of the welcome which can be given to it by a mature religion. What we have to mention now is that technology itself can be a quasi-religion. 'Technology has sacred overtones in the minds of many,' one sociologist observes. 'To contravene the values of technology in favor of, say, nationalism or economic profits can seem as impious to a scientist today as contravention of religious ends, in the name of economic gain, did to a medieval theologian.'[2] This quasi-religious veneration for the conspicuous use of science has, indeed, encouraged the diversion of fantastic proportions of the total resources of the Soviet Union and the United States in the race to the moon. Here—in a modern version of the moon-worship against which the prophets of Israel's God thundered—is epitomised the belief that technological advance should take precedence over such causes as consumer-goods for the masses, or food for the children of the under-developed world. But we may wonder how many of our

[1] The quotations are from pp. 78, 23 of the Pelican edition of Jacob Bronowski, *Science and Human Values* (London, 1964). It is only fair to add that in his 1964 Preface Dr. Bronowski wrote: 'I would, were I beginning again, give some space also to a discussion of those values which are not generated by the practice of science—the values of tenderness, of kindliness, of human intimacy and love.'
[2] Robert A. Nisbet in *Religion and Social Conflict*, ed. R. Lee and M. E. Marty (New York, 1964), p. 12.

contemporaries would actually vote for that allocation of resources; or, at least, we may wonder how many would vote to reach the moon at all costs, were it not for the motivation in the moon-race of a greater quasi-religion, which goes by the name of patriotic pride. We may suspect that even in this age of triumphant technology, not many manage to sustain a devotion to applied science as the central enthusiasm of a lifetime. Technology is valued because it 'delivers the goods', to feed and heal and comfort people; but many people fear that technology, if worshipped by itself, would produce a waist-high culture. So the contemporary cry goes up: to learn the wisdom of the heart, neither science nor the application of science is enough.

The clergy preach to more or less empty pews while the people, leaving their household gadgets behind, seek the God of the open air in considerable discomfort; and if the countryside cannot be reached, gardening may be more successful than theology in teaching the citizen on what he depends. And temperaments which are not in love with raw nature can find profound satisfactions through the contemplation of *nature interpreted through art*. The vast increase in popular enjoyment of the arts, so evident in the American enthusiasm for 'culture', cannot be due only to the spread of television, broadcasting, tourism, public libraries, paperback publishing and schools; part of the explanation of this enrichment of contemporary life seems to be that art speaks to depths of the personality where the old religion once spoke. Supremely through its growing love of serious music has our time been enabled to commune with the suffering and beauty, the order and grace in the world. Music struggles with mystery and music delights in goodness, as the sacred scriptures did for previous generations. So the art of man can interpret the world—can console and celebrate; and this is for many an effective (because not a self-conscious or artificial) substitute for the ceremonies and atmosphere of the old religion.

Estimates of nature or of art—especially estimates from a religious point of view—should, of course, be made with due caution, but fortunately we need not plumb the philosophical depths here. If by 'religion' we mean a creed of the kind which Sir Julian Huxley advocates—if we mean a quasi-religion of nature, or of man in nature, with no transcendent God—then of course a mountain-top or a picture-gallery or a concert-hall is the most likely cathedral of this religious atheism; and it is obvious that the interpretation of man's basic religious sense according to the categories of a godless humanism by concentrating on the worship of nature or of art has attracted many of the finest spirits of our time. But if we are asked to believe that an atheist's love of nature or of art can be an adequate substitute for the traditional worship of the transcendent God, then some reasons for hesitation must be offered.

The love of nature, the love of art and the love of God can flourish together. A close and loving observation of nature is evident in the psalms of the Bible and in the teaching of Jesus. While the art of the Hebrews and of the early Christians was far from great, it is a matter of history that Western painting and music—to say nothing of Western drama and prose—were nutured in the very churches where architecture rose to the heights of beauty, and no story in the world has inspired so much, or such good, art as the story of Jesus. The recent breakdown of the Church's patronage of the arts has robbed worshippers of a major source of inspiration, and has been a factor in the feeling which many artists have that their society does not care what they do. Some of the most important movements in modern Christianity have been those which have sought to reconcile the churches and the arts in integrity, as media through which the great truth about the world may be celebrated. In various ways, therefore, it may be said that Christianity is so deeply in love with the world that it is a religion of beauty.

On the other hand, history forbids us to assume an *identity* between the love of nature, the love of art and the love of God. Aesthetic response and religious response are so intimately related that it is not easy to be precise about the distinction between the two, but the importance of seeing a distinction may be learned in the tragic history of the distortion of artistic integrity to fit the demands of religious sentiment or ecclesiastical censorship. The debasement of art by religion is a familiar enough story, and it is clear that such prostitution is avoided only when mutual respect, freedom and integrity mark the marriage of religious insight and aesthetic vision to make religious art. Now that art has escaped so widely from the tutelage of religion, we need to remember from the history of art that art has good reason to be suspicious of religion's arrogance.

But another reason for emphasising the distinction between the aesthetic and the religious is that neither nature nor art can happily perform all the tasks which traditional religion has allocated to God. The strict prohibition of artistic images of God in Judaism or Islam, and a long history of 'iconoclasm' (image-breaking) and Puritanism in Christianity, bear witness to religion's suspicion of art. An individual may indeed regard the enjoyment of nature and art as a substitute for religious faith, and at least for a time this substitute may seem satisfactory or superior. But the limitations of art are liable to manifest themselves in an individual's character by producing a superficial aestheticism, which is the debasement of the artistic sense just as pietism is the debasement of the religious sense. These limitations also appear in the inadequacy of secular art to integrate a whole society, taking over the job done by traditional religion.

The first of these crucial defects is the remoteness of nature or art from the field of *personal relations*—from the field which remains the primary concern of human nature. Modern psychology confirms what common observation suggests: that almost all men and women derive almost all their deepest energies and satisfaction from their relations with their fellows. The pure nature-lover or artist, with little or no need of such fulfilment through society, is, like the pure scientist, in a small minority. The contemplation of nature or of art can calm troubled breasts and ennoble mean hearts, but it is not a real alternative to the speaking

of heart to heart. Traditional religion has in fact offered a
vast stimulus to human fellowship and a detailed and urgent
commentary on personal relations, and if it is to be effective
a new religion must show similar warmth towards the
personal. And how intolerably banal that sounds! It would
be better to think about those great if sad last days of Leo
Tolstoy, who gave up his art for Christ and the peasants.

The second crucial defect in the aesthetic as an alternative
to the traditionally religious has appeared in the failure of
nature and of art to give *a satisfactory significance to personal
lives*. For what is the purpose of human life? It has often
been answered: to contemplate nature or art. But the human
spirit in every age, including our own, is often left dissatisfied even by those natural glories. This dissatisfaction
may come as the life of the senses ebbs away in old age—but
also when a person is in the prime of strength. It may come
in a bitter loneliness—but also as a search for the ultimate
meaning of experienced love. Man in his obstinate belief
may seek to enter the most fascinating of all relationships—
the worship of the eternal God who, while perfect in his
beauty, is also personal in his capacity to respond to love.
Such belief may be dying out under the impact of secularisation, but we can recall from the past how many of the
greatest artists, musicians, etc., have confessed that for
them, in their celebration of the glory which they saw, the
natural glories have not been enough. They have said that
only God, with nature as his temporary garment and with
art as the dim mirror of his beauty, can satisfy the human
spirit. In our own time some great artists, musicians and
writers have shared in that religious confession; and the
alternative has been shown plainly enough, for many
novelists and dramatists by their pictures of the desolation
of life and death under atheism (and even by their own
miseries and suicides) have told the true story of man's
restless heart.

Even this superficial discussion may be enough to suggest
that nature has its limits as the basis of a new religion, for the
worship of it does not mean so much to so many as the

worship of the eternal God meant in the old religion. These limits of nature may come to be accepted as the limits of man's useful concern, but meanwhile the religious quest of the secular century continues.

Secular Social Gospels

If nature is dissatisfying because impersonal, where can we find a substitute for the 'dead' God of Western religion? Many in our time have tried to reassure themselves emotionally through the ceremonies and the atmosphere of political movements which, while rejecting God, have developed the conviction of Jews and Christians that a glorious Kingdom is to come on earth. The Jews have paid very dearly in Europe during our savage time for giving birth to that Messianic hope, and no theme in the church history of the twentieth century looms larger than Christianity's rivalry with political totalitarianism.

In Chapter 2 we considered briefly why *Communism* has been the most militant of these political quasi-religions. It has often been pointed out that the atheist Marx never entirely escaped the influence of his Jewish ancestry, and of Protestant theology mainly as communicated through the philosophical idealism of Hegel. History for Marx had a purpose, a purpose which people must serve if their lives were to have meaning. This purpose was opposed by many forces, but its triumph in the end was inevitable, and to speed that triumph men must join actively in the work of the one fellowship which is aware of the secret of history. The doctrines and scriptures of that fellowship must be kept clean as weapons in the fight. A day would come when the patient waiting of the oppressed would be rewarded. It would be a day of plenty, a day both of freedom and of justice for all, when the fulfilment for which men at present sought in vain through work would be granted to them in a perfect society. The class system would wither away. The State itself would wither away. Since each individual would receive from the community according to his needs, there would be no room for envy. Since each people would live in affluence, there would be no cause to provoke war or to encourage colonialism. All these are religious themes, going back to the Old Testament prophets (and to Zoroaster in Persia). These were the themes of the triumph of Light over Darkness, and these were some of the ancient details of the menu at the Messianic Feast. Marx gave these themes a secular twist, but he believed in them passionately, and the history of the twentieth century shows that it has been the religious intensity of Marxist faith, rather than the accuracy of its analysis of the future development of capitalism (which has turned out to be incorrect in almost every respect), that has filled the religious vacuum left by the spiritual bankruptcy of the ecclesiastical institutions of Russia and China and by the despair of the secularised intelligentsia in the West.

But we have only to recall the apocalyptic hopes of Karl Marx as the world moves towards the centenary of his death to realise that Schweitzer's Jesus was not more mistaken than he. Marxism has brought economic progress by its ruthless industrialisation, but when it has approached plenty, freedom and justice for all it has ceased to be Marxist. What has withered away has been Marxist dogmatism, through the development within the 'socialist' country of a more liberal and *bourgeois* atmosphere, with prosperity leading to private property and to private ideas. The power of dogmatic Marxism has been seen to rest to a large extent on the power of a police more efficient than the capitalistic police whom Marx denounced. The weapon in its hand in the fight for social progress was the dictatorship of the proletariat, but that weapon turned out in practice to be the dictatorship of the Party over the whole community including the proletariat, ruling by terror; and the Party's rule of terror has become almost everywhere notorious and hated. Marxism has also been seen to depend on an indoctrination of the people through the control of schools and of all means of publicity, and through the suppression of free speech—all of which has seemed a good deal more formidable, and a good deal more repugnant, than the preaching of the clergymen whom Marx attacked as the allies of the nineteenth-century police.[1]

Marxism as a quasi-religion is now in the midst of the Chinese chapter in its astonishing story (perhaps with the Indian and Latin American chapters to come). In Russia, and to some extent in Eastern Europe also, it is viewed much as the Christian tradition is viewed by most Western Europeans: as an impressive relic from the past, which few can now accept literally but which even fewer know how to replace. In Western Europe, dogmatic Marxism is a spent force.[2] The poor of France and Italy may still vote Communist as the best available means of protest against an unjust society, but Democratic Socialism seems the clear victor in its long struggle with Communism on Europe's political Left. In Britain and North America, Communism stands no chance at all in the electorate. The enthusiasm of Western European or Anglo-Saxon intellectuals for Soviet Russia as a 'new civilisation' has not survived the successive shocks of the age of Stalin and its aftermath in the bloody suppression of the Hungarian and Czech risings.[3]

Western intellectuals have therefore sought other consolations for the emptiness which they have found in modern life, and their approach to social problems has become more realistic, more empirical. Instead of Karl Marx's Newer Testament, we get such a book as Baroness Wootton's plea for more research in her *Testament for Social Science* (London, 1950). The development of the

[1] Nicolas Berdyaev, a Christian prophet who was a Marxist as a young man but who was sickened by the Communist Party's brutalities, often drew attention to the eschatological element in the Russian Revolution, and linked this with the frustrated idealism of Russian Christians. On the day of his death he completed his last presentation of this theme: *The Realm of the Spirit and the Realm of Caesar* (1949; Eng. trans., London, 1952).

[2] For a French Communist's willingness to listen to some Christian criticisms, see Roger Garaudy, *The Turning Point of Socialism* (1969; Eng. trans., 1970). For such heresies, M. Garaudy was expelled from the Party.

[3] A well-known book of essays by ex-Communists was *The God that Failed*, ed. R. H. S. Crossman (London, 1950).

social sciences to something like the status and usefulness of the natural sciences is indeed urgent in our civilisation, and already immense benefits have come to mankind from such research and from its clear-headed application to modern social problems. But research is not religion, nor is it an effective substitute for religion's power; and when it comes to asking by what vision of destiny men shall live, the Baroness joins the British Humanist Association, which we have seen to be faced by problems as a quasi-church for the secular West. Meanwhile the Western masses, rightly or wrongly desiring a strong substitute for the old faith, have turned to other quasi-religions.

Among these movements, the most powerful has been *nationalism*, once described (by Edward Shillito) as 'man's other religion'. 'By nationalism,' Dr. Max Warren wrote, 'I mean that deep inner attitude of mind which distinguishes one group of people, large or small, calling for an exclusive loyalty, which in the last analysis limits humanity to that group, and which tends all too easily to treat inhumanly those outside this group.'[1] The examples of Confucianist China and Shintoist Japan are enough to remind us that this attitude has not been exclusively Western, but Western nationalism has certainly flourished as a quasi-religion in our time. Communism itself has made most progress where it has run with the mighty wind of nationalism (as in Russia or China, countries which have always been intensely patriotic) rather than against it (as in Russian-occupied Eastern Europe). When Marxist dogmatism has fully withered away, the Russian and Chinese nationalisms may be left as its (bitterly quarrelling) heirs.

When the twentieth century began, very few intellectuals prophesied that the coming age would include the spectacle of peoples sacrificing their personal freedom and reason on the altar of the State. Yet millions in this century have been glad to do so. Europe in 1914 was a continent itching for war, because the patriotism of the European powers, of the

[1] *The Missionary Movement from Britain in Modern History* (1966), p. 120.

British and of the Irish, had reached fever pitch. 'National self-determination' was the sacred principle in the peace-making of 1918–20. When peace did not bring prosperity or dignity men turned to Communist, Socialist or Fascist nationalism because it claimed the power to end the exploitation of the people by putting the key instruments of production and distribution, and the mass media of publicity, into the hands of the State's nominees. 'Nothing outside the State, nothing above the State or against the State; everything in the State and for the State' was the motto of Mussolini's Fascists, and the Fascist march on Rome in 1922 inaugurated a Right-wing totalitarianism with which was a quasi-religion of 'blood and soil', no less militant than the atheistic Communism to which it was so loudly opposed. Here was if we may use in an unintended sense the title of the classic expression of Nazi neopaganism 'the myth of the twentieth century'.[1] The rulers of the totalitarian states got their way by violence, trickery and tyranny, but at the time millions agreed to this because their souls as well as their bellies were empty; they needed price as well as food. In the 1940s, 1950s and 1960s a type of nationalism arose which was as fierce as anything in Europe's history: this was the nationalism of the peoples who had won independence from the European empires, but were determined to advance out of primitive tribalism by a basic Westernisation. They used nationalism as the West's most potent export.

Nationalism has not been a religion according to the *Oxford English Dictionary*'s definition of religion as the 'recognition on the part of man of some higher unseen power as having control of his destiny, and as being entitled to obedience, reverence and worship'. But nationalism, whether European or ex-colonial, is a quasi-religion, because it provides visible powers as substitutes for the divine: leaders who are acclaimed as fathers, saviours, prophets, philosophers and magicians, the architects of a country's wealth and virtue. This Messianic nationalism

[1] Alfred Rosenberg's notorious book was published in Munich in 1930.

has used many methods reminiscent of religion: initiation ceremonies at birth and coming-of-age, youth movements, adult cells, public rallies such as those at Nuremberg under Hitler, scriptural slogans such as the thoughts of Mao Tse-tung, sacred songs such as *Lead, Kindly Light* as the anthem of the Convention People's Party during its dictatorial rule of Ghana, temples such as the lavish Congress Halls built in many capitals, statues to be a focus for worship such as the representations of Stalin in colossal concrete, or of Nkrumah with the text inscribed beneath for the instruction of Ghana: 'Seek ye first the political Kingdom.' Nationalism has been sternly puritanical in advocating the practice of those virtues which do not conflict with the interests of a totalitarian state or of its rulers. Firm faith and hard work have been demanded from every citizen, and, apart from the fate of the minority who are unteachable and damned, citizens have been promised a glory which will come to their society, if not to themselves. Nationalism has not hesitated to offer a glowing vision of Utopia, compensating for all the struggles of the liberation necessary to deliver the country from an evil regime—and compensating also for the natural, accidental or planned shortages of consumer goods and for the heroic labours necessary to build the new society. Nationalism, evoking the idealistic spirit of self-sacrifice, has made a religious impact on our time, and it is not too much to detect in its appeal the ghost of God sitting crowned on the grave of supernatural religion.[1]

Some Western countries have escaped, or have out-grown, the conspicuous hysteria of nationalism, but that does not mean that they have no public philosophy. It simply means that their public philosophy is harder to define —and may be harder to maintain as a valid long-term alternative to the religious faith which survives in their midst. This vaguer public philosophy does make for human happiness; its problem is that, in the absence of a vital public faith, it finds itself called to do duty as a quasi-religion,

[1] See C. J. Hayes, *Nationalism: A Religion* (New York, 1960).

where 'gracious living' is believed to depend on the acquisition of a large number of goods.

Many people in the West rebel against this cult of goods. One generation of the young therefore likes to think of itself as 'beat', envying the beatitude which is claimed by those who 'opt out' of modern life. The protest of the next generation of youth can take more exciting forms. Marijuana, heroin and LSD have been widely peddled in recent years as a means of obtaining the ecstasies of religious mysticism without the need to discipline oneself in prayer. Aldous Huxley suggested (or seemed to suggest) that Westerners in a hurry, unwilling to spend time on all the processes of the Eastern religion which he commended, might take a dose in order to see God;[1] and since Aldous Huxley a thousand lesser prophets have promoted the drug cult as a means of instant beatitude.[2] It is arguable whether this hippy cult is, or is not, less dangerous than the cult of violence which currently appeals as an alternative outlet for youth's revolt.

Those who disapprove of such habits in the young may find a purpose in life in the lodges of Freemasonry and of the other Orders which bring middle-aged men together. Freemasonry, with its world-wide membership of six millions, clearly meets a need. Its European and Latin American branches ('the Grand Orient' tradition) have played an important part in the history of the century as a focus of militant opposition to the Roman Catholic Church. English-speaking Freemasonry has no such anti-clerical basis; indeed, it insists on belief in God. But all these Orders do seem to be fairly described as substitutes for the churches. If only a social need was being met, bodies such as the Rotary Clubs, without ritual and secrecy, would be enough; but what exists is a religious need. Both the younger generation and the middle-aged are—as many popular songs affirm—looking for something.

[1] See his *The Doors of Perception* (New York, 1954).
[2] For a Christian assessment of this phenomenon, see R. C. Zaehner, *Drugs, Mysticism and Make-Believe* (London, 1972).

If secular people discover that neither drugs nor rituals will do as substitutes for religion, but still desire a cause with which they can identify themselves, they can watch a sports team. If they need a myth of the good defeating the bad, they can watch a Western. If they need more individual heroes, they can adore the stars of entertainment. If they still need a cosmic vision to surround their lives, they can study 'what the stars foretell' in many magazines or journals which find no space for religious sermons. For astrology flourishes in the West as in the East, 'luck' and 'fate' are taken seriously, and a substantial proportion of the public appears to hold magical views of reality.

Indeed, Western society, as observed in daily experience or as analysed by those few sociologists who have had the courage to make an accurate study of the real opinions of advanced peoples, is scarcely 'secular' in the style which is attributed to it by philosophers (and even theologians) who hail the triumph of reason and experimental science. In fact Western society is dominated by passing fashions in which people find some identity and security—and these are fashions of opinion as much as of dress. 'In many respects,' a sociologist observes about contemporary England, the doctrines of the Church are much more sophisticated than average thinking, and the problem is too little education and not too much. It would be absurd to suppose that a population widely nurtured on the *Daily Express* and *Old Moore's Almanack* finds the New Testament an intellectual insult or Thomism not compatible with modern logic.' On the scepticism of the English intelligentsia he remarks: 'These prejudices are not genuinely understood so much as simply imbibed with the *New Statesman* as the appropriate atmosphere for those who aspire to be intellectual.' He concludes: 'Technically sophisticated societies are capable of living by belief systems emotionally and intellectually crass to the point of nausea.'[1]

And we have still not mentioned sex. That part of evolution which is considered by the Western belief system as

[1] David Martin, *A Sociology of English Religion*, pp. 114–15.

most suitable for worship is the distinction between male and female, as leading to the reproduction of the species. The rather elevated literature of the Humanist Associations may not fully emphasise this, but the truth may be that it is only through sex that the creative thrust of evolution is able to excite human nature deeply. We can worship the mystery of sex, and an expression of our worship can be the physical or mental enjoyment of the sexual act. Here is the quasi-religion of modern prophets so diverse as D. H. Lawrence, Havelock Ellis and Mr. Hefner, the pundit of *Playboy*.

This new awareness of sex is indeed a powerful formulation of the 'Life Force', and it has on the whole brought a clear benefit to humanity, for it has rolled away a great burden of ignorance, shame, guilt and misery produced by the Puritanical denial of the centrality of sex in human life. But even sex as a symbol of the evolutionary process is (over the years) often less satisfying than the traditional symbolism of God the Creator—for the creative power of nature in sex, however impressive, glorious and delightful, involves men and women in emotions which can gradually turn out to be destructive and even tedious. Sex if placed not only at the centre but also at the crown of life, sex if regarded as the object not only of honour and joy but also of a cult, sex if welcomed not only as grace and as fun but also as the one purpose in an aimless life, sex if worshipped can damage many other activities which men and women tend to think are valuable; and when it has satiated men and women, sex loses even its fascination. There may be signs of a new Puritanism arising among us. Often enough in the history of religion eroticism has served as a substitute for supernaturalism, and has in the end been discarded, usually in a wave of hatred for the flesh. Much human experience suggests that sexual energy, while it enters powerfully and inextricably into many activities which are not openly sexual (any realistic picture of man must now be post-Freudian), can be disciplined and sublimated outside marriage—and experience suggests also that marriage is itself not a purely sexual arrangement. History, we may reasonably (if tritely) conclude, teaches that sex should be enjoyed and used, not worshipped.

So it is that we find a London psychiatrist reminding us that 'sex can become a god, and often does so; and a great deal of psychotherapeutic work with people of middle age is concerned with the withdrawal of the projection of the god image from sexuality'.[1] And when Harvey Cox reads *Playboy*, where men use girls as playthings, he concludes: 'It is precisely because these magazines are antisexual that they deserve the most searching kind of theological criticism.'[2]

Certainly those who thoughtfully adhere to supernatural religion may join the independently reflective secular humanists in hoping that the spread of education will erode the power of these soft substitutes for God. Most of the pleasures just described are, of course, harmless enough in their proper places, and they or their equivalents flourished in the epochs when traditional religion integrated society. The point of the criticism which is often made of them by dissatisfied Westerners is that their place should not be God's place, in a cult. These things (many feel) should not be the things for which man lives. For if these things turn out to be principal competitors with Judaism and Christianity as giving significance to human life, it will indeed be hard to attach much importance to the idea of human progress.

That has, of course, been repeated by many moralists. What is not so often stressed is the degree to which the younger generation in the West in the 1970s is itself idealistic in rejecting these glossy prisons of the soul. The older generation may prefer to concentrate on the small minority of the Western young which relies on drugs or enjoys violence in the course of political protest or is promiscuous in its enjoyment of sexual intercourse; here, the older generation can play a moralising role while at the same time

---

[1] Anthony Storr in *Christian Essays in Psychiatry*, p. 80.
[2] *The Secular City*, p. 199. But Professor Cox has contributed articles about religion to *Playboy*.

gratifying its curiosity about (and envy of) the physical appetites of the young—a posture as old as history. But the serious point to be made is that youth seems to be as idealistic today as it ever was, even if drugs to supplement (or replace) alcohol and tobacco are more freely available, and even if contraceptives remove some of the obstacles to youth's traditionally hot sexual desires. Personal relations—including the relations between men and women, whites and coloureds, the middle classes and the workers—are often taken with a deep seriousness. The word 'love' is pounded out with as much intensity of meaning as ever in the past. Marriage comes early, and great hopes surround it. The crude competitiveness, the triviality, the artificiality and the emptiness of peace, and the horror and futility of war, arouse as great a disgust with adult society as similar characteristics did when past societies called forth young reformers. It is even possible to find in the new 'jeaneration' a new and better stage in man's evolution.[1]

Since the collapse of Communism in the West the slogans of political protest have been generally felt to be unable to absorb, carry and justify this great mass of youthful idealism and energy; yet the religious vacuum of our time in the West is shown by the fact that it does not occur to most of the young that they, these splendid rebels against materialism, are a generation seeking a religion—a crusade in search of a cross. Religion to the bulk of this generation means a blind or hypocritical conservatism, and above all it means an illusion. Most of the young do not take seriously the gimmicks by which some clergymen seek to be relevant to teenage fashions; and most of the young know little and care less about the churches from which these clergymen come. They would ask: 'What are the churches now, if they are not the tombs and monuments of God?'[2]

[1] Charles A. Reich, *The Greening of America* (New York, 1970), was an enthusiastic portrait of the new generation.
[2] Friedrich Neitzsche, *The Joyful Wisdom*, p. 169.

New Spiritualisms

In our time in the West, one of the substitutes for religion has been Spiritualism. At first sight, this seems simply the opposite of materialism. On closer inspection, however, spiritualism can be seen as a supplement to materialism, for it claims that death itself is powerless to destroy the humanity whose glory is celebrated by secular humanism, and it interprets eternity in the language of material prosperity.

In the Spiritualist movement, the great problem to be addressed by religion has been seen not as the creation of material plenty but as the survival of physical death. The age-old attempt to pierce the mystery of the grave has been organised afresh in characteristically twentieth-century ways: at the intellectual level through psychical research using scientific methods as fully as possible; in the organisational efficiency of the Spiritualist Churches through the distribution of literature, the convening of rallies, the formation of groups and the support of expert leaders; and, finally, through a warmly compassionate approach to the griefs of individuals mourning the loss of loved ones. It is typical of the religious inadequacy of the West that in so many contacts with the dead as described by Spiritualists the majesty of God's heaven, or the bliss of the nothingness of the Buddhist's *Nirvana*, has been replaced by a profusion of trivialities—as the dead express, or are made to express, their continued concern for the details of earthly existence and for the domestic side of the after-life where these details are reproduced.

The new Spiritualism is thus to a large extent the old materialism projected beyond death. G. N. M. Tyrrell, in one of the most thoughtful presentations of the lessons to be learned from psychical research,[1] declared: 'When speaking of a future life, the finite type of existence which psychical research appears to point to, must be clearly distinguished from the immortality which is the goal of the mystic and

[1] *The Personality of Man* (London, 1945), chapter 30.

which consists in attainment of union with the divine . . .
It has been frequently stressed that telepathy and precog-
nition give us glimpses of an extended realm of *nature*. Why
should not a future life be another type of natural finite
existence? . . . The idea that dying does not launch us into
a religious sphere is quite simple once we have grasped the
idea that "nature" need not come to an end when it ceases
to be visible.' Tyrrell urged that the Christian churches
should welcome these ideas, since 'the traditional conception of the supernatural has now become a stumbling block
in the way of any reconciliation between science and religion'.

Since the churches have on the whole clung to the old
orthodoxy, it is symptomatic of the religious need of our
time that with few external aids Spiritualism has established
itself as, in some sense, an underground church, and has
sometimes been a setting for a spiritual life which the saints
of the old faiths would have recognised. Here sensitive
spirits have been able to exercise the wonderful human
powers which the old faiths called mystical and miraculous
—and have done so in the context of a ministry of healing
and teaching. Here intellectuals have been able to contemplate 'para-normal' powers in human nature which at
present lie beyond the reach of the sciences and outside the
scope of the usual philosophical attempts to explain man's
mind—as witness the keen interest taken in psychical
research by British philosophers as distinguished as C. D.
Broad,[1] and by some psychologists.[2] Here ordinary mortals
have found reassurance about their places in the universe,
and a fellowship with the living as well as with the departed.[3]
Their grief for a dead God, as well as for husbands or children or friends, has been calmed if not cured. To many
thousands, and perhaps to millions, the most important
achievement of the modern age has been its proof that at

[1] *Religion, Philosophy and Psychical Research* (London, 1953);
Lectures on Psychical Research (London, 1962).
[2] See D. J. West, *Psychical Research Today* (2nd edn., London, 1962),
and *Science and ESP*, ed. J. R. Smythies (London, 1967).
[3] See G. K. Nelson, *Spiritualism and Society* (London, 1969).

least some people, for at least some time, can transcend their material limitations and can even survive death.

Not only death has preoccupied Westerners as a challenge to their material prosperity. No religious history of our time would be complete without some mention of the general fascination with medical problems, which has included widespread interest in 'para-normal' healing. Our age in the West has been the first period in history to try to make medical care available to all, although the attempt has not yet fully succeeded. This massive programme of social welfare has been accompanied by spectacular advances in medical science, extending its power to the diseases of the mind and rescuing uncountable numbers of children and adults from the death which would have been their sure fate in any previous century. But in the eyes of many thousands, and perhaps of millions, all this glory of orthodox medicine has been dimmed by the religious impressiveness of various medical heresies. Our time has been as interested as earlier periods were in the possibility that a man of faith (or at least of 'positive thinking') may order his emotional life better than the unbeliever, may gain a strange mastery over his body and its ills, and may even bring health to others.

From Rasputin at the Imperial Russian court to a faith-healer in the back streets of Chicago, many a strange personality has been found among those who have ministered to the Western desire to be cured without the doctors. But this movement has not departed entirely on personal magnetism. The modern literature of unorthodox medicine is enormous. In Christian Science, Mrs. Mary Baker Eddy founded a religious body which is in many ways exactly what we should expect as a replacement of the historic churches, and despite its founder's death in 1910 this body has greatly prospered. The First Church of Christ, Scientist, Boston, or more precisely its Board of Trustees, wields an executive authority which the Vatican might envy, and the *Osservatore Romano* is as a newspaper less respected than the *Christian Science Monitor*. The Christian Science

Reading Rooms found in many places in the English-speaking, middle-class world do much to ensure that Mrs. Eddy's book *Science and Health* is revered and used as the indispensable key and supplement to the Christian Bible. But for all its efficiency, this movement seems to owe its spread largely to the testimonies of people who have found light, health and happiness through Christian Science. We cannot wonder that the agnostic historian H. A. L. Fisher entitled the book which he wrote about it in 1929: *Our New Religion.*[1] Basically its teaching is that matter is unreal beside spirit, and that diseases of the body are illusions produced by mental sickness; thus if the mind is made and kept healthy in accordance with Mrs. Eddy's teaching, the body will also be healthy. For this belief some Christian Scientists have laid down their lives, refusing medical treatment when gravely ill.

We have here, argued and institutionalised, what William James at the beginning of the century called 'the religion of healthy-mindedness'. The interest in 'para-normal' approaches to death and disease, resulting in the churches of Spiritualism and Christian Science, springs from the feeling that the churches have abdicated from their proper concerns. Here is an apparently spiritual Gospel, a Gospel of personal survival and health, and the churches are criticised for capitulating to the climate of the secular century by their concentration on the social Gospel. However, this Gospel is by itself no more adequate to sustain a new religion than is the social Gospel's baptism of a current philosophy of nationalism or internationalism, individualism or socialism.

What is lacking in the spiritual and the social Gospels, in comparison with the great religions of the past, is a vision of reality comprehensive enough, and profound enough, to be the truth which converts great numbers of people, or which seems to them the very basis of a truthful and integrated account of the world. Through this enthusiastic

[1] A more recent study is by C. S. Braden, *Christian Science Today* (Dallas, 1958).

acceptance such a vision unites, disciplines and energises a definite fellowship of adherents; and through this fellowship it can change or build a whole society. The Spiritualists are right to say that the social Gospel is not such a vision, for it deals with the temporary. It neglects that essential strain in religion which is 'other-worldly'—which teaches that political and economic arrangements, however important, are as nothing compared with the soul's eternal destiny. Caesar, however excellent a ruler he may be, however useful and honourable, cannot cover everything, and is not entitled to the complete self-surrender of immortal spirits. This applies even to the Caesar of the welfare state. On the other hand, the spiritual Gospel provides only a trivial commentary on life apart from the overcoming of disease and death. Thus we find G. N. M. Tyrrell complaining about Christianity's involvement in this world: 'Would it not have been natural to insist that the Kingdom of Heaven is a spiritual state and not a state of society to be some day achieved in this world; that Christianity never promised that the world will be any better than it is today and, although we may hope it will be, that religion would be no whit perturbed if it were not?'[1] The spiritual Gospel neglects that strain in religion which teaches that the vision of ultimate reality heals not only the individual but also society as a whole, beginning with the Church, and conquers not only physical death and disease but also that vast state of man's alienation from the true source of blessedness which is usually called sin. Above all, the spiritual Gospel can easily become a Gospel about the powers inherent in man during his life on earth and after it (for a limited time?). God need not come into it. H. H. Price sensibly concludes that 'religious people are compelled to postulate the existence, in some human beings at least, of what may be called super-sensory cognitive capacities', but that this telepathy between people is not at all the same

---

[1] *The Personality of Man* (Penguin edn., London, 1954), p. 283. In some expert students, 'intellectual inhibitions' have not been weakened by psychical research. See, e.g., C. E. M. Hansel, *ESP: A Scientific Evaluation* (New York, 1966).

as the sense of the divine. Psychical research, he points out, does nothing at all to establish the existence of God. 'It only weakens the powerful intellectual inhibitions which at present prevent the question from being investigated.'[1]

To sum up: neither the social nor the spiritual Gospel ends in the old vision of earth and heaven united in the eternal joy of the Communion of Saints, the City of God. Neither Gospel evokes more than a fraction of those intellectual, aesthetic and moral energies, those emotional and corporate forces, which have built up worship in the traditional religions.

New Religious Movements

In this situation, many in the West have reached the conclusion that there can be no substitute for religion, and they have interpreted 'religion' in the old sense as the attempt of the human spirit to commune with a reality greater than it and greater even than nature as a whole. This definitely religious interest, continuing in our society, accounts for the appeal of the new spiritual movements which deviate from the traditional churches but retain many characteristics of Christianity. New movements have flourished in the twentieth-century West because their religion seems to be rooted in Western soil, either as a religion of the oppressed or more comfortably.[2]

An example of indigenous Western religion is Mormonism with its new scriptures revealing the ancient history of America, tracing the Red Indians to Hebrews who crossed the Atlantic after the fall of the Kingdom of Judah, and recounting how the risen Christ planted the Gospel and the Church in that continent. This teaching, which began in the 1820s, has become largely respectable after the admission of the State of Utah to the United States in 1895, and its

---

[1] *Some Aspects of the Conflict between Science and Religion* (Cambridge, 1953), pp. 47–9.
[2] See, e.g., Horton Davies, *Christian Deviations: The Challenge of the New Spiritual Movements* (1954; revd. edn., London, 1965).

evangelism in many places in our century may be seen from its present statistics: this Church of Jesus Christ of the Latter-Day Saints numbers almost two million full members.[1]

Two million adherents are also claimed by a movement of more recent origin: British Israel, which teaches that the white citizens of Great Britain and its former empire (including the United States) are descended from the ten 'lost' tribes of Israel and are the legitimate heirs of the political promises made by God to Abraham.

Larger numbers appear to have been influenced by a movement very different in its claims also largely middle-class in its ethos: Moral Rearmament. Originally known as 'a First Century Christian Fellowship', this movement had by the time of the death of its founder, Frank Buchman, in 1961, ceased to be distinctively Christian, but its religious basis may be seen in some continuing characteristics. It has waged its campaigns to counteract the West's loss of morale during the economic depression of the 1920s and 1930s and more recently to influence the international conflict between the American or Western ideology and Communism. It has taught the 'Four Absolutes'—truth, honesty, unselfishness and love—and also the need to turn to God for guidance in daily life; but in its enthusiasm it has spread stories of miraculous changes in individuals and in extremely difficult political or industrial situations brought about by the conferences and plays which are its chief means of propaganda.[2]

We have just mentioned three movements which have attempted to replace historic Christianity. Many more 'Holiness Churches' and far more bizarre movements, have arisen, particularly in the United States, around prophets of shorter-lived effectiveness.[3] Whether they originate

---

[1] See Thomas O'Dea, *The Mormons* (Chicago, 1957).

[2] See a. W. Eister, *Drawing Room Conversion: A Sociological Account of the Oxford Group Movement* (Durham, M. C., 1950); Tom Driberg, *The Mystery of M.R.A.* (London, 1964).

[3] See Christopher Evans, *Cults of Unreason* (London, 1973), for an account of movements such as Scientology.

among the oppressed or among the comfortable, whether they look for the coming of the Kingdom or say that it is among us if only we will read between the lines of our newspapers, whether they ignore or invoke 'science', such movements have in common a falsity which is obvious to almost all whose minds have been trained to think, and their incompatibility with education seems to rule them out as faiths for the future. It may be that if the West moves further from its Christian past, more successful religious movements will arise to interpret Western man's new spiritual pilgrimage. Such a movement would need a new prophet, even a new Christ. A number of writers have speculated about the possibility. Some, like Nevil Shute in his novel *Round the Bend* (London, 1951), have suggested that the new incarnation of God will come out of Asia to relate Eastern wisdom to the civilisation symbolised by the aeroplane. Other writers, like Pierre Berton in his Canadian best-seller, have speculated about a Western Christ to come: 'some spiritual genius . . . who will take all the incredible laws, postures and myths of today's Church and turn them inside out . . . Such a man would by sacrifice and commitment work his modern miracles. He would have to be a man of vigour, humour, passion, concern, guts, and, above all, action . . . It is axiomatic that he would be reviled as the most dangerous of heretics . . . And it is in the cards that society would find some modern means of crucifying him . . . Yet there would be one or two who, at the moment of his death, would be moved to the point that they would commit their own lives to his ideals.'[1] But in the history of the world only two men, Gautama and Muhammed, have established their rivalry with Jesus over centuries and for millions as the revealer and bearer of ultimate reality among men; and new Messiahs are liable to be judged by a somewhat alarming standard in the post-Christian West, as may be seen by the limited success which has come to the Bahai faith since its announcement that Christ had

[1] Pierre Berton, *The Comfortable Pew* (Toronto, 1965; British edn., 1966), pp. 143–4.

returned to West Asia in 1863, in the person of Bahaullah.[1] However unfairly, Europe and America are liable to insist not only that a new Messiah must be crucified, but also that on the third day he must rise again.

In his brilliantly written book of 1929, *A Preface to Morals*, Walter Lippmann referred to 'the gifts of a vital religion which can bring the whole of a man into adjustment with the whole of his relevant experience'. He commented: 'Our forefathers had such a religion. They quarrelled a good deal about the details, but they had no doubt that there was an order in the universe which justified their lives because they were a part of it. The acids of modernity have dissolved that order for many of us, and there are some in consequence who think that the needs which religion fulfilled have also been dissolved. But however self-sufficient the eugenic and perfectly educated man of the distant future may be, our present experience is that the needs remain. In failing to meet them, it is plain that we have succeeded only in sub-stituting trivial illusions for majestic faiths. For while the modern emancipated man may wonder how anyone ever believed that in this universe of stars and atoms and multitudinous life, there is a drama in progress of which the principal event was enacted in Palestine nineteen hundred years ago, it is not really a stranger fable than many which he so readily accepts.'[2] And many who recall the social and religious tumult which has come since Walter Lippmann wrote those words, and which he has chronicled with dis-tinction, would say that as a diagnosis of the mind of the West those words still stand.

Not even Mr. Lippmann's own sketch of a humanist morality has filled the vacuum, for it presented as 'maturity' a rejection of man's ultimate hope. 'A man may take you into the open at night and show you the stars, but unless he feels the vast indifference of the universe to his own fate, and has placed himself in the perspective of cold and illimitable space, he has not looked maturely on the

[1] See John Ferraby, *All Things Made New* (London, 1957).
[2] p. 8.

heavens.'[1] Here the Mr. Lippmann of 1929 echoed Bertrand Russell's despair as the foundation of 'A Free Man's Worship'.[2] That famous essay of 1902, however, displayed the fervour of a Victorian preacher, rather than the ice-cold neutrality of a modern logician. On the one hand, the 'firm foundation of unyielding despair' must be laid by accepting the truth that man's 'origin, his growth, his hopes and fears, his loves and his beliefs, are but the outcome of accidental collocations of atoms' and are all 'destined to extinction'. On the other hand, the 'free man's worship' is 'to burn with passion for eternal things' and to treat others so that 'wherever a spark of the divine fire kindled in their hearts, we were ready with encouragement, with sympathy, with brave words in which high courage glowed'. This attitude—like Russell's willingness to allow his life, even in old age, to be agitated by a passionate involvement in public affairs—shows a despair touched by faith, hope and love.

Mr. Lippmann suggested 'that the function of high religion is to reveal to men the quality of mature experience, that high religion is a prophecy and anticipation of what life is like when desire is in perfect harmony with reality'.[3] In effect, this definition makes religion the grand debunker of desire. Reality is grim; religion has to adjust men to it. This is a twentieth-century revival of the Stoic philosophy of the ancient Roman empire, as we see when *A Preface to Morals* gives a highly Stoic definition of the 'mature' man. Such a man 'would take the world as it comes, and within himself remain quite unperturbed. . . . Since nothing gnawed at his vitals, neither doubt nor ambition, not frustration, nor fear, he would move easily through life.'[4] But the history of Stoicism gives the answer to this kind of hope. Stoicism was outlived by the very Christians whom its favourite philosopher, the Emperor Marcus Aurelius, despised and persecuted, because Christianity had what Stoicism lacked and

[1] p. 187.
[2] Bertrand Russell, *Mysticism and Logic*, chapter 3.
[3] p. 193.
[4] pp. 329–30.

what human nature wanted. It had *joy*. This joy was based
on the conviction that, ultimately, 'reality' is not indifferent
to the fate of a sparrow, still less of a person. 'High religion'
which contains this joy teaches that mortal men desire too
little, not too much. As a maturer Walter Lippmann has
come to acknowledge in subsequent writings, for better or
for worse it is a religion of joy, of 'peace with God' that the
American people insists on having in our time. And in
recent writings Mr. Lippmann has indicated his growing
sympathy with the churches which repeat the Christian
Gospel's offer of joy.

We may add that not only the American churchgoer is
left dissatisfied by a modern Stoicism. A British 'humanist'
such as Professor R. W. Hepburn states that 'given flaws
of logic or evidence, much needs to be abandoned' in Christianity; but at the same time he gives a nostalgic sigh which
is, if anything, louder than Walter Lippmann's. 'There may
survive, however, moral concepts of a richness that shows
up the meagreness of the humanist's own. And there may
survive ways of seeing humanity, transfiguration of the
supposedly familiar world, which—even when we are quite
unable to assimilate or domesticate them—can haunt and
trouble and goad the imagination.'[1]

Here, it seems, is the real reason why the replacement of
Christianity is so hard to achieve. Many observers, while
sharing much of the conviction of Lippmann or Hepburn
about the need to abandon the old, *see no real alternative
to the renewal of the Jewish-Christian tradition*, if 'high
religion' is to come alive for the modern West. History
teaches them how massive is the passion of heroism and
saintliness which builds a religion, and how vast is the mechanism of tradition which sustains it across the centuries; and
their knowledge of the world as it is teaches them that if
other faiths are to be compared with Christianity in this
context, *no alternative to Christian belief can make good its
claim*. Such observers are often oppressed by the odour of

[1] R. W. Hepburn in *Objections to Humanism*, ed. H. J. Blackham
(London, 1963), p. 54.

decay given off by the contemporary churches, and their hearts are liable to break when they consider the plight of Christianity; but then these observers may turn to contemplate Christianity's rivals, and once again it becomes clear to them where the hope lies.[1]

Can a revival come after an almost complete abandonment of the old churches? The longing to recover the primitive vitality of the ancestral faith while discarding most of its traditional organisation has inspired a widespread movement of new churches, sects and 'assemblies' in the West. These bodies are very varied in their beliefs and backgrounds, but many of the strongest accept the label 'Pentecostalism'. Conservative—indeed, often Fundamentalist—in its attitude to the Bible, Pentecostalism holds that the ardour of genuine Christianity, as presented in the Bible, is accompanied by phenomena such as 'speaking with tongues' and 'faith healing'. Thus every Christian ought to know from his own experience the ecstasies and extraordinary powers which came to the apostles at Pentecost. This modern 'Baptism of the Holy Spirit' was experienced first in Los Angeles in 1907, but belief in it now unites a worldwide movement whose evangelism has had special success in the vacuum left by the corruption of Roman Catholicism in Latin America.[2] Pentecostalism has often voiced a protest against degrading social and economic circumstances; but its spiritual joy and power are now appealing both to considerable numbers of people with a middle-class background and to many who remain within the historic churches. And even when Pentecostal Churches are organ-

---

[1] Mr. Leslie Paul, who in his autobiography first popularised the phrase 'angry young man' and then bravely immersed himself in a prolonged study of the finance and administration of the Church of England, might be understood from his writings in the ecclesiastical field as a prophet of doom on the institutional Church. But in his philosophical work, e.g. in his *Alternatives to Christian Belief* (New York, 1967), he analyses the failure of these alternatives to answer the meaninglessness and misery which (on the evidence of the serious secular literature of our time) he finds to be characteristic of the human situation.

[2] See W. J. Hollenweger, *The Pentecostals* (London, 1972); Steve Durasoff, *Bright Wind of the Spirit* (New York, 1972).

ised separately it does not follow that they will always be sectarian. As with many previous religious movements, the sense of inner confidence, the Puritan moral progress and the ability to co-operate in a cause—qualities which result from the success of the sect—tend to bring consequences which the first enthusiasts did not expect. The sect's members rise to a superior social class; the sect itself is gradually transformed into a respectable, organised and educated denomination. This process has been well expounded by Dr. Bryan Wilson.[1] Although this authority on secretarianism, shows himself to be astonishingly ignorant about the traditional churches, which he constantly compares to their disadvantage with the sects, yet the future of Christianity does seem to depend on the churches more than on the sects. This is not only because the churches still have a numerical advantage over the sects (this applies even in Latin America), but also because, as Dr. Wilson shows, the sects develop into respectable denominations.

When we glanced at religion in the United States in Chapter 2, we concluded that the over-simple distinction between the rebellious vitality of the sect and the established vagueness of the National Church must be refined to take account of the denomination, a body which is vigorous and self-aware without being sectarian in the sense of being fanatically exclusive. It is significant that most reformers of the denominations in the twentieth century have chosen to work from within these semi-established churches; there have been remarkably few serious attempts to found new bodies. Indeed, many of these reformers have emphasised the importance of reunion between the denominations. This ecumenical movement of Christian reunion has been the antithesis of sectarianism, yet it has probably been more effective than the sects as a focus for Christian renewal—and many Pentecostalists are now joining the ecumenical movement; some of them are becoming members of the

[1] See Bryan Wilson, *Sects and Society* and *Religious Sects* (London, 1961 and 1970), and the essays which he edited on *Patterns of Sectarianism* (London, 1967).

World Council of Churches. It may be that the future of the Christian community, and therefore the main future of 'high religion' at least in the West, will lie in a process which looks very small amid the great dramas of our time, and very tame amid the exciting novelties: the renewal (dare we not say: the Pentecostal renewal?) of the denominations.

Our survey of these new quasi-religions and religious sects suggests, in brief, that Matthew Arnold's famous saying is as true in the twentieth century as it was in the nineteenth: 'Two things about the Christian religion must surely be clear to anybody with eyes in his head. One is, that men cannot do without it; the other, that they cannot do with it as it is.'[1] An American sociologist, E. A. Shils, has written a penetrating survey of the limits of secularisation.[2] He concludes: 'The need for order, and for meaning in order, is too fundamental in man for the human race as a whole to allow itself to be bereft of the rich and elaborate scheme of metaphorical interpretation of existence which is made available by the great world religions. The spread of education and of scientific knowledge, as well as the improved level of material well-being, will not eradicate them unless those who have these religions in their charge lose their self-confidence because of the distrust the highly educated hold toward the inherited metaphors.' We may now draw one conclusion. *A renewed Christianity would still have a chance.* And so, in Part Two of this book, we may turn to see what is going on today inside the Christian religion. How is its fellowship being reshaped? How is its faith being restated? How do contemporary Christians struggle to receive 'more truth'— which is their only hope if their religion is ever again to be the living faith of the Western millions? To these difficult questions, all of which have been very widely and thoroughly discussed, we may—with an impertinence made necessary by the need to be brief—suggest some tentative answers.

[1] Matthew Arnold, *God and the Bible* (London, 1875), p. xiv.
[2] In *The Religious Situation: 1968*, ed. D. R. Cutler, pp. 733–48.

PART TWO

CHAPTER SEVEN

A New Shape for the Christian Church

Reunion and Renewal

Many people who would call themselves Christians would say that Christianity needs no separate fellowship at all. 'You can be a Christian without going to church' is a very popular slogan. And many practising members of the churches would say that Christianity now needs a fellowship with a shape different from any church's present shape. Throughout the century discontent with the churches has been voiced by Christians. It came to one climax after the First World War, when it seemed possible to remake the churches as well as the nations in order to serve democracy; and in the 1960s the second climax began.[1]

The fact that Christianity is divided has contributed significantly to this prevailing sense that the churches need renewal. For one thing, there has been no united front in conservative Christianity. When it has been proclaimed authoritatively that 'the Church teaches . . .', the inevitable question has arisen: *which church?* As the world has been reminded by the tragedies in Northern Ireland—which admittedly are not solely or mainly religious in origin—the

[1] Instead of attempting to compile a bibliography of authoritative works, I may mention that I edited three reports on ecumenical conferences: *Unity Begins at Home* (1964), *Christians in a New World* (1966) and *The British Churches Turn to the Future* (1973). All were published by the SCM Press, London. I also contributed a chapter to *The Ecumenical Advance, 1948–68*, ed. H. F. Fey (London, 1970).

most conservative Christians have also been those most prone to fight each other, rather than to work out a joint approach to the modern world.

Many have drawn the conclusions that something has disintegrated at the very centre of a religion which is so deeply divided, and that the reunion of Christians, so far from being mainly a task for diplomacy and administration, should be accompanied by far-reaching changes. Among those who have seen Christian disunity as a challenge to a radical renewal have been many leaders of the churches. This emphasis has been prominent in the work of the World Council of Churches, which chose as the theme of its Fourth Assembly in Uppsala in 1968 the declaration attributed to Christ in the Revelation of St. John the Divine: 'Behold, I make all things new.' More strikingly still, Pope John XXIII and a clear majority of the two thousand prelates who assembled for the Second Vatican Council in 1962 saw that the Roman Catholic Church must open itself to the criticisms of others, and must commit itself to *aggiornamento* (renewal). The gatherings of the World Council of Churches and of the Roman Catholic bishops might easily have become occasions for self-congratulation, like most meetings of political movements. Instead, they have publicly and irrevocably expressed the conviction that the disunity of Christians points to many other scandals now afflicting institutional Christianity; and they have confessed their own sins as well as the sins of fellow-Christians. The road to unity has thus drawn the churches out of their isolated securities into a pilgrimage where the way is tough, the company strange and the destination scarcely known.

Millions of words of modern Christian self-criticism have been spoken or printed, but it is not easy to trace a strong thread running through the debates. Clearly we need a new Reformation. Few, if any, of the major theologians of the twentieth century have avoided comparisons with Luther and Calvin. But wanting does not make a Reformation, and it is difficult to find in these debates a realistic hope of a renewal on a scale sufficient to create a new religious situation. An ecumenical leader has voiced the despair of so many reformers: 'If somebody has sufficient courage to make a study of cynicism, he should buy the reports of all major ecumenical gatherings, read them, and see what the churches said together. Then he should go to the balcony of his house and look over his city at the churches that are standing there, from which steeples have risen to heaven since the Middle Ages, and see how nothing has happened to them.'[1] But the smallness of the change achieved in comparison with the eloquence of the reformers is not only the fault of the leaders of the churches; it also brings home to us the difficulty which has been experienced by many interested members of churches in gaining from the debates a clear and practical programme of reform. So much of the prophecy has seemed either vaguely idealistic or cruelly destructive. Conferences have come, and conferences have gone; books have exploded, and books have been forgotten; and the local churches, sullenly resentful or cheerfully ignorant, have remained much as they were before the prophets arose. The world has remained largely indifferent to the churches' internal debates, except when these could provide material for a brief melodrama of modern progress *versus* clerical reaction, or when they seemed to touch on public questionings about political or sexual morality. The humiliation of the Christian Church is the great fact which stands out, and it often seems that the only solid achievement by Christians in our age has been their acquisition of a spirit of penitent humility.

However, even that modest achievement is something significant. What needs most to be remembered against the background of history is the rapidity with which the tree of new life has begun to grow in this humble soil; and we can remember this when we contrast our time with the nineteenth century.

The nineteenth century saw great activity in the churches of Europe and America, and in comparison with the lethargy

[1] Albert van den Heuvel, *The Humiliation of the Church* (Philadelphia, 1966), p. 51.

prevailing over much of the previous century it might be described as the time of the Christian counter-attack. It was a 'century of hope' in theological as well as in secular terms. Many new religious activities were made possible by the secular advances. Missionaries could travel the globe in the new steamers; preachers could stir evening congregations thanks to gas-light; new churches could be built and new societies could be organised. But the religion of the West in the nineteenth century was essentially conservative. In its most self-revealing intimacies it was nostalgic. It built many thousands of churches, but most of them copied the architecture of the Middle Ages. And in many ways that era of hope and expansion, with its conservative basis, is today a burden on Christian consciences. Their muscular confidence —all the righteousness and all the energy which we sum up by the word Victorian—must often seem superior to our own age of general anxiety, of intellectual confusion and of religious failure. In particular, the prosperity of the churches in the nineteenth century is now apt to arouse the envy of hard-pressed clergymen and doubtful laymen.

Yet there was an inherent weakness in nineteenth-century religion. Essentially, what happened then was the application of modern methods to old patterns of belief and behaviour; and these patterns were already doomed by the very modernity which gave them a temporary revival. In ethics, the old patterns of behaviour traditionally derived from Christian belief were still widely respected (often by hypocrisy, 'the tribute which vice pays to virtue'), but they were being undermined by the shift in the social forces and by the questioning of the intellectual foundations of belief. The replacement of an Emerson or a Ruskin by a Lippmann or a Camus was inevitable, and those who adhered to some form of Christian belief could not expect to be spared all consequences of the growing revolution in morals. The modern insistence on education and amusement was satisfied partially and temporarily through the activities of the churches, with impressive results for the statistics of organised religion, but the steady growth of truly modern forms of education and amusement was bound to take the crowds from the churches in the long run. Many of the middle class went to church in order to demonstrate their respectability; but a secular life in a suburb would do this better. Many of the working-class, struggling to rise above degradation, used their local churches as means of relief and self-improvement; but their esteem for the churches depended on their own poverty, not on much conviction about the churches' teaching. Their sons and daughters, often housed in characterless but comfortable new areas, would inevitably turn for material welfare to the machinery of the democratic state, and would seldom feel any need for the churches as allies in the social struggle.

This insecure, even artificial, character of much nineteenth-century churchgoing can now be seen to have been associated with another basic defect: its quarrelsomeness. Often basically uncertain about what in the old religious tradition was really appropriate to a rapidly changing world, nineteenth-century Christians seem to have felt obliged to should all the louder in order to cry up their rival wares. Their religion was often truculently controversial. It spent much energy in fighting atheism or moral ungodliness, and was seldom too selective in its choice of weapons for those fights; but it spent even more passion on controversies between Christians, even between Christians of the same denomination. The Roman Catholic Church was the most militant, to its gain and loss; but the same spirit resulted in naked competition among the Protestants of America, and in England the spirit of controversy flared up in disputes between the Established Church and the Nonconformists (over the control of religious education, over the compulsory payment of agricultural tithes to the parish priests and even over the right to be buried in the parish churchyards). These competitions and controversies were still fierce enough to blacken at least the first decade of the twentieth century.

Half a century later, there was far less nostalgia and far less truculence in all the denominations. In a sense the churches, too, have 'come of age'; they are sadder but wiser, less hearty, less brash, less self-confident, but perhaps no less effective in the mature religion of the spirit. The rise of a maturer charity may be attributed in part to a decline of interest in the religious positions taken up by past generations. The feeling grows that a new age is here. The old answers are, many think, irrelevant—because the old questions are not being asked. In the Roman Catholic Church, for example, the theological freeze which set in with the condemnation of modernism in the first decade of this century was thawed in the dialogue with Protestantism, and even with secularism, which began in the 1950s and 1960s; and in the 1970s, we can see that Roman Catholics learn, to the great profit of themselves and of the world, when they begin to listen before teaching. Within the non-Roman churches the hatchets have been buried for a longer time, and more deeply. A trend which is the central theme of their twentieth-century history slowly moves all the churches towards a reconciliation and a reunion which must jeopardise all their cherished institutions, and the costliness of this change explains its slowness.

The coming together of almost all the Presbyterians into a united Church of Scotland (1929) and of the different Wesleyan traditions into the Methodist Church (1932) were no small achievements in Britain. The union of Presbyterians, Methodists and Congregationalists to form the United Church of Canada (1925), and of these three traditions with the Anglicans to form the United Church of South India (1947), made history even more decisively. In the United States there have been significant unions of Protestants who were already heirs of one 'confessional' tradition (for example, they were all Lutherans) but who were divided into separate churches because of differences in ethnic origins (for example, they were of German or Swedish stock), in colour of skin or in theological convictions (they were liberal or conservative).

Such unions—and still more, the many inter-church conversations which have not produced successful reunion schemes—may seem trivial in comparison with the size of the century's challenge to institutional Christianity, but it needs to be remembered that willingness to consider reunion would have been inconceivable if there had not been a humble spirit of self-criticism within the institutions. Ever since the Lausanne Conference on Faith and Order in 1927, it has been clear that a United Church could not emerge without the acceptance of the unfamiliar, and subsequent ecumenical history could be summed up as the progress of this unpalatable idea. Presbyterians have recognised that not all questions can be answered by referring back to the Scottish Reformation of 1560; Methodists have broken away from loyalty to the local chapel and to the memory of John Wesley in order to ask how Methodism might best serve the Gospel in the twentieth century; Congregationalists have forsaken the cherished principle of the independence of the local congregation in order that Christians might combine for their contemporary tasks; and Anglicans have been willing to rethink and reshape institutions so venerable as episcopacy or (in England) the privileged establishment of the Church by the State. Baptists, while more conservative and usually standing apart from full reunion (specially the Southern Baptists of the United States), have not entirely lacked the ecumenical vision.

The search for Christian unity has, indeed, so far been the chief way by which the twentieth century has advanced towards Christian renewal. This is not to say that reunion will automatically result in renewal. On the contrary, the coming together of denominations into a Church apparently big and successful can increase any complacency and remoteness already existing in their leadership, and can result in institutional rigidity. It has been said again and again that no such intention is, or should be, in the minds of those who promote the cause of Christian reunion, and on the basis of some historical evidence it can be argued that a Church which is large in numbers can also be rich in the diversity of the attitudes to be found in its membership. Yet the danger of uniformity is certainly present in any scheme for merging religious institutions and deserves more attention than it generally receives in the flush of ecumenical enthusiasm.

The World Council of Churches in its Assembly at New Delhi in 1961 accepted as a definition of 'the unity we seek' the idea that in each place all Christians should be brought together into one fellowship 'joining in common prayer and having a corporate life'. This definition may have been influenced unduly by the example of South India, where as a result of the comity agreements between the missionary societies the Protestants in a district tended to come from one denominational tradition. For the planning of Christian strategy in a Western city the New Delhi definition leaves all the crucial questions unanswered, except that it rightly implies that congregations should recognise each other, occasionally worship and witness together, and continuously co-operate for certain specialised tasks. Fewer congregations would be needed in a united Church, but many studies in religious sociology suggest that at the local level it is best not to merge *all* worshippers into a monolithic association, for a variety of religious communities can appeal to different neighbourhoods, to different temperaments and to different classes.

This kind of question illustrates another danger: that the reunion negotiations between the churches, with all the theological, pastoral, liturgical and administrative problems involved, will absorb over a long period energies which might have been devoted to relating the churches to the society around them. The introspection may continue when the formal reunion has been achieved. Although the Church of South India, for example, has made some progress in its contribution to the total life of India since it achieved unity in 1947, this outreach in service and evangelism has been less than many of its friends had hoped, and the basic explanation seems to be its continuing preoccupation with reunion problems—with problems, that is, which arise out of a Western theology and style of life rather than out of the living faith and culture of its Hindu neighbours. We have to take the warning that Christian reunion is not a panacea for all the diseases which afflict institutional Christianity.

But it must be repeated that reunion will often be the spearhead of renewal in the churches. Two reasons can be given for this.

First, the very sobriety of the discussions involved as denominations come together should remind us that, in order to make progress, *churches like individuals must start where they are and move one step at a time*. The habits of a church, as of an individual, grow into a mass of inertia. Radical pressures can thrust forward dramatically if instead of trying to alter these habits they try to create the ecclesiastical equivalent of Utopia: a Church new and pure. Many articles or books have been written in our time to voice the impatience of Christians with the Church as it is. Some actual communities have been founded to embody a radical group's vision of a purified Christianity. These utterances and experiments have had a great value in disturbing complacency. Yet much of all this brave adventure has got nowhere, for the whole experience of the century cries aloud that, in religion as in politics, Utopia never comes to this earth. No Christian body is ever totally renewed and purified, so that the Christian who waits for that event before committing himself to any church has to wait until he joins the celestial choir. Even the prophets of reform have their own limitations and weaknesses, their own conceits and follies which time reveals all too painfully, so that many in our time have become disillusioned on personal grounds with the prophetic call to purity. Even experiments in twentieth-century discipleship lose their freshness, and need institutional structures if they are to continue their work; and those structures lead to fresh complaints that the happy pioneering days are over and the Spirit has again been quenched. And during all the impatience and experimentation of the radical minority, the great bulk of the people who are interested in religion does not come into close contact with these experiments, but forms its impressions of Christianity from what is routine and dull, particularly from the everyday behaviour of parents, teachers, clergy and lay friends or colleagues. If the impact of Christianity on the life of the total community is to be strengthened, it is therefore necessary to pay attention to possibly tedious problems raised by the ordinary life of the churches. When the pattern of life in those churches is unsatisfactory, a preliminary impact is necessary, with a force large enough to disturb the pattern. The experience of the century has shown that, in religion as elsewhere in social life, no challenge to entrenched institutionalism is sufficiently powerful except the challenge of a definite plan to unite the existing institutions with each other. Only this apparently dull, administrative proposal brings about the necessary self-examination in churches from top to bottom, as leaders and led alike are driven to ask: what is essential?

Moreover, it is highly desirable that the problem of Christian disunity should be one of the first of the practical problems to be tackled, for *their lack of unity erects many obstacles for the churches in their approach to the people*. When the tide is flowing strongly in favour of churchgoing (at least in the middle classes), these obstacles are scarcely noticeable. The denominations of Victorian England or of the contemporary United States seemed to flourish because of their competitiveness. (At least, this applies to the towns; the division of a village by the building of several houses of worship has seldom been other than tragic.) But when the tide of fashionable religion recedes, or before it begins to flow, we see clearly that competition is on the whole bad for the churches. The need of a denomination to maintain a network of buildings and officials covering the country, when in any one area supporters are few, absorbs almost all that denomination's energy. It causes an introversion which is none the less real because it is thought to be inevitable, and which is greater than the danger of absorption in reunion negotiations. Complacent self-absorption is the disease; reunion is the beginning of the cure.

Despite many problems which would demand attention,

it is probable that a United Church is better able than any of the divided denominations to plan a reasonable strategy and to make a reasonable use of its resources. The hope for the Church of South India, for example, is that greater strength will come if it has the patience to maintain through the problems of union the evangelistic vision in which its union was conceived. It seems beyond question that, if the actual performance of the Church of South India has to some extent been a disappointment, the prospects would have been far worse if Indian nationalism in recent years had been able to say that Christianity consisted of small, divisive sects, each looking to the West for guidance and support. The fate of the Christian mission in China is a vivid warning. But the matter scarcely needs arguing. The need of Christian unity has for too long been recognised as urgent in Asia and Africa—which was why the modern ecumenical movement began in the 'comity' agreements between Protestant missionary societies, in conferences of Protestant missionaries, and in co-operation over education, literature, etc.

Even in the prosperous denominations of the United States, where apparently competition seems good for religion, there are aspects of disunity which many Christians consider scandalous. One such aspect is the very appearance of adjacent churches competing for custom. Such rivalry seems remote from the New Testament's description of the fellowship of the Church as the Body of Christ, and devout Americans for whom that description is significant have their consciences burdened. The dependence of each local church on local popularity, while it has kept American religion in touch with the needs of the people, has contributed to the spiritual and intellectual debasement of popular religion to which Americans are increasingly sensitive. The question coming to the fore in the United States, as the movement for Christian unity slowly gathers strength, is how this movement can increase the practical effectiveness of the Christian mission. One consideration which is being stressed is that, as the movement for 'inter-faith' co-operation has already enabled the American religious bodies to speak and act together to a limited extent, so a further unity would enable a fuller witness and service, reaching out to the whole society of the United States. A crucial defect in the denominational pattern of American religion has resulted from the pressure on the churches to think primarily of the needs of their own members (with the largely unspoken fear that dissatisfied customers would transfer their membership to a rival), instead of considering the religious task within the whole local community and the whole state. There has been a contrast between the lavish provision made for the internal life of their congregations in the churches of the United States, and the relative poverty of attempts to influence the national life in secular spheres.

In secularised Europe, particularly in Britain, religious worship and instruction through television, sound radio and the schools are the chief links connecting the Christian Gospel with the bulk of the people, and it is usually recognised that the use of these public media should be shared by members of different denominations. But special, often insuperable, problems have arisen in Catholic–Protestant co-operation, and even when the worship and instruction are interdenominational there remains the great problem of linking children or adults influenced through these media to actual congregations in which their faith might deepen and grow. The last mentioned problem may have been as significant as any other factor in ensuring that the vast amount of religious instruction put out by Britain's radios and schools has brought few recruits into the churches, although it has checked the general process of secularisation. Historians may well judge that a major defeat of Christianity in England was the failure of the English churches to agree about religious instruction in the nation's schools. Not until 1870 was it fully recognised that the Church of England could not educate the people in schools under its own control. Not until 1944 did the Church of England and the Free Churches agree on arrangements for the religious life of the state schools, and even then the syllabus of religious instruction, by concentrating on the Bible as the common bond of the denominations, was dangerously remote from the real interests of the children. It is not practical for churchmen to seek a remedy through the expansion of church-controlled schools, although the Church of England and the Roman Catholic Church both still conduct large educational efforts. The main hope of a more vital role for religion in the schools lies in adventurous co-operation between Christians prepared to sink the rival denominational traditions in order to talk the language of a new generation about what interests that generation.

The Emerging Church

Although it is difficult to see a continuous thread and a realistic hope in the century's ecumenical and other debates about the nature of the Christian Church, it is not impossible. On the contrary, enough agreement is emerging to enable us to glimpse what a Church may look like if, while remaining imperfect, it is substantially renewed and reunited—and to persuade us that the prospect may be more real at the end of the twentieth century than it was at the beginning.

'The vision that arises,' ran the famous Lambeth Appeal from the Anglican bishops in 1920, 'is one of a Church genuinely Catholic, loyal to all Truth . . .' But that appeal for Christian unity, brave and moving as it was, did not begin far enough back, and this largely accounts for its failure to secure solid results after initial enthusiasm. Too much of this century's debate about the Church has been dominated by the question of institutional Catholicity, regarded as continuity with the early and medieval Church, *versus* institutional modernity; or by the question of the intellectual tradition, whether Scriptural or ecclesiastical, *versus* other parts of intellectual truth. Too much effort has been put too soon into the attempt to reconcile these elements. The more profitable vision that arises in the debate is of *a Church genuinely Christian.*

Such a Church would approximate, as closely as is possible for sinful mortals, to the singlemindedness implied in Dietrich Bonhoeffer's arresting phrase for the Church: 'Christ existing as a community'. In some sense it would be an 'extension of the Incarnation', to use another bold phrase popular in some of the century's Anglican theology. It would recover for the life of Christians, as scholarship has recovered in theology, the New Testament's sense that the Lord who speaks to the churches is continuous with the Lord who spoke in Galilee. But this centrality of Christ in the Church, this dependence of the Church on the continuing life of Christ at its heart, would be experienced and interpreted like the life of Christ in the flesh and like the first disciples' reaction to their Lord. That is, the presence would be personal: it would be communicated through personal friendship of the Lord for the disciples, of the disciples for each other, and of the disciples for those who would turn to them; it would evoke a personal response, changing with circumstances, liable to misunderstandings and to failures of love, prevailing only because the personal appeal of the Lord Jesus and his saints was so attractive that it was able to persuade into discipleship without destroying the freedom of personal response.

The 'extension of the Incarnation'—if that is at all an appropriate way of speaking of the Christian Church—must, it now seems, involve the abolition of legislative categories to describe the authority found in the Church, the abolition of the emphasis on discipline in the work of the Church's officers, and the abolition of mechanical ways of talking about the grace to be tasted in the Church's worship and life. Many modern Christians have been profoundly dissatisfied both with the rigorous and formal emphasis in Roman Catholicism, and also with Protestantism—whether Protestantism is 'orthodox', emphasising the 'wholly other' remoteness of the biblical God, or 'liberal', emphasising the practical duties of daily life. Such Christians have sought a more spiritual religion, emphasising the contemplation of the eternal glory as every man's right. Such a search has often been accompanied by a recovered respect for the Eastern Orthodox tradition, but a very powerful statement of the cause of spiritual religion can come from Christians who remain entirely within the Western Church's devotional heritage. A personal, devotional and pastoral interpretation of the Church's role—a vision of the Church as servant rather than lord—probably represents the attitude of most churchmen today, but it runs up against centuries of legalism.

The influence of Latin law on Christendom has, we may recall, produced in Christianity much of the rigour which Jesus attacked fiercely when he saw it in the corruptions of his native Judaism. Although Jesus never laid down a clear administrative pattern for the disciples whom he called to follow him and to be his 'apostles' or envoys, Roman Catholics, and Catholic-minded people elsewhere, have insisted that his voice must continue legislating through the authorised succession of Popes and bishops and that all Christians must obey these judges; and the Calvinist tradition has affirmed that the Reformed, Presbyterian organisation of the Church is clearly laid down in the Bible. Although Jesus never hesitated to reinterpret the Old Testament boldly and never wrote a book himself, although he taught in short stories and in vivid exaggerations (that is, in Semitic hyperboles), and although the early Christians seem to have had few scruples in adding to or changing these words of the historical Jesus in order to express what they believed was the teaching of the Divine Spirit in the Church, Christianity has become a code.

The key question is now: *can Christianity be a community, but not a code?* The neo-orthodox reaction of the 1930s against Liberal Protestant individualism now belongs to history. What has survived from it has not been an insistence on a particular organisation, such as may be found in countless volumes of Catholic polemic from that period. We do not observe in many now the mood which made Dietrich Bonhoeffer defend the 'Confessing' Church against the 'German' Christians who compromised with Hitler: 'Whoever knowingly cuts himself off from the Confessing

Church in Germany cuts himself off from salvation.'[1] Even in Roman Catholicism there has been a profound change of tone between the defiant wartime Encyclical on the Church of Pius XII, *Corpus Christi Mysticum* (1943), and the Pastoral Constitution on the Church which was the central achievement of the Second Vatican Council. The Encyclical called Catholics to their own discipline amid far worse terrors, and it called the world to a sanity which could be restored only by embracing the true Church; the Constitution, while abandoning no Roman Catholic claim, saw the Church as the fraternity of the faithful, almost all lay and including (in an ill-defined sense) even Christians who had not submitted to the Pope. The Constitution saw Christians, including ecclesiastical officers, as 'holy' in the sense that they had been accepted by God; but there were sinners needing constant forgiveness and renewal. It saw the Church as 'apostolic', for the whole Church was sent into the whole world to demonstrate the Gospel of love. What has survived the rebirth of the corporate emphasis has been the conviction that the Church is more than a voluntary association, for in its Spirit-empowered fellowship it was intended by Jesus as the prolongation of his work. The Church which wrote the New Testament felt the power of its living Lord in its own life—and if Christianity is not to be reduced to rootless, shapeless democracy, the Lordship of Christ over the Church must be recovered for our time. Many are coming to the conclusion that one way of bearing witness to this Lordship is to recover the leadership of the ministers of the Church—but it must be a leadership with a difference.

In traditional theology, the ordained 'ministry' has been interpreted as embodying Christ's three-fold 'office' or role as prophet, priest and king—yet the word 'minister' comes from the Latin meaning 'servant'. In the Roman Catholic Church and elsewhere, the 'order' of deacons has been re-

[1] Bonhoeffer's article of 1936 on 'The Question of the Boundaries of the Church and Church Union' was translated in *The Way to Freedom*, ed. E. H. Robertson (London, 1966), pp. 75–96.

garded as a mere preparation for the priesthood—yet the word 'deacon' comes from the Greek meaning 'servant'. It is clear that the domineering clericalism which has affected almost all the churches has been a betrayal of the very idea of the Christian minister, and it is not surprising that a revolt has resulted.

Many young men who might have been ordained in a previous generation have preferred to serve the community, and therefore God, by a ministry or diaconate as school-teachers or social workers. They have believed that even in a business career there will be more opportunities of giving effective service than would be likely to come their way if they were in the full-time service of a local church, pre-occupied with worship or 'services'. There is an obvious truth in this emphasis on the role of the layman as a servant of the world for Christ's sake, and increasingly the more profound and creative thinking of Christians about the jobs of the Church's full-time employees is being set in the con-text of a theology of the laity. Other lines of argument which appeal to the younger generation are those which conclude that, if a man does decide to be ordained, it should be either as a 'part-time priest' or as a specialist working outside the local church. It is ominous for the future of the American local church that such arguments are so often heard in the seminaries where the ministers of tomorrow are trained, but there is obvious truth in this insistence on the Church's need of a flexible strategy in a rapidly changing world.

If the isolation of the institutional Church from the everyday life of laymen is the major challenge, it follows that the acceptance of *honorary clergy*, who earn their livings in secular jobs, can be more than a device for getting 'ser-vices' taken during a shortage of professionals; it can be a deliberate step to render a service both to the Church and to the world by recognising some men who have volunteered to carry in their own persons the tensions which come with an allegiance to both. Within the institutional Church, such men can make the voice of the world heard; within the secular world, they can have the thought-provoking strangeness of men set apart for God. Within the Church, they can help to break down the isolation of the professional clergy and can bring laymen out of lonely puzzlement and ineffectiveness into groups concerned with the realities of the world; and within the world they may be able to bring many through friendship to a knowledge of Christ and the Church.

If such are possible roles for large numbers of honorary clergy, the need of *specialist professionals* in the ordained ministry, but not primarily in local churches, is even more apparent. In previous centuries—when parochial clergy were often themselves farmers and identified with the daily work of their parishioners—those few institutions which separated laymen from the routine of the village or town often had their own clergy. Such institutions were schools, colleges, hospitals and the armed forces. It is logical that in a much more complex, more education-conscious and more industry-shaped society more clergymen should feel called to work outside the old routine. Perhaps the most healthy, although also the most painful, experiments in the twentieth-century Church have been those which have taken dedicated men into factories either as 'worker-priests', identified with their mates in the labour movement, or as the professional members of an industrial mission. If the Church is to be vital in an industrial society, there must be many future experiments in new forms of 'ministry'. Among these experiments must be work reaching the controllers of industrial society—careful, humble work, in which theology is combined with a knowledge of economic and social problems.

But realism suggests that *a professional clergy serving a neighbourhood through its local church* remains indispensable. Despite all the attention which has rightly been given to the worker-priests and to the industrial missions, probably the most effective service given to the working class in the twentieth century has been given by the Christians who have staffed many thousands of unromantic churches in artisan housing areas. A literature has grown about the 'down town' churches of America, but equally good work has been done by Christians who have no memorial. Writing by American Christians tends to play down the suburban church in contrast with the 'down town' church, but here again we have to be on our guard against inverted snobbery: suburbanites also have souls, and it is not irrelevant to mention that the comfortable suburb may have a longer future than the industrial slum. The work involved in reaching, befriending and caring pastorally for thousands of people, whether in an artisan or in a middle-class area, does justify the full-time dedication of a man who is educated, trained and equipped. As automation reduces the physical labour needed in manufacturing, the 'service industries' will absorb more and more manpower; and it would be ironical if in this situation a Church professing to love people as individuals were to be left without a corps of efficient professionals willing and able to give their energies to pastoral care. The tasks confronting Christian theology in a secular world are enough in themselves to justify the separation of many thousands of teachers who will give themselves to study and who will have the time and the experience needed to advise laymen in their own quest for religious truth. As the intellectual status of religion becomes increasingly open to question, and as society becomes more educated, it would be tragic if the Church were to be unable to supply for work of education anyone who had more than an amateur's experience in this field. And as the ordained 'ministry', called to these pastoral and intellectual tasks, suffers under inevitable strains, it is surely right that there should be a few men set apart as pastors of the pastors and as teachers of the teachers, whether these men be called professors, chairmen, secretaries or bishops.

Against the idea of the priesthood as a separate caste, mediating between God and men and removed from the normal experience of men by a special training and dress and by the enforcement of celibacy, Protestantism insisted on the priesthood of all believers; and against the idea of the bishop as a feudal lord or as a civil servant, Protestantism

healthily reasserted the equality of all ordained ministers.
Presbyterianism in particular worked out an alternative to
the Catholic structure of the ordained ministry. The minister
in his parish would be surrounded, and it was hoped
supported, by 'elders', each of whom would have a definite
role in the running of the church and a special responsibility for a part of the parish. He would also have the company, and it was hoped the inspiration, of neighbouring
ministers in a group of parishes formed into a 'presbytery'.
This presbytery would be represented in a provincial or
national Assembly, the highest court of the Church. This
system lessened the dangers inherent in the individualism
of the Catholic priest or bishop, who was the monarch of
his petty kingdom but might not be able to turn to any other
human being for friendship and help in intimate equality.
After many abstract arguments and practical controversies,
the Protestant and Presbyterian view of the ministry has
begun to prevail among most Christians. There is a growing
awareness of the spiritual value of a group of priests,
ministers or (the most ancient and useful word) 'presbyters',
with 'deacons' or 'elders' or other assistants, as a team at the
heart of the work of a parish. More and more experiments
are also being tried out which combine the clergy of a
neighbourhood in a larger team, whether in a city or town
whose social unity cuts across the divisions of parishes
or in the thinly populated countryside. A vision of the whole
city or of the whole rural district, a grasp of its urgent social
problems, a recruitment of a task-force of Christians to help
in these problems: all these things may be possible for the
team but seldom for the individual. In the larger team, the
main responsibility for the normal service of a parish remains
with its own clergy, but in addition specialists can be appointed to serve the whole area in education, youth work,
hospital or industrial chaplaincies, etc., and both the
normal and the specialist work can be undergirded by
worship, by common study and discussion of the Bible and
by the useful or pleasant exchanges of friendship. In the
French Catholic Church, the spearhead of mission is seen

to be the *équipe*, or team of priests; for if the priests' fellow-ship is outgoing it can help to communicate the joy of love.

It is in such a setting that the work of a bishop comes alive: no longer as a lord but as a leader who is 'first among equals'. A bishop can play a vital part in keeping the specialist experiments of the Church in touch with each other and with the routine of the local churches; and a bishop who serves the clergy of the local churches by being the chief co-ordinator of their work, by being available for advice out of his experience in detailed problems, and by taking trouble to strengthen worship and study, shows why neither a committee nor an executive on a temporary appointment can be so effective as a bishop in the practical tasks of a pastor of the pastors and a teacher of the teachers.

Much more could be said about the ordained 'ministry' on its mysteriously spiritual side, but what matters most now is that the ordained, instead of talking about themselves, should *serve* more effectively. In some such ways as those which have just been hinted at, an understanding of the Servant-Lord may be recovered through the 'ministry' of the ordained and lay leaders of the Servant Church.

Worship and Education

Among both Catholics and Protestants, one of the dynamic thrusts of the Spirit in the Church of our time has been through the 'liturgical' movement, to renew worship. This movement can be understood as a retreat into an unreal, ecclesiastical world, or as a return to the primitive days of the Church for archaeological reasons, and this it often has been; but it need not be, for its essence is *an understanding of the worship of the Church as a drama in which all who take part renew their faith in the Lordship of Christ*.

This was the attitude of the primitive Christian community, but for many in the twentieth century it has become an interpretation authentically their own. The recovery of ancient usages has been only a symbol of this deeper recovery. The liturgical movement understands worship as a corporate activity, and so breaks down the separation of the Catholic priesthood or of the Protestant preaching ministry as a caste holier than the rest. The liturgical movement understands the whole of an act of worship as one drama, and so avoids claiming that the worship is valid only if the priest (or preacher) utters some semi-magical formula. The words which the congregation speaks or sings express a deep involvement in the action. The presence of the Lord Jesus can be felt in response to this strongly corporate, articulately expressed faith: the mechanism can be explained psychologically without it being necessary for us to dismiss a faith so deeply rooted in history, so closely involved in the problems of daily life, as neurotic or hallucinatory. Thus Baptism is honoured in the liturgical movement by being rescued from its semi-magical status as something 'done' to babies like an innoculation, and by being understood primarily as the reception of adults or children into the fellowship of the Christian community which is represented both in the Baptism and in the subsequent education of the baptised. The 'Eucharist' (from the Greek for 'Thanksgiving') is restored as the principal act of worship, but as a Holy Communion in which all jointly recall and re-enact the death-and-resurrection climax of the life of Jesus in the flesh, so that through the symbolism of the bread, dedicated and broken, and the wine, dedicated and outpoured, all may together receive the spiritual presence of the eternally living Christ. Babies, and bread and wine which are manufactured—nothing could be more obviously of the earth, yet through the sacramental drama they are made the vehicles of Christ's presence on earth. The sacramentalism which has grown in many parts of the Christian Church during this century has largely escaped from the superstitions which could fairly be attributed to much popular Catholicism in older days; and under strong pressures from secularisation it has demonstrated its ability to sustain many in the Christian fellowship which is incorporated by Baptism and fed by the Eucharist.

In the first days of Christianity, the celebration of the

Eucharist took place in the course of a meal (the *Agape* or 'love-feast') and before or after a normal day's work (this was, of course, before the Lord's Day, the weekly co-memoration of his resurrection, had become the new Sabbath, the day of rest, in Christendom). These two facts about the primitive Church have helped to inspire twentieth-century efforts to rescue sacramental worship from an excessively religious atmosphere of unreality. First, the Eucharist has been followed by a breakfast or other social gathering when the communicants may meet each other as friends, so that the complaint 'no one ever spoke to me' may be less justified. It is possible that bolder experiments may be needed, returning to that primitive custom by which the bread was blessed and broken, and the wine blessed and poured, as a 'grace' at a meal, making clear the holiness of all food, drink and friendship in God's world. The old rules about fasting before Holy Communion have already been relaxed in the Roman Catholic Church and elsewhere, partly because (outside the North American pattern of Sunday morning at church) Sunday evening may be a convenient time for worship. Second, in many local churches ways are being tested to follow the congregation's service in church by service to the community outside. A church or group of churches may provide a Sunday school for the neighbourhood's children, a youth club with regular and tactful leadership, a coffee bar for teenagers and for others who wander our towns 'looking for something', a housing association to help people towards better homes, a group where young mothers can help each other, some social stimulus for women whose husbands are away at work, a system for visiting the lonely and a club to which they are welcomed, a centre for psychological advice (specially over marriage problems), or a simple organisation to supplement the social services by helping the old, the sick and the housebound. When the Eucharist inspires such activities, it can be seen to be what it always has been in theory: a strengthening of effective love, an equipment for Christ's soldiers.

Here again, much more could be said on the mysteriously spiritual side; but here again, too much has already been said—and too little has been done, to show the Eucharist as the people's food.

A radical personalism when applied to the Church's organisation and worship thus removes the over-heavy emphasis on the institutional and intellectual elements in the Christian religion. But this is not to deny that it is good for the disciples of Jesus to come together in order to think about their faith. On the contrary: it is to say that recent history shows how urgently Christians need new educational methods. For centuries Christian education has been confined almost entirely to the duty of listening as a child to a teacher, and as an adult to a preacher; and the nineteenth century was the great age of the Sunday school and the sermon. Our time, however, has seen in many places a decline in the amateur Sunday schools, and has found that religious instruction, even when given by qualified teachers in school hours, usually does not persuade most of the pupils of the truth of the religion being taught. During the twentieth century there have been some great and many good preachers, but both the world and the Church have taken less interest in pulpit oratory. These generalisations apply more to Britain and Continental Europe than to the United States, but the level of concern about 'Christian education' in the American churches indicates a sense that, despite the immense expenditure of human talent and of money, all is not well. The search for more effective forms of education is for the most part still at the experimental stage, but a consensus does begin to emerge that education, like worship, is meant to be a drama shared by the whole group—and is meant to be rooted in that group's ordinary life. Thus in a school, memorisation of the Bible is only a fraction of the educational task. Plays for young children and discussions among older pupils can do far more to enable the teacher to contribute relevantly to the class in terms relevant to the children's own abilities to imagine and conceptualise their intellectual questions and their psychological needs.

A new look at adult education is equally important, for if it ever was possible for a Christian to go through the wilderness and storms of life like a camel, on the strength of an education acquired as a child and haphazardly supplemented by nibbling at sermons, that is a plain impossibility in a world changing so rapidly. The churches have given to adult education a very low status among their priorities, and the alienation of so much adult thought from the world of the sermon has been the penalty paid. Only slowly and spasmodically are methods being worked out which involve laymen in a sustained and systematic course of training. For adults as for children, work in a group with freedom to question and contribute is normally essential if the teaching is to be relevant, but this presents a greater rather than smaller challenge to the teacher, and it requires the retraining of those clergymen who are familiar only with the authoritarian monologue of the pulpit.

It is often pointed out that laymen also are to blame: they are not willing to give time and energy to a deeper study of religion. The answer emerging to this objection is that the churches must rethink their priorities, sacrificing other activities in order to encourage adult education. Each local church needs rooms where armchairs face each other, instead of pews facing a pulpit. There laymen, respected as thinking adults, may come to terms with some theological and ethical teaching and may be able to absorb the truths in such teaching through an open and free discussion. Many (although not all) sermons in church can be sacrificed in order to make room for such education.

Each local church needs also to meet outside its own premises, in the homes of its members and their neighbours. At times Holy Communion may be celebrated on the kitchen table, or the Bible studied in the living room, but the pattern need not be formal. It is in such intimately small meetings that strangers can be welcomed and friends made, and it is out of the discussion, fellowship and prayer of such 'house-churches' that a spontaneous wish may come to enter the Church's larger congregations. More and more churchmen in our time are coming to see that such groups are an essential part of the Christian's education at the deeply personal level, and that a congregation without them can be impersonal.

But increasingly modern Christians are recognising also the importance of occupational groups and problems. The world of the local church is usually the world of the suburban home; whether on its own premises or in 'house churches' its discussions may be remote from the work to which the men (and many of the women) give so much of their lives, partly because each job has its own problems—or at least its own expressions of the basic human problems. It is particularly in the discussion of the ethical and other tensions arising in a job away from home that the 'lay colleges' are vital. In these 'lay colleges' laymen—not only churchgoers— can feel quite free to speak just what is in their minds. Often this is nothing specifically theologian or religious but it may reveal their frustrations in living, and the Church as an independent agency can have a useful role in sponsoring such probes into embarrassments. What is the purpose in my work for society and myself? What are the injustices, dishonesties and inefficiencies in the organisation which thwart the most satisfying human behaviour? How can relationships with colleagues and the public be improved? Such are some of the questions which arise. An answer may come slowly, both through the group's own discussions and through the contributions made by those who are more expert than the average layman in theology, psychology and ethics. Many new houses for lay conferences and training courses, adequately equipped with staffs, libraries, etc., are needed, and some have already been founded. The churches of the United States have a long tradition of 'conference centers', and have strengthened that tradition since the Second World War. From the ruins of that war, there dramatically arose in Germany a serious and increasingly elaborate attempt to bring laymen together in Evangelical Academies; and in the Netherlands and other parts of Europe, this German initiative has been taken up by Protestants and Catholics. But elsewhere in the world, lay colleges exist more precariously.

A more educated, leisured and richer society may support such methods of Christian training, and a more united Church may be able to provide for them out of the economies elsewhere; but at the present stage of the twentieth century, it is impossible for the honest observer to do more than to record that there seems no alternative to a massive expansion of adult education if the churches are not to abdicate from the intellectual life of the modern world. The most hopeful signs that this challenge is being taken seriously come from the United States, but the American style of 'lay training' is acknowledged to contain many defects, while apart from occasional 'missions' or 'campaigns'—which all too easily are unrelated to local realities and to the deepest problems of laymen—pathetically little is done in this field by the churches of, for example, Britain.

So we return to worship, as religion must always return. For if new houses for study and discussion are needed, so also are new centres for the deepening of the life of prayer. The Roman Catholic, Orthodox and Anglican churches have a long tradition of monastic houses and 'retreat' houses where lay people are welcome to take part in the spiritual life of the resident community and to give time to private prayer, under guidance or alone. In recent years it has been seen that such houses need to welcome experimental methods in a definitely lay atmosphere, without forcing the monastic pattern on to lay people whose minds may be full of harsh problems thrown at them by contemporary experience. Some new patterns of monastic or semi-monastic life have been worked out by communities which are convinced that the medieval style of discipline is basically relevant to our disintegrated age, but must be adjusted in modern conditions. Few recent developments in Protestantism have attracted so much spontaneous interest and loyalty as the Taizé Community in France and the Iona Community in the Church of Scotland.

It is in this context that the future of the great houses of prayer should perhaps be seen. In Europe many of these cathedrals or large churches have been inherited from the pious or proud church-builders of the Middle Ages; tourists flock to them in ever-increasing numbers, but tourism is not accepted as their sole purpose. In America, and to some extent in Europe also, massive new churches have been built within this century, and the future will have to face the question, what cause they can serve apart from being examples of architectural skill. It is often said that such cathedrals are follies now that Christendom is over, and clearly new building projects deserve to be scrutinised. But at a time when new houses are clearly needed for lay conferences and for private prayer, a role may be discerned for some buildings which teach worship by their own majesty. Aesthetic standards are being raised in the whole population, and these great churches can make a relevant contribution precisely by aiming at excellence—in their beauty as buildings, in the art old or new which they house, in choral or instrumental music, in the regular offering of the praise of God and in special acts of worship where the aspirations of the community may be dramatised.

The current mood of contempt for the local church must pass if Christianity is to have a strong future, but from the 'house church' to the cathedral new structures of the Church need to be developed, supplementing the local church. What has just been written may seem visionary, but every sentence has behind it a substantial body of discussion and of experiment somewhere in the world.

Catholic Substance and Protestant Principle

Paul Tillich spoke about modern history as essentially 'the Protestant era' because it is based on the questioning of inherited traditions. The key idea in the work of the Royal Society in seventeenth-century London, for example, was experimentation. Instead of consulting authorities such as Aristotle or Galen, the scientists would examine nature for themselves; and Thomas Sprat, the Bishop of Rochester who wrote the history of the Royal Society, explicitly compared this appeal to nature with the Protestant appeal to Scripture, behind and if necessary against all ecclesiastical traditions. But Tillich also saw that Scripture was too remote and ambiguous to provide the sole basis of a living religion. The message of the Bible must be conveyed to our time by generation after generation whose experience was in its essence identical with the experience of the prophets and apostles; and it must be expressed in our time through the living voice of a teacher and, above all, through the life and worship of a religious community. Tillich, for all his insistence on a Protestantism based on the psychological drama and 'ultimate concern' of each individual, never forgot his Lutheran childhood—or the debt of Martin Luther to the Church of the Middle Ages. He therefore spoke also about the importance of 'Catholic substance'. By this phrase he meant that tradition of people and buildings, myths and rituals, dogmas and customs, which nurtured the Protestant individual, which spoke to him at a level deeper than everyday reasoning, and which by its own depth encouraged him to interpret the meaning of its symbolism of the ultimate for his own concern and for his own existence.[1]

Tillich was by no means isolated among modern Protestants in his guarded respect for 'Catholic substance'.[2] The adoption of many traditional customs of worship (prominence for the altar, candles, surplices, etc.) and of ancient prayers and hymns such as *Te Deum Laudamus* in the churches of the Free Church tradition has coincided with an emphasis in Catholic circles that the ardour of devotion, the dignity of ordered worship and the beauty of disciplined holiness constitute the true spirit and splendour of Catholicism—not any institutional or doctrinal rigidity or any frigidly 'correct' copying of the past. This increase of

---

[1] See the essays by Paul Tillich, *The Protestant Era* (Chicago, 1948) and his dialogues with students, *Ultimate Concern* (New York, 1965).
[2] See, e.g., Martin E. Marty, *Protestantism* (New York, 1972). This contains an extensive bibliography.

traditionalism in the atmosphere of worship has been accompanied by a breakdown of individualism in matters of belief. For the triumph of criticism is only one fact about the twentieth century; another is the triumph of collectivism. The days of the lonely Protestant getting instruction from his Bible without help from priests or commentators seem to be drawing to a close, despite the remaining power of Fundamentalism; and the appeal to tested experience instead of the sacred book, the new essence of Protestantism, seems to result in practice in a willingness by laymen to learn from each other in discussion and from the experts, whether this learning process is conducted mainly through the local churches (as in the United States) or through broadcasting and television (as in Britain). The community is needed if the message of the Bible is to be heard as relevant. The twentieth-century Christian community is needed—for other laymen can speak convincingly about what the message of the Bible has meant to them in their lives, and the ordained leaders of the Church can attempt to bring all these diversities into a living whole. But the community of the other Christian centuries is also needed in the background, and here theologians can be useful. Thus within non-fundamentalist Protestantism the tendency has been to abandon the battle-cry of the sixteenth-century Reformation, *sola scriptura* ('test all doctrines by Scripture alone'), and to substitute for it a more subtle appeal to a more comprehensive tradition embodying the total fact of the Christian community of all times and places. But the question remains: what is the significance of the tradition now? *What is Catholicism for us today?*

'It is not of Catholicism in the grip of the exploiter, but of Catholicism as a living and lived religion, as a school of souls, that modernists are thinking . . . It is the spirit of Christ that has again and again saved the Church from the hands of her worldly oppressors within and without . . . It is easy to quench a glimmering light caught by the eyes of a few; but not the light of the noonday sun—of knowledge that has become objective and valid for all. It is through knowledge of this kind that God has inaugurated a new epoch in man's intellectual life . . . Shall He do less for man's spiritual life when the times are ripe? And are they not ripening?' So in the 1900s George Tyrrell voiced a hope which, at the time, he seemed to take to a tragic grave.[1]

Before the 1960s the question 'What is Catholicism?' might have been answered in one of three ways. Catholicism might have been defined as that which has been believed everywhere and always by all Christians. However, in Christian history few propositions have enjoyed popularity on that scale, and a solid institution could not be built on the basis of them. Secondly, Catholicism might have been defined as the reproduction of at least the most important elements in the Church of the first few centuries, particularly its doctrinal councils (although the authorities might have disagreed about the dates of the period to be imitated); this was the appeal to antiquity. Thirdly, Catholicism might have been defined as the devotional and doctrinal system developed by the Papacy and its obedient sons in the Counter-Reformation of the sixteenth century and in the Catholic Revival of the nineteenth.

But the Second Vatican Council and the debates around it have introduced the possibility of a more comprehensive understanding of Catholicism. It was not that the Council, or more than a few Roman Catholic theologians commenting on it, clearly envisaged the possibility that the full-orbed Faith might not have been delivered to the primitive saints and transmitted from them through all the Christian generations. No disagreement between the early Church and the modern Church of Rome was stated, and any intention of changing doctrine was always explicitly renounced. The infallibility of the Pope when teaching faith or morals *ex cathedra* was assumed. Nevertheless, the Church was no longer immobile. The Church, instead, seemed to be a mystery not fully disclosed: a company of sinners on pil-

---

[1] *Christianity at the Crossroads* (London, 1909), pp. 280–2. For the background, see A. R. Vidler, *A Variety of Catholic Modernists* (Cambridge, 1970).

grimage, 'human, all-too-human', as well as the holy People
of God whose redemption has already been purchased. No
period, ancient or modern, was held up as perfect. Instead,
with penitence for any errors (a penitence voiced by Popes
John and Paul), the Roman Catholic Church turned in
humility to the tasks of the future. In the great words of the
Pastoral Constitution on the Church in the Modern
World: 'Inspired by no earthly ambition, the Church seeks
but one solitary goal: to carry forward the work of Christ
himself under the lead of the befriending Spirit. And Christ
entered this world to give witness to the truth, to rescue and
not to sit in judgment, to serve and not to be served.' The
concessions made by Vatican II to the good will of non-
Christians and to the Christianity of non-Catholics were
vital to progress, but in the long run are likely to count for
less than this overall emphasis on hope as well as memory.[1]

In making these concessions to present realities and in
turning to the future, Catholicism has begun to recognise
that it is incomplete. Neither the Church around the Mediter-
ranean in the fourth century nor the Church of the Middle
Ages in Western Europe (as reorganised in the Counter-
Reformation) is now seen as a model to be copied everywhere
and always. On the contrary, reunion with the Eastern
Orthodox or Western Protestant churches has been seen as
more than a matter of their absorption into Rome; and the
possibility has been welcomed of a genuinely African or
Asian or Latin American spirituality, abandoning many of
the European or North American patterns of life and
thought and re-clothing the Gospel. The Second Vatican
Council talked in Latin, but the diversity of peoples represented among the bishops at the Council meant that it was
impossible for Catholicism to preserve the place of Latin, or
much other uniformity, in its fast developing life.

The revolution in the understanding of Catholicism may
be summed up by emphasising that the word 'Catholic'
means basically the same as 'ecumenical'; that is, it means

[1] Much was due to the personal influence of John XXIII. See Meriol
Trevor, *Pope John* (London, 1967).

'universal' (the two words derive from Greek). And the modern history of the word 'ecumenical' enables us to state the revolution in the total understanding of the Church's task in the world. For many years 'ecumenical' was used to describe the world-wide body of Christians; thus the Second Vatican Council was summoned as an Ecumenical Council. Then it was applied to the special aspect of Christian reunion. In recent years, however, it has been expanded to cover the whole inhabited earth, the Greek *oikoumene*. The essence of Catholicism may thus be defined as the belief that as Christians hasten to the ends of the earth and to the ends of time, they will meet there more and more of Christ, until an ecumenical wholeness is given. As Dr. Hans-Reudi Weber has written: 'On this way to the centre and to the frontiers Christians and churches discover that unity which is both God's will and his gift. The ecumenical concern for unity sees church unity as the first fruit of the promised unity of all. It commits us to the struggle for manifesting this unity among Christians and in the whole of humanity. It aims not at conservative reunion or static uniformity, but at the growth into the wholeness of God's rich economy of grace.'[1]

The Church in the World

The main contribution of the Church to the twentieth-century world will, it seems, like in the quality of its own fellowship and thinking. The Church will remain a minority, but it may be a creative minority if its own members can give evidence that they have found here relationships between loving people, and quests of free minds, superior to those normal in the world. 'The Christian Community,' as Emil Brunner once wrote, 'is the great miracle of history, and history is the proof that the gates of hell shall not prevail against it. There can hardly be a more overwhelming personal experience of this miracle than when it is granted to one to greet brothers in Christ in the far east and far

[1] *Asia and the Ecumenical Movement* (London, 1966), p. 44.

west and in many lands inhabited by men of other races, tongues and cultures, and to strengthen one's faith by uniting with them in common prayer to the one Lord. The institutions which we call churches . . . have built up the shell in which this precious kernel has been contained and preserved'—although also, as Brunner went on to say, concealed.[1] The World Conference on Church, Community and State, which met at Oxford in 1937 on the eve of war, with Martin Niemöller who was to have been a chief speaker already in prison, was one of these 'overwhelming' experiences, and it was remembered most for its message that 'the first duty of the Church, and its greatest service to the world, is that it be in very deed *the Church*—confessing the true faith, committed to the fulfilment of the will of Christ, its only Lord, and united in him in a fellowship of love and service'. The message of the conference added: 'We do not call the world to be like ourselves, for we are already too like the world.' It is therefore neither surprising nor entirely regrettable that so much of the energy of Christians in our time has been given to what seem to be the internal affairs of the churches—to their reunion and renewal. Various factors are involved here. Placed as it is among many other communities or associations in a pluralist society, and having to adjust to the end of a monolithic Christendom, the Church must be more self-conscious than it was in many past centuries. And the self-consciousness which is inevitable may turn out to be beneficial. Many voices are still heard, in the 1970s as in the early years of the century, protesting that the Church is not needed nowadays—that it is enough for a modern follower of Jesus to make his own prayer (or vaguer meditation) in secret and to live his own life, answerable only to his conscience. Such voices do not take the ethos of secularisation with sufficient seriousness. The 'secular' civilisation which is built on modern science is in some ways the heir of Christianity, as we have seen; and if it is free of the ideologies which can be more narrow than the

[1] *The Misunderstanding of the Church* (1951; Eng. trans., London, 1952), p. 116.

religions which they replace—if it is really *pluralist*, really open to all the truths glimpsed by its members—it will not wish to persecute the Church. But if Christianity is to make its own characteristic contribution to this pluralist society, it must (it seems) do so after a certain amount of spiritual reflection and human fellowship in circumstances which are shaped by itself—otherwise the salt of the earth loses its savour, as Jesus himself warned. And if the individual Christian is to play in modern society a role which is related responsibly both to his fellow-men and to his God, the need of a definitely Christian preparation for the tasks of the world, a preparation which is renewed in forgiveness after successive failures, becomes a personal necessity for him—otherwise he will for practical purposes cease to be a disciple, his spirituality choked by the cares of the world or withered by the long noonday sun like the growing crop in the parable of Jesus. In the modern world, more and more Christians are coming to see that taking the secular seriously means re-thinking, not abandoning, what belongs distinctively to the Church of Jesus Christ.

Few, if any, churches in the modern world have been more effective as national churches than the Church of Scotland, and it is worth recalling the noble words of the Articles Declaratory of the Constitution of the Church of Scotland in Matters Spiritual, as accepted by Act of Parliament in 1921. In these Articles, 'the Lord Jesus Christ' is declared to be 'King and Head of His Church'. Therefore the Articles continue: 'The Church of Scotland, while acknowledging the Divine appointment and authority of the civil magistrate within his own sphere, and holding that the nation acting in its corporate capacity ought to render homage to God and promote in all appropriate ways the interests of His Kingdom, declares that it receives from its Head and from him alone the right and power subject to no civil authority to legislate, and to adjudicate finally, in all matters of doctrine, worship, government and discipline in the Church, including the right to determine all questions concerning membership and office in the Church.' It is clear that in other countries a satisfactory adjustment of the relations of Church and State cannot be reached on any other foundation, although the precise details of the Scottish settlement may not be reproduced. And it seems probable that both Church and State would benefit greatly in many countries from such an establishment of a free National Church.

Indeed, it is precisely through its own distinctive fellowship that the Church can make a much needed contribution to contemporary society, and it is only on the basis of a measure of success in establishing such a fellowship that the Church may reasonably expect to be listened to when it pronounces on the affairs of the world. The need of the world to become one world has been emphasised by so many prophets that the cry has become a platitude, but in a divided world the growing unity of Christians from many nations is one of the few efforts to reach a global community which have solid and tested achievements to show. If not the 'great new fact of our era', as Archbishop William Temple fulsomely called it in 1942, it is still deeply significant. The fellowship expressed in the World Council of Churches, and the internationalism of the Roman Catholic Church, by their sheer existence and continuance under strain are modern miracles of faith.

Nor is the unity of the Church instructive and useful to the world only at the level of international politics. Locally a small and unglamorous congregation of Christians can bring into a real unity representatives of deeply divided classes, races and generations; it can hold together people from very different cultural and intellectual backgrounds; it can even hold together people with clashing personal temperaments. Similar things are done in secular organisations and in non-Christian religions, and the Church often fails to do them: but the fact remains that very few other bodies, if any, have attempted to build unity on the same scale as the Christian Churches—out of many millions of ordinary people, not merely combining them for speeches or prayers but making them an active fellowship where individuals co-operate over a long period of time, in a deeply personal encounter without ceasing to be themselves. In such congregations of the Church we learn why Herbert Butterfield surveyed the Christian contribution to the civilisation of Europe in these terms: 'It was by bringing society in general from the lower to the higher level of religious experience that the Church most promoted the cause of civilisation itself, and most affected the character of our western world. Those who preached the Gospel for the sake of the Gospel, leaving the further consequences of their action to Providence, have always served the world better than they knew, better than those who worked with mundane purposes in mind—sometimes they served the world better than they desired or intended to do . . . Those who . . . nurse the pieties, spread New Testament love and affirm the spiritual nature of man are . . . guarding the very fountain.'[1]

In the double schools of discipleship in the Church and apostleship in the world, the individual Christian is gradually trained into maturity. All religion, including the Christian religion, can be used as an escape from reality into fantasy; but we saw in earlier chapters that we are not compelled to conclude that a wish for fantasy was the origin of all religion, and as we observe many religious believers living and working in the modern world we may incline to the conclusion that, whatever may be the truth of their beliefs, their religion has strengthened them as human beings. Religious believers have a special stimulus to co-operate with others and to give themselves to the worthwhile duties of the moment, for they believe that their companions are also the sons and daughters of God—and they believe also that their work, however unromantic or unrewarding, is also the work of God. Being human themselves, they seek satisfactions from their life and work, and from the admiration of others, but when these are not forthcoming they do not entirely despair, for the secret springs of their lives are their desires (however feeble and intermittent) to

[1] *Christianity in European History*, pp. 25, 55.

live and work for God's sake. When they are helpless through sickness or age, religious believers can stabilise their anxieties on the faith that 'man's extremity is God's opportunity'; but the 'coming of age' of man as the son of God means also that man's strength—the delightful fulness of his powers of body and mind—is also God's opportunity for the accomplishment of great purposes for mankind. And what is true of the maturing effects of all real faith in God is specially true of the faith which finds its special inspiration through the embodiment of God in the man Jesus. In ways which can seldom be predicted the sheer attractiveness of the saints may draw non-Christians into a desire to know more about Christ and Christ's Church— specially when the Christians are willing to discard weapons and uniforms which are no longer serviceable.

When the purpose of the Church is seen as the maturing of disciples into apostles, and as the service rather than the conquest of the world, then the true character of the Church's contribution to social progress may be seen more clearly.

Catholic Action in Modern Society

The reluctance to accept the world as having its own dignity in its creation by God, and the desire to impose the Church's own notions on all the world, have died hard in our century. We think most readily of the pretence in much Roman Catholic teaching that the world must return to the Church for the cure of all its troubles. Paradoxically enough, the Second Vatican Council's decree on Modern Communications was a typical example of that failure to communicate the Gospel by a failure to take seriously the persons and structures to whom the Gospel was addressed. Through much Roman Catholic thinking there has been a tendency to say that a movement could serve God only if it wore a Christian, and preferably a Roman Catholic, label, and was controlled by faithful Catholics, and preferably by bishops.

This tendency can be seen in the twentieth-century move-

ment known as Catholic Action. The progress of this movement was perhaps the Church's greatest achievement in the
late 1920s and early 1930s, and in the 1970s we can see in it
some great strengths. Its vision is that the whole of
Christianity should be taken into the whole of life, and its
realism is that this cannot be done unless youth, workers,
businessmen, farmers, intellectuals, etc., come together into
groups which supplement the devotional groups of a parish
church. Both the vision and the realism are superior to
Liberal Protestantism's naïve reliance on the Christian
conscience of the individual. However, the position of the
clergy has been a major problem for Catholic Action. Often
this movement has encouraged lay initiatives, as in the 'see,
judge, act' procedure by which the small 'sections' of the
Jeunesse Ouvrière Chrétienne have since the 1920s trained
young Belgian and French workers into mature responsibility and militant faith. But the 'Jocists' have been only one
side of Catholic Action. Another side is suggested by *Opus
Dei*, which began in Spain. *Opus Dei* is probably for the most
part blameless enough, but it comes under suspicion because
its members, many of whom hold high positions in Spanish
life, are held to be a secret society under clerical control, a
Catholic equivalent of Freemasonry. One of the reasons for
insisting that 'Catholic Action is the property of the hierarchy' was to lessen the danger of laymen giving a Catholic
label to party politics (as in the *Action Française* movement);
and another danger in mind was that social action might
lead to indifference to religious truths (which was why
Cardinal Hinsley in England in 1941 had to abandon his
idea of making the *Sword of the Spirit* movement interdenominational). But Pius XI, who defined Catholic
Action as the participation of the laity in the apostolic
mission of the Pope and bishops, cannot be said to have
grasped fully the independence of the twentieth-century
layman. (He was himself a scholarly official of the ecclesiastical libraries in Milan and Rome, until at the age of sixty-
one he was sent as Papal representative in war-torn Poland,
becoming Pope only four years later; and as Pope—he made

a courageous Pope—he was preoccupied by the need for Catholic discipline in response to political totalitarianism.) The suspicion of clericalism interfering in lay life probably accounts for the fact that Catholic Action has disappointed the high hopes of its founders, and the clergy's authority over these lay groups may be reconsidered in the period into which the Roman Catholic Church is moving after the Second Vatican Council (although, to be sure, no layman voted in that Council).

Connected with Catholic Action has been the network of Christian Democratic political parties and labour movements. Before 1919 there were Centre Parties in many European states, for the most part small and concerned for the political defence of the Church and its schools, and other groups sought an understanding between the Church and the working-class. Amid the problems of post-war reconstruction a socially concerned and progressive lay Catholicism became a stronger political force through the Popular Party of Italy inspired by Guiseppe Toniolo, and through the Centre Party in Germany—only to be abandoned as the Vatican and the bishops made their peace with Mussolini and Hitler. In 1945 'Christian Democracy' was resurrected in order to lead the reconstruction of Europe with Di Gasperi in Italy, Adenauer in Germany, etc. But even in this triumph the movement was ambiguous. On the one hand, uninhibited Catholic lay leadership was necessary in order to fill the vacuum left by the collapse of Nazi and Fascist governments, in the face of the threat of Communism. On the other hand, the gift of a Christian label to short-term, partisan objectives, and the interference by the clergy in political intrigues and elections, were standing invitations to an anti-clerical reaction. Most Protestants, specially in the English-speaking world, would regard this type of Christian activity as justified only in an emergency of the kind which certainly existed in post-1945 Europe (as in the Italian general election of 1948, when it took a Pope to defeat the Communists), but which has now largely passed outside the Communist world.

If we seek to assess the general effect of Catholic social teaching, again the truthful answer seems complex. On the one hand, since Leo XIII issued the Encyclical *Rerum Novarum* in 1891 an impressive body of teaching has been built up. That Encyclical, which was reaffirmed forty and seventy years later (*Quadragesimo Anno*, 1931, and *Mater et Magistra*, 1961) defended the 'natural' right to private property, it praised the family and the Church as the chief educators, and it denounced the growing power of the State; on the other hand, it also defended the right of workers to organise themselves in order to obtain a 'just' wage related to the needs of the worker's family. The ideal held up by these Encyclicals, and by many Roman Catholic writers who applied their principles to economic problems, was that of co-operation between capital and labour in running an industry for the benefit of all. Not the bureaucracy of the State, but a 'guild' of those who worked with hand or brain within the industry itself, was to be the guardian of social justice and the architect of distributed prosperity. This solution for the internal problems of industrial democracies was followed up under John XXIII (*Pacem in Terris*, 1963) and Paul VI (*Populorum Progressio*, 1967); these Encyclicals pleaded for peace in the nuclear age and for justice for the undernourished masses of the underdeveloped nations. Such guidance from the Popes has maintained the courage of Roman Catholics who have offered radical criticism of the selfishness and brutality of the West in this century. Papal leadership has provided a charter for the participation of working-class Roman Catholics in the cause of their own class, and has probably made many other religious believers pause before a too complete identification with the cause of social reaction.

On the other hand, there has been a gap between the ideals of these Papal Encyclicals and the realities of Roman Catholic involvement in the often sordid life of our time. In the eyes of many, the Papacy itself has been prevented from rising to the full height of its prophetic stature by its obligation to put first the Roman Catholic Church's own freedom. The Popes have been Italians, and Vatican City has been a small state within Rome; the Popes have been fathers to millions of Catholics living under tyrannies; and it is not surprising that Pius XI and Pius XII sought to get along with Mussolini and Hitler. When the Fascists and Nazis denied freedom to the Church, and in particular when they claimed sole control over the education of the young, the Popes protested vigorously, but it is significant that Pius XI never plainly condemned the Italian invasion of Abyssinia, while his Encyclical *Mit Brennender Sorge*, denouncing the neo-paganism of the Nazis, was less thorough than his condemnation of Communism, issued five days later in 1937 (*Divini Redemptoris*). Pius XII was essentially a diplomat; he spent the years 1917–29 as Papal nuncio in Germany, and was then Secretary of State at the Vatican for nine years. He has been accused of cowardice in not protesting publicly against the Nazis' extermination of the Jews, and the debate about that charge is worth considering because it shows up a widespread uneasiness about the role of the Papacy. It can be replied that Catholics (including Pope Pius) rescued many Jews, and that a more general protest would almost certainly not have rescued any more. But the very ugly fact remains that German Catholics generally applauded Hitler's policies except when these damaged the Church. Only seven of them sought exemption from military service on grounds of conscience. Dr. Guenter Lewy, after a carefully documented study, concluded that the general silence of the neutral Pope and the patriotic bishops about the iniquities of Nazism 'reflected not so much a personal failure to be courageous and to uphold the cause of justice, but the demands of an institution which for close on two thousand years has put its survival as a channel in the salvation of individual souls before the moral demands of its own Gospel'.[1] The Catholic Church has seldom hesitated to 'interfere' in politics when urgent moral or spiritual questions have seemed to be at stake—and has on occasion used its weapons very severely (for example, in Italy against

[1] *The Catholic Church and Nazi Germany* (New York, 1964), p. 244.

the anti-clericals before 1929 and against the Communists under Pius XII). The Catholic Church in Germany in 1933 possessed great resources for influencing public opinion, and although gradually deprived of these it had enough influence left in the 1940s to make a difference. What might have been done may be seen from the sermon of Bishop (later Cardinal) Galen which in 1941 stopped the Nazis' euthanasia of non-Jewish 'defectives'. About eight hundred Catholic priests perished in German concentration camps for offences against the Nazis; there were some heroes.

During and after 1945 the crucial moral challenge concerned the use of weapons of indiscriminate destruction. Here again the Papacy was tame, and no lead came from the American Catholic bishops; and the financial reliance of the Church on American public opinion cannot be ruled out as irrelevant. Not until the Encyclical *Pacem in Terris* and Chapter V of the Second Vatican Council's Pastoral Constitution on the Church in the Modern World did the Roman Catholic Church go beyond a generalised condemnation of war, and even then American Catholic leadership made no effective move to alert the public to the moral aspects of the possession of a nuclear arsenal and the use of savage weapons in Vietnam. The contrast with the condemnation of contraceptives was striking. All this is understandable in the harsh conditions which have existed for the diplomacy of the Papacy and the Catholic Church since 1914, but the practical compromises may be remembered more vividly than the eloquent appeals.

In the Roman Catholic Church's contribution to the problems of the underdeveloped countries, a compassion for the poor, accompanied by much missionary self-sacrifice, has been evident. But most students of these problems hold that the compassion for the poor would have been infinitely more effective if it had been accompanied by encouragement to limit families, and by the active participation of the higher clergy in the struggle of the peasants against poverty, disease, squalor and ignorance. Tragically, the Church by its fight against public money for family planning facilities, by its lack of enthusiasm for public education and by its blessings on some of the worst exploiters (we think of Sicily and Latin America), may be judged by history to have impeded the progress of those peoples whose needs have been stated eloquently by recent Popes.

It is difficult to be sure just what has been the effect on Western industrial and political life of the Popes' social ideals. Christian Democratic governments in Europe have not effectively applied them when they have had their opportunities, and in the United States the National Catholic Welfare Conference, despite some excellent statements, has not been as consistently courageous in achieving social justice as in denouncing immoral films. As for 'social action' by Catholics: the development of specifically 'Christian' trade unions in some countries may have weakened, by dividing, the working-class protest. Many Catholics have looked nostalgically back at the peasants and craft-guilds of the Middle Ages, and realistic comment on contemporary industry has been rare. The small minority of 'the Catholic Left' may be justified in arguing that only a massive extension of State power can secure social justice in practice. If that is so, then the great suspicion of socialism which marked the Papal Encyclicals—at least before John XXIII's blessing on 'socialisation'—may have been a disastrous discouragement of what was really needed: Christian Socialism.

Perhaps a just verdict on the social record of the Roman Catholic Church in the twentieth century cannot be reached without using paradoxes. On the one hand, the emphasis was right—international peace, justice for the workers, co-operation between labour and management, justice for the poor nations, co-operation between them and the rich— and it was authentically prophetic to proclaim this emphasis through tragic days when nations, classes and races seemed determined on each other's ruin. On the other hand, the rhetoric of the Papal Encyclicals, and of lesser Roman Catholic writing, could suitably have been made rather less grand, for much of its commentary on social problems was unrealistic and its influence on the course of the century was small.

Protestant Social Thought

However, the classic example in the twentieth century of a 'Christian' attempt to force some debatable opinions on society at large arose not from Roman Catholicism but from American Protestantism. The prohibition of alcholic liquor sprang directly from church-inspired crusades for temperance. It was enacted as an Amendment to the Constitution in 1919, and not repealed until 1933. Prohibition, although it was an intolerable interference with liberty and although it led to many social evils by driving the drink trade underground, was part of an idealism which should not be despised. Drunkenness among industrial workers had been both a symptom of their 'alienation'—to use the Marxist analysis of that ruthless stage of capitalism—and a contribution to the plight of themselves and their families. The American churches had given far less support to labour's protest than the workers had wanted; the churches had been sadly dependent on the support of the capitalists. But the history of the time shows that the churches' fight against liquor was accompanied by some prophetic attacks by their leaders and assemblies on brutalities of the industrial system. The Social Creed of the Churches, adopted by the Federal Council of Churches in 1908 and strengthened by revision in 1912 and 1932, included warnings against specific policies or acts of injustice; and a similar statement came from the National Catholic Welfare Conference. The controversial Christian report on the steel strike of 1919 was by no means an isolated case of church spokesmen standing up for labour's right to unionism and collective action in days when such things were liable to be denounced as creeping Bolshevism.

The main motive which led to the 'noble experiment' of Prohibition was, however, a naïve belief that the machinery of the State could be used to enforce righteousness. The same criminal innocence in the assessment of human nature and of political reality lay behind the (admittedly short-lived) Inter-Church World Movement in 1919 with a billion-dollar programme to survey 'all the facts about the religious, social, moral, physical and economic environments of humanity throughout the world', so that 'from these facts a unified program shall be worked out in which all can concur'.[1] Innocence inspired the American churches in their undiscriminating endorsement of the war in 1917. Innocence also inspired their pacifism which encouraged their country's holier-than-thou isolation from the problems of the world until the world, deprived of effective American influence, drifted through the agonies of Manchuria and China, Ethiopia and Spain, to the Nazi conquest of Europe and the Japanese sinking of the American fleet in Pearl Harbour. And much innocence has continued through the bitterly cold war against Communism, leading many American Christians into a dangerous identification of American foreign policy with the cause of the Kingdom of God.

It was against the danger of such romanticism that Reinhold Niebuhr protested. The most mature Christian commentator on the social agonies and dilemmas of the twentieth century, he made his name by his warning in his book *Moral Man and Immoral Society* (New York, 1932) that the conflicts of power needed more than optimism about the power of ideals to counteract vested interests. At first Niebuhr used the Marxist critique of conflict and change in society, toying with the belief that the proletariat might be exempt from the immorality of social groups. As a minister in industrial Detroit he had come to see that all the well-known philanthropy of a Henry Ford was in vain if Ford's automobile factories could be closed for 'retooling' without care for the destitution to which many fathers of families were reduced by this economic action; and he had gradually broken with the pacifism of the main 'Social Gospel' movement because he believed that the possessors of such power could not be dispossessed without militant unionism in a class struggle.[1] But gradually Niebuhr also saw through socialism's illusions about the perfectibility of human nature, and turning from all dreams of Utopia in his 1939–40 Gifford Lectures on *The Nature and Destiny of Man* he explored the classic themes of sin and salvation. Man's dignity, Niebuhr came to teach, lay in his freedom. Man is 'subject to the necessities of nature, of sexual and racial limitation, of geography and climate, and of the dominant drives of his own creaturely nature'; but 'when man rises above the necessities and limits of nature he is not inevitably bound in his actions to the norms and universalities of "reason" '. Man is *free*: free to love, to worship, to dream and to create beyond reason, but also free to grab, hate and destroy. His dignity has the same ground as his sin. Thus Niebuhr could joke that his early book should have been entitled *Immoral Man and Even More Immoral Society*.[2] Applying this profound analysis of human sinfulness to the problems of establishing social justice through a long period which has brought one unprecedented problem after another to the intelligence and conscience of his people, Niebuhr directed the eyes of many in the intellectual community in America to a God who alone is free from the ambiguities of historical movements, and who alone is above sin and 'beyond tragedy'. But it was a sign of his greatness in his old age he was willing to re-think the classical Christian concepts such as 'Original Sin' which were unintelligible to most of the laymen whom he wished to reach.[3]

Reinhold Niebuhr, for all his awareness of the limitations

---

[1] See his *Leaves from the Notebook of a Tamed Cynic* (Chicago, 1929).

[2] See, e.g., Niebuhr's intellectual autobiography in *Reinhold Niebuhr: His Religious, Social and Political Thought*, ed. C. W. Kegley and R. W. Bretall (New York, 1961).

[3] Some of Reinhold Niebuhr's later essays were collected in *Christian Realism and Political Problems* (New York, 1954) and *Man's Nature and his Communities* (New York, 1965).

of historical movements, never contracted out of the intellectual and political work involved in them. He came to support Roosevelt's New Deal for the United States, and to urge a decisive stand against both Nazism and Stalinism abroad, without the illusion that success over poverty at home or tyranny abroad would usher in Paradise. He proclaimed the duties of the American government, but also advocated many restraints on it. His rejection of pacifism, his acceptance of power despite its sinfulness, and his profound meditation on the connections between 'pragmatic' justice and the 'impossible' ethic of love, were first inspired by his acceptance of the Marxist insistence on the power of the workers as the one remedy for the evils of American capitalism; but these teachings reached the height of their influence in relation to international affairs in the first era of nuclear power.

Niebuhr's style was marked by a relish for paradox. He frequently pointed out how, thanks to the presence of sin everywhere, no cause on earth can be trusted utterly—not even the cause of American democracy, not even the cause of the institutional Church. This realism was a major contribution to an age which (particularly among Americans and among Christians) often saw moralising used as a screen to cover unpleasant facts—and which (as in Communism) was burdened by violent tyrannies motivated by puritanical ethics. Ruthlessness in the cause of morality has been a nauseating characteristic of the twentieth century. Much sentimentality or hypocrisy might have been checked among moralists, and much misery might have been spared to the masses who have been the victims of various moralising panaceas imposed by force of arms or public opinion, if a realistic analysis of the kind offered by Niebuhr had more widely taken the place of the simple-minded application of 'morality' to politics too often urged by preachers and publicists in the name of Christ. If this insistence on paradox and subtlety has sometimes made Niebuhr's eloquence obscure to the simple-minded, it is precisely this wrestling with the obstinate facts that has commended this thought to the sophisticated, including many intellectuals who do not share his Christian faith in an eternal absolute beyond the temporal paradoxes. And the influence of Niebuhr has been great on the fairly sophisticated churchmen who have commented on our troubled age through the various Councils of Churches—although the study of Christian ethics has been starved in the Protestant churches outside the United States, and it has been given to tragically few (if any) ecclesiastics or theologians to speak to men of affairs with anything like Reinhold Niebuhr's effectiveness.

History may judge that the best comment on our age has come from the assemblies and agencies of the World Council of Churches and from the national councils associated with it. In part this comment has been in the shape of a costly concern for the relief of the victims of wars and disasters and for the resettlement of refugees. In part it has come as the churches have provided a platform for the legitimate aspirations of the Afro-Asian Revolution. In the areas of 'rapid social change' the World Council of Churches has sponsored an intensive programme of study and action intended to equip Christians to enter more fully into the tasks of building modern nations; and in the richer countries the World Council, with its associated national councils, has put its influence behind the fights for civil rights for coloured minorities, and for greater economic equality for the coloured and hungry majority of the peoples of the world. Together with this emphasis on the supreme importance of the tension between the 'haves' and the 'have-nots' for the future peace of the world, there has gone a constant warning against the total horrors of nuclear, bacteriological or chemical war and a constant pressure in favour of risky initiatives in disarmament. This pressure against war has (unlike the pacifism of the 1920s and 1930s) sympathised with the dilemmas of the statesmen who are caught in an evil situation for which they are not entirely to blame; and it has been backed up by a consistent argument that the ideological conflict between capitalism and Com-

munism, the West and the East of the world, was not serious
enough to justify the use of the Bomb.

A striking development of the 1960s was an outburst of
bold thinking by Protestant Christians about the character
and content of their ethical decisions in the personal problems of life. This new crisis in ethics had been building up
because Christians had noticed—some more acutely than
others—that new decisions had been demanded by new
situations created by scientific progress. The dominance of
power politics by nuclear weapons forced the old issues of
pacifism or patriotism with a new intensity for many consciences and led to a new debate about whether those
weapons should be 'renounced', or kept as a deterrent against
aggression, or wielded as instruments of war against military
forces, or even, at the last extreme of horror, hurled like
obscene parodies of the thunderbolts of Zeus to punish
civilian populations. Some of the new situations posed the
most intimate of questions. The advance of medical
science's capacity to alter the course of nature caused many
to wonder whether personality should be regarded as sacred
in all circumstances, or whether, in the interests of those
around them, people might legitimately be conceived by
artificial insemination, or aborted before birth, or altered in
their characters by brain surgery or drugs, or killed when
judged to be too old or weak. Even the comparatively
trivial ethical problems involved in heart transplants caused
many to discuss the meaning of personality in the surgeon's
age of miracles. The availability of contraceptives produced
another debate about whether sexual intercourse could now
be treated as hand-shakes had been in the old Western
society, or whether it should be tolerated or encouraged
between homosexuals, or whether it should be confined to
men and women who might marry, or whether, within
marriage, it could be enjoyed for years without any thought
of rearing children. From the nuclear graves of an over-
mighty civilisation to the cradles of a scientifically planned
family, modern progress thus threw down new challenges
to traditional ethics, changing patterns of work and family

life, politics and social security, recreation and transport, reminded people that all ethical codes have been relative to their social environment; and these new situations caused many to probe the ethical dimensions of *all* situations in real life. Many Protestants asked: do we now need a 'situation ethics'? They meant by this: do modern people need a 'new morality' in which personal decisions are taken not by referring to long-established rules but by fresh choices inspired by the wish to find the most loving' or the most 'sensitive' or the most 'authentic' action?

In this debate, some agreements seem to be emerging from the smoke of a wordy battle. One agreement is that action guided by love is certainly nearer to Christian ethics than is an unthinking or unfeeling obedience to a moral code which may be irrelevant to the situation in which action is needed. Another agreement is that a humble concern to 'do the loving thing' for the benefit of one's neighbour is nearer to Christian discipleship than is the Pharisaism which is the constant temptation of those who righteously adhere to the laws laid down in a textbook. If the freshness of love, with its honesty, courage and creative power, can be recovered for a Christianity grown stale, cold and irrelevant, then the challenge of 'situation ethics' will generally be thought to have been not only healthy but also vital to the maintenance of religious inspiration for the conduct of the free adult. But, perhaps inevitably, much that has been said under the banner of the 'new morality' has been said in such a way as to suggest a view of human nature which is pathetically irrelevant to the stuff of life. 'The new morality' has often seemed to be based on an optimism about the power of individuals to love intelligently—a view no less disastrous than was the optimism of the social Gospel about the power of societies to establish the reign of love. An analysis of this new phase in Christian ethics no less devastating than Niebuhr's in the 1930s is widely seen to be needed. That analysis, when it comes, is likely to proceed by asking the question: *what is the real situation* in which a decision about the use of nuclear weapons or contraceptives, about the transformation or termination of a human life, must be made? And the real situation is likely to be seen as involving more than the emotions of the principal actors in the immediate drama. The interests of society and of future generations will almost always deserve extremely serious consideration, and the wisdom of society and of past generations will almost always deserve more attention than the individual in his enthusiasm is liable to offer at once. Above all, a believer in God will say on reflection (or under the pressure of other believers) that the will of God should be reckoned the decisive factor in the real situation; for putting God first is the heart of what it means to be ethical in a Christian context, with the aid of the Christian community. Such deeper considerations will not necessarily restore old patterns of ethical behaviour; new situations may indeed call for new decisions. But they will deepen the debate, by doing what the Bible does, by reminding optimists of the depth and breadth of sinful selfishness, by pointing to the mystery of man as the son of God, and by exploring the world as the scene of the coming of the Kingdom of God.[1]

[1] The best introduction to this debate is provided in the two books by Joseph Fletcher, *Situation Ethics* and *Moral Responsibility* (Philadelphia, 1966–67), and the best presentation of the resources of ethical thinking by Christians of various schools is that made in *A Dictionary of Christian Ethics*, ed. John Macquarrie (London, 1967).

CHAPTER EIGHT

A New Statement of Christian Belief

Communicating with the Modern World

When twentieth-century Christians talk with their contemporaries, what should they talk seriously about?

Although we might not suspect this when reading most
Christian theology, most of the raw material used by the
Christian Church's only ultimate Master was not philosophical or doctrinal or ecclesiastical, but was the life of plants
and birds, shepherds and merchants, kings and children. The
parables of Jesus belong to a Palestine which is remote from
the modern town-dweller, and the Spirit promised by Jesus
to his disciples has to be claimed to inspire parables and
symbols for the modern world. One necessary task of the
Christian imagination is to relate old parables or symbols to
new questions (or to old questions in a new dress), but the
creation of new parables or symbols cannot be shirked by
Christians who would continue the prophetic and artistic
courage of their Master. The renewal of the Christian
imagination is thus an urgent priority if the Church is to
communicate with our time. Already the twentieth century
has so developed that some of the most distinguished poets
in the English language in the age of Eliot and Auden are
Christian believers. New hymns have been sung, and new
religious plays performed; and a renaissance in church
architecture (specially in France and Sweden), with some
first-class painting or tapestry design or stained glass, have
opened up the hope of new arts. The communication of the
Christian Gospel will remain excessively academic until

these arts, and the art of new speech, sweep over the living people. Only in this way can the Church repeat what Jesus did: which was, not to lay down for all to accept a dogmatic proposition about an experience, but means of popular art to intensify the experience itself. By telling parables, Jesus opened the eyes of some to look for themselves on nature as the good work of God, and on life as a drama in which people act as they do because people are in some ways like God (fathers like the Father, etc.). Only in this *earthed* style of teaching can the Church, like Jesus, begin where people are, and thus slowly lead people into a creative conversation.

It is, therefore, of much more than academic interest that the reconstruction of the parables of Jesus in their original setting, and the detection of the detailed changes which these parables underwent as the early Christians pondered and expounded them afresh, have been among the positive achievements of the modern critical study of the New Testament. Discussing the dynamic and endlessly fertile art of Jesus, based as this was on loving observation of daily life, Professor Amos Wilder wrote: 'In the Jesus of the parables we have a humanity in which uniquely the heart of man is recognised, as is not the case in all such humanisms, and yet in a way which is universal.'[1]

Science and Religion

At this stage we had better pause to say that we are not meaning to recommend a pious sentimentality or a new vintage of theological jargon. From the theological ferment earlier in the century, there survives this warning from Max Weber: 'The need of literary, academic or café-society intellectuals to include religious feelings in the inventory of their sources of impressions and sensations, and among their topics for discussion, has never yet given rise to a new religion. Nor can a religious renascence be generated by the need of authors to compose books, or by the far more effective need of clever publishers to sell books.'[2]

[1] A. N. Wilder, *Early Christian Rhetoric* (London, 1964), p. 96.
[2] *The Sociology of Religion*, p. 137.

The communication of Christianity must take place in a period when the West's intellectual life is dominated by *science*. If Christian believers are to be at all numerous and at all intelligent, they must include many whose minds have been shaped by science. Even Christian theologians, who are usually (but not always) without a scientific background, tend to be conscious of the scientific atmosphere of the intellectual world around them. It is natural that laymen and theologians alike should often think it necessary to relate religion to science, as ways of knowing and speaking.

Clearly, the attitudes, procedures and languages of science and religion are very different. Science forms theories and tests them by experiments. Its language is public; anyone with sufficient patience, intelligence and knowledge may rethink the theories and repeat the experiments. Brave talk by religious believers about theology as a science betrays an inadequate understanding of the profound contrast between science and religious language, between the discipline of the scientist and the discipline of the man of God. For religious language is essentially a personal language. It is one man's, or one society's, interpretation of an event as a disclosure of the divine. The interpretation is made in terms of the rest of that one man's experience. Even the social character of religion does not make it truly public, for societies differ greatly in their religious traditions which influence their members. Even the event which is interpreted by religion may not be a public event, at least not in the form in which religion claims that it took place. It may be a private ecstasy; or it may be an everyday event which only the prophet has seen as 'charged with the grandeur of God'; or it may be a miracle which can be proclaimed in the witness of the believer but which cannot be admitted into scientific history-writing. Religious language comes alive for a hearer when that hearer decides to accept the event which it interprets as connecting momentously with lesser events which he has already interpreted out of his own experience, and the decision must always be with the hearer (influenced by the community around him). Something of all this highly emotional process is preserved from generation to generation by the models or symbols in a religious tradition, and because they have such an emotional content these models and symbols come to be regarded as sacred. Religious believers come to feel that the symbols which are dear to them should not be compared with everyday objects, and any proposal to replace them by fresh symbols is liable to be regarded as blasphemous, whereas science makes progress by its willingness to scrap old theories. Science and religion are very different ways of describing the world.

Yet the difference between religion and science, although profound, can never be complete. Religion attempts to describe an unearthly and therefore largely unknowable source of light for the world, and it shows the world as mysteriously bathed in that light, looking the same and yet different in comparison with the world as seen and described in the light of the common day. But the world cannot be completely divided. It remains one world, seen in these sacred and secular lights, and therefore religious believers who are also intelligent thinkers can never give up the attempt to compare the two views, religious and scientific, in order to see the one world with the fullest possible clarity.

It is healthy that there has recently been some discussion of religion and science among religious believers who are also trained scientists. Since we have already confessed the average theologian's ignorance of science, we may add that not many scientists have taken theology's discipline seriously enough. Among scientists religion is often left unexamined; for most scientists, this neglect amounts to the rejection of traditional religion, but among some scientists who are religious believers their lack of time for theology may result in an almost childishly naïve traditionalism—or in a faith so vague that it is not in conflict with knowledge because not in contact with it. But some effort has recently been put into the difficult comparison by suitably equipped thinkers.

One theme which often emerges is that both the religious and the scientific communities demand that candidates for entry should be initiated into that community's customs. Sympathetic humility and self-forgetful perseverance are indispensable if any newcomer is to gain access to the secrets of either religion or science. And another frequent theme in this well-informed comparison is that, when its secrets have been penetrated, neither religion nor science turns out to be a straightforward account of the obviously real world. Each discipline, into which the newcomer must be initiated by stages, at the end confesses that it is unable to picture its world with complete accuracy. For the sake of its own thought and for the sake of communication, each discipline therefore uses *models* which can represent intelligibly some aspects of the mysterious reality. The use of the idea of fatherhood to describe God in religion is the use of one model; another model is the scientific picture of the atom as (in the nineteenth century) a hard billiard ball or as (in our time) a miniature planetary system. And the willingness to study such models humbly, with the intention of learning from them, may be the greatest test of the newcomer's desire to become mature in the discipline.

Both science and religion can to some extent overcome the inadequacy of any one model by 'qualifying' that model —that is, by placing it alongside others; and both science and religion often expect the vital disclosure to come to a humble student only through his study of a combination of models. Thus the physicist studies an electron by means of mental models which describe it as behaving now like a particle, and now like a wave; the truth about the electron cannot be expressed more simply. Not only the electron but light itself is said to have some particle-like and some wave-like qualities, and the physicist cannot say anything simpler about it. The student of science has to accept this situation and proceed through it. In a way not altogether dissimilar, the religious believer may find it necessary to use a combination of models in order to express a truth greater than any one of them. For example, light has often been used as a symbol in religion. It may be pictured as the light of a growing dawn, or as the light of a threatened candle, meaning that the light which comes from God begins to illuminate the world (the world being either responsive or hostile). But light may also be pictured as the noonday brightness suffusing the world, meaning that the light comes from a God who is open to the world and reaches a world which is open to God. Thus God's transcendence over nature and men, yet also his being in everything and everyone, may be pictured by a union of apparently contradictory symbols.[1]

These are examples of the inadequacies in single models being corrected, but the student must be prepared for some hard thought before the disclosure will come. He must make sure that the two models, placed side by side, are not *essentially* contradictory; and having ascertained that he must discover what exactly are the features in the different models which are most useful in the task of understanding the total truth. We cannot wonder that, in religion as in science, no impatient person stands a chance.[2]

But while we grant that both religion and science use models, we may still hesitate to say that religious models are useful instruments in a true description of the real world. We have so many warnings from the past that religious doctrines may be used as substitutes for science, or as denials of science. It is therefore necessary to affirm that no proposition should be regarded as authoritative for science simply because religion claims that it has been 'revealed', and that no proposition, however sacred it may be for religion, should be preserved when it has been disproved by science. Such affirmations are not only necessary in logic; they are also needed in practice, for many Christians in the twentieth century have continued to exalt a dogmatic system over science. The conflicts of religion

[1] An excellent study of light as a religious symbol forms Chapter 9 of John Macquarrie, *God-Talk* (London, 1967). But the classic modern treatment of imagery in religion remains Edwyn Bevan, *Symbolism and Belief* (London, 1938).
[2] Some elements in a comparison of religious with scientific models were suggested by Ian T. Ramsey in *Religious Language* (London, 1957) and elsewhere. I wrote a memoir of *Ian Ramsey* (London, 1973).

and science are not yet over. However, the crucial question for religion is not the occurrence of this or that event which religion may have affirmed and science may have denied (such as the creation of the world in 4004 B.C., or the 'special' creation of Adam from whom all men are descended). The crucial question is: *what is the character of reality as a whole?*

To this question about reality as a whole science provides no answer, for science is the study of particular events or objects. The scientist is no more (and no less) qualified than the non-scientist in discussing 'the riddle of the universe'. Ernst Haeckel's widely influential book of that title, translated in 1900, was not science, although it used much evidence from Darwinian biology and other science. It was a controversially philosophical work, tracing the iron laws which controlled the evolution of the universe and denouncing the idea of an active God as a 'gaseous vertebrate'; and it explicitly advocated a new quasi-religion, 'monism'. *The Survival of God in the Scientific Age* (London, 1966) by Alan Isaacs may be cited as a popular book which also made no secret of its atheistic interpretation of the evidence provided by science. But after working through the evidence about the evolution of matter, the evolution of mind and the evolution of the concept of God, Dr. Isaacs conceded the vital point that the basic interpretation of it by religion cannot be disproved, however many mistakes religious teachers can be shown to have made. 'The religious organizations,' Dr. Isaacs wrote, 'being committed to "truth" by revelation, find it impossible to see themselves as a temporary bridging operation between the emotional past and the rational future—or as an extra branch of the secular social services. And they may, of course, be right—the agnostic has no grounds for ruling out the truth of revelation. All that he can be certain of is that in the present context of the nuclear age the religions are rapidly losing their support.'[1] By Haeckel's standards, the anti-religious conclusion reached by Dr. Isaacs was no conclusion at all:

[1] p. 207.

'Perhaps our greatest gift to posterity is that we have released our children from the fear of the supernatural. The concept of God is still available for those who need it—and those who do not, have no longer to be ashamed, and no longer to be afraid.'[1]

We must therefore state here that the uncertainty of science destroys only the attempt to prove God from nature; it does *not* destroy belief in God as a valid option. Some 'natural' religion has to be rejected as claiming too much; but precisely because nature is ambiguous, atheism also deserves to be checked if it dogmatically claims to be the only possible 'scientific' attitude. The thoughtful believer is allowed the same freedom which the agnostic rightly claims for himself. And the believer's is a more honourable freedom than Dr. Isaacs implies. The thoughtful believer is the man who gives his support to religion not because it is fashionable, but because it seems true to him; and he believes religion to be essentially true because he needs the concept of God (or its equivalent in Eastern religion) *in order to interpret his own experience.*

Religion is therefore associated with a world-view which is different from the scientific attitude, although not essentially incompatible with it—just as atheism is different from the scientific attitude, although the same person can, of course, be both an atheist and a scientist. The believer chooses to view reality in one way, although when he is acting as a scientist he is as ready as the next man to pursue his investigations so far as possible 'without bringing religion into it'. His choice is neither arbitrary nor irrational, for it results from his thinking about his experience. Even in a laboratory experiment, the personal factor enters into scientific work, for many scientific theories are born in 'hunches' and are only slowly formulated and tested. But a closer analogy to religious faith within science arises out of the status of a scientist as a human being, who has to choose whether or not he is to work on a particular project, serve a particular company, university or government, or to

[1] p. 215.

marry a particular girl; in these life-determining decisions the scientist, like the next man, has to proceed on the basis of intuitions which he may find it hard to express or to rationalise. And it is in the experience of making such decisions, about religion or about secular life, that a man comes to see most clearly where freedom is left in the age of science. There has been something ludicrous about the enthusiasm with which religious believers have greeted various developments in modern physics, believing that this or that new model in science allowed room for the freedom of man's mind or of God's will. For example, Heisenberg's 'indeterminacy principle'—his discovery that the elementary particles of the atom behaved in ways which could not be predicted—was hailed as demonstrating the freedom of God to act providentially in an otherwise law-abiding world. But such descriptions of matter at its most microscopic descriptions which may one day be improved) have nothing to do with the decision for or against a religious inter- pretation of the whole of reality. The freedom that can be known in the world is the freedom experienced by the person who decides, and this freedom is real amid many factors which profoundly influence personal decisions. Here is the freedom with which a scientist decides whether or not to make the atomic bomb; and here is the freedom with which an individual challenged by a religion decides whether or not to accept its claims.

The decision for or against religious faith is made by the total person, and however reasonable it may be it arises from levels of the personality deeper than the reason. *In this choice, the total person takes a view of total reality.* Religious believers, in addition to jumping at the latest developments in physics, have often made themselves ridiculous by finding gaps, especially in biology, into which their God could be inserted while the rest was left to science. For example, there has often been a religious emphasis on an alleged lack of continuity between mind and matter, so that mind could be described as a miraculous creation by God. But the advance of science is constantly filling in such gaps, so that the God of the gaps quickly becomes redundant. Instead of thinking of *gaps*, it seems to be more useful to think of *levels* in nature. At one level, the parts go their separate ways, but at the next level, the parts combine into a system, and it is out of that organisation—not out of the introduction of a totally new part—that novelty emerges. Nature is increasingly studied as a continuous whole, as a system of systems from the smallest to the greatest. Organic life, for example, or mental activity, while each is seen to be distinctive, is each regarded from a scientific point of view as matter organised at a new level of complexity: 'life' or 'mind' is not a totally new miracle. It is always possible for the scientist to emphasise the old level at the expense of the new, and to reduce the whole system to the alliance of its parts, forgetting that the system works in a new way. Thus biology need not be pursued as the study of living organisms as they exist and behave; it may be reduced to the levels of physics and chemistry, and it often has been. Psychology need not be pursued as the study of the mind of man; it, too, may be reduced to lower scientific levels, as it was by J. B. Watson and other 'behaviourists'. Such 'reductionism' can, of course, be criticised on strictly scientific grounds. The religious believer may or may not be a reductionist when studying any one level in science, but he is a man who sees, beyond all the levels described by science, a level which may be pictured, with the aid of symbols or models, as the level of the activity of God.

This level beyond science is the level of 'miracle'. The true miracle for the believer who accepts the scientific attitude while going beyond it is not the sudden entry of God into the world, reversing in a special case the operation of a 'natural law' which is otherwise inflexible. The believer is content to leave each allegedy special case to a specially careful study of the evidence. The believer may well interpret his own experience of God in such a way that the possibility of God altering normal procedures is not ruled out, and the believer who has such an understanding of God may rightly point out that the so-called 'laws' of nature need not be inflexible, for they really express the norms in the statistics of humanly observed phenomena, not unchanging decrees issued by nature. But all believers hold that God normally works through normal procedures rather than emergency actions, and the believer if he is sensitive to the possibility of error in claims about 'miracles' will not rest his whole faith on one special case proving to be utterly abnormal. The great miracle for the believer in the age of science is *reality as a whole*. 'Miracle' comes from the Latin for 'wonder'. Reality as a whole is wonderful to the believer, for the mystery of its source, character and destiny is illuminated for him by the models provided by his religion.[1]

Christian Faith and Current Philosophies

The religion which is communicated by parables or models must also be interpreted by a philosophy which is as clear and convincing as possible. Jesus himself was no philosopher, and no philosophical system can be an essential consequence of his teaching—certainly not the philosophy of St. Thomas Aquinas, which was a brilliant but temporary feat of the Middle Ages, seeking to harmonise the God of Jesus with the God of Aristotle. A. N. Whitehead was surely right in his famous description of Christianity (here contrasted with Buddhism) as 'a religion seeking a metaphysic'.[2] The Christian religion can awaken personal faith by the appeal of its symbols, supremely by the symbol which is provided by the whole life of Jesus; and the intellectual arguments follow the impact of these symbols on the whole person. Faith, in brief, is existential (and so is unbelief). But some genuinely intellectual arguments there must be, specially as society becomes more educated. 'Faith' must, in St. Anselm's famous phrase, 'seek understanding'— analysing itself, drawing conclusions from its intuitions, and testing itself against all other ways of looking at the

[1] The best introduction to the field is Ian Barbour, *Issues in Science and Religion* (New York, 1966).
[2] *Religion in the Making* (New York, 1926), p. 50.

evidence. A philosophy which follows faith must also examine the secular philosophy of the day—regarding this as the intellectual expression of the attitudes which, largely because of facts which sociology or psychology may usefully analyse, are dominant in the period.

In the twentieth century there has been a series of dialogues between Christian theology and secular philosophy. At first the conversation was between a 'Christocentric metaphysic' of the kind which William Temple embodied, and the philosophical idealism then reigning in the universities with its confident talk about the evolution of mind, value and God; then the conversation was between a 'biblical realism' of the kind proclaimed in Europe by Karl Barth and in America by Reinhold Niebuhr, and the existentialism which studied the nature of the person's decision for or against such a faith; and more recently the dialogue has been between a rather less confident faith, founded on a critical understanding of the Bible, and the philosophy which coldly analyses the language of metaphysical claims. When we see what nonsense is still paraded as wisdom in our world, we need not regret that most of the energy of the professional philosophers, at least in the English-speaking universities, has recently been devoted to this analysis of words, rather than to a love of the higher-flying wisdom. But a new phase in the endless dialogue has now begun.

Some theologians, sensitive to the social and psychological impact of our century, have tried to work out a way of talking about God which is not metaphysical at all, even not 'religious', but which is, in their favourite word, 'secular' —more secular than the anti-God philosophy of secularism, because more open to the realities of experience. In a sketch for a book which he did not live to write, Dietrich Bonhoeffer mentioned that 'the transcendental is not infinite and unattainable tasks, but the neighbour who is within reach in any given situation'.[1] Followers of Bonhoeffer have tried to develop an understanding of transcendence as the encounter with the neighbour, and these

[1] *Letters and Papers from Prison*, p. 381.

attempts have healthily recognised the truth, as old as Christianity, that we cannot claim to know or love the transcendent God unless we know and love the human neighbour. Such awareness of the independent, and to the end mysterious, reality of the other person is specially valuable in the age of technology, when personal relations may be atrophied by our concentration on our masterly manipulation of inanimate objects. Thus a student of science may need reminding that his girl is not like his test-tubes.[1] But encounter with the neighbour cannot be the *total* content of transcendence, unless we really are going to reduce theology to anthropology, stopping with man as well as starting with him. Ronald Gregor Smith has recorded an occasion when he put the crucial question, in a conversation with Martin Buber. 'I said something to the effect that it was not clear to me how "the eternal Thou" was to be understood as implicated in each relational event. How could this be proved? "Proved?" he replied. "You know that it is so." Now, long afterwards, I understand that this *knowing* of which he spoke was a trustful, believing knowing.'[2] In other words, through the neighbour some of us experience the transcendent God—and others of us (the more thoroughly secular) experience only the neighbour. The division remains between religious faith and religious unbelief. 'If faith cannot be demonstrated, neither can it be disproved. It remains faith, and by its mere existence it involves a total response'.[3]

Some recent theologians have sought to present Christianity in a larger, although still 'this-worldly', setting —as a political rather than personal matter, as an interpretation of this world's history. The prophets of Israel and Jesus himself saw God in the events of history, and not at all in metaphysical speculation—in the events of the world, and not primarily in the rituals of the temple. It is therefore

[1] John Macmurray's Gifford Lectures on *Persons in Relation* (London, 1961) may be regarded as the crown of personalist philosophy.
[2] R. Gregor Smith, *Martin Buber* (London, 1966), p. 22.
[3] R. Gregor Smith, *Secular Christianity*, p. 58.

healthy when Christians discern the hand of God in the great drama of our age. Such Christians do not regard the enormous expansions of human intelligence and knowledge, the new freedom of mind and speech and the spread of popular education, the triumphs of the natural and social sciences, and the beginnings of a true psychology, as threats to be denounced and resisted; instead, they regard these things as great new acts of God.

But more and more widely it is being agreed that the real progress of our civilisation—its true humanism, in the sense of serving the full development and deep happiness of the human race—will demand that more people in the secular city face openly the question of what their humanity means. This must include the question whether they and their neighbours are, or are not, meant to live in the light of a destiny as citizens of the eternal City of God. The Christian in John Bunyan's seventeenth-century *Pilgrim's Progress* made the mistake of dismissing the world which included his wife, children and neighbours as 'the City of Destruction', but a twentieth-century Christian has still to regard the path of life as in some sense a road which takes himself, his family, his neighbours and the whole human race to a destination which he believes to be the Celestial City. Others will not share his belief, and the debate between faith and unbelief is likely to continue until the Celestial City is reached (or turns out to be a mirage in the desert of a pointless universe). But if one thing is clear as the believing pilgrim struggles along the road, it is that secular urban planning is not the same activity as theology's quest for the ultimate.

Religious belief may, therefore, legitimately protest that the object of its concern is really *ultimate*: it is more than the human neighbour, and more than the secular city. Religious faith may also rightly affirm that its object is more than the sum total of the natural world already around us. Sometimes religion in our time has been reduced to little more than a sense of perspective. Religion has been described as urging us not to be anxious about the details, but instead to 'see life steadily and see it whole'. In our century's more optimistic moments, such a religion has been presented as a vision of the glorious whole; and in our century's blacker moods, it has been presented as liberation from narrow cares or temporary despairs. These elements are certainly present in religion as most believers in the modern West would understand religion; but, when all this has been said in praise of religion, most believers will still feel that religion's grand object has been left out of such descriptions. The vision offered by the Western religious tradition to perplexed or despairing minds is a vision of a power which is greater than any person or object in the universe, and greater even than the sum total of objects and people; and in the long run the value of this religious tradition stands or falls with the truth of this vision. It is necessary to emphasise this point, which seems obvious enough to almost all those who look at religion from outside, because in our time a number of those standing within the religious world, including theologians, have obscured it; they have argued that religion may rightly claim to provide emotional re-assurance or ethical inspiration, but not information about what really is.

Most of those who stand outside religion, as well as most of those who worship within it, would suppose that the vision just mentioned does constitute religion's central claim to truthfulness and therefore to usefulness. But in our time the word 'God' has lost much of its former power, not only for those who have been thoroughly secularised, but also for many of those who have felt the psychological impact of our secular century while remaining in the religious tradition. It is not surprising that some theologians have wished to show afresh the basic strength of the idea of God, but to discard outmoded elements in traditional talk about God. Such theologians have turned to current philosophical movements for help. Here, however, we shall not offer an elaborate exposition of the philosophical school in question; we shall merely provide the briefest outline of how the philosophical tradition is likely to be relevant to the fundamental problems of the person who is interested in religion without being a professional philosopher. We may excuse ourselves for our lack of philosophical refinement by recalling that our purpose is to see the broad relevance of these ideas to theology and through theology to the religious life of the age. The philosophies which we have in mind are the philosophy of Being, associated with the German thinker, Martin Heidegger, and the philosophy of Process, associated with the Anglo-American thinker, A. N. Whitehead.

Being and Process

For the philosophy of Being—which is extremely hard to state clearly—the clue may be provided by Wittgenstein's remark that 'not *how* the world is, is the mystical, but *that* it is'.[1] As Leibniz asked in the eighteenth century: 'Why are there entities at all, and not just nothing?' Any observation of nature, or any incident in life, may awaken that question in us, but the wonder of sheer Being may be experienced most sharply when we consider its alternative: the destruction of what was. Since we are samples of Being, the wonder may come home to us by meditation on our own deaths, when 'to be or not to be' becomes for us the question of all questions. Man knows that he has been thrown into life, and man knows that he will die, and man wonders whether he will die entirely—and man asks whether there is any point in it all. Such questions may lead the questioner to meditate on the mystery of the 'Being' which all existent things and persons have in common; and so the questioner may be led to sense, and to contemplate, what is in the mystical tradition called the source of Being, or the power of Being, or the ground of Being, or Being itself. According to most parts of the great mystical tradition, Being itself may be deeper than all things, and stronger than all their deaths. The religious name for 'Being itself' is 'God'; but it is impossible to answer the question 'What is Being?', for

[1] *Tractatus Logico-Philosophicus*, p. 187.

Being is not a 'what' or something, and 'Being itself' cannot be expressed except through symbols or models. Even to say that 'Being exists' suggests a confusion between Being and mere existence. Yet Being may be revealed. Anything in the universe can become a symbol or model for the mystery of 'Being itself'; any 'what' can disclose it to us; at any moment the discovery of the deep truth may occur; and the greatest symbol is a rational, spiritual person—a person who bears the mystery of Being in his existence, a person who may learn what it means *to be* by looking into himself.

Paul Tillich in his *Systematic Theology* (3 vols., New York, 1951–63), and John Macquarrie in his *Principles of Christian Theology* (New York, 1966), related this philosophy of Being to traditional Christianity's doctrines, and the passionately eloquent and deeply moving sermons of Tillich[1] and of Rudolf Bultmann[2] related it to the doubts and anxieties of twentieth-century man. Such books show how this basically mystical or aesthetic understanding of existence can bring out the deep reality of many of the affirmations which the Christian wishes to make about God and about Jesus. Theology when preached in this way can help a modern man towards 'authentic existence'. Courage can replace despair arising from a sense of meaninglessness, and concern for what ultimately matters can replace a man's temporary, illusory satisfactions provided by trivial, material objects.

The philosophy of Process is definitely interested in *how* the world is—although it, too, is basically mystical or aesthetic.[3]

It begins with the failure of science to detect a purpose in every part of the universe. Modern science in its early days struck up a friendship with Christian theology on the basis of an agreement that the beauty of a designed order could

[1] *The Shaking of the Foundations* (New York, 1948); *The Boundaries of Our Being* (London, 1973).
[2] *This World and Beyond* (1956; Eng. trans., New York, 1958).
[3] The relevance of this philosophy for Christians was summed up in two short books, *God in Process* by Norman Pittenger and *Exploration into God* by John Robinson (both London, 1967).

be seen in every part of creation; but the experience of the limitations of purpose, or at least of the limitations of science, has become an overwhelming psychological fact in the nineteenth and twentieth centuries. The Process philosophy starts from that experience, and it is perhaps not too fanciful to say that this philosophy interprets the whole of reality through using a model provided by the achievements of modern science: the model of the successful experiment. The whole universe is interpreted as a process where failures or accidents apparently occur, but where gradually these failures and accidents are seen to be less significant than the victory at the end. The ultimate victory comes with the coming of that beauty of order, which 'natural' theology used to teach was present from the beginning.

This Process philosophy sees a beauty and a goodness in the world. And it sees this beauty and goodness as more significant than the disorder and evil which are also in the world; for in the world it sees human intelligence and love, and it sees that these mental or spiritual activities of man are, at least in their essential physical basis, continuous with the rest of the universe, mind emerging out of matter. The philosophy of Process therefore interprets the whole of reality in the light of the fact that evolution has produced thought and love in man. Such a philosophy can have a very powerful religious significance, interpreting all the universe. For if the power of intelligent love is taken as the clue to the meaning of this whole vast process, then the power which runs through evolution (and through the whole universe) can itself be understood as persuasive and not coercive. In other words, God (or whatever other name we may give to the ultimate reality) may be seen as the supreme example—the 'chief exemplification' in Whitehead's phrase—of intelligence and love, not of mere power.

The relevance of this Process philosophy to the idea of God has been seen by Process philosophers in at least two ways—ways which are essentially different. Some philosophers of this school equate God with the natural process itself, either as this process already is or as it is coming to be.

Such philosophers belong to a tradition at least as old as the seventeenth-century Spinoza. On this showing, God *is* the universe as the spiritual power of love prevails in the universe. But others (and Whitehead was among them) think that the reality of God is greater than the reality of the natural process. They find room—even if to some it may appear a rather obscure room—for the transcendence of God (who to Whitehead was a 'real entity'). On the basis of either understanding of the meaning of the word 'God', Process philosophers can suggest a picture of nature as God's growing body, but the second, fuller, understanding of the nature of God is more satisfying religiously to those brought up in the Western tradition, for it sees God as the transcendent Lover and the whole process of the universe as the expression of this divine Love. A vision of God such as we find in Whitehead seems rooted in the essential validity of the West's traditional religious vision. 'The fact of the religious vision, and its history of persistent expansion,' he wrote, 'is our one ground for optimism. Without it human life is a flash of occasional enjoyments lighting up a mass of pain and misery.'[1] Whitehead therefore respected the West's religious vision of the transcendent God, whether or not his philosophy found adequate room for it.

Both the philosophy of Being and the philosophy of Process deserve to be taken seriously, for they are twentieth-century expansions of older styles of philosophical or religious argument. They both appeal to the new self-consciousness of twentieth-century man, who is aware of the wonder of his existence, and of the power of his mind, against a background which often tempts him to despair. The philosophy of Being, with its deep emphasis on a static peace and perfection at the heart of things, seems likely to appeal more to a deeply disturbed society, and the philosophy of Process, which emphasises 'becoming' and tends to view change as progress, seems likely to appeal to a society which is cautiously optimistic; and in fact we do find that Martin Heidegger the German, and Paul Tillich the German-

[1] *Science and the Modern World*, p. 275.

American, wrote and spoke about Being in the period from 1914 to around 1960, when Germany was in the throes of a destructive crisis and when the United States was under the threat of total war, whereas Whitehead and his disciples have emerged as the apostles of Process from more peacefully academic (and scientifically minded) circles in Britain or America. But both philosophies have in common a concern to relate twentieth-century man to his total environment. They seek to show modern man his roots; and in this they fulfil one of the age-old tasks of religion. They try to demonstrate that man is not a lonely stranger in the universe; on the contrary, his life is united with all that is, and his mind is at home in the evolution out of which it came.

Such philosophies may in their different ways give a contemporary significance to the mythical account of the creation at the beginning of the Bible. That account has often been regarded as arising out of a pseudo-scientific knowledge of the origins of the universe, or out of a religious speculation about them. But the first chapter of the Old Testament seems to have been one of the last chapters to be written, and it seems to have arisen not out of science or out of speculation but out of the experience of Israel. That experience had a double climax: the Exodus from Egypt, and the Exile in Babylon. In those crises, Israel was confronted by two great empires, and Yahweh the one God of Israel was pitted against strange, mighty gods. Under immense pressures the faith of Israel held fast. Moses in relation to Egypt, and the unknown prophet known as Second Isaiah in relation to Babylon, interpreted the people's experience so as to disclose to them the unique Lordship of the one God, and the *Genesis* model of God the Creator survives to embody that crisis in religion. This model will not help the twentieth century to decide whether the universe began with one primeval nucleus and a 'big bang', or whether the creation of atoms is steady and continuous; that is a question best left to the astronomers. But the ancient model may help the twentieth century to see whether it, too, discovers the God of the Bible to be the conqueror in its own tribulations because he is the source of its own existence. As Bultmann wrote, 'the affirmation that God is Creator . . . cannot be made as a neutral statement, but only as thanksgiving and surrender'.[1]

The age of science has to ask what in its own experience is similar to the experience which created the biblical myth. The philosophies of Being and of Process point to the answer, which is that estrangement or alienation, although felt in our time as perhaps never before, is not the deepest experience of modern man. Paul Tillich in particular has seen the grace of God ('Being itself') as coming to modern man in every moment when man feels that there is an infinite power in the universe which accepts and sustains his finitude, and an inexhaustible love which accepts and transforms his anxiety; and Professor Macquarrie's large-scale reconstruction of Christian doctrine is made on the simple basis that God is Being experienced as gracious. Without this basis, Macquarrie argues, a Christian existentialist's analysis of human existence cannot be a Gospel; for without this basis, the last word about the human situation is a word of anxiety.

This experience of communion with a goodness at the heart of life comes to people in moments of intensely personal joy such as the delights of marriage or parenthood, or in aesthetic ecstasies such as a full response to great music—rather than in the routine of intellectual work; but there is an aspect of science which can help intellectuals whose personal life may be impoverished to appreciate what is being said in these philosophies. Science may itself provide this relevant experience, for science is the correspondence between the mind of man and external reality. There are limits to the capacity of the mind, and one of these limits is the 'givenness' of the whole universe (no one can tell how the primeval nucleus came to be); another of the limits is the unpredictability of the behaviour of the most elementary particles; but the mind can travel far before it comes up against such a limit. Up the telescope or down the microscope, the material of science seems to be orderly and responsive to the mind of

[1] *Jesus Christ and Mythology*, p. 69.

man. The universe expands continuously at a speed which is faster than the speed of light, yet the mind of man can reach where even his aided eye cannot. At a level humbler than the microscope can reveal, the dance of the atoms in the stream of energy still seems to have a pattern which the mind can grasp. After its fantastic adventures, the inquiring mind still seems to be at home. This experience does not automatically produce religious orthodoxy, but it appears to have played a part in making a considerable number of the century's distinguished scientists religiously sensitive. In a period when the artists have normally felt angry because they have been isolated rebels against society, and when many ordinary people have been the victims of anxiety because the social order has not given them enough support, many of the scientists who have most effectively applied their intellects to nature have been most profoundly moved to a contented humility before the miracle of their success.

The Reality of God and Christ

At the end of his book on the possible answers to contemporary anxiety, *The Courage to Be* (New York, 1952), Paul Tillich wrote: 'The courage to be is rooted in the God who appears when God has disappeared in the anxiety of doubt.' We need to sense the force of this insistence by a great theologian that the real God is beyond all the images of God which are liable to disappear once questioned. Tillich's philosophical way of speaking should not conceal his intention of continuing the protest of the Bible. Included in his prophetic distrust of all images was a specially powerful protest against one particular form of religious triviality: the sentimental tendency to regard God as *one person among others*, the childish tendency which ends in the picture (still popular among many adults) of God as the 'Old Man in the Sky'. Tillich here supplied the austere correction which both the prophets and the mystics have always offered to the simple sentimentality of the devout, but in fairness to him we should see that he was not undevout himself. He did address his prayers to God as 'Father', and his protest against a trivial conception of the divine personality arose out of a desire to stress the power of God. God, Tillich taught, cannot be merely one person among others—because God is in every person. Implied in Tillich's protest against the sentimental picture of the Old Man in the Sky was also a rejection of the more intellectual tendency to regard God as *one object among others*—the highest part of the universe, but only a part. This tendency can result in the philosophical concept of God as the First Cause. The First Cause is an object in philosophical speculation which may or may not be there in actual reality (it is hard to tell); but anyway the First Cause is inert and remote. Or this tendency can result in the acknowledgement of God's presence only in a series of fitful interventions from the supernatural sphere, as when a watchmaker corrects a watch which normally he leaves alone, or as when in a Greek tragedy a god appears at the end to clear up the man-made mess (*deus ex machina*). Even orthodox and devout Christians may reveal a trivial conception of God when they speak of God 'entering history' at the incarnation. God, Tillich taught, is everywhere; God is in all that is. As a Protestant prophet, Tillich taught that religious faith must be deepened in sensitivity to the depths of the mystery of Being. Such a purifying insistence on the wonder of God's reality seems now absolutely vital to the future of faith in God.

From its negative protest, however, modern theology may be emerging into a few positive affirmations. Faith in our time meets God's presence in this life, for no other life is yet available to us—*and faith finds God to be not a mere aspect or part of this existence but the inexhaustible mystery of 'Being itself'*. Faith watches God's work in history and gains through this work a vision of eternity. Thus the 'high' God—high in the sense that this God is 'Being itself'—is also near; and yet when he is near, God is known as 'high' above all persons and all things. Faith declares that we may sense the presence of this God anywhere, in the secular world primarily, but also within religion. God shows himself to us, and we are grasped by him. We can answer him and obey him, but we can never fully describe how he has come to us, and still less can we describe him as he really is. In our time as for Moses in the Old Testament, the secret of the Lord remains with the Lord; his full name is not given to us, and his nature will be revealed only as he will gradually show himself more fully to us when we obey him. And what is even more astonishing for faith: God treats us as adults, we can easily escape from his grasp, and again and again, even when we obey him as sons, he withdraws in order to teach us to stand on our own feet and not to cling to him in childish dependence. In our time, therefore, faith does not reach certainty; faith experiences much of that sense of godlessness which is described as the 'death' of God; yet faith perseveres.

Faith in God perseveres, for, despite the validity of the protest against the idolatrous tendency to reduce the Creator to the level of being one person among many other people, the faith of Western monotheism finds itself still compelled to affirm that God cannot be *less* than personal. The Source and Ground of all that is cannot be inferior to any person in intelligence or will, freedom or love. Despite the inability of any symbolism to reveal perfectly the perfect Being, this faith still finds that personality is the key symbol in beginning to understand God; and one of the reasons for using this personal category in the language of faith is the experience of faith that God, who is more than personal, becomes 'a person' when he comes to meet us.

But *has* God come? We may put the difficulty by saying that although he was the greatest theologian of our century only a small minority has found Karl Barth's way of making the Christian faith worth noticing again to be permanently convincing.

Barth's failure may be attributed partly to his style, the eloquence of an excited preacher—a style which in our time falls strangely on the ears both of the intelligentsia and of the intellectually simple. But about Barth supremely it is true to say that the style is the man. In his fully developed and academically supported *Church Dogmatics* as in his moving

addresses to the inmates of Basle Prison,[1] Barth deliberately
began not with a discussion of the possibility of Christian
faith in terms of the hearer's own experience, but with an
announcement of a fact repeated from the Bible. He scorned
to discuss possibilities; he was gripped by what for him was
the all-embracing and all-deciding reality, the glorious
reality of God in Jesus Christ. He believed that single-minded
concentration on the Word of God as the one object to be
considered in preaching or theology is what could deliver
those human activities from speculation and sentimentality.
Thus, and only thus, the task of the preacher or the theologian could become manly and joyous. The scientist studies
one object; and Barth called on the preacher or the theologian to be disciplined and objective in something like the
same way. Up to a point, this approach was successful.
Barth's own torrential eloquence was manly and joyous, and
the truth to which he was devoted appealed through his
personality. This impact was the equivalent—at a far more
intelligent level—of the effect on a mass audience of the
evangelism conducted by Billy Graham in Barth's later years.
But many continued to ask questions which they cannot
abandon without denying all their life to this date. Karl
Barth (like Billy Graham) was not so helpful there.

For all its many merits, Barth's presentation of Christ
suffered from his dogmatic approach. Great emphasis was
placed for example, on, the eternal decree of God the Father
to be 'with men' and 'for men' through God the Son, who is
called 'Jesus Christ' even before the birth of the 'God-Man'.
The purpose behind the whole created universe is that it
should be a theatre for the fulfilment of this decree, and the
meaning of all history is that in history a People of God
should respond to God's choice of them (their 'election').
This divine decree has the incidental merit of ruling out the
speculation of the sixteenth-century John Calvin (who was
greatly honoured by Barth in other connections) that God
had predestined some to everlasting damnation. According

[1] *Deliverance to the Captives* (1959; Eng. trans., London, 1961);
Call for God (1965; Eng. trans., London, 1967).

to Barth, the decree was revealed during the days in which the risen Christ taught his disciples, before his ascension. In those great days the first Christians also learned *how* God had been 'with men' and 'for men'. Here Barth did mainly echo Calvin, for his presentation of the saving act of God is made through an emphasis on Jesus Christ's sufferings on the cross under 'the wrath of God'. But *all* men, Barth said, were loved by God from the beginning; *all* men sinned and therefore deserved damnation; Jesus Christ when he suffered and died bore the punishment on behalf of *all*, and therefore *all* have been reconciled to God, whether they accept it or not. On the cross God took man's place; therefore, in heaven man may share God's place. For Barth, this was the 'incomprehensible miracle' at the heart of the Gospel.[1] Barth differed significantly from Calvin in a clearer stress on God's love as the centre of the cross. God for him was by no means a remote judge, for God was fully in the Crucified; indeed, God the Son, the eternal Second Person of the Trinity, is 'the Subject' who is the centre of the manhood of Jesus.

The trouble about this whole proclamation of Jesus Christ by Karl Barth is that it means little or nothing to modern men whose minds do not move in response to talk about religious metaphysics and religious sacrifices. Not even the genius and attractiveness of Barth can permanently remedy this basic defect. The language of Barth can be deeply meaningful to minds formed by the orthodox tradition of Christianity, and such believers may compare Barth's theology to its advantage with the theology of Calvin, etc. But to those who begin at another place, Barth offered no concessions and no connections. He frankly spoke of faith as a miracle, and his concern was that the faith should not be betrayed in the attempt to make it palatable. And many Christians who in our time share Barth's desire to witness to the God of the Bible find that the basic arrogance in such theology is an arrogance which is essentially different in its

[1] E.g., *Dogmatics in Outline* (1947; Eng. trans., New York, 1949), p. 115.

whole mood from the Bible's firm and unsentimental teaching. The Christ they know did not dismiss the earthy, doubting layman with the 'Take it or leave it' of Karl Barth. And they agree with Dietrich Bonhoeffer's letter of 5 May 1944: 'Barth was the first theologian to begin the criticism of religion, and that remains his really great merit; but he put in its place a positivist doctrine of revelation which says, in effect, "Like it or lump it": virgin birth, Trinity, or anything else; each is an equally significant and necessary part of the whole, which must simply be swallowed as a whole or not at all. That is not biblical.'[1]

Bonhoeffer (whose own academic writing on the problem of the nature of Christ can scarcely be described as unsophisticated) was indicating his great sympathy with many modern questioners. If they are agnostic about many of the details in the earthly life of Jesus, such questioners are even more sceptical about the ability of human minds to describe with precision the links between that life and the home life (in technical theology, the 'aseity') of God. Bultmann's contention seems likely to prevail that theology 'cannot speak of God as he is in himself, but only of what he does for us'.[2] Among many theologians there is an impatience with the metaphysical dogmas of the past. This leads to a questioning of the contemporary relevance of the fifth-century Chalcedonian Definition of the divine and human natures in Christ, and it leads also to an ashamed disgust with the virtual tritheism (three gods) of much popular Trinitarianism. When Barth tells us that the Word of God was 'the Subject' in the person of Jesus, and that the Word derives from the communion of the Three Persons of the Trinity with each other in eternity, such theologians dare to ask: does even Barth know what he is talking about? How can any mortal man be confident that he has understood the unique personality of Jesus? How dare he seem to be at home in the home life of God?

[1] *Letters and Papers from Prison*, p. 286.
[2] *The Theology of Rudolf Bultmann*, ed. C. W. Kegley (New York, 1966), p. 273.

Theologians who confess their ignorance about most aspects of this mystery may, however, believe and teach that in an utterly unique manner 'God was in Christ'; that God was present in Jesus without removing that Son of God from among the sons of men; that God acting mightily through that holy, loving life, so as to reveal his glory and so as to save the world. Thus Bishop Hugh Montefiore has written: 'His knowledge was human knowledge, his actions were human actions. Yet in Jesus the divine activity was fully present so far as is possible to human personality . . . We are exactly translating the essence of Chalcedon into a different thought-form. We have not rid ourselves altogether of the concept of substance, but we cannot theologize about it, since the Being of God is transcendent to our existence.'[1] Or Professor John Hick writes that the Divine Love 'caused' the love of Jesus, much as the radiant energy of the sun causes the light which falls on the earth, so that 'Jesus was God's attitude to mankind incarnate'.[2] Jesus seems to have been extremely reticent about his self-consciousness, and no doubt he was sharply aware of the inadequacy of all the traditional titles which his followers were to apply to him. But Jesus did believe that his mission was unique and all-important, so that the simple Christology which we have just outlined may be considered both necessary and enough. In Norman Pittenger's words, 'one group of Christians has tended to say that this person is God living and acting humanly. Another has tended to say that this person is the Man in whom God lives and acts. The difference between the two ways of phrasing the fact which Christians have encountered has led to almost interminable theological argument, which has been as little enlightening as it has been little edifying.'[3]

What our time needs, therefore, in the reconstruction of a distinctively Christian faith is the centrality of a *credible* Christ as the enfleshed Word of God. This recovery must

[1] *Soundings*, ed. A. R. Vidler (Cambridge, 1962), p. 171.
[2] *Prospect for Theology*, ed. F. G. Healey (London, 1967), p. 164.
[3] *The Word Incarnate* (London, 1959), p. 12.

take account of biblical scholarship, which with its patient
learning and courageous honesty has been one of the most
strenuous forms taken by the free intellectual life of our
century; and it must be patient to relate itself to all our
century's difficulties with Christian orthodoxy. Much has
been questioned or destroyed by modern biblical scholarship, but what remains? We need to try to answer Dietrich
Bonhoeffer's question: *Who is Christ for us today?*[1]

At least since Albert Schweitzer's *Quest of the Historical
Jesus*, it has been generally acknowledged by scholars that
Jesus taught about the supernatural and world-transforming
Kingdom of God, and that he lived and died in order that
this Kingdom might come on earth as in heaven. The
supreme question has been what this message and life can
mean for an age which does not think in the language of
the first-century Jewish apocalyptic hope. The facts that
Schweitzer grossly exaggerated Jesus's identification with
the cruder forms of that hope, and that he failed to work out
for himself a philosophy with any real resemblance to the
teaching of Jesus about God, have not blinded the more
thoughtful to the urgency of the challenge. What has begun
to emerge from the massive debate among the theologians
has been a consensus that the Kingdom means the fully
acknowledged sovereignty of God, and that Jesus regarded
his work as the decisive stage in the inauguration of this
Kingdom. That was why in so many of his parables he
warned his original hearers that the greatest conceivable
crisis was upon them. It is also agreed that Jesus summoned
men to enter the Kingdom by following him along the way of
the cross, and promised them that God would bring in his
own Kingdom fully in his own way and at his own time.
Finally, it is agreed that after the death of Jesus his resurrection became for Christians *the* sign that the Kingdom of
which he had spoken had been inaugurated, and was
triumphing.

Because other words have to be produced to express this

[1] I made an attempt in my *What is Real in Christianity?* (London,
1972).

message today, we may refer to some of the preconditions of understanding this message. Here we must agree with the insistence of Karl Barth that it is only a new life that will lead to a new understanding of God. There must be a thorough turning, a conversion; a thorough renewal, a rebirth; for it is only a life of attempted obedience to the ethical teaching of Jesus, lived in spiritual fellowship with him, that will give a person in our time a clear enough vision of the world as it is meant to be, and of the Sovereign Lord who means this. Only the experiences of this discipleship will give men a sufficient foretaste of the victory of God over evil —a victory which is not complete in this age of the world but which is surely coming when all the purposes of God have been worked out. The experiences of the disciple are not sufficient in themselves to supply this vision; they only become sufficient when brought to the Master in a continuing and developing relationship. Thus the centrality of Christ in Christian thought involves the centrality of Christian prayer in Christian life. Nor are the experiences of the disciple sufficient to satisfy all of a man's natural curiosity; they are adequate only to sustain the disciple along the road to the end. And when the disciple has contributed what he can to the victory of God, he will find that it has been very little, so that when Christian prayer moves from communion with God through Christ to consider the needs of the world, the disciple learns that his chief contribution is to express in prayer the world's greatest (although largely unacknowledged) need: 'Thy Kingdom come, thy will be done.'

In the course of such a discipline, what does the disciple begin to discover about the significance of the teaching of Jesus about the Kingdom of God? After all our criticisms of the great theologians of our century, it would be foolish for us to pretend to possess the answers to the vast problems at which we have glanced. (Albert Schweitzer used to say that the day when the meaning of the Kingdom of God was agreed on would be the day when the two streams of dogmatic and liberal theology flowed together.[1]) But in due humility

[1] Henry Clark, *The Philosophy of Albert Schweitzer*, p. 210.

we may mention a few of the discoveries which have been reflected and vindicated in some recent theology. For in other hands than ours, under an inspiration greater than any given to our own age, these themes might become the battle-cries of a new Reformation, the affirmations of a faith able to fire the hearts of the millions.[1]

The Message of Hope

First, the disciple learns that the Gospel is a message of hope.[2]

At the end of his notoriously brief discussion of 'The Message of Jesus', Bultmann put its essence very clearly. 'For Jesus, God became a *God at hand*. He is the power, here and now, who as Lord and Father enfolds every man—limiting and commanding him . . . For Jesus, man is de-secularized by God's direct pronouncement to him, which tears him out of all security of any kind and places him at the brink of the End.'[3] Such a Gospel, however brief, is not vague; and Bultmann does regard it as the task of the Christian Church in each generation to repeat and interpret this message of Jesus. Asked what was the Gospel for an industrial society as represented by the steel workers of Sheffield, Bultmann wrote in a private letter: 'The basic sin is man's self-will and his intention of trying to live by his own wisdom and power . . . The grace of God releases him . . . The surrender of self-will to God occurs in actual life through loving one's neighbour . . . To such surrender to the grace of God and to the neighbour, the Gospel promises freedom, power and life . . . We hand everything over to the grace of God, who gives us what is to come.'[4]

[1] And I am particularly grateful to the Archbishop of Canterbury, Dr. A. M. Ramsey, who wrote in a careful review (*Frontier*, February 1970): 'He is asking by what road we may so approach the mystery of the New Testament as to put ourselves to school with it most meaningfully to ourselves and our contemporaries . . . I would say that the last chapter of the book is all about the Holy Spirit or about nothing.'

[2] I have expanded this brief section in my *The Last Things Now* (London, 1969).

[3] *The Theology of the New Testament*, vol. i, pp. 23–5.

[4] *The Honest to God Debate*, p. 138.

'What is to come' has been the theme of much Christian thought in recent years, for of theology, when it has been vital, has had to come to terms with the totalitarianisms of Communism and National Socialism, and with the longer-lived intoxications of technical and social progress in the democratic age of science. All these were philosophies of history—'eschatological' because concerned to proclaim which things were ultimate. The twentieth century has been eschatological in its inner drive, and the twentieth-century Church has had to think about the contemporary relevance of the eschatological myths and symbols which it has inherited from a vanished (but no less turbulent) world. The World Council of Churches, for example, made 'hope' the theme of its Assembly at Evanston in 1954, and the Second Vatican Council repeated in a different context many of the agreements of that Assembly. Theologians in their reflections, after many one-sided emphases and mutual accusations, have increasingly come to see that various elements in the Christian hope should be held together in an eschatology for our time.

First, many of the hopes of history can be endorsed, for the energy in such creative hopes should be interpreted as coming from the Creator. In particular, the revolutionary hope of our own time may be seen as connected profoundly with the energetic optimism of the Christian Gospel. Jesus dared to live in joy because he trusted that his Father would show himself as King; and the central inspiration in the progress of the modern world is connected with that confident trust. Christians believe in a progressive and revolutionary God, who is 'above' yet who always calls men into a better future on the good earth. As Teilhard de Chardin liked to put it, 'the synthesis between the (Christian) God "above" and the (Marxist) God "in front": here is the only God whom we can henceforth adore in spirit and in truth.'[1]

Second, the hopes of evolution should be endorsed as they hold before us realistic prospects of technical and cultural

[1] Quoted in *Evolution, Marxism and Christianity*, ed. B. Towers and A. Dyson (London, 1967), p. 73.

advance in the two thousand million years ahead of *homo sapiens*. The full emergence of man, his 'hominisation' in Teilhard's phrase, is not complete, but a promise of complete 'hominisation' may be heard if the hand of God is seen in the processes of evolution to date; and the twentieth-century Christian may set his faith in that perspective. But fearful dangers remain in both contemporary and evolutionary hopes, and the certainty of death—the death of the individual, the death of the race, the death of the planet—lies at the end.

Therefore, Christian theology rightly continues to put its main emphasis on the third great element in Christian hope, which is the confidence that the glory of God will sustain the glory of man through the death which comes to every man and to every part of the universe. 'The last enemy that shall be destroyed is death . . . that God may be all in all,' wrote Teilhard on the last page of his journal before his death in New York on Easter Day, 1955.[1] Here one of the greatest Catholic prophets to the twentieth century is at one with a great Protestant prophet, Bonhoeffer. Here is faith in the eternal 'Lord of heaven and earth', who loves the man whom he has made and, having loved him, will not throw him away. This God remains the 'Lord of the living'—through death itself. Here, resting man's whole hope on God's reality and rule, is the most sublime affirmation of the destiny of *homo sapiens*. Since Copernicus man has lost his physical centrality in the universe; since Darwin man has lost his uniqueness in creation; since Marx and Freud man has lost his rationality as the control of his conduct; yet here, in the very simple faith that God loves for ever the man whose character has been shaped by all the influences of the world (influences which Darwin, Marx, Freud and a host of others may analyse), is the modern translation of the old myth of the glory of man in the resurrection of the body. Here, all but totally incredible in the splendour of its courage, is faith in eternal life as the consummation of the whole story of the

[1] Teilhard de Chardin, *The Future of Man* (1959; Eng. trans., London, 1964), p. 309.

whole man in the whole universe. 'The world as we see it is strictly unintelligible,' wrote William Temple in a letter when he had just become Archbishop of Canterbury. 'We can only have faith that it will become intelligible when the divine purpose, which is the explanation of it, is accomplished.'[1]

'Theologically,' Temple noted, 'this is a greater emphasis on eschatology.' 'The eschatological,' Jurgen Moltmann has written more recently, 'is not one element of Christianity, but it is the medium of Christian faith as such, the key in which everything is set, the glow that suffuses everything here in the dawn of an expected new day. For Christian faith lives from the raising of the crucified Christ, and strains after the promises of the universal future of Christ . . . Christianity is to be understood as the community of those who on the ground of the resurrection of Christ wait for the Kingdom of God and whose life is determined by this expectation.'[2]

This summary of Christian eschatology by a biblically based theologian may be compared with a famous passage written by A. N. Whitehead, with a significant silence about the resurrection of Christ. 'The essence of Christianity,' wrote Whitehead, 'is the appeal to the life of Christ as a revelation of the nature of God and of his agency in the world'—and for Whitehead, this was the life of Christ: 'the Mother, the child, and the bare manger: the lowly man, homeless and self-forgetful, with his message of peace, love and sympathy: the suffering, the agony and the tender words as life ebbed, the final despair: and the whole with the authority of supreme victory'. And Whitehead added: 'Can there be any doubt that the power of Christianity lies in its revelation in act of that which Plato divined in theory?'[3] Our answer must be that such doubt is possible. What Whitehead called the 'persuasive love' revealed by Christ and by Plato as the final power in the world has been for Christians the 'revelation in act' of *the living and triumphant God*. A philosophy which ignores the mystery of Easter, and which uses Bethlehem and

[1] F. A. Iremonger, *William Temple*, p. 538 .
[2] *Theology of Hope* (1965; Eng. trans., London, 1967), pp. 16, 326.
[3] *Adventures of Ideas*, pp. 213–14.

Calvary as illustrations of Plato's teaching, must be asked whether it has really included in its system the biblical proclamation of this God. Whitehead neglected Easter as a foretaste of the victory of the living God at the End; and this neglect was all the more regrettable because his philosophy suggested important reinterpretations of the traditional ideas or pictures of eternal glory.

We may sum up an austere and subtle philosophy by saying that, according to Whitehead, immortality consists in being remembered by God; and eternity consists in the permanence given in the 'consequent nature' of God to the 'perishing of occasions'. Such reinterpretations may indicate a way for Christian believers to avoid the selfish sentimentality of the idea of heaven as 'pie in the sky when I die'. Whitehead's theories may seem too close to the nihilism of Gautama's *Nirvana*; they may suggest a view of human destiny which values the personality and its environment less highly than did the traditional Christian doctrines. Christians will wish to insist that the comparison of God's eternity with man's memory provides only one 'model' to help us in the exploration of an inexhaustible mystery. But such reinterpretations, if connected with the Easter mystery, might be developed in a way which communicated with a new power the traditional emphasis that the only ultimate hope of man (and the surrounding creation) is of resurrection into the endless glory of God.

For if God is the God of Easter, if God is the Father who remembers the crucifixion in order to forgive it, if God is the Lord of history who brings the highest joy out of the deepest tragedy and who pours an invincible assurance into those whose hearts have been broken, if God is the Lover who began the whole process of the universe out of love and who can be trusted to make the best of it, why should the destiny of being remembered *by this God* be less than the destiny of the 'survival' claimed by Spiritualism? Why should history as a contribution to the life of this God be less significant than history 'going on for ever'? The transforming power of the human memory already foreshadows the glory which could cover the whole story of man in the universe, when God the Creator in his mercy remembers.

One of the most interesting of contemporary American theologians has offered the following sketch of a 'demythologised eschatology', leading to a new vision of the resurrection to eternal life as the greatest hope in the Christian message. 'Because God's love, radically unlike ours, is pure and unbounded, and because he therefore can and does participate fully in the being of all his creatures, the present moment for him never slips into the past as it does for us. Instead, every moment retains its vividness and intensity for ever within his completely perfect love and judgment. He knows all things for just what they are, and he continues to know and cherish them throughout the endless ages of the future in all the richness of their actual being. In other words, because God not only *affects*, but is also *affected by*, whatever exists, all things are in every present quite literally resurrected or restored in his own everlasting life, from which they can never more be cast out. This, I hold, is the promise of faith: that, whatever else may befall us and however long or short may be the span of our lives, either here or hereafter, we are each embraced in every moment within God's boundless love and thereby have the ultimate destiny of endless life in and through him. In this sense, the promise of faith, which is already known to the Christian in his present encounter with Jesus Christ, is the promise of victory over death.'[1]

The Message of Patience

A message of hope, on earth and in God's eternal life, may be heard as the message of the Kingdom of God in our time. But Christian hope cannot be Christian unless it includes some understanding of the tragedy which culminates in death, for the central Christian experience is of Easter illuminating Good Friday; and this dimension of Christianity continues to be relevant in a world 'come of age'.[2]

[1] Schubert M. Ogden, *The Reality of God* (New York, 1967), p. 226.
[2] I tried to work this out in my *God's Cross in Our World* (London, 1963).

Better than any drama written out of twentieth-century despair, the story of the crucifixion of Jesus teaches the tragic sense of life and closes the road to Utopia. The cross shows how history with all its hopes can lead to disaster; Hebrew religion and Roman law, representing the best in history, tortured to death the embodiment of God. And now Christians see that in the crimes and follies of history, the crucifixion of the best goes on. No one who reads history in the light of that cross will be found prophesying a future for man in which human nature will inevitably create and support progress. The crucifixion of Jesus is a tragedy which shows man as too little for his destiny, which shows to what depths human nature can so easily fall, which shows how little the world's pomps and vanities are worth, and which purges our emotions by pity and terror. But the cross is also something more than that, and the message of the cross, the message of Christian patience, is something more than the teaching of the tragic sense of life. Those modern thinkers who have asserted that Christianity is in the last analysis incompatible with tragedy are right, if by Christianity we mean essentially what the New Testament means. According to the New Testament the crucifixion is a revelation not only of the tragedy of mortal man, but also of the victory of the eternal God in this tragic world. Facile optimism stands rebuked; the broad and easy road to a secular Utopia is closed; yet the road to the Kingdom of God is open, *and that road goes through Calvary*.

This, it would seem, is the Christian understanding of the cross. Jesus seems to have gone to his death voluntarily (presumably he could have avoided getting into the situation which brought it about, had he so wished), and the simplest explanation of the attitude of Jesus to his death seems to be the one which the gospels give: which is, that Jesus believed that a life which was so lived as to incur charges of blasphemy and treason, and yet was defenceless—a life which inevitably led to the punishment of crucifixion—had to be lived in that way if the victorious love of God was to be demonstrated in a tragic world. Was that belief right? The correctness of the belief of Jesus will be accepted most readily by those who accept the witness of the New Testament that the crucifixion was followed by a further act, in which God upheld the faith of the crucified Servant by showing him to the faith of the disciples as the risen Lord. If we are to go beyond an interpretation of the cross as a moving tragedy, this will be through accepting the resurrection as a separate event—whatever its mechanism may have been. It is in the light of Easter that the tragic Friday is seen as 'Good'; it is in the light of Easter that the whole story of man is seen as a love story with a happy ending, as the Divine Comedy.

A Gospel of the cross built on these New Testament foundations, and shining in that Easter light, will always proclaim a message of hope first; it will preach patience within this hope. It will always be invincibly optimistic. And here we have to note that it is precisely the optimism of Christianity that has dismayed many secular thinkers of our time whose central experience has been one of disillusionment with lesser hopes. Thus Albert Camus made this comment: 'There is, of course, an act of metaphysical rebellion at the beginning of Christianity, but the resurrection of Christ and the annunciation of the Kingdom of Heaven interpreted as a promise of eternal life are the answers that render it futile.'[1]

A number of religious thinkers influential in our time have seemed to suggest that Christianity should accordingly be refashioned as the Divine Tragedy. It is the defeat of the purposes of the Sovereign Father on the cross, they have implied, that should lead to a deeper understanding of the suffering of God in this tragic world. Such a theology certainly seems to be more Christian than does the doctrine —with a far larger history in Christianity—which complacently declares that God is already completely in control, his Kingdom come, his will done, his glory and power manifest, in every detail of the universe. It also seems preferable to the doctrine—also highly honoured in Christian history, although owing more to Aristotle than to the Bible

[1] In a footnote in *The Rebel* (Eng. trans., London, 1962), p. 27.

—that God is affected neither by the tragedies not by the triumphs of his creatures, but remains the passionless Source, the unmoved Mover. We shall wish to say that the tragedy in life is opposed to God—so that, although every event is permitted by him, not every event equally reflects God's loving will. Here, it may be, is the reality behind the New Testament's myths of the battles with the demons. We shall also wish to say that God is involved in the struggles of his creatures; his infinite being bears a real relationship to their suffering in time, and his perfection includes the triumphant completion of his creation in the perfection of his creatures. Here, it may be, is the truth behind the Bible's naïve pictures of the sorrow, anger and joy of the God who is in covenant with man. But if we are to remain loyal to the message of the Bible, we shall not wish to deny the perfect eternity of God the Creator; nor to deny that this perfect eternity, this source from which creation emerges, is best glimpsed when through the suffering and sorrow, and beyond all the tragedy of history, the last word is joy. We shall wish to affirm as the distinctively Christian understanding of the cross that the transcendent God was in the crucified Christ, triumphantly transforming the suffering to joy.

The cross of Jesus, seen in this Easter light, reveals the inexhaustible patience of the transcendent, and in the end victorious, God. For his own purposes, which are beyond our full understanding, the Almighty Father has chosen to postpone his triumph until the incomprehensibly vast and complex process of evolution has reached its goal. God's choice of such a universe costs his children an agony; and this cost we see when there is no miracle to rescue the crucified Jesus. But God's choice also costs him something; and this cost we see in the Jesus who on the cross is the Model or Image or Word of the transcendent, eternal, triumphantly joyful God who now suffers. Jesus spoke of the Father as the One who gives of his own to his children, and who gives his children freedom and lets them be if that is what they want, and who waits, and who in their distress runs to them. Jesus claimed that through his life God was showing this patient love, and as we look back we can see the love shown supremely in the patience to death—the patience which through its humility conquered.

This vision of the patience of the God of Calvary has consequences for our lives, now that we are 'come of age', called to live as God's adult sons and fellow-workers. Recent Christian thought has rightly rejoiced over the progress of our time, and has interpreted this rapid change as the means by which God is acting to awaken the world and to confer on all mankind the privileges of adulthood. Many Christians rightly wish to be involved in the thrill of this hope and achievement, for the delight in it has an eternal source. But after all the changes in society human hearts will still be broken; and during and after these changes, the call for human endurance will remain. For many Christians it therefore matters that they should be confident that this patience, like the hope, has its basis in the eternal joy. It matters that the 'Lord of heaven and earth' calls men to share not only his continuing creativity, but also the suffering involved, in the cross which, as Pascal said, will remain until the end of the world.

Dietrich Bonhoeffer, whose phrase about man's 'coming of age' has run through so much recent Christian thought, was trained in a strictly pious discipline and a rigorously intellectual theology. Much of his adult life was spent as a leader of the Confessing Church. When the war came he found himself involved in the anti-Nazi resistance alongside many men who did not share his ecclesiastical background. For a time this political movement held high promise for Bonhoeffer; it seemed possible that the Nazis could be removed and an honourable peace negotiated. When he was arrested and imprisoned because of his share in this conspiracy, Bonhoeffer still hoped that the evil tyrant might be killed and further tragedy averted; and to the end he did not repent of his involvement in the struggles of political and military power, in the secular hopes of worldly success. But in prison he learned that success was not necessary for the disciple who would, in hope and patience, take his part in

God's creativity and suffering. On the day after the unsuccessful attempt of his fellow-conspirators to assassinate Hitler in 1944, when his own doom was now sealed short of a miracle which never came, Bonhoeffer wrote a word for our secular century with its glittering accomplishments but recurrent tragedies, a word about the triumphant God of Calvary. 'I am still discovering, right up to this moment, that it is only by living completely in this world that one learns to have faith. One must completely abandon any attempt to make something of oneself . . . By this-world-liness I mean living unreservedly in life's duties, problems, successes and failures, experiences and perplexities. In so doing we throw ourselves completely into the arms of God, taking seriously, not our own suffering, but those of God in the world . . . How can success make us arrogant, or failure lead us astray, when we share in God's sufferings through a life of this kind?'[1]

To share the Christian faith today is therefore nothing else than this: *to choose to share the faith of Jesus Christ in God the Father who cares and suffers, and who will make known his power and joy as King on earth as in heaven.* Such a faith can be shared by modern minds sensitive to all the criticisms of Christianity mentioned in this book, and to all the changes brought about by this largely secular century. To that faith a future generation, inspired by the self-revealing God, may contribute the fresh vitality and power which this chapter has lacked; on that foundation a more stable fellowship of believers may be built in a more creative epoch; and in that fellowship our children or their descendants, while not escaping either the burdens or the excitements of continuous change, may find a greater peace than has marked the religious life of our century so far.

[1] *Letters and Papers from Prison*, pp. 369–70. For the background, see Eberhard Bethge, *Dietrich Bonhoeffer* (Eng. edn., London, 1970).

General Index

Titles of books are not listed. See second index for modern authors.

Index of Authors